Praise for

Deena Katz's Complete Guide to Practice Management

Tips, Tools, and Templates for the Financial Adviser

by Deena B. Katz

"The power behind these very practical tools and tips is that they are rooted in Deena Katz's solid track record of accomplishment. She matches the theory with the reality of the business."
— DALE E. BROWN, CAE
President & CEO, Financial Services Institute, Inc.

"Deena is a true leader in the financial advice industry who has helped build a hugely successful practice (Evensky & Katz), and who now helps educate future planners at Texas Tech University. Her experience-driven insights and perspectives, along with various tools and solutions, are now available to you in her new book. Any advisory firm can benefit from it."
— TOM BRADLEY
President, TD AMERITRADE Institutional

"Deena Katz is one of the genuine icons in the independent advisory world. After making Evensky & Katz into one of the preeminent advisory firms in the country, she's turned her knowledge and experience toward helping other independent advisers run more efficient practices to better serve their clients. She is a valuable, and valued, resource for the industry."
— BOB CLARK
Former Editor in Chief, *Dow Jones Investment Advisor*
and *Financial Planning* magazines

"Never has so much useful, practical information been compiled in one place for the financial advisory practice."
— BOB VERES
Publisher, *Inside Information* newsletter
www.bobveres.com

"The chapter 'The Killer Process' alone is worth the price of the book. Systemizing your practice is one of the major keys to success in this business, and Deena gives you a step-by-step guide for doing exactly that."
— DAVID J. DRUCKER, MBA, CFP
President, Drucker Knowledge Systems
Principal, Virtual Office News LLC

"Deena Katz continues to make important contributions to the business of financial advice. She brings years of practical experience in forming, merging, and growing a successful advisory firm, combined with insight she has gained as a teacher of financial-planning principals to college students. The result is a reference that advisers at every level will find helpful to have handy when trying to sort through critical practice-management decisions."
— MARK TIBERGIEN
Chief Executive Officer, Pershing Advisor Solutions LLC

DEENA KATZ'S

COMPLETE GUIDE TO
PRACTICE MANAGEMENT

Also available from
Bloomberg Press

Family
by James E. Hughes Jr.

Family Wealth
by James E. Hughes Jr.

Getting Started as a Financial Planner
by Jeffrey H. Rattiner

How to Value, Buy, or Sell a Financial-Advisory Practice
by Mark C. Tibergien and Owen Dahl

The Investment Think Tank
edited by Harold Evensky and Deena B. Katz

Managing Concentrated Stock Wealth
by Tim Kochis

Money Well Spent
by Paul Brest and Hal Harvey

Practice Made Perfect
by Mark C. Tibergien and Rebecca Pomering

Retirement Income Redesigned
edited by Harold Evensky and Deena B. Katz

A complete list of our titles is available at
www.bloomberg.com/books

DEENA KATZ'S

COMPLETE GUIDE TO
PRACTICE MANAGEMENT

TIPS, TOOLS, AND TEMPLATES
FOR THE FINANCIAL ADVISER

DEENA B. KATZ

Bloomberg Press
New York

BLOOMBERG, BLOOMBERG ANYWHERE, BLOOMBERG.COM, BLOOMBERG MARKET ESSEN-TIALS, *Bloomberg Markets,* BLOOMBERG NEWS, BLOOMBERG PRESS, BLOOMBERG PROFES-SIONAL, BLOOMBERG RADIO, BLOOMBERG TELEVISION, and BLOOMBERG TRADEBOOK are trademarks and service marks of Bloomberg Finance L.P. ("BFLP"), a Delaware limited partnership, or its sub-sidiaries. The BLOOMBERG PROFESSIONAL service (the "BPS") is owned and distributed locally by BFLP and its subsidiaries in all jurisdictions other than Argentina, Bermuda, China, India, Japan, and Korea (the "BLP Countries"). BFLP is a wholly-owned subsidiary of Bloomberg L.P. ("BLP"). BLP provides BFLP with all global marketing and operational support and service for these products and distributes the BPS either directly or through a non-BFLP subsidiary in the BLP Countries. All rights reserved.

This publication contains the author's opinions and is designed to provide accurate and authoritative informa-tion. It is sold with the understanding that the author, publisher, and Bloomberg L.P. are not engaged in rendering legal, accounting, investment-planning, or other professional advice. The reader should seek the services of a qualified professional for such advice; the author, publisher, and Bloomberg L.P. cannot be held responsible for any loss incurred as a result of specific investments or planning decisions made by the reader.

Portions of this book have been previously published in *Deena Katz on Practice Management,* ISBN 157660070X and *Deena Katz's Tools and Templates for Your Practice,* ISBN 157660084X.

First edition published 2009
1 3 5 7 9 10 8 6 4 2

Library of Congress Cataloging-in-Publication Data

Katz, Deena B.
Deena Katz's complete guide to practice management : tips, tools, and templates for the financial adviser / Deena B. Katz.
   p. cm.
  Includes bibliographical references and index.
  Summary: "This edition is a revised and updated consolidation of two previously published books, Deena Katz on Practice Management and Deena Katz's Tools and Templates for Your Practice. This new expanded volume includes Katz's most recently tested approaches to managing a financial practice and the latest most ef-fective ways of communicating with clients"--Provided by publisher.
  ISBN 978-1-57660-308-6 (alk. paper)
  1. Financial planners--Handbooks, manuals, etc. 2. Investment advisors--Handbooks, manuals, etc. 3. Finance, Personal--Handbooks, manuals, etc. 4. Business enterprises--Finance--Handbooks, manuals, etc. I. Katz, Deena B., Deena Katz on practice management for financial advisers, planners, and wealth managers. II. Katz, Deena B., Deena Katz's tools and templates for your practice. III. Title.

HG179.5.K38 2009
332.6'2068--dc22   2008041700

Acquired by Mary Ann McGuigan
Edited by Dru-Ann Chuchran

To Sarah, Daniel, Amanda, and Josh,
who always sit in my corner

For downloadable versions of the figures included in
Deena Katz's Complete Guide to Practice Management,
go to www.bloombergbooks.com/katz_complete_guide.

In the pop-up box, enter:
Username: Bloomberg
Password: Forms

CONTENTS

ACKNOWLEDGMENTS

Each time I start writing a book, I call upon my many friends in this industry for ideas and counsel. Each time they give time and talent. They do it because they sincerely want this profession to remain strong and grow. They do it because this is a sharing profession and somewhere along the line, someone made a big difference in their professional lives that helped them reach their own personal success. So, to all of you, I sincerely thank you, not only for your contribution to this book but for your continued dedication to this industry.

I want to thank my Evensky & Katz family who have let me experiment on them all these years and who have become the next generation of really superb planners. I'm really proud of you.

Additionally, I want to acknowledge my new Texas Tech Personal Financial Planning family who welcomed me into the academic world and shared their invaluable insight into the development of the professional planner.

This book is a culmination of many hours of work from Amanda Newton, Sarah Tiprigan, Daniel Tiprigan, and Josh Mungavin, my student support team. However, this book would not read this well without the amazing magic touch of my editor, Dru-Ann Chuchran, who has a talent for making me sound really smart.

Finally, thanks to Harold, my bershert, who encourages, indulges and challenges me to be a better planner, educator, and person.

INTRODUCTION

When Bloomberg Press contacted me about updating the book *Deena Katz's Tools and Templates for Your Practice*, I envisioned changing some data, adding a few things, and taking out some ideas that I don't believe any more. As time went on, I found that I was raiding material from my first practice management book, *Deena Katz on Practice Management*, because I realized that unless you look at your practice holistically, you could leave gaping holes in your planning strategies. So, I went back to Bloomberg and offered to put these two books together, updating them and creating a comprehensive look at professional financial practices. The result is this effort: too big to carry around, but small enough to occupy desk space to serve as your personal consultant when you could use another adviser's viewpoint.

I have divided this book into four major sections: The Business, The Staff, The Client, and The Process. Each section has several chapters to help dig a little deeper into areas I think are important to you as a practitioner. I offer ideas at many different levels so you can pick and choose according to the maturity of your practice. And, as in the *Tools* book, I include forms, worksheets, and templates to get you started. Although I have dropped a few of the initial forms from *Tools*, the ones I have kept have been updated where necessary. Also, I have added new forms and worksheets that I think you'll find useful.

After writing my first two books, I continued to learn as a practitioner, sometimes changing my ideas. For example, my recommendation for providing minimal bonuses has been tossed out in favor of a more sophisticated and appropriate compensation structure. I found that I have evolved, as I am sure you will as experience and expertise deepen. It's good to be constantly learning, jettisoning outdated ideas for new and improved ones. I hope you find that too.

I could not possibly thank all the people who have had a positive influence on me professionally and personally, but I do thank one person in particular: my wonderful husband, Harold. I will say that, as you read this book, if you find an idea or a thought that sounds familiar, it may be one we've talked about together over the years. One great aspect of this business is that we share generously—our thoughts, ideas, and dreams. Thanks to all of you who share.

THE BUSINESS

Successful entrepreneurs constantly reevaluate and refine current practices. Moving water never stagnates. This section is concerned with firming up the foundation of your practice by reexamining your core values, mission, and vision. It will discuss the importance of selecting your business model and will provide recommendations related to managing business crises and planning for succession.

To be a good leader, you have to have a clear
set of values you implant in the company.
—Herb Kelleher, chairman of Southwest Airlines

Psychological studies indicate that people develop their attitudes toward money at a relatively early age. This process is rarely scientific and almost never rational.

Isadore Katz, a business genius and financial success, who was also my mentor and father-in-law, inadvertently taught me an important lesson about determining value. Isadore loved the stock market. Well into his eighties he would sit by the pool with the *Wall Street Journal* in one hand and a small radio dispensing market reports in the other.

When he reached his midseventies, Isadore's driving skills had begun to fade and his sons persuaded him to buy a limousine. Daily, his driver would take him downtown to his club to play cards with his pals, and then drive him home again in the evening. One day, his driver was sick. Isadore's youngest son called to tell his dad to take a taxi to the club since his chauffeur would not be available. "I'll take the bus," Isadore told his son, "I'm not going to pay that kind of money for a cab just to go downtown."

In a time-pressured world, people will pay for all sorts of services including personal chefs, exercise trainers, dog walkers, and house sitters. There is even a scooper service in my town, called Tech Poop. You can guess what they are picking up.

There is no practical way to determine, much less control, how people assign value to various services. What matters is that you value what you do, because if you don't believe that your advice or service is desirable, prospects won't either. How you feel about your work is transmitted immediately to people.

One of my first clients was a United Airlines captain. At the time, United pilots were entertaining the possibility of a strike, since negotiations for their new contract were not going well. At one of our appointments I remarked that considering the responsibility pilots have in the air, I'd give pilots any salary increase they wanted and not bat an eye. Surprisingly, my client didn't agree. "The money I make is already obscene," he remarked. "I'm just a glorified bus driver."

In one statement, my view of him as a professional was altered by his own perception of himself. My client went on to explain that when he started flying commercially, he was working in a 727 cockpit with a copilot and an engineer, all three of them busy virtually every minute of a flight. He had recently been promoted to captain of a 737. This cockpit was more automated and required only two people. With fewer activities, he often felt like a glorified bus driver.

Consider how technology affects how you see yourself and your value to your clients. In my earlier days of practice, there wasn't much financial planning software, no performance database, and no optimizers. We had to scramble for information on mutual funds, fund managers, and fund performance. We relied heavily on marketing material and anything we could glean from a prospectus. When I prepared a review, I literally sat with copies of my client's nine mutual fund statements and typed relevant information onto a single sheet so I could provide a consolidated report. We couldn't handle many clients because the data gathering and report preparation took forever. We were in the publishing business, not the planning business. Compared to those days, my practice activities today are a breeze. There is no doubt that the personal computer and companies like Charles Schwab and Morningstar have put advisers like me in business. But, by themselves, they won't keep me in business.

I asked financial adviser Eleanor Blayney, formerly of Sullivan, Bruyette, Speros & Blayney (SBSB), now Harris SBSB, for her perception of her value to clients. "I know I add a great deal to their lives, but in the back of my mind I keep thinking, what am I missing? Why should I be paid so well for this? It's fun and it's easy." The ease of preparing physical reports leads us to forget how hard we worked (and continue to work) to acquire our specialized knowledge and skills. Our value to clients is not derived from the easily prepared reports. Our value is reflected in our clients' success in meeting their goals, assisted by our knowledge and skills. Vladimir Horowitz made playing the piano look effortless. What his audience actually heard, and paid for, was his expertise, training, and talent sharpened by the endless hours he spent practicing.

 ## We Need to Express Our Value to Clients in Benefits, Not Features

More than one adviser I know describes his value in the statement, "My clients sleep well at night." Telling our clients we design well-balanced (deadly dull and boring) portfolios is less effective than telling them that if they follow our advice they will sleep soundly.

That's why you shouldn't give clients the impression that performance is the value you add to their lives. In fact, if you believe in asset allocation and diversification, you guarantee that your clients' returns underperform the hot market of the moment. Diversification requires including asset classes that are poorly correlated. The possibility of making a killing is what your client gives up to sleep well at night. On the other hand—here comes the benefit—when a single market is depressed, diversification will buoy returns. Stated as a value to clients, you help them avoid getting battered in the market. We tell prospects, "We can't make you rich, but we won't make you poor. Our job is to help you enjoy life and sleep well at night." In our firm, we demonstrate our value by keeping our clients from chasing returns in bull markets and from bailing out in bear markets. All of our interaction and communication with clients revolves around managing their expectations. I think this is such an important issue that I have devoted Chapter 14 to it.

John Guy of Wealth Planning & Management in Indianapolis, Indiana, has an interesting perspective on the value of an adviser. "My guess is that over the course of a long-term relationship, a financial adviser is likely to render at least one piece of immensely valuable advice. The advice usually arises from coincidence, even when the adviser understands investment markets and the client's personal situation. Usually, the value of advice is not recognized at the time it is delivered. Instead, it is recognized months or years later."[1]

Until the recent ugly downturn, wild market volatility has been prevalent. The Dow is down 500 points one day, up 300 the next. The first time this happened, in 1997–98, we called our clients and then followed up with a soothing letter. After several incidents of this, many of our clients suggested we save the postage. "I know you're doing your best work, now," one of my clients told me, "but why don't you concentrate on some of your newer clients? I've already been on this roller-coaster ride and it doesn't make me sick to my stomach anymore."

Since the beginning of the millennium, market volatility has not changed much, but I believe that investors have. Some have become immune to the daily pendulum swings, but most recognize that they need professional help in responding to market movements. Certainly, as American investors gray, they're more willing to accept professional advice to preserve their future lifestyles. This can only be good for the financial advisory profession. Later in this book I will discuss communication techniques you can use with clients who are still jumpy about market volatility.

Not every prospect will find value in your services. Like Isadore, they may be unwilling to pay for services that they believe they can get elsewhere "for free." "Why should I pay you," they ask, "when I can get all this information on the Internet and do it myself at a discount broker?" When you encounter these people, and it appears that you are not speaking the same language, move on. I'm fascinated to hear advisers tell me about their "conversion ratio." Conversion should not be a part of your job description. If you are presenting yourself and your business effectively, prospects either understand your philosophy and appreciate your value or they do not. To me, conversion presupposes resistance. Clients I've successfully "converted" were never satisfactory relationships for me.

Most Advisers Spend Little Time Defining Themselves and Building Their Practices

The clearer the adviser is about what he does, the better he is able to explain it to a prospect. It helped me to sit down, enumerate my ideal client in detail, and describe what I could do for that client. This thinking process became the basis for developing my core values, mission and vision statements, and ultimately, our company philosophy.

In speaking with other advisers, I discovered that we have no consistent way of developing these essential components of our business. In fact, many used different names for the same idea. For example: core belief, core value, and core purpose all seemed to describe the same fundamental concept. Because I often refer to "building a practice," I thought a building analogy would be useful in clarifying how successful practices are developed. Therefore, the following are, in order of priority, descriptions of the four statements that I believe must be in place in order to "construct" successful practices.

1. **One thing.** There is a huge range of services and products one might offer in a financial planning business. In order to be successful, you must determine at the outset the unique service you propose to provide. What will set you apart from everyone else? For what will you be known? I refer to this as your *one thing*. In building a practice, this is your preliminary survey, the staking out with words the idea that describes your *one thing*.

2. **Core values.** What fundamental beliefs underlie the philosophy and policies of your company? Your firm's core values are analogous to the foundation of your practice, a largely unseen but essential underpinning.

3. **Mission statement.** Once you have determined your one thing and your core values, you must describe how you wish your practice to look. Analogous to the plans for a building, a mission statement provides the basis for the design of your company.

4. **Vision statement.** If a mission statement is analogous to a building's blueprints, a vision statement is the equivalent of an architectural rendering of the completed practice. The vision statement describes what the practice will look like once the practice is successfully established.

One Thing

My partners, Harold Evensky and Peter Brown, began their partnership in 1985, five years before I joined them. When I arrived, there were eight advisers with the planning practice and twenty registered representatives with our broker-dealer, which Harold and Peter had started in order to eat while they waited for financial planning to earn them a living.

If you had asked them individually to describe their client base, their assessments would have been as diverse as the descriptions of blindfolded men feeling different parts of an elephant. Although we suspected we shared the same basic philosophy, we had never formally shared it with one another. So we never expressed it uniformly to our clients. We assumed that having a common name, one brochure, and a similar work product was enough. Consequently, we had a practice of people who had their own enterprises. We were not a business. We shared the same vague image of the future, but we weren't sure how to bring that vision into focus.

One evening after a lengthy "reorganization" meeting, Peter, Harold, and I went to see the movie *City Slickers*. In the film, Billy Crystal's character discusses the meaning of life with an old cowboy. "The secret of life," says the cowboy, "is *one thing*." "What is that *one thing?*" asks Billy. "That's for you to find out," says the old cowboy. Another "ah-ha" for me. We hadn't figured out what our *one thing* was. As a result, we hadn't been able to communicate it to our advisers and staff, much less to our prospects and clients.

Starting (or reviving) your own practice begins with finding out what your *one thing* is and then explaining it to those around you. The financial planning industry today is made up of specialties. Even if you are a comprehensive planner, that too is now a specialty, much the same as family practice is for a physician. These days my partners and I call ourselves wealth managers. To me, this is a specialty within financial planning, describing our holistic approach to our investment advisory services that I'll explain in more detail in the next chapter.

Joe Kopczynski, president of Universal Advisory Services, formerly in Albuquerque, says his *one thing* is comprehensive planning—not conventional comprehensive planning, either. He has negotiated leases, mortgages, and even HMO contracts for his physician clients. "It all comes down to trust. Clients who trust you want you to help them in many other aspects of their lives, not just the financial part." Joe says he grew up in corporate America where people are taught to stay professional by keeping at arm's length from colleagues and clients. "That just doesn't make sense to me. It's vital to have trust and accountability at all levels. For that, you've got to roll up your sleeves and get involved." Joe uses a multifamily office as a model for the services and relationships he develops with clients. His model includes far more servicing than in many planning practices, with business consulting and personal mentoring. Joe's *one thing* is to become the primary guide for all aspects of his clients' personal and business planning.

Dave Diesslin, of Diesslin & Associates in Fort Worth, Texas, is also a comprehensive planner. His *one thing* is instilling confidence. "We know that we add value and that we communicate well. Our clients have confidence in our ability to support them and confidence in the role we fulfill in their lives."

As I interviewed practitioners around the world, most described their *one thing* in such terms as engendering trust and confidence, maintaining personal relationships, or providing superior personal service to their clients. Some expressed their *one thing* in terms of actions, specifically offering special services. No one suggested that producing fancy reports or voluminous analyses was the key to their success.

When Charlie Haines of Charles D. Haines, LLC from Birmingham, Alabama, reviewed his client base, he made a startling discovery. The demographics and buoyant economy of the past few years had produced a group of successful but unhappy people. "I've got to address that situation, so now we require that all our clients spend two hours with a family therapist who discusses issues of money, preparation for retirement, and wealth transfers." Charlie finds that using a professional helps facilitate the planning process and his relationship with his clients. "Sometime between the retirement planning meeting and the estate planning meeting, we tell our clients, 'We want to get your reaction to the first chapter of the rest of your life. We would like to have a family therapist at that meeting, since she is more skilled at facilitating these discussions than we are.'" No one has turned them down.

Although Charlie feels it is essential to deal with the psychological and behavioral aspects of a client's life, he warns that there is a big danger in our industry of overstepping our bounds. Planners by nature are "counseling-oriented financial nerds. Unless we are trained as counselors or therapists, we shouldn't attempt to function like them. We wouldn't dream of practicing as an attorney unless we had a JD. We need to treat professional counseling in the same manner."

Our *one thing* is expressed in the tag line my firm uses under our company name: "Planning to Live Well." This line describes the unique function that we believe we have in our clients' lives. We plan, and assist our clients, to help them achieve their chosen lifestyles. This line also describes our relationship with our partners and staff. We measure our success not by the money we make, but by the quality of life enjoyed by everyone who works with us or for us.

 Core Values

When you've figured out the *one thing* that defines you and your organization, you must develop from it the foundation on which you build your business practices. I refer to these fundamentals as "core values." Core values simply state your permanent personal and business principles. We've expanded our *one thing* into these simple bullet points:

- **Teamwork.** Working together for common goals
- **Quality in execution.** Do it once; do it well
- **Ethics.** Honesty and professionalism
- **Critical review.** Unrelenting pursuit of excellence
- **Enjoyment.** Supplying the resources and physical environment that bring out the best in people

Everyone in our office has a copy of our core values. These are internal and not shared with clients, but we use them constantly as a compass and a reality check. Many of the planners I spoke with share the same attitudes about these statements. I've included two here to give you a sense of how unique, yet similar, firms' core values can be.

☐ SAMPLE CORE VALUE STATEMENTS

RTD Financial Advisors
Philadelphia, Pennsylvania

- A passion to help
- Place client's needs first
- Absolute honesty and integrity
- Competency is necessary before advice is given
- Empower our employees
- Treat everyone with fairness, respect, and dignity
- Contribute to the profession
- Make a profit

RegentAtlantic Capital
Chatham, New Jersey

- The client comes first. Always.
- A constant pursuit of excellence
- Extraordinary colleagues and partnerships
- Leadership, creativity, and innovation
- Open, honest communication
- Absolute integrity, objectivity, and reliability
- Mutual trust, respect, and dignity

David Bugen of RegentAtlantic Capital explains that the core values of his company are so integral to its practice that employees make every important decision in the context of those core values. For example, David told me, "Before we place our investment policy in the hands of our clients, we always ask ourselves, 'Is this the best we can do?'"

 ## Mission Statements

After you have developed your *one thing* into core values, you will need to devise a mission statement. Your mission statement ensures that everyone in your practice is focused on the same goals. It should be just long enough to express your position, but not so long as to be tedious. As with your core values, every significant business decision you make should be consistent with your mission. Joe Kopczynski said it very well when he told me, "It's extremely important for those of us who manage other people's money to understand who we are, to make sure we don't deviate from who we are and who we've told the client we are."

In military terms, the mission is to accomplish some goal, usually to overtake a target. Your mission statement is a broad plan of action to help you overtake your target market.

I wrote my first mission statement alone: "To provide financial education, direction, and planning for women who have previously left financial decisions to their spouses or who are in a life transition and require guidance to empowerment." Writing it clarified the goals for my practice and gave me a sense of direction, much like a financial plan does for our clients. At the time I started my practice, I enjoyed working with women clients. Some were widows, some divorced, and some business owners. When thinking about the commonality of this diverse group, I described it as "women in transition." My ideal client was a woman, aged fifty and older, who needed education, constant hand-holding, and emotional support. This was a woman who had never played an active part in her family's financial decisions, but was abruptly left with these responsibilities through divorce or widowhood. Because of my background in social work, education, and finance, I felt uniquely qualified to provide this type of advice.

When my partners and I formed our new company, we wrote our *one thing* as, "We are financial planners with a unique expertise in the area of investment planning for conservative clients." We referred to this as "wealth management." We then prepared a new mission statement. "We are financial planners and we want to make a comfortable income doing what we like while helping our clients get where they want to go." Okay, we weren't very sophisticated, but it was a start. It is important for everyone involved in your practice to understand why you are in business (the *one thing*), what your fundamental beliefs are (core values), and what you are trying to accomplish (the mission statement). Use these statements as your reality checks, especially when you find opportunities to engage in activities that may seem peripheral to your primary business.

Roy Diliberto of RTD Financial Advisors has distilled his *one thing* and mission into one brief statement that defines the purpose of his company: "Improve the quality of our clients' lives." Every challenge Roy meets is measured against this statement. Roy tells about one of his clients who experienced moments of literal paralysis thinking about the chaos that the year 2000 could bring. "He envisioned deteriorating markets and recession. He wasn't sleeping nights. He just wanted us to move everything to cash. I thought about it, then went back to our core purpose: to improve the quality of our clients' lives. If I move his money to cash, will it improve the quality of his life? Absolutely; he will sleep nights. Will it improve his portfolio? No, but he already has enough to accomplish his primary goals. Improving his portfolio is not consistent with our mission. We moved him to cash." Notice that Roy's statement does not say, "to improve the quality of our clients' financial lives." Roy specifically looks holistically at his clients' lives.

During our reorganization stages, we determined that we did not want to have a large practice with many advisers. Coincidentally, around this time, the media began a campaign to educate the consumer about fee-only planning. My Uncle Walt always advised, "If you see a right hook coming, lean into it; it will lessen the blow." If the media were going to strike a blow for "fee-only," we'd be crazy not to lean into it. We decided we were going to be fee-only and our *one thing* would be to provide fee-only holistic investment planning. This meant two very big changes. One, we needed to sell our broker-dealer. Two, we needed to take on clients with more assets to manage so we could afford to provide fee-only planning. To accomplish these goals, we realized that we needed to "grow down." Not everyone attached to our broker-dealer shared our fee-only vision. Similarly, we met with the advisers in our planning practice to determine who wished to make the leap to fee-only with us.

We are not opposed to other forms of compensation. The fee-only approach simply works best for our practice. I am not suggesting that you adopt this style. Instead, you need to be clear about your *one thing,* and then adapt your compensation structure to it. I will say that it is important to understand that current trends are moving toward a fee-based environment. Much of this movement has to do with investor demand for unbiased advice, best delivered, I believe, in a fee-based environment. Think of this: You go to your doctor and he tells you that you have the flu. He tells you that he will give you a prescription for the best flu medicine on the market. He then tells you that, in the interest of full disclosure, he gets 5 percent of the price of the medicine for each prescription he writes. At this point, you are probably wondering if this is the best medicine and in your best interest, or if it is the best medicine in the doctor's best interest. As soon as there is an incentive, no matter how incidental to the advice, there can be questions about the advice itself. I also believe there may be conflicts of interest in all areas. For example, if I recommend a certain custodian to my clients, it may be seen as a conflict of interest. The important task for you as an adviser is to figure out how you can most comfortably operate your business and do it with complete disclosure and the highest ethics.

At our first company retreat, we redesigned our initial mission statement. It was a powerful team-building effort, with all the partners and staff contributing ideas. Each year we revisit it to ensure that it still communicates our purpose. We use our mission statement as our strategic planning guide. As we set our goals for each year, we measure them against this mission statement. For years, our mission statement read, "E&K is the preeminent provider of fee-only wealth management services to individuals, qualified and public plans, nonprofits, foundations, and trusts with financial assets of two to fifty million dollars."

It was a comprehensive affirmation of what we wanted to be when we grew up and what we were trying to accomplish for our staff, our clients, and ourselves.

Today, our mission statement reads:

Our mission is to partner with clients to enable them to achieve their financial goals through objective planning and management of investment assets. Our purpose is to help build, manage, and preserve your wealth. We are fiduciaries. We put our client's interest first, act with integrity and honesty, and strive for excellence in every facet of our practice. Our success is not measured by performance statistics, but rather by our clients' success in achieving their goals.

Whether you write your mission statement alone at the kitchen table or craft it during a company retreat, it should still answer several questions:

- Who do you want to be?
- What do you expect to do?
- For whom will you do it?
- What needs will you fulfill?

☐ SAMPLE MISSION STATEMENTS

Here are three mission statements from some of the best planners around the world. All describe planning firms, yet each description is unique, reflecting the nature of each practice.

Norton Partners, Clevedon, United Kingdom

To provide an excellent financial planning and tax service to our clients, to be recognized as true professionals in our field, to enjoy what we are doing, and to provide such value to our clients that they cheerfully pay our fees and recommend us to their friends.

Blankinship & Foster, Solana Beach, California

To provide our clients with the best financial planning and investment management advice and services available.

To work with integrity, candor, and imagination with our clients, their advisers, and our employees.

To help each of our employees attain his or her best level of achievement and professional satisfaction.

To set a standard of excellence in our profession reflecting the importance of our work and assisting tomorrow's planners and investment advisers to achieve the highest public regard.

Sullivan, Bruyette, Speros & Blayney, McLean, Virginia

At Sullivan, Bruyette, Speros & Blayney, Inc., our mission is to be indispensable in helping our clients make smart financial decisions through uncompromising integrity, trust, and personalized service.

I particularly like the "cheerfully pay our fees" that Norton Partners uses. David Norton, who recently passed away, confided that he frequently told prospects, "We're not cheap, but we're good; take your choice." This is an interesting positioning statement. Russ Alan Prince, who has done a great deal of work analyzing high-net-worth individuals, suggests exactly this statement in his book, *Cultivating the Affluent,* when he says, "Certainly the knowledge that the cost of services is not a major factor in selecting an investment manager is valuable; it indicates that financial providers will succeed with the affluent by marketing themselves as good, not cheap."[2] By the way, Russ has a new book that you will want to read, *The Middle-Class Millionaire: The Rise of the New Rich and How They Are Changing America.*[3]

Eleanor Blayney says that the essence of the SBSB mission statement is for the firm to be indispensable to its clients. SBSB's partners frequently visit this statement and make business changes as they continually recalibrate their view of how to be "indispensable." SBSB provides tax planning as well as financial planning and asset management services. Since SBSB devised its first mission statement, it has changed a good deal, and the partners have now written one for each of the service areas of their business.

"It [the mission statement] seemed corny at first, but it grows on you once you begin to understand the different ways you can interpret it," Eleanor confides. "We want our staff to feel its importance, so at our annual retreat we make new employees sing the mission statement to the tune of their alma mater fight song."

Blankinship & Foster in Solana Beach, California, includes its mission statement in its brochure. "We want prospects to know immediately what they may expect from us," Jack Blankinship says. The firm's mission statement addresses the clients and their other advisers, as well as the profession as a whole.

Good mission statements are not universal. They do need to reflect your business specifically and be free of business jargon and mindless buzzwords. Be careful that the statement is clear, concise, and reflects the essence of you and your firm.

Let's look at five pizza companies and their statements.

1. Pizza Hut is the family pizza place.
2. Papa John's will create superior brand loyalty, i.e., "raving fans," through (a) authentic, superior-quality products, (b) legendary customer service, and (c) exceptional community service.
3. Domino's: Exceptional People On A Mission To Be The Best Pizza Delivery Company In The World. This is part of Domino's Vision and Guiding Principles.
4. Little Caesars: To be the best take-home pizza chain by exceeding customer expectations with extraordinary value, great-tasting products, and outstanding people while providing strong returns to our stakeholders.
5. Archie's: Passionate for Pizza.

Each statement reflects the nature of the company and emphasizes the aspects it deems most important. Pizza Hut wants to emphasize its family environment; the product is secondary. Papa John's focuses on superior brand loyalty through customer and community service. Domino's wants to be "the best pizza delivery company." Period. They don't say anything about the product; rather, they only speak about the process. Little Caesars is interested in being the best "take-home" chain and, particularly, being the best by providing strong returns to

Mission Statement   **worksheet**

If you aim at nothing, you'll surely get there. Your mission statement adds focus to your business and succinctly reminds you, your staff, and your target market who you are and what you do.

	Formulating Questions	Answers
1.	Who are you?	
2.	What business are you in?	
3.	Who do you serve?	
4.	What makes you different from competitors?	
5.	What are the unique benefits of working with you?	

Mission Statement:

FIGURE 1.1 Mission Statement Worksheet

its stakeholders. Archie's is the only firm that focuses on the product of pizza; it is just passionate about it.

When you think about your firm and what best describes it, be sure that you include these thoughts when you craft your mission statement. We have provided a mission statement worksheet to help you think through your own statement (**Figure 1.1**). Once you've completed it, you're ready to proceed to vision statements.

It is essential that the mission statement become an integral part of your business practices. It should serve as your benchmark to gauge progress, as well as function as your reality check when you have decisions to make.

Samuel Goldwyn, well-known movie mogul, had a single statement hanging on the wall behind his desk. When anyone came in to pitch a new movie idea, recommend new actors, or ask for changes in a script, he'd listen intently, then turn around to read the line, "Will it sell tickets?" Goldwyn knew he wasn't in the movie business; he knew he was in the business of selling tickets. Each decision he made needed to reflect that belief. As Mark Hurley, president of Fiduciary Network would say, "You are not in the financial advisory business; you are in the business of getting people to pay you for financial advice." Big difference.

The Vision Statement

As if all these statements about who you are and what you do aren't enough, I am going to ask you to consider one more, the vision statement. At one of our retreats, an adviser asked, "We think we know what we want to be when we grow

Vision Statement

worksheet

- Your vision statement dictates where you and your firm intend to be in the future. A vision is a statement about what your organization wants to become. It should resonate with all members of the organization and help them feel proud, excited, and part of something much bigger than themselves. A vision should stretch the organization's capabilities and image of itself. It gives shape and direction to the organization's future. Use the strategic framework and answer the question, "What is your preferred future for this firm?" An example of an answer: "Year after year, Westin and its people will be regarded as the best and most sought after hotel and resort management group in North America." (Westin Hotels & Resorts)

Formulating Questions	Answers
1. Who will you be?	
2. What business will you be doing?	
3. Who will you serve or continue to serve?	
4. How will you be known in the marketplace?	
5. What unique benefits will you provide?	

Vision Statement:

■ **FIGURE 1.2** Vision Statement Worksheet

up, but where are we really going?" We have found it invaluable to supplement our mission statement with a vision that indicates what we expect to happen as a consequence of the mission. The vision statement should be specific and goal oriented, for example, "Amberton Wealth Advisory will be the dominant independent fee-only advisory firm in the greater metropolitan McKeesport area, serving high-net-worth professionals and their families." We've included a vision statement worksheet for you as well (**Figure 1.2**). Notice that the questions for a mission and vision are similar, except one addresses where you are now; the other covers where you want to be. Your answers will direct the path of the development of your firm.

It is vital that your staff be a part of the development of your mission and vision. Eleanor Blayney admits that those who were involved in the drafting of their company's statements feel differently about them than those who were not. Retreats are great opportunities for drafting or refining these statements. I'll discuss them in Chapter 9.

Philosophy Statement

While I believe it is imperative for a successful practice to have in place the four ideas I've just discussed—*one thing,* core values, mission, and vision—there is an optional statement that you might find useful. We refer to this as our "philosophy statement." In this, we outline our basic approach to the advice and service we've developed in advising others about their money. While the prior four statements are primarily used internally in our firm, we have reproduced our philosophy statement as a special statement that we share with prospects and clients. Although I have included an edited copy of our philosophy statement here, you can find the full text in my partner Harold Evensky's book *Wealth Management.*[4]

EVENSKY & KATZ PHILOSOPHY

The entire staff of Evensky & Katz participates, at different levels, in the development of our philosophy.

All members of the firm are committed to its consistent implementation.

We are committed to the financial planning process

- **Goal setting.** We believe that our clients must set their own goals. It is our responsibility to educate them in the process and to assist them to define, quantify, and prioritize their goals.

- **Rule-of-thumb planning.** We believe that "rule-of-thumb" planning (such as that retirement income should equal 80 percent of preretirement income) is an incompetent and unprofessional method in planning for a client's financial independence.

- **Cash flow.** We believe that our clients need total return, not dividends or interest. The traditional concept of an "income" portfolio is archaic and places unnecessary and inappropriate restrictions on portfolio design.

- **Capital needs analysis assumptions.** We believe that "conservative" assumptions are a dangerous myth. As an example, if we should be "conservative" and not include any social security income for a client in our retirement planning calculation, the result might well be the projection of a significant shortfall in the resources necessary for retirement. That, in turn, could lead to a recommendation that the client either significantly reduce his or her current standard of living, delay retirement, and/or invest more aggressively. A "conservative" assumption might well result in an inappropriate and aggressive solution. We believe in making intelligent assumptions, not relying on fundamentally unsound, "conservative" defaults.

We are committed to professionalism

- All of our advisers are either certified financial planners (CFPs), certificants, or in the process of becoming CFP certificants, and are expected to be active participants in our professional organizations. Continuing education is mandatory for all of our professional staff.

We are committed to our clients' individual needs

- Our primary allegiance is to our client. If commitment on the part of the client is not forthcoming, we will not agree to an engagement.

We are committed to a fundamental investment philosophy that includes the following elements:

- **Risk and return.** We believe in appropriate measures of risk and return.

- **Efficient market hypothesis.** We believe in the weak form.

- **Value over growth.** We believe in Fama/French research.

- **Active versus passive.** We believe it is not either/or; we use both.

- **Asset allocation.** We believe that the portfolio policy is the primary determinant of the variability of long-term portfolio performance.

- **Optimization.** We believe that mathematical optimization is the appropriate method for designing a strategic-asset-allocation model. However, we also believe that an optimizer is simply a tool, to be used by a knowledgeable adviser.

- **Arithmetic versus geometric returns.** We believe in using geometric returns for historical analysis and future estimates.

- **Time diversification.** We believe that the concept of time diversification is appropriate in its conclusion that the relative risk of increasing equity exposure decreases as the time horizon of the goal increases.

We are committed to customized investment implementation

- **Policy.** We believe that an investment policy should be written and should be customized to the needs of our client. It should describe our client's goals and discuss his risk tolerance.

- **Managers.** We believe that professional money managers will provide results far superior to a client's or wealth manager's direct security selection and management. With rare exception, separate account management (including wrap accounts) is inefficient and expensive.

- **Ongoing management.** We believe that there should be a regular review of a client's situation to determine if he is continuing to move toward achieving his goals.

We accept fiduciary responsibility

- We believe that we are uniquely qualified to integrate the skills and talents of financial planning with investment skills, knowledge, and technology previously available only to large institutional clients, for the benefit of our clients.

Ross Levin's philosophy statement reflects both Ross's personality and his business style. Ross explained that he and his staff spent the better part of last year creating and revising Accredited Investors' philosophy statement. Today, it is a compilation of their mission, core values, and philosophy.

Ross's prospects receive a copy of his philosophy statement prior to their first visit so there is no misunderstanding of what he and his staff believe or how they will work with them. This is their first step in managing client expectations.

☐ ACCREDITED INVESTORS PHILOSOPHY STATEMENT

We believe in comprehensive professional financial planning. Our purpose is to help you determine what is important to you and bring congruity between your actions and your values. Our expectation is to build a committed relationship with you over your lifetime.

We believe:

- Financial planning involves maximizing your wealth. At Accredited Investors we define wealth as integrating all of your resources—**financial, emotional, physical, and spiritual.**

- We help you strike a healthy balance between all of your resources throughout your life via **Life Planning.**

- The level of communication between us will determine success. Financial planning is personal, so we often ask that you share with us some of the many things that you don't share with anyone but your family.

- We believe in integrating the five key areas of financial planning—**Asset Protection, Disability and Income Planning, Debt Management, Asset Management, and Estate Management.** We believe all of these areas are integral for achieving your personal financial success.

- We do not believe in timing the market. We believe that if your time horizon is greater than three years, you should accept some of the volatility risks of the stock market. For those needs that occur in less than three years, you should not accept this risk.

- We believe that if we make mistakes, we must correct them. But first, we must know of them. Please talk to us so that we may do so.

- We believe that a competent and fulfilled staff is critical to execute our mission. We treat our staff with respect and ask that you would as well.

- We believe that we should like and trust each other. If that ever stops happening, we believe our relationship needs to be reevaluated.

- We believe that you should be as involved in your plan as we are. This means that we will often ask you for help in gathering information or talking with other advisers who may have this information.

- We believe in the value of synergy. A competent, healthy communication and exchange of ideas between all related advisers is essential to achieving the desired success for you.

Get Busy

By now, you should have enough material to design, develop, or just renew your own core values, mission, and vision statements. Start with your *one thing* and work from there. A good building is never built until the architect blends the dream with the details.

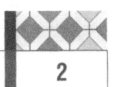
*Most importantly, to successfully develop a serious business,
you need a process, a practice, by which to obtain that information
and, once obtained, a method with which to put that information
to use in your business productively.*
—Michael Gerber, author of *The E-Myth*

Financial planning practices have largely evolved from a sales model originally developed in the late 1960s. At that time, some stockbrokers and insurance agents began to recognize the need to address a broad spectrum of financial issues for their clients. For these forward-looking advisers, it was clear that clients' needs were interrelated and interdependent. And from a business perspective, planning for clients ultimately resulted in selling financial products. In the early 1970s, a group of advisers originated the certified financial planner (CFP) designation based on a six-step planning process. This disciplined approach gave birth to the comprehensive financial plan.

My first financial plan was 103 pages. I figured it was my responsibility to tell the client everything about herself and her financial life that I could. My client looked at the plan, flipped through it, and exclaimed, "Oh my goodness, you published!" It took me fifteen years and many more clients to realize that a financial plan is not for the client; it's for me. I want to know as much as I can about my clients so I can guide them in making intelligent decisions. I need to understand what motivates them to spend, save, work, and play so that I can help them achieve their life goals, whatever they are.

As the financial planning profession matured, so did our practices. I found myself doing more modular plans, such as college funding, retirement planning, and investment planning. What clients wanted, I realized, were answers to very specific questions. How can I pay for my child's college education? When can I retire? How can I expand my investments? These I could answer without requiring them to pay me to do a full-blown plan that discussed their property-casualty insurance and disability needs.

In the late 1980s, the planning community discovered asset management. What the clients *really* wanted to know, we reasoned, was how to *invest their money*. Many planners embraced asset management like a long-lost relative. Companies like Schwab and Fidelity Investments put us in business by allowing us to consolidate positions, download trading activity, and produce our own performance reports. A roaring bull market made us look brilliant. Business for planners never looked better.

In the late 1990s many of us became concerned that if we abandoned the financial planning aspects of our practices, we were betting the farm on market performance. Further, to the extent we believe in and use asset allocation and diversification principles in our practices, we guarantee that our client's performance will never be as good as any one well-performing asset class. The answer is what I call "holistic planning." I've described that as comprehensive planning without killing any trees. We just don't print the 103 pages anymore. "Plans," says Ross Levin, "should be process driven, not paper driven."

For example, when I was producing comprehensive plans, I took the responsibility for sending out the client's property-casualty to be reviewed by an agent who specialized in property and casualty. I did evaluations and wrote extensive reports on disability and life insurance needs. Ten years ago, I'd identify the risk exposures and direct the client to knowledgeable insurance agents. My plans would hover between ten and fifteen pages, and the meat was in the action plan section. Today, planning has become collaborative and interactive, using software and tools that will allow clients to "play" with different scenarios, becoming invested in the results. Our delivery is online, and the focus is on the process of planning, not the product (the plan). We engage as many other professionals as we need to (accountants, attorneys, and insurance agents) to complete the implementation.

The most important part of my professional service is not anything written on paper. It's the counseling, the coaching, the listening, and the caring, as well as the knowledgeable and intelligent planning that I wrap into my relationships with clients. The responsibility I take for maintaining and improving the quality of their lives is what they value and pay me for.

Don't get me wrong. I am not suggesting that a planner does not have to possess the technical capabilities. I am saying that an adviser must be able to synthesize complex and sophisticated concepts and communicate them effectively to clients, while maintaining an environment of caring and trust.

As the financial planning profession has matured, many planners have added more client services to their service mix, until ultimately a service model has developed as an alternative to the traditional sales model. This service model, even in cases where its compensation is commission based, promotes a client-centered relationship rather than a product-centered one. Structurally, the service model tends to fit more with entrepreneurial practices.

The most recent trend is the increasing participation of advisers from related financial fields, such as banking, brokering, accounting, and law. The result is the emergence of what I'll call the "professional model." This model incorporates the attributes of a service orientation with the traditional attributes of a professional relationship (for example, credentialed professionals, confidentiality, a fiduciary relationship, fee-based compensation, and structurally independent practices that do not represent any one financial institution or product). Steve Moeller, of American Business Visions, maintains that the financial adviser of the future will practice "comprehensive wealth management," consulting on financial, tax, and estate planning, and counseling, teaching, and providing business advice and investment management services.[1]

Today, practices based on sales, service, and professional models are all viable alternatives. The trend is clear, however. The market is increasingly deserting sales-based practices for service and professional alternatives. "No longer is our business about products, or sales of products—our business is about advice, delivered in a way that cannot be duplicated by computers or toll-free phone numbers," says Lew Walker. "Information is not knowledge, judgment, or empathy." The market you serve and your personal business style should determine the choice of a practice model. But it pays to know the pros and cons of each model before you choose.

Compensation Structures

The media have fueled the differences between the sales and service models and the professional model by suggesting to the public that the only competent adviser is one who has no conflict of interest. They frequently suggest that advisers compensated by commissions or a combination of fees and commission cannot act in the client's best interest. This controversy regarding fees and commissions has existed for twenty years among advisers. I believe that all advisers have conflicts of interest. We would be less than truthful if we did not admit it. For example, I choose to use Schwab and Fidelity as third-party custodial partners for the convenience of back-office operations. There are other discount brokers, and they may be even less expensive for my clients. This is surely a conflict. The clients who want to work with me are expected to have a relationship with Schwab or Fidelity as well. To my mind, the measure of who is a professional, giving quality advice, is one of competence, the value of services delivered, disclosure, and ethics, not compensation. However, the marketing reality is that there is a certain professionalism that the public associates with fee-only planning, and this is a perception that someone accepting commissions must overcome.

How Do You Charge for Your Services?

Many years ago, Bob Veres, editor of the monthly publication *Inside Information*, suggested that fee advisers should think about lowering their assets-under-management fees to 20 or 30 basis points, then charge a separate fee for their financial planning work. This unbundling would let the clients know what they are paying for. Those who do not want or need the planning don't pay for it.

Our services are bundled with the asset management fee. We refer to it as a "retainer." Many fee planners I've interviewed also use this method and would not be comfortable changing. "I roll it all up into an asset management fee. I don't want a client to do so much self-diagnosis," says Charlie Haines. Charlie is concerned, as are many advisers, that clients will not want to pay outright for the financial planning services, skimping on the important planning aspects.

I once had an attorney who used one of those little meters attached to his phone that kept track of the time for each call. He charged me for every fifteen-minute increment, whether we were on the phone, in his office, whatever. I thought long and hard each time I needed to pick up the phone for a quick question, which discouraged me from calling. I would have much preferred if he had just charged a retainer. I think this nickel-and-diming of a client is a barrier to maintaining a good relationship.

Joe Kopczynski charged a fee based on net worth. He felt that basing the fee on performance is sending the wrong message to the client. He admits many clients balk at this. One prospect told him, "I made my million dollars, and you had nothing to do with it. Why should I pay you for that?" Most of his clients warm to the arrangement, though, when Joe tells them that he's responsible for helping them preserve that million.

"In one day," says Joe, "I might scout out a new building my client wants to buy, help secure a mortgage for another, and negotiate fees with an HMO for a third. Most of my clients are doctors so I have become an expert at supporting them and their unique needs." Joe has cultivated a relationship with a local bank so that when his clients need mortgages, he can provide the personal financial information and then personally escort them to the bank to complete the deal, making the whole process relatively painless.

Joe's expertise in negotiating HMO contracts has become notorious in his town of Albuquerque, New Mexico. "Doctors want to spend their time with their patients, not battling with other providers. To me and my clients, this is what comprehensive planning means."

The Sales Model

The commission-based sales model generally works well for a client in the middle-income market whose net worth is under $250,000. I am constantly amazed at the media touting fee-only planning for the general public. Frankly, we can't charge enough for our time to satisfy this market on a fee-only basis. Lew Wallensky, of Lewis Wallensky & Associates in Los Angeles, in an interview with *Investment Advisor* magazine, said it best, "Do you know what I call financial planners who say, 'Talk to me anytime about anything'? I call them poor." Moreover, someone with a net worth of less than $250,000 may find it difficult to pay an annual ongoing fee.

Practitioners using this model are typically employees or agents of major financial services firms. Compensation structure is based on commissions and fee income from the proprietary offerings of their corporate partner. These advisers generally serve large numbers of clients. The critical business decision is the establishment of a strong corporate relationship, because most of the practitioner's income will be determined by the sale of products selected by the corporate partner.

This structure has many advantages—minimal start-up costs, strong marketing, compliance procedures, back-office support, and minimal requirements for management of support staff. These advantages come with many disadvantages—including a lack of control over the allocation of resources, limited product choice, and, most important, the inability to independently represent the client's interest. This structure is best suited to a practitioner with significant sales skills who wishes to serve a large, relatively unsophisticated middle-income market.

The Service Model

Practitioners following this model are generally independent entrepreneurs. They typically maintain a relationship with a financial services firm that provides services related to commission-based products. The service model has a number of attributes in common with the sales model. Advisers must have securities and insurance licenses. They also must have a corporate relationship, usually with a broker-dealer. The primary differences are an increased flexibility in the choice of the compensation structure offered to clients (i.e., both fee and commission) and fewer restrictions with regard to the products available to their clients. Because of the higher level of personal service, these practices are more restricted in the number of clients an individual practitioner can manage.

The most successful practitioners utilizing this model have in common a number of attributes: They are client (as opposed to product) oriented, and they follow the financial planning process in determining their product recommendations. In order to position themselves for marketing purposes as well as to expand their professional competence, most have or work toward obtaining recognized credentials such as the CFP and the ChFC (chartered financial consultant).

Most service-based practices are composed of practitioners who move from the large organization or who start as a sole practitioner associated with a less restrictive broker-dealer. Don't kid yourself. Even if you work with a broker-dealer, you are a sole practitioner. You are expected to develop a book of business, and although you may have supervision and support, you are essentially building a raft of relationships that depend very much upon you. The best part about this arrangement is that you probably have a great deal of flexibility in the way you work. You develop your own style and philosophy. You may add support staff, but the cost burden and practice success is solely dependent upon you and your personality. You can make decisions without having to run them by another person.

This structure is best suited for a practitioner who wants to serve a limited market (for example, two hundred to five hundred clients) of middle- and upper-middle-income clients and for those who wish to transition in the future to the professional model.

The Professional Model

The attributes of the professional model generally include a fee-only (or migration towards fee-only) practice committed to the financial planning process. The firm's professionals are credentialed (often with multiple credentials) and consider themselves to be acting in a fiduciary capacity. The practice typically prides itself on its total independence (no mandatory affiliations), sophisticated and customized planning and implementation, and commitment to confidentiality.

This is the profile of the practice often touted by the media, and its model is very client oriented and service intensive. It is not economically feasible for practitioners serving the general market. It is most appropriate for a client base consisting of clients with very high incomes and/or a significant net worth.

Many planners I've talked with who provide holistic professional planning feel the need to limit their client base to a range between 80 and 150. Judy Shine of Shine Investment Advisory Services in Englewood, Colorado, emphatically states that she will take no more than one hundred clients. Her intensive involvement with her clients prevents her from handling any more than that. "I am staying small by choice. I am not interested in being overburdened with managing a huge staff, nor am I interested in having clients who I don't know and like very well."

While the sole-practitioner management structure is common for service and professional practices, the growth of such solo practices will be limited. One solution is to expand the entrepreneurial base via partnership. This is an extremely important decision, so I have devoted Chapter 9 to it.

Pricing and Fees

Let's look at pricing strategies for a moment. Although the asset management fee is very popular among registered investment advisers (RIAs), the fact is, it does not come without its difficulties. High-net-worth clients are more inclined to accept this pricing strategy, since they are used to paying fees for other services, such as accounting or legal work. Clients with smaller incomes and net worth may not find it of value or even economically feasible to work with this method. While there are advisers who work with middle-income clients (check out Sheryl Garrett's website, www.garrettplanningnetwork.com), most advisers cannot afford to deliver services to middle-income clients without some kind of commission strategy.

The common pricing methods for asset management and financial planning, and examples of each, follow:

- **Percentage of assets**—By individual service

    —Asset management: 0.35 bp

    —Planning: 60 bp

- **Fee for initial service**—Percentage of assets

    —Planning: $1,500

    —Asset management: 1 percent

- **Percentage of assets for investment management**—Fees for all others

    —Initial fee: $1,000

    —Asset management: 0.50 bp

    —Reporting and meetings: $500 per hour

- **Retainer fees**—Services priced by fixed fee

    —Priced by complexity and service mix

- **Fees based on net worth**—Net worth calculation

These fee arrangements have worked fairly well for years, but I believe as we get into the "next phase," the "decumulation" phase of planning for our clients, we are likely to see a major overhaul in the delivery and pricing of services, largely because as clients began to withdraw significantly from their portfolios, it will be more and more difficult to maintain the fee structure.

Unbundling

I've talked about bundled services, but as Veres suggested above, it might be a more viable alternative to unbundle your offerings so clients can control their costs. Let me relate a story that illustrates the idea of unbundling and how it affects your practice. I needed a new bedroom quilt for our bed, so I went shopping in search of one

I had seen in a magazine. Sure enough, at the first store, I spied the quilt, colorful and inviting, and searched for a saleswoman so I could purchase it. "This is lovely," she agreed. "But it is only sold as part of our 'Bed-in-the-Bag' collection." I had never heard of that. She explained that the quilt was sold with pillow shams, sheets, pillowcases, and a dust ruffle, all in one bag. "I don't want the other stuff," I said, "I just want the quilt." "Sorry," she said, "it's only sold this way." I couldn't believe that I could not just get the item I wanted, and so I trekked to five more stores before I resorted to the vast resources of the Internet. Surely I could find it there. After a fruitless three-hour search, I finally came to realize that if I wanted that quilt, I simply had to buy the whole bag, which I did. I hated the sheets, the dust ruffle was too short for the bed, and the pillowcases were king-size and I only used standard ones on my bed. I gave away everything else and only kept the item I wanted in the first place.

It then occurred to me that advisers are often putting their clients in the same situation. We create these complicated, all-inclusive bundled offerings, for one fee, when our clients just don't want, or even value, anything beyond our basic services. I remember telling one of our clients about our auto-leasing/purchase program. "We'll negotiate for you, and all you need to do is drop by the office to sign the paper work and pick up the keys." He looked at me horrified. "I love negotiating for cars; I don't need that." Continuing, I added, "We will provide reports to you on demand." "Great," he commented, "Now when I get up at 3:00 a.m. for a bathroom visit, I can call you and order a new retirement projection. No thanks." It was at that point we explored many ways to deliver value (and services) to clients that are not just our standardized deliverables.

Conventional asset management pricing also leads to some complications. For example, most of us tell our clients we want them to invest for the long term. We spend innumerable hours explaining long-term-return expectations, short-term volatility, and long-term benchmarks. Then, each quarter we invoice the clients based on the current value of their investments. They can't help but focus on short-term performance when we are cramming it down their throats quarterly, with a nice little bill attached to it.

I don't have an answer for this, and probably as you do, I just have a lot of questions. In the meantime, here are the pros and cons of unbundling your offerings:

Pros
- Revenue stability
- Matching fees to cost causation
- Encouraging market entry and participation
- Cost allocation information

Cons
- Challenge of isolating services that are of value
- Difficult to price
- Impact on current revenue
- Impact on current clients
- Infrastructure requirements
- Marketing confusion

Business Plans

Once you've determined the business model for your practice (or it already exists) and have made some decisions about your pricing and service offerings, it's time to develop a business plan. I don't believe in cumbersome business plans, unless you are looking for outside investors or you have a very mature practice that demands it. There are plenty of books, software programs, and other resources available to help you prepare a business plan. I prefer to use a simple model of my own (**Figure 2.1**—see p. vi). Whatever you use, it is important to have a plan and refer to it frequently. Remember, who else, but financial planners, should understand the value of good planning? Perhaps the most important parts of the plan are the five-year vision, the six-month action plan, and the twelve-month budget. Almost all successful planners I know have business plans, some more elaborate than others.

Creating the Business Plan

Start with the basics. Who you are, why you are in business, what your target market is, and what you provide for your clients. If you went through the process of developing core values and a mission statement, you will already have thought these through. The first section of the plan should include the following:

- Charter date and revision dates of the business plan
- Charter (the formal name of the company)
- Mission statement (who do you want to be?)
- Services and products
- Types of clients
- Where the business operates

The next section of the business plan, under the heading, Long-Term Objectives and Strategies, should include your five-year plan. What is your ultimate goal for this company? What will this company be when it grows up? What is your vision? Then consider operational issues:

- What will your fee structure be?
- Will you use a third-party provider?
- Will you have a relationship with a broker-dealer?
- Will you use individual stocks, bonds, and/or mutual funds? What due diligence will you institute in the selection of these investment vehicles?
- What are your regulatory and legal considerations?
- What services will you be providing?
- What are your personnel requirements?

Next, tackle your marketing plan. How will you reach your ideal client? At this stage you do not have to detail your entire marketing strategy. Frankly, marketing strategies require a plan of their own. In this section, state whether you will do seminars, cultivate spheres of influence, use direct mailing tactics, etc. Also state who will be responsible for marketing and whether additional personnel are required. We will look at marketing plans in detail in the next chapter.

Once your five-year vision plan is developed, prepare a shorter-term action plan. I find it easier to accomplish things if I break them down into near-term goals, so I suggest devising a six-month action plan. In that section, discuss where you will concentrate your efforts during the next six months. Will the actions be external, for example, implementing marketing plans, or will they be internal, such as developing systems or training personnel. Be specific and create benchmarks to check your progress.

Finally, you will want to address your twelve-month budget. What is your expected budget for the year? Project your income and estimate how many new clients you expect to gain. What new expenditures do you expect? When you have completed your one-year projections, follow the same procedures to develop projections for your five-year plan. Quantify these plans by estimating the following, for example:

- Expected new income
- Expected number of new clients
- Expected salaries
- Expected additional expenditures for software and advertising
- Budget summary

I will discuss how you should set up your books to help track your profitability in Chapter 6, so at this point, include the chart of accounts that you are currently using. If you are just starting out, refer to **Figure 2.2**.

 ## Business Structure—Not-So-Usual Suspects

The discussion so far has made the implicit assumption that a practitioner has settled on a legal structure that will be similar to that of the typical planning office (i.e., a simple corporation, a partnership, a limited liability corporation or partnership, or a sole-proprietorship). You will want to discuss your unique needs with your accountant or attorney. Specifically, keep in mind where you may want this firm to go—adding partners or what your succession or exit strategies may be. The most flexible arrangement is best. While most practitioners will opt to follow the traditional path, others may wish to consider creative alternative structures, some of which I've included here.

The Trust Company

Tom Bray, formerly of Legacy Wealth Partners in Overland Park, Kansas, described his company as a "plain vanilla RIA, with Schwab, no-load funds, and doing the big book, you know, comprehensive financial planning." That was

FIGURE 2.2 Sample Income Statement

Your Company, LLC Income Statement For Year Ended 12/31/06		
Revenue		
Asset Management Fees	-	0.0%
Planning & Consulting Fees	$580,383	12.8%
Securities Commissions - Current	-	0.0%
Securities Trials	-	0.0%
Insurance Commissions - New or 1st Year	1,426,924	31.6%
Insurance Renewals, Allowances & Bonuses	1,918,458	42.4%
Other Fees	596,553	13.2%
Total Revenue	4,522,317	100.0%
Direct Expenses		
Professional Compensation	655,258	14.5%
Commissions Paid	-	0.0%
Owner's Draws or Base Compensation	1,139,877	25.2%
Other Direct Expense	-	0.0%
Total Direct Expense	$1,795,135	39.7%
Gross Margin	$2,727,183	60.3%
Overhead		
Advertising/Public Relations/Marketing	17,710	0.4%
Auto Expenses	986	0.0%
Business Tax & Licenses	16,339	0.4%
Charitable Contributions	2,837	0.1%
Client Appreciation	1,107	0.0%
Compliance	-	0.0%
Depreciation/Amortization	4,333	0.1%
Dues	2,253	0.0%
Employee Benefits	71,910	1.6%
Employee Salaries	814,011	18.0%
Equipment Leases/Purchases	11,361	0.3%
Hardware Expense	29,750	0.7%
Insurance	4,133	0.1%
Office Expense	78,717	1.7%
Payroll Taxes	15,562	0.3%
Professional Services	4,048	0.1%
Quotation & Research Services	-	0.0%
Rent	106,641	2.4%
Repairs & Maintenance	28,242	0.6%
Software Expense	1,912	0.0%
Training & Continuing Education	22,598	0.5%
Travel & Entertainment	4,430	0.1%
Utilities/Phone/Fax/Online Service	26,558	0.6%
All Other Expenses	323,384	7.2%
Total Overhead	1,588,823	35.1%
Operating Profit	1,138,360	25.2%
Other Income/(Expenses)		
Other Income	1,520	0.0%
Other Expense (--)	-	0.0%
Owner's Bonus	-569,939	-12.6%
Total Other Income/(Expense)	-568,419	-12.6%
Profit Before Taxes	569,941	12.6%
Pretax Income Per Owner	2,279,757	50.4%

before Tom created National Advisors Trust, a federally charted trust company, which now has 135 shareholders, comprising advisory firms located throughout the nation. Tom worked with middle- to upper-middle income clients who, in his estimation, will one day need dynasty trusts to handle all the assets they will acquire over their lifetimes. Tom was interested in providing a range of services for middle America—a family office, of sorts, for the little guys. He also knew that if this group continued to grow their assets, he would need to provide for multigenerational transfers. Conventional custodial arrangements cannot facilitate this as well as a trust company can.

A trust company is a departure from the traditional financial planning or asset management business. It has several advantages, including the ability to capture all of the client's assets through custodial accounts, trust accounts, and agency (individual) accounts. There are three major considerations to be addressed prior to opening a trust company: accepting fiduciary responsibility, meeting significant capital requirements, and engaging in highly regulated activities. For example, Tom explains that bank examiners will visit annually, provide a list of items they need to see, examine them, and then leave. The job of maintaining the structural legal requirements is made easier by his administration software, SunGard, one of the few proprietary trust software programs available that's efficient and user friendly.

On the downside, operating a trust company is much more expensive than running a conventional financial planning office. The software is proprietary, specialized, and costly. There are increased accounting costs, since a trust company must file audited financials. Additionally, trust companies require specialized, increased insurance coverage.

You don't have to open your own trust company to have specialized trust services, however. Jeffrey Lauterbach, director of National Philanthropic Trust, maintains that while advisers need the flexibility of a trust company, the development of the practice on this business model is divergent from the original purpose of a planning practice. "It's like everything else: you probably should concentrate on what you do best, and use support systems when you can. Trust services are a tool."

Strategic Alliances and Co-Advisory Relationships

The only commodities advisers ultimately have are their time and knowledge. You might take a tip from major corporations that have increasingly been using strategic alliances to leverage their resources. A strategic alliance is a formal business arrangement, usually between two or more complementary organizations.

Many firms have tried co-advisory relationships, but the ones that really work are those that truly have no overlap in services. A financial planner can form an alliance with an accountant, as long as the accountant does not want to do financial planning work, or if the planner confines himself to one aspect of the client relationship, such as the investment piece.

Similarly, advisers can leverage their time by taking on strategic alliances (or superclient relationships) with banks, accountants, and law firms. This allows the practice to grow, but does not increase the time the adviser needs to make available for face-to-face meetings. In effect, the practice takes on a $10-million or possibly a $100-million client. Additionally, these relationships allow the adviser to increase leverage with vendors, to have more clout with providers, and to have increased resources for more research and more specialized staff.

If you are considering such an arrangement, the services you provide to another organization can range from designing the portfolio models and making recommendations to providing full back-office support. Whatever you decide, systematize all activities as much as possible to ensure that you have the control you need to accomplish the tasks. Remember, you still have responsibility for the clients, even if you don't see them personally.

Unless you are working with a federally chartered bank, your co-adviser will need to become a registered investment adviser. The ADV Part II form of both firms must explain the relationship. Shared clients will need to receive copies of ADVs from both entities and sign a disclosure statement that acknowledges the relationship between the co-advisers and the activities to be performed by each. I will discuss securities registration and ADV forms later.

The co-advisory contract should outline the function of each entity, determine the fee structure, and provide for recourse and termination if the relationship is not working.

You will want to standardize your forms and procedures to ensure consistency in the client relationships. Our co-advisers, for example, are trained to use our proprietary risk-coaching questionnaire as part of their education process with each client. In this way, we know that aspects of risk have been evaluated and discussed by our co-advisers in the format we would use.

Consider your fee structure carefully. If you are still required to meet directly with clients, your fee should reflect this. However, if you are providing only investment expertise and reporting, your fees can be lower.

The structure of these relationships can be complicated. Be sure to get competent legal advice, and as with any partnership arrangement, plan for termination if it doesn't work.

Your Style Is You

Your business should be comfortable and consistent with your personality and style, a reflection of you. Clients gravitate to advisers with whom they find empathy and trust. If you're not comfortable with how you've structured your business, they won't be either.

So you were misquoted, but did they spell your name right?
—Harold Evensky, chairman of Evensky & Katz

No matter how long you've been in business, if your practice is growing to include services that you have not provided before, or if you are just refining your practice, there is no better way to reposition yourself than to use the media and public relations to gain credibility.

Of course you'll want to think it through before you start. Many years ago a planner friend contacted one of his local papers, offering to serve as a local resource expert in financial affairs for the paper. My friend sent in his résumé, which happened to include a statement that he was listed in *Who's Who in American Finance and Industry*. The paper responded by printing an article blasting my friend for sending such a presumptuous letter and attacking the credibility of listings in *Who's Who*.

When Mark Hurley, then president of Undiscovered Managers, produced his white paper, "The Future of the Financial Advisory Business and the Delivery of Advice to the Semi-Affluent Investor,"[1] in 1999, it was met with mixed reviews. In 2005, he revisited the issue, in the paper "Back to the Future: The Continuing Evolution of the Financial Advisory Business," and although he came to the same conclusions, the paper was better received because many things he predicted had started to move in that direction. (If you want to read them, visit www.jpmorganfunds.com.)

As the last several years have unfolded, many of the things that Mark predicted have come true. Mark's premise is that the industry is changing rapidly. With consolidation and new entrants, competition will be the theme of the future. The biggest change will be that advisory firms will no longer get clients for free.

Until now, we have not had to spend money for clients; they fell in the door. Roy Diliberto of RTD Financial Advisors, in Philadelphia, once described his marketing plan to me as "watching the phone ring." In recent months he complains that he is doing more watching than answering. Many advisers I've spoken with have commented that their conventional referral sources (for example, CPAs) are now their competition. To meet this increased competition, many advisers are hiring marketers and developing marketing teams to beat the bushes and get potential clients in the door.

Historically we've been entrepreneurs, quite comfortable wearing fifteen different hats, including marketer, planner, bean counter, analyst, and trash collector. However, in my experience, very few people are really good at everything. We usually fall into one of two camps: rainmakers or "brainmakers." You will need to decide which role is best for you and your practice. Are you better at obtaining and handling relationships or managing the practice? However you see yourself in your practice, in the future with the new competitive environment, you must have a marketing plan. You will also need to have a designated marketing person as well. That person might be you.

If so, you'll need to delegate some of your other activities to someone else. See Chapter 4 for some help on this concept. Even if you have no desire to increase your practice, you'll probably need to consider a designated marketer just to stay in business.

 ## The Marketing Plan

There are thousands of marketing resources available to you, including books, websites, and professional consultants. I won't pretend to compete with any of these. I am not a marketing expert. Most planners I know aren't either. And most of us do not have the time to research everything about marketing or the resources to hire marketing consultants. If you too are on your own, here are a few tips to consider in developing your marketing plan: Even if you do ultimately hire an expert, developing a basic marketing plan ahead of time will provide a handle for these issues and make the process easier and more cost efficient.

The first step in any plan is to determine your target market. I often ask advisers how they define their target market, and I get broad and very general descriptions. "Retirees" is not a target market, particularly since many people will not fit your ideal client. You can shoot a BB gun in the woods, and I guarantee you will hit something, but instead of the tree you were looking for, you could hit the bear standing beside it.

Start with writing your ideal client description. If you could work with anyone of your choosing, who would that be? What attributes would you like to see? Years ago, I completed a description of the characteristics of my own "ideal client":

- $1–10 million liquid investable assets—single account
- Long-term investment horizon
- No cash flow needs from the portfolio
- Sheltered assets
- Delegator
- Perceives self as conservative investor
- Recognizes they have limited investment experience/knowledge
- Individuals or institutions
- Nice people
- Clients who value what we do

I also listed clients I would *never* want to work with:

- Do-it-yourselfers
- Return chasers
- Unpleasant personalities
- Clients who do not value advice
- Clients who are not the primary decision makers

■ | **FIGURE 3.1** Customer Profile

customer **profile**

PLEASE FILL IN (YOU CAN TYPE RIGHT ON THE LINE)

Complete this form based on the similar characteristics of your best customers.

	EXAMPLE	
AGE RANGE:	35–49	
GENDER:		
• Male • Female	Male	
HOUSEHOLD INCOME (Average)	$175M	
NET WORTH (Average)	$400M	
EDUCATION: % of total		
• High School • College • Graduate	Graduate	
OCCUPATION:		
• Professional	Professional	
• Self-employed		
• Business executive		
BEHAVIORAL PROFILE:		
• Conservative		
• Moderate		
• Aggressive	Aggressive	
INVESTMENT TIME HORIZON:		
• Long term	Long term	
• Short term		
INVESTMENT CHARACTER:		
• Family needs/obligations (education, etc.)		
• Personal freedom/comfort		
• Relieve financial worries		
• Influence/power/prestige		
• Make money	Make money	
• Risk level		
• Challenge		
NOTE OTHER IMPORTANT CHARACTERISTICS OF THIS CUSTOMER		

Source: Fidelity Investments Institutional Brokerage Group

This exercise helps keep you focused on client relationships that are meaningful to you. It also keeps you from being distracted by "opportunity clients" whose only real value to you is in what you think *might* occur in their relationship with you.

If you have current clients, interview your staff and current clients to better define the market you are interested in. For example, when we wanted to expand our services to doctors we had targeted, we interviewed our current doctor clients to find out what issues were important to them and how we could get better visibility among physicians. From those chats we determined that it is important to differentiate our marketing according to medical specialty and practice size. Fidelity Investments Institutional Brokerage Group has allowed me to share their "Customer Profile" (see **Figure 3.1**) to help you target a desirable market. It's a great format because it allows you to immediately see any client patterns. The idea is to look at your existing client base for a pattern of client types.

JPMorgan has a similar approach (see **Figure 3.2**). First, divide your client base depending on whether they are task or relationship oriented. Next, divide them according to how standardized or customized your relationship needs to be. You can plot these following the axes shown in the illustration above. You then can get a sense of whom you want to target as clients and how.

Once you have your ideal client documented and your target market confirmed, you can then begin to formulate your marketing plan.

First, determine your resources. Marketing in any form takes human and financial capital. Be realistic in budgeting for a dedicated marketer; good ones don't come cheap, and they will need staff support. If you elect to serve as your firm's marketing guru, remember that you will limit your ability to function elsewhere (and probably in a more valuable capacity) in your business. I've learned from the experience of successful global financial services firms that good marketers don't cost money; they make money. Next, target your resources to specific

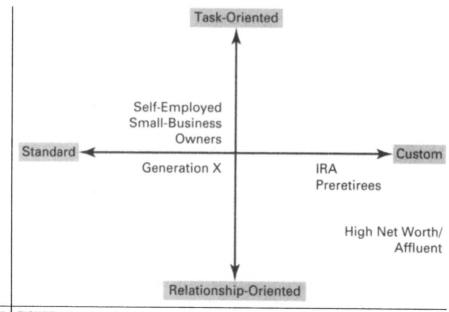

■ | **FIGURE 3.2** Mapping Client Groups by Type *Source: JPMorgan Fleming Asset Management with assistance from William M. Mercer*

activities and goals. It's not enough to say that you have $30,000 for marketing this year. You'll need to know how you will match that money to a specific seminar, mailing, or other marketing activity. I have provided a marketing budget worksheet (**Figure 3.3**) to help you think through where you want to spend your marketing money and how much you will dedicate to each effort.

Also, just as we benchmark our managers' performance, benchmark (by careful recording of the source and quality of new business) your marketing results in order to avoid ongoing funding of nonproductive campaigns. I have provided a worksheet that will track your effectiveness with each initiative and help you decide whether you want to continue or shelve the efforts going forward (**Figure 3.4**).

Consider how you can get free or low-cost help. Many practitioners have confirmed the same experience we've had. Local college or university marketing students can provide valuable and cost-efficient help in developing and implementing a marketing program. Prepare a preliminary plan, describing in some detail the target market you wish to reach. Contact the dean of the business school or chair of the marketing department to discuss the possibility of student interns or a class project directed toward your goal.

Look to your service providers for assistance. The best resources for helping you design a marketing plan are likely underutilized. There is fierce competition among product and service providers for relationships with successful practitioners. The better companies have learned that they can best get your attention by helping you be successful. Take advantage of their willingness to help. Check with your broker-dealer or custodian to see what tools they have available for you.

You may also want to consider using joint marketing efforts to leverage effectiveness. Search for opportunities to partner with others (both other planners and related professionals) in your area to reduce costs and gain higher visibility. For example, you and several advisers can get together to sponsor a special event to introduce your expertise to the public. Successful examples include:

Women's Expo. A program with speakers, products, and services (including health and nutrition specialists) specifically for women.

Fiduciary Management. A program targeted at fiduciaries for trust and Employee Retirement Income Security Act (ERISA) accounts. Participants include attorneys with an expertise in fiduciary law.

Financial Planning for Physicians in Independent Practice. This program includes experts in practice management, insurance, and Medicare reimbursements.

While a "joint" program means you have to share the exposure, developing a program with multiple professionals not only leverages your marketing budget, it helps position the program as a "public" event rather than simply your firm's marketing vehicle.

In the next chapter, I talk extensively about using public relations to supplement your marketing efforts. These efforts can give you the credibility that you need to boost interest in you and your firm, so make sure to include a robust public relations program in your marketing plan. Most of the senior advisers I know have built excellent relationships with the media and have used those relationships to gain credibility and expand their businesses.

The biggest part of your marketing plan is tracking your progress. As I noted earlier, marketing is only worthwhile if it works. It's important to know what

■ | **FIGURE 3.3** Marketing Budget Worksheet

Marketing Budget
worksheet

	Estimated Costs	Actual Costs	Actual vs. Estimate	Percent of Budget
ADVERTISING				
Print Ads (per ad)				
DIRECT MAIL				
Design				
Printing				
Mailing/Postage				
Demographic Mailing Lists				
BROCHURES				
Design				
Printing				
PUBLIC RELATIONS				
Press Kit Design/Distribution				
Write Articles				
SEMINAR/EVENTS				
Seminars—Topic Presentation Development				
Event Venue/Meals				
Invitation Printing/Mailings/Ads				
Demographic Mailing Lists				
CLIENT GIFTS				
Holiday Gifts				
Holiday/Special Event Dinners				
TOTAL				

Timeline worksheet

Use this worksheet to plan your marketing activities.

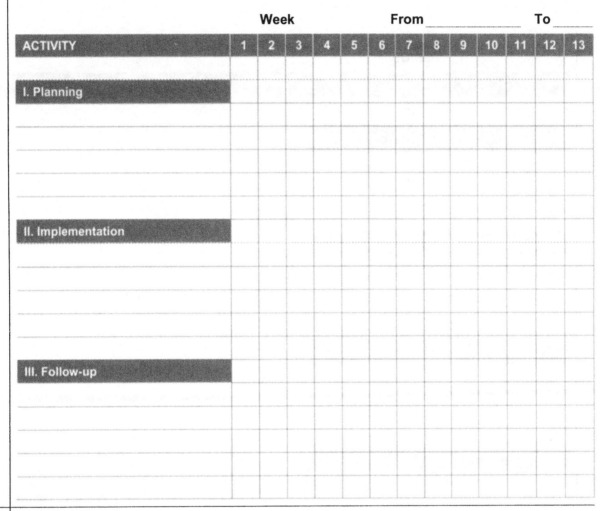

Week **From** _____ **To** _____

ACTIVITY	1	2	3	4	5	6	7	8	9	10	11	12	13
I. Planning													
II. Implementation													
III. Follow-up													

■ **FIGURE 3.4** Timeline Worksheet

works for you and what doesn't. Monitor and benchmark, ask new clients how they heard about you, and keep the results in a database.

I have included a very basic marketing plan for your use that is loosely based on material that Fidelity Institutional used to make available for their advisers. This marketing plan has two worksheets to help you think through your marketing initiatives. The first will help you plan what steps you need to take to get ready for your marketing program. The Timeline worksheet is divided into thirteen weeks. During the initial week of your marketing plan, you will be preparing contact lists, seminar scripts, brochures, or any other material that you will need to carry out your objectives. Toward the end of those weeks, you will be executing the plan.

Impact Review
worksheet

Use this worksheet to track the impact of your marketing efforts.

TIME
PERIOD _____

ACTIVITY	Responses	Interest	Prospects	Clients
Direct Mail				
Public Relations				
Seminars/Events				
Website				
Other				

■ | FIGURE 3.5 Impact Review Worksheet

Know what you are planning to do on a week-by-week basis so that you won't arrive at a critical moment and find that you are unprepared.

One of the most important pieces of your marketing plan is the Impact Review (**Figure 3.5**). This form allows you to review your efforts and decide what is

SWOT Analysis

Strengths
- Your specialist marketing expertise
- A new, innovative product or service
- Location of your business
- Quality processes and procedures
- Any other aspect of your business that adds value to your product or service

Opportunities
- A developing market such as the Internet
- Mergers, joint ventures, or strategic alliances
- Moving into new market segments that offer improved profits
- A new international market
- A market vacated by an ineffective competitor

Threats
- A new competitor in your home market
- Price wars with competitors
- A competitor has a new, innovative product or service
- Competitors have superior access to channels of distribution
- Taxation is introduced on your product or service

Weaknesses
- Lack of marketing expertise
- Undifferentiated products or services (i.e., in relation to your competitors)
- Location of your business
- Poor quality goods or services
- Damaged reputation

■ **FIGURE 3.6** SWOT Analysis

working and what isn't. Don't throw away any of your marketing effort ideas. I find that just because something doesn't work right now, that doesn't mean it won't ever work. You may try it again next year.

The essential parts of your plan should be the following: (Please see Figures 3.1 through 3.11.)

- SWOT analysis (**Figure 3.6** and **Figure 3.7**)
- Ideal client profile (**Figure 3.8**)
- Target market profile
- Current client segmentation (**Figure 3.9**)
- Growth objectives (**Figure 3.10**)
- Positioning and value proposition (**Figure 3.11**)
- Budget
- Implementation timeline
- Impact review

Although I do not talk about all these documents in this chapter, I do cover all of them in this book, so you should be able to design your marketing plan easily by pulling all of your worksheets together from various parts of this book (and see p. vi).

FIGURE 3.7 SWOT Analysis Worksheet

SWOT Analysis
worksheet

STRENGTHS:
(For example: Good reputation, superior service)

- _____
- _____
- _____

WEAKNESSES:
(For example: Weak sales force)

- _____
- _____
- _____

OPPORTUNITIES:
(For example: Expanded market due to fee business)

- _____
- _____
- _____

THREATS:
(For example: Local bank advertising new wealth management division)

- _____
- _____
- _____

FIGURE 3.8 Target Client Profile

Target Client Profile

Use this sheet for prospective client relationships.

Prospects	Excellent Opportunity	Good Opportunity	Fair Opportunity
Referrals:			
• Client			
• Center of Influence			
• Vendors			
Seminars			
Direct Mail			
PR			
Other			
Age Range			
Education			
Occupation:			
• Professional, Business Owner, Retired, Other			
Household Income			
Net Worth			
Investable Assets			
Investment Goals/Objectives:			
• Retirement/Financial Freedom			
• Family Obligations— College/Eldercare			
• Wealth Accumulation and Management			
• Other			
Investment Style			
• Delegator			
• Consultative/Sharing			
• Do-It-Yourself			

Client Segmentation
worksheet

Use this sheet for current client relationships.

Prospects	Service Level A	Service Level B	Service Level C
Age			
Education			
Occupation: • Professional, Business Owner, Retired, Other			
Household Income			
Net Worth			
Investable Assets			
Revenue to Firm			

Investment Goals/Objectives:
  • Retirement/Financial Freedom
  • Family Obligations— College/Eldercare
  • Wealth Accumulation and Management
  • Other			

Investment Style:
  • Delegator
  • Consultative/Sharing
  • Do-It-Yourself			

■ | **FIGURE 3.9** Client Segmentation Worksheet

 Put Your Plan to the SWOT Test

A good marketing plan will maximize strengths, compensate for weaknesses, take advantage of opportunities, and minimize threats. Take your plan through the SWOT (which stands for strengths, weaknesses, opportunities, and threats) analysis and recognize where you might need to make changes. Look at your plan from six different perspectives.

Here are examples of the issues you should address in your SWOT analysis:

Growth Strategies
worksheet

Market Segment_____

Objectives	Strategies

Market Segment_____

Objectives	Strategies

Market Segment_____

Objectives	Strategies

■ FIGURE 3.10 Growth Strategies Worksheet

Internal

- **Staff.** What is the number of staff, their education, experience, credentials, and interests?
- **Technology.** What types of hardware and software do you have? Are you using these to their fullest capabilities?
- **Facilities.** List your location, size, layout, attributes (for example, kitchen, conference space)

Positioning Statement worksheet

If you aim at nothing, you'll surely get there. Your positioning statement adds focus to your business and succinctly reminds your target market who you are and what you do.

	Formulating Questions	Answers
1.	Who are you?	
2.	What business are you in?	
3.	Whom do you serve?	
4.	What makes you different from competitors?	
5.	What are the unique benefits of working with you?	

Positioning Statement:

■ | **FIGURE 3.11** Positioning Statement Worksheet

External

- **Vendors.** List relationships with vendors, such as fund companies, financial services providers, and technology providers.
- **Professionals.** Do you have formal or informal relationships with accounting firms, law firms, trust companies, and banks?
- **Organizations.** What are your relationships with other professionals, regulatory agencies, nonprofits, and businesses?
- **Clients.** What are their skills and businesses? Are you making the most of your clients' knowledge and ideas? For example, one of my clients has her own advertising and public relations company in New York. We pass ideas by her creative brain every chance we get. Do you have or should you establish a client advisory panel?

Present

- **Vendors.** What present relationships are working well?
- **Professionals.** What professional relationships (accountants, attorneys) are working well?
- **Organizations.** With what organizations do you retain memberships, such as the Financial Planning Association (FPA), the CFA Institute, or Rotary?

- **Clients.** What clients can you rely upon as a resource? For example, we have six physician clients in established practices who we use as a focus group to create services for others like them.

Future

- **Vendors.** How can you use these relationships in the future? For example, you might establish a relationship with an insurance vendor experienced in underwriting medical disability or extensive property and casualty coverage if you do not presently have such a relationship.

- **Professionals.** Should you formalize current relationships, by either outsourcing or bringing these professionals in-house? Should you add more specialized resources? For example, should you establish a relationship with a law firm specializing in representing physicians in medical malpractice cases? Another example: should you consider moving your accounting relationship to a CPA firm with a well-established physician practice (if you are targeting physicians) and add in-house expertise in medical practice management?

- **Organizations.** Consider more active participation. You could become chair of the local FPA public relations committee, join the chamber of commerce and become a member of the new member committee and the entertainment committee, join the Planned Giving Council of the local hospital, or sit on the board of a community foundation.

Positive

- **Vendors.** What resources do your vendors provide in support of your practice? For example, our financial services vendor provides significant target marketing education support; our primary mutual fund company developed a database to assist us in evaluating our specific market opportunities.

- **Professionals.** What value do you receive from your professional relationships? For example, your new accounting firm and law practice affiliates may be interested in developing new business and willing to provide support gratis in return for possible referrals.

- **Organizations.** Are your current membership organizations providing support for your practice or insurance arm?

- **Clients.** Have any clients indicated a willingness to participate in an advisory role?

Negative

- **Vendors.** Are your vendors becoming your competition? Many financial services firms are beginning to provide direct client advice in areas across the country.

- **Professionals.** Are your current accounting and legal relationships establishing their own financial planning practices?

- **Organizations.** What competition do you have from organizations? For example, perhaps a local hospital Planned Giving Committee has an entrenched executive committee.

- **Clients.** What are the negatives in your current client base? For example, if you are targeting physicians, do you have a relatively low number of physician clients in independent practice? Is your client base so widely varied that it is impossible for you to see a target market or a market trend?

The process of the SWOT analysis will help you clarify many of the issues you need to address when developing your marketing plan. Consider sharing your ideas with key staff or partners for their perspectives.

Become Growth Obsessed

Mark Hurley, who is now president of Fiduciary Network, suggests that independent firms that are good at marketing efforts create a marketing culture. That is, everyone is involved in the marketing efforts, there is an organizational commitment to marketing, and a portion of the compensation for everyone is tied to individual goals and firmwide goals. As you formulate your marketing plan, include everyone in the design and responsibilities. You will be surprised how focused your company can be on new business when everyone has some job or responsibility for bringing in new business, especially when they are compensated in some way for it.

I believe that too many firms are retention focused, not growth focused. Naturally, you want to keep your current clients happy so that they will stay with you year after year. But unless you are deliberately farming your current clients for new business, you are probably not making the most of those relationships. I know advisers who clearly state to clients, "Your fees are not the only way I get paid. I also get paid by taking on new clients that you refer to me. Do you know any others that I might help?" Advisers who are successfully growing their practices have learned how to balance the retention with growth.

Spheres of Influence

Hurley believes that a marketing program that incorporates a systematic networking program will find more success than looking for your target clients one at a time. "Think about it," says Mark. "In times of volatility, or fears of recession, or any economic downturn, you can contact your influencers and give them information that will make them look pretty smart to their clients. What professional doesn't want that?"

Mark Hurley's "Six Elements of a Systematic Networking Program" looks like this:

1. Develop a target list of referral sources.

   a. Attorneys

   b. Accountants

   c. Insurance agents/mortgage brokers

   d. Affiliation groups

   e. Professional associations

   f. Executive recruiters

   g. Charitable organizations

2. Have a written marketing plan.

   a. Schedule, objectives, milestones

   b. Avoid anonymous contacts.

3. Design a tracking system.

   a. Activity, contacts, meetings

   b. Updated, maintained for attribution

   c. Information handoff

4. Incorporate a "rapid response" mechanism.

   a. Advise on major news stories.

   b. Excuse for additional contact

   c. Manage the story and the perception of your firm.

5. Insist on participation by all firm professionals.

   a. Fundamental mentality shift

   b. Relationship managers, client service personnel

6. Ensure that senior management is involved and focused on marketing.

   a. Annual preparation of plan

   b. Monthly review of participation efforts

   c. Ongoing adjustments to plan

As with any worthwhile effort, consistency is imperative. If you cannot maintain the firmwide enthusiasm for the marketing process, you can easily fall back into old habits. Only you can decide how important your marketing efforts are to the success of your business.

We own the paper; we own the ink.
—Bob Clark, former editor in chief of *Investment Advisor*

Visibility means credibility. Gaining visibility is an important challenge for any adviser. Larry Chambers, writer and author of the workbook, *Attraction Marketing*, told me that "celebrities earn a premium because they are better known than other members of their profession." Visibility builds credibility, which brings clients. Larry's visibility hierarchy looks like the illustration in **Figure 4.1**. You'll notice that four of the seven items listed in the Chambers Visibility Hierarchy involve the media, and none of them is "I started noticing your paid ads after three or four repeat impressions."

Larry's hierarchy confirms just how important media exposure is for us in developing our business. Unfortunately, all too often media are equated with advertising. Few practitioners have the resources to compete with the financial gorillas in advertising. The good news is that we don't have to.

Dr. Martha Rogers, a partner at Peppers & Rogers Group of Stamford, Connecticut, has coauthored an exceptionally insightful book called *Enterprise One to One*.[1] The book's premise is that your marketing should not consist of blitzing a huge audience, offering the same thing to many. Instead, the goal should be to provide an array of services to one customer at a time. Think about your practice. It is built on relationships with individuals.

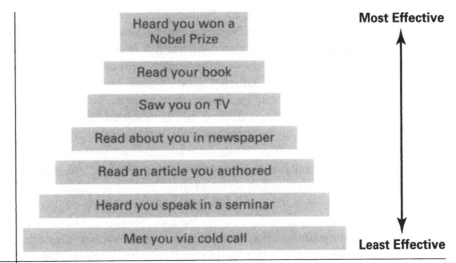

■ **FIGURE 4.1** The Chambers Visibility Hierarchy *Source: Larry Chambers*

You get to know them, educate them, watch over their money, and help them meet their goals. We've spent years convincing people that they are unique. Their goals are different from anyone else's. In fact, twenty years ago, one of the standard lines I used was, "You wouldn't take your neighbor's prescription medicine. Why would you take his investment advice? What's good for him isn't necessarily good for you." Yet, as soon as the prospect became my client, I began to treat him the way I treated my other clients. I made a financial plan for him, which essentially looked the same as every other plan I wrote. I put him in the same investments as every other client, and my reports to him were exactly the same as those that everyone else received. I justified this by explaining that standardization was necessary to ensure that each client received the best service. Furthermore, I could help more people, using mass production. Horse puckey! What I was doing was institutionalizing and standardizing a very personal, unique relationship. My service was a system, and my clients were being processed through the system. Henry Ford's first customers could have any color car they wanted as long as it was black. My clients could have any service as long as it was the one I offered.

Mark Ralphs, of Financial Advisory Consultants in the United Kingdom, told me that he can work with, at most, fifty clients. When the number of clients gets perilously close to that, he reviews his client base to determine if anyone should be graduated, or he stops entering into new relationships. "I realized early on that I can only be effective in the lives of so many people. But while they are clients, I am the adviser of the whole person, not just their financial affairs."

Judy Shine, of Shine Investment Advisory Services in Englewood, Colorado, explains that her company remains small by choice. Her client base is limited to people whose needs and circumstances are similar, but her relationship with each one is dictated by the services and support they believe they require. "In a way," explains Judy, "my client base has defined me."

Believe It!

I am not a marketing expert. Neither are any of the advisers I know. But, we've got two things going for us. We believe in the service we have to offer our clients, and because we are able to communicate that, our clients trust us. We are constantly repositioning ourselves—with prospects, with our clients, and with the media.

When I was a kid, my sister Sharon had a Tupperware distributorship. Tupperware was sold on a home party system. My sister's sales force would go into a home, set up a display, and demonstrate the use of various plastic storage containers to the attendees while serving them coffee and cookies. One day, Sharon took me along while she trained a new salesperson. Sharon and her trainee set up the display and sat down with cups of coffee. The party attendees wandered to the table and picked up the brightly colored containers. Soon they were telling each other how they used this piece and how they loved that one. Many sat down and filled out an order form on the spot. Sharon and her trainee drank coffee and kibitzed with the other women. Later I asked her why she didn't get up and demonstrate the pieces like the other salespeople I'd seen. "Deena," she said, "when you believe in your product, it doesn't have to be sold. It's bought."

I apply this concept to our services. Our clients come to us for our expertise and advice. I used to have difficulty giving an answer to the question, "What is your performance?" This question is plain enough to the money manager who needs to maximize returns and who, in fact, stakes his reputation on making the list of the top ten mutual funds of the last ten minutes. But I meandered through my answers, giving performance numbers for different asset classes, explaining that overall performance is based on the percentage of exposure to each class. It was a miserable response. My clients wanted a number. I was giving theory.

Today, the very first statement I make goes something like this, "If we work together, we will teach you that performance is not the primary criterion for a successful portfolio. We will teach you the value of a consistent return over time and how that return can help you reach your goals. After all, isn't achieving your goals your primary concern? Wouldn't that make your portfolio a success?" I firmly believe my services consist of helping clients sleep well at night while they achieve their goals. I don't promise performance. I don't promise to beat any market. In fact, when one asset class is booming, I can promise that their portfolios will not do as well as that one asset class. Asset allocation does not maximize the client's total return; it helps them reach their goals. From the very first meeting, my main responsibility is to get that message across. I believe it will improve their lives, and I tell them so.

Joe Kopczynski believes that his honesty helps manage the client's expectations as well. "When someone knows what you know, it really changes things. I sit down with a prospect and tell them about every screw-up I've ever made. I want people to know that they are dealing with human beings." My partner Harold tells new clients with large accounts that need to be transferred, "I guarantee you that somewhere along the line someone will mess up one or more of the transfers. I also guarantee you that we'll monitor the process, assume the responsibility, and see that, in the end, everything comes over properly." David Diesslin goes right to the heart of their expectations and asks them, "If we look ahead five years, what will have made this relationship a success?"

The Art of Marketing

Adviser practices have changed over the past thirty to forty years, but sadly, our marketing techniques have not. Most advisers were successful in their practices despite their inability to market themselves effectively. Today, the competitive landscape demands that we have a structured marketing plan, a targeted prospect base, and a dedicated marketing professional or business development officer to professionally acquire new business. If marketing is not core to your skills, consider hiring.

Promote the Whole, Not the "Core" Business

I am originally from Chicago, home to McDonald's corporate headquarters. Some of my clients worked for McDonald's. In fact, I had the pleasure of visiting Hamburger University one year. Imagine my shock to learn that McDonald's

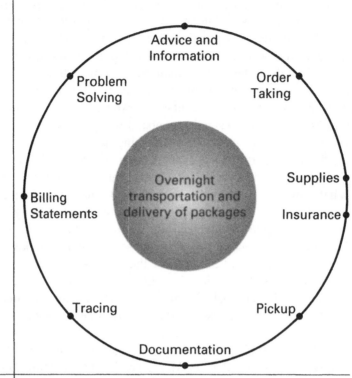

FIGURE 4.2 Core and Ancillary Services of FedEx
Source: FedEx

is not in the hamburger business. They will tell you that they are in the thirty-minute-eating-experience business that happens to include hamburgers. One of their most famous tag lines is, "You deserve a break today." It does not say, "You deserve a hamburger today." Although their core business is food, they provide toys, playgrounds, consistency, and an atmosphere for taking a break from a busy day.

Successful advisers have figured out that they are not just in the investment advisory business. Just look at Ross Levin's philosophy statement in Chapter 1. ". . . we define wealth as integrating all your resources—financial, emotional, physical, and spiritual." Ross is not confining his practice to one aspect of his clients' lives.

Paul Brady of Brady & Associates in Australia says he's a lifestyle consultant. David Diesslin is a self-described client coach. Judy Lau, president of the Wilmington, Delaware, financial planning firm Lau Associates, and Judy Shine position themselves as counselors. Smart advisers know that they cannot segregate a client's financial life from the rest of his life. Successful advisers have found ways to incorporate that concept into their practices.

The illustration above (**Figure 4.2**) can help determine how you can position yourself in the marketplace. The picture represents the core and supplementary service elements of FedEx. As you can see, FedEx does not merely position itself as an overnight transportation and delivery service company. It is in the corporate support business.

On a blank piece of paper, draw your own circles and write your core business in the center. Then list around the outer circle all the supplemental services you provide clients. Review all the supplementary services and, ignoring for a moment what is written in the core circle, try to devise a statement that focuses on those supplemental services. This exercise may help you position your practice in an entirely different way—the way a client perceives it.

Years ago my partner Harold was to deliver two speeches, back-to-back, on two coasts. Upon arriving in San Francisco, he discovered that he had not brought his overheads for his second talk, which was in New Jersey. It was a Saturday, and I had the responsibility of getting his materials to him in New Jersey on a Sunday so that they would be available for his talk at 8:00 a.m. Monday. I called FedEx and explained my dilemma. The support I received from their representative was amazing. "I think we can make this work," he told me. "It happens that we have Sunday delivery at the Newark airport. Is he going to Newark?" I was relieved to say that he was. "Great. Now," he said, "is he a member of any airline club?" Yes, he was a member of the American Airlines Admirals Club. "Wonderful," he told me, "they have one at the Newark airport. Here is the address of the local FedEx office in your town. You deliver your package by 7:00 p.m., addressed in care of the Admirals Club at Newark. Then call the Admirals Club in Newark and tell them to expect your package and hold it until your partner arrives. He can pick it up when his flight arrives from San Francisco." FedEx is definitely not just in the overnight package delivery business. And their employee understood that.

If this sounds as though I am dismissing financial knowledge, expertise, and skill in favor of counseling and hand-holding, rest assured I am not. Obviously, financial advice is the core of your business, and you must do it all very well. McDonald's makes good hamburgers. FedEx delivers packages fast and efficiently. If they didn't, neither would survive. You just don't have to promote your core service as if it were the only thing you do.

Who Is Your Competition?

In the mid-1980s, I joined the RotaryOne Club in Chicago. At one of my first meetings, I met the regional director of Delta Air Lines. In an attempt to make small talk, I asked him who he considered to be his competition. Since Chicago is the home of United Airlines, I naturally assumed he would name United. He looked me straight in the eye and said, "AT&T. In the future, teleconferencing will probably eliminate the need for much of the business travel." I was shocked at his insight, and began wondering what it meant for my business.

Your competition probably does not come from the obvious quarters. Step out of the box and figure out who it is. Then you can prepare to meet it head on. At our firm, we have determined that our competition is not from other advisers, but from a local trust company. They have a one-hundred-year-old tradition of service and fine china in their private dining room. Their fees are high and their returns are mediocre, but their service is impressive. That's where we've attacked. We can't compete with our own private dining room, but we do have superior, attentive service, intensive customer care, and a classy gourmet restaurant nearby, where my nephew is the chef.

Position and Promote Subtly

Many years ago, I got a little booklet in the mail. It was twenty pages on how to create a good business plan. Initially, I didn't pay any attention to who sent it, nor did I much care. Still, it contained some good information, so I stuck it away for future reference. Then another one arrived, this time about hiring and recruiting. Then I received another about designing office space, then one more about business succession. I began to look them over carefully. They were damned good. They were from Chase Vista Funds. Chase didn't write the books; they hired experts to pen them. The last page in each one explained that as a financial company, they understood my needs and wanted to be a partner in my success. There was not one statement in any of those books that touts the excellence of their funds, or their performance. I'm sure they have that material, but that's not what they sent to me. Through these books, this company was subtly telling me that they did not see me as just a distribution channel for their funds. They saw me as a partner in our mutual future success. The positioning was powerful. I had never looked at these funds before, but I made it a point to visit them at the next industry show. Imagine the impact on your prospects when you position your services as different from those of your competitors.

Courting the Media

No matter the level to which you feel you need to take your visibility, you are going to want some media exposure. The more formalized you make your approach to the media, the better success you'll have. First, recognize that there are different kinds of media to target. Aside from the obvious printed media, there are broadcast and Internet media as well.

Let's start with some general hints about positioning yourself with the media.

 ## Use Public Relations Wisely

My partner Harold is probably the most widely quoted financial adviser in the nation. He got there because he worked hard at establishing relationships with the media. He stays popular because he learned the value of the "fifteen-second quotable." Harold says he realized years ago that in order to compete with far larger companies, he needed visibility and credibility. While advertising can certainly develop visibility, it is costly and in our industry does not address issues of reputation or status. Good public relations can. He figured that the best way to reach the media was to write to them. So, he began to address letters to specific journalists, commenting on some of their columns. If he found an item of interest, he'd write to compliment them on their effort, and then add an additional tidbit to suggest related areas for stories that they may want to pursue in the future, while at the same time demonstrating knowledge of the subject. The journalists he wrote to would file his letters for future reference.

After he started getting calls from the media, he realized that he wouldn't get more unless his remarks were thoughtful, pointed, and memorable. One day while watching a morning news show, it struck him that the best interviewees speak in fifteen-second sound bites. They must sound intelligent, and they must have something to offer that makes the experience richer for the listener. These attributes are no less important when working with the print media, since reporters are usually on deadline, have limited space to make their point, and must consistently be informative.

It also occurred to Harold that he could not be an expert on every subject, but he could be a good resource. He spent the time and energy to compile a list of other financial service professionals and their expertise. When he received a call that he did not feel comfortable fielding, he would offer another name. Soon, journalists on deadline would call him asking for sources.

You Need a Plan

Not everyone sees the value of good public relations. I think it's essential for growth, but it does take time. If you decide to cultivate the media, you will need to develop a public relations plan. It should include the following information:

- Your organization. Who are you and what sets you apart?

- Public relations objective. How do you want to influence public opinion?

- Current public exposure. How much and what type of exposure do you have now?

- Expected public exposure. What exposure do you want to have, specifically?

- A defined target audience. Who are you trying to reach?

- A fully developed strategy. What steps will you take to accomplish this plan? Once you have a plan in place, you will need to have specific action items before you can get started.

- An evaluation of your publicity strengths. What are your oral and writing skills?

- A design for a media package. It should include your biographical sketch, a brochure, and reprints on your firm and its principals.

- A media list. These are the people you want to get to. Don't just use the books in the library. Construct your own by reading the publications and watching and listening to the programs that the audience you wish to reach will be reading, hearing, and seeing. Notice who's writing the stories and producing the programs.

Additional actions you can take to further your public relations plan might include the following:

- Join a local community or service organization like Rotary or Kiwanis to raise your visibility.

- Contribute your time and talent to professional organizations at both the local and national levels. This will raise your visibility within your profession and attract industry media.

- Develop your speaking abilities by giving lectures or conducting seminars.

Hone Your Skills

After you've made all these preparations, you still must decide how you will act and react when that first call arrives. Many of the advisers I interviewed for this book have enjoyed good relationships with the media. I have compiled a list of their best suggestions:

- Be aware. Read everything your clients are likely to read. You should be familiar with what the public is reading and thinking. Your value to the media will be your ability to integrate the issues of concern to the general reader with your own professional expertise.

- Be available and prompt. Reporters generally need answers "now." Make sure your office knows where to find you if you get a call. If you are not available, reporters will move on to the next source.

- Be professional. Don't make negative comments about others in the profession.

- Be prepared. Always ask journalists if they have a deadline. If you are not comfortable speaking spontaneously, ask to make an appointment to discuss the subject later.

- Be honest. If you don't know, don't answer. However, ask the reporter if he or she would like you to find someone who does know. If the reporter says yes, do so *immediately*. If you are unsuccessful, let the reporter know posthaste.

- Be clear and concise. Journalists rarely have time for long stories or ramblings. They will let you know if they do.

- Be controversial. Stick your neck out. Say something worth hearing. If you're really a professional, you presumably have opinions on professional issues. Be prepared to defend them after they appear in print.

- Be interesting. Pithy comments will likely wind up in print. News today is as much entertainment as it is information. Recommending that investors buy low and sell high is a good way to send a reporter on to a new source.

- Be confidential. Don't offer details about specific clients or their circumstances without first discussing it with the clients.

- Be circumspect. Don't say anything that you would not want to be made public. If you have to preface your statements with, "This is off the record," you probably should not say it in the first place.

- Be respectful. Good reporters are also professionals. Credit them with knowing more about their profession than you do. Don't try to persuade them to refocus a story. They know why they're asking the questions they are; you don't.

- Be realistic. You won't always be quoted in a story even if you have been interviewed. Life's not fair, but if you're patient you'll get your fair share.

- Be responsive. If you're misquoted, determine whether the mistake is serious enough to do something about. You then have two choices: You can ignore it, while vowing never to speak to that reporter again, or you can write a nonconfrontational letter, stating, "I appreciate your interest in my thoughts. However, it seems that I did not express myself clearly because the quote you used in your article did not reflect my point. What I was trying to say was . . ."

Why Bother?

I attended a session on public relations for financial service professionals not long ago. One of the planners explained that he had all the business he wanted and couldn't figure out why he would want to spend time courting the media. We all agreed that this might not be the most effective use of his time now. This is for you to decide. If you believe that your client base is stable, and you can attract new clients without establishing even a local media presence, then by all means, forget it.

Bear in mind that the financial advisory profession is changing rapidly. Conventional marketing techniques may not be enough to ensure growth and can even be counterproductive if you're selling the wrong features. Subtle positioning of your practice, as well as effective use of public relations, can poise your business for dynamic growth.

Lou Stanasolovich of Legend Financial Advisors in Pittsburgh compiled a list of reporters in publications that he'd like to reach and then sent each of them a letter similar to the one below:

> This letter is to introduce you to our firm, Legend Financial Advisors, Inc. Attached is a fact sheet about the firm and our services as well as biographies of our financial advisers.
>
> Also attached are several briefs (story ideas) on current financial planning and investment market issues. We make briefs available on a monthly basis with the hope that you will find them valuable in identifying emerging issues. Each brief lists how to contact us directly by phone if you require more information, want to follow up on one of the topics, or want to discuss any other topic that you may be interested in for a story.

Lou reports that he gets several calls a month from reporters following up on an interesting idea he's sent their way. You can get ideas for stories by jotting down issues that your clients have asked you to address over the past few days or weeks. Look for trends in their queries, as well as items that you thought were different or challenging to tackle. Lou cautions that this approach takes work. Each month you need to come up with some substantive ideas to send.

Tucker Hewes of Hewes Communications in New York City agrees that sending story ideas to the media is a good way to stimulate interest. Tucker cautions, though, that cultivating media relationships is not for everyone. "Most advisers don't know why they are doing it. Ask yourself, what are you going to get—higher visibility, credibility, and article reprints to send your clients? Is this what you are aiming for? Are you really going to get new clients from this effort?" Tucker also believes that planners seldom stay with their public relations plan. "They sit down one weekend, write a few press releases, and then next month they get busy and forget all about it." Tucker's tips:

- If it's news, such as hiring a new staff employee, issue a press release.

- If it's an idea or a comment, one-on-one contact is the best.

- Forget the *Wall Street Journal*. Make a list of a handful of newspaper writers in your hometown, contact them, get to know them and send them ideas. Reporters like to feel that they are getting exclusive information. They know that when a press release shows up, everybody has it. If you call or e-mail them with a good idea, they know you've singled them out.

- Watch your expectations. There are really very few planners who are quoted on a regular basis by the financial press.

- Keep a current press list. Reporters move around a lot so you need to periodically check the phone numbers, addresses, and e-mail addresses to keep them current.

- Follow up, follow up, and follow up. Like everything else, this plan takes constant attention.

- Be sure you have the skills for this. Just because you want to talk with the press doesn't mean they want to talk with you. Be brutally honest about your ability to communicate effectively. Don't try it if you don't enjoy it.

- Have patience. Courting the media is all about cultivating relationships, and this takes time.

Here are some other ideas for getting media attention:

- Regularly attend professional conferences and conventions. Reporters and correspondents are there to get a perspective on these meetings, and they want new contacts.

- Speak at these professional gatherings. The media tend to be interested in profiling a good speaker who has a good story.

Broadcast Media

Many public television stations around the country have cable programs. As a professional, you have unique knowledge that can be a valuable commodity for their programming. It's your job to let them know you're available and how you might be a resource. In Miami, the local PBS station provides community-access programming. Students are the camera and crew. A few years ago, through this program, I produced my own series, *Financial Fitness*, in conjunction with the local chapter of the International Association for Financial Planning (IAFP), now the FPA. The IAFP members were talk show participants. We covered such topics as "You Can't Take It with You, But Who Gets It When You Go?" (estate planning issues) and "The Taxman Cometh" (end of the year tax planning). Explore what's available in your area.

Bob Glovsky of Mintz Levin Financial Advisors appeared on his own radio program every week for eight years. Bob says that certain people like the anonymity of radio or television to ask questions they might feel intimidated to ask an adviser face-to-face. A radio show, he says, also gives an opportunity to reach a wide range of people and to "feel them out" before they visit in a formal appointment.

The Internet

There's a whole new world of media that you can target on the Internet. In many ways this contact is easier—simply leave an e-mail with comments, ideas, and issues. Here are some favorites of planners I know.

Morningstar	www.morningstar.com
Morningstar Advisor	www.morningstaradvisor.com
SmartPros	www.pro2net.com
Horsesmouth	www.horsesmouth.com
TheStreet.com	www.thestreet.com
SmartMoney	www.smartmoney.com
Bloomberg	www.bloomberg.com
MarketWatch	www.marketwatch.com

Media Referral Programs

The following organizations have media referral programs. Essentially, you can sign up, declaring areas in which you consider yourself an expert. When they get specific media calls, they'll refer to you.

CFP Board of Standards: www.cfp.net (800-487-1497)

American Institute of Certified Public Accountants (AICPA): www.aicpa.org (212-596-6111)

FPA: www.fpanet.org (800-322-4237)

National Association of Personal Financial Advisors (NAPFA): www.napfa .org (847-483-5400)

Society of Financial Service Professionals (SFSP): www.financialpro.org (610-526-2521)

Preparing for Media Calls

Once your name has hit a reporter's computer screen, you'll need to start brushing up on events of the day that might be newsworthy.

- Skim the financial press each morning, making notes on interesting items.
- Choose a financial website that gives you up-to-the-minute news in a format you like.
- Visit the financial professional sites listed above to see what professionals are talking about.
- Keep a resource file with interesting articles and information that you can get to quickly if your phone rings and a writer wants a comment.

- Read what your prospective clients read, not just the *Wall Street Journal* and *Barron's*. Successful, media-savvy planners read the publications their clients read—*Money, SmartMoney, Kiplinger's Personal Finance*, and similar publications—cover to cover.

Preparing for Interviews

A few years ago Schwab Institutional gave a few of us advisers an opportunity to spend a day with their consulting PR firm, Edelman Public Relations. The workshop leaders for Edelman gave some interesting advice about interviews: "An interview is only an opportunity if it provides a platform to showcase your expertise and firm." This was a different perspective for me. I thought the object was to get your name in the paper. They were telling us that we should "grant" interviews only if it suits our purposes. The second bit of advice I found valuable was that "the point of the interview isn't to answer the reporter's questions. The point of an interview should be because you have something to communicate. Determine your objective, then balance everything you say against it." Frankly, this discussion helped many of us present ourselves as less "desperate" for media exposure. Some other gems from the Edelman pros:

- Know who your audience is, and direct your answers to them when you speak to reporters.
- Focus on the message you have, not on the messenger (reporter).
- Anticipate the questions. Few people handle impromptu questions effectively.
- Keep it simple and to the point. Sound bites are good.

There are plenty of public relations books out there, but two I believe are essential: Larry Chambers's *The Guide to Financial Public Relations: How to Stand Out in the Midst of Competitive Clutter*[2] and Beth Chapman's *Get Media Smart!: Create News Coverage That Builds Business*.[3] Larry has shared some great material on gaining credibility to be found later in this chapter. You can get Larry's book at your local bookstore or through online booksellers on the Internet. Monthly retainer fees for Larry's public relations and media services average between $5,500 and $10,000 per month, plus expenses.

Beth's resource package comes with an audiotape and learning guide to walk you through your own self-directed media program. She details how you should include a PR plan in your marketing plan. You can get a copy of this or any of her many products by contacting her at Ink & Air (I love that name!), 508-479-1033, or www.inkair.com. Monthly retainer fees for her full-service public relations and media strategies average between $3,000 and $5,000 per month, plus expenses. Her "Get Media Smart!" professional development program is currently $49.95. Both Beth's and Larry's products and services are well worth the money (and I don't get a cut). Explore them now.

Press Releases

Earlier in this chapter, Tucker Hewes warned against overuse of press releases. But there are times when they are very useful for a specific event. For example, the following press release was sent after recent stock market volatility:

FOR IMMEDIATE RELEASE   Contact: Martina Schramm
                                       Tel: (305) 448-8882 x 235
                              E-Mail: Martina@evenskykatz.com

Worried Over Market Volatility? Consider the Can-of-Tuna Strategy

With the market's current volatility, one prominent wealth manager's simple advice makes sense, calms nerves, and may help you prosper.

(Feb.1, 2008, Coral Gables, Florida) If the stock market's volatility has you on edge, the simplest advice can be the wisest. In his January 2008 market letter, Harold R. Evensky, president of Evensky & Katz Wealth Management, a Coral Gables, Florida–based firm, reminds investors in his own easy-to-understand fashion how lower stock prices offer "sale price" opportunities.

Well-aware that investors often have the urge to sell their assets when stock prices are declining, Evensky offers his readers this simple investing strategy advice in his letter to clients entitled, "Thoughts on Recent Market Volatility":

"If tuna fish normally sells for $1 per can, you'd go to the grocery and buy just the amount you need for current consumption. If the price went up to $2 a can, you'd probably cut way back on your purchase of tuna fish. And, if it went on sale at fifty cents a can, you'd think, 'Wow! This is a real bargain!' and you'd buy cases to stock up at that great sale price."

Evensky knows that no one likes seeing his or her nest egg dwindle but understands the value inherent in a declining market. "Unfortunately, as generations of markets and decades of research confirm, the only way to make money in the market is to be in the market through thick and thin," he said.

For more information, contact Martina Schramm at (305) 448-8882 x 235.

To read Evensky's January 30, 2008, market letter, "Thoughts on Recent Market Volatility," visit www.evensky.com/default.asp?P=332288, and click NewsLetters & Commentary in the left-hand panel to download the letter.

About Evensky & Katz Wealth Management
Evensky & Katz is nationally known for its skill in wealth management and financial planning. Providing clients with traditional wealth management services as well as comprehensive tax, insurance, and estate planning services and generational wealth transfer and charitable planning advice, the firm offers fee-based wealth management services to corporate executives, professionals, physicians, business owners, retirees, and other affluent clients. Utilizing a team approach in analyzing and planning a client's investment portfolio, recommendations are based solely on your specific needs, circumstances, and goals. The firm is registered with the U.S. Securities and Exchange Commission. All advisors are Certified Financial Planner practitioners with a wealth of planning and investing experience. All are active members of the Financial Planning Association.

# # #

Notice that a press release is in a specific format, with the contact person's name at the top right-hand corner and crosshatch marks at the end. Try to keep

FIGURE 4.3 Announcement Card

Continuing the practice of fee-only financial planning and investment management,

James L. Budros CFP, ChFC
Peggy M. Ruhlin CPA, CFP

BUDROS & RUHLIN, INC.

are pleased to announce

Daniel B. Roe, CFP

has joined the firm's executive staff
April 1, 1996

1650 Lake Shore Drive Suite 150
Columbus, Ohio 43204.4895

telephone (614) 481.6900
facsimile (614) 481.6919

Source: Budros & Ruhlin

your press release to one page. Larry Chambers's book has a great section on press releases, including a checklist to make sure you do it right.

Announcements

Announcement cards work well, particularly if you have an event to publicize. Budros, Ruhlin & Roe sends a simple announcement card (see **Figure 4.3**), accomplishing two things at once: announcing the milestone and reminding us of what they do.

A few years ago, Jack Blankinship of Blankinship & Foster sent the following letter, similar to a press release in format, to his clients and professional acquaintances. Jack's letter subtly let people know that his company has been honored before, which adds even more prestige to the firm.

PRESS RELEASE   August 15, 2000

Once again a national magazine has honored our firm.

The August issue of *Medical Economics* is now on the newsstands with its exclusive list of the "150 best financial advisers for doctors."

A total of nine planners were named, including Blankinship & Foster, for the state of California. Two of the nine are in San Diego.

This is the second time *Medical Economics* has published its list of "best financial advisers." The first was in 1998.

We are honored to be named again in 2000.

Announcements are still announcements, so if you really want to get some attention, you might want to consider something a bit more offbeat. When we returned to our former name after a named partner left, we sent this announcement (see **Figure 4.4**) to some (not all) of our clients. We got lots of attention and plenty of laughs.

Do It Yourself

I left one of the best recommendations for last. All the earlier strategies depend on getting the media to accept your expertise and write about it. Why not take control yourself?

Years ago, a professor in one of my marketing courses gave us a project. We each had $5,000 to market our business. (Okay, so this was quite a few years ago.) Our job was to figure out how we were going to spend it effectively. Some set aside money for newspaper advertising, while some spent money on fancy brochures and fine stationery. Not one of us came up with the professor's solution: "Publish a book. It will make you an authority and give you instant credibility." In hindsight, I believe he was right. Being quoted in the press can give you instant credibility, but being an author gives you instant celebrity, or at least an instant of celebrity when you need to draw on it. You can self-publish a booklet, eighty pages or so, to hand out to your prospects and use in seminars. It's impressive, and you'll distinguish yourself from others in the business.

"If you can't commit to a book," says professional financial writer Larry Chambers, "write articles." Larry has developed an interactive CD that walks you through writing an article with the ease of a professional. Larry's advice on writing about problems in an industry may help you target a certain market. For example, you could write an article about financial issues for a physician. You can find out more about Larry and *Attraction Marketing* at www.lchambers.com. When I asked Larry for some material for this book about writing an article, he graciously allowed me to adapt a piece from his book. This is good stuff.

How to Write a Problem-Solution Article

How does your service solve industry or consumer problems? A published article in a targeted periodical that educates, informs, or solves a problem can be very effective in generating new business. Readers are much more likely to respond favorably to a solution to a problem from someone who communicates expertise than from someone who is pushing a firm or product.

Design the article to explain the complexities of a problem in a certain industry. This draws readers and increases your chance of getting published. Your goal should be to create a feeling within the reader that he or she has discovered something new and useful.

Don't write self-serving articles. If an article sounds like you're trying to sell something or be manipulative, you are! Instead, address a problem, pose a question

---

THE DWEEB, THE CURMUDGEON, AND THE DRAGON LADY

[HAROLD EVENSKY, PETER BROWN, AND DEENA KATZ]

ANNOUNCE THE RENAISSANCE OF

EVENSKY, BROWN & KATZ

FINANCIAL ADVISORS

241 Sevilla Avenue, Suite 902   305-448-8882
Coral Gables, Florida 33134   FAX 305-448-1326
January 1999   EBK@EVENSKY.COM

■ **FIGURE 4.4** Offbeat Announcement *Source: Evensky & Katz*

or series of questions, or explain an opportunity. Begin with a brief introduction of only a sentence or two, and then get right into the how-to of the article. Educate, solve a problem, or reveal an advantageous situation. Success sells success. Highly educated professionals are always looking for timely information that will increase their wealth of knowledge.

— Outline the article. Carefully determine who your readers are and what the point of the article will be. Identify the main premise you want the readers to learn.

— Identify the problems or concerns that the readers have in common.

— State the problem.

— Identify three related problems that are a result of the main problem.

— Provide steps and actions to correct the problem.

— Discuss any relevant discoveries or recent developments that the readers wouldn't likely have heard about yet.

— Write a personal experience story that shows the problem and how you solved it.

— Use a call to action, when appropriate.

— Summarize your article.

— Reread. Does the ending answer the question that you posed at the beginning? That's the built-in test.

If you are not a writer or have great ideas but can't seem to get them to paper, there are some alternatives for you. Get a writer to help you: Dian Vujovich at mismutual@aol.com and Janet Ashkenasy at editor@janeta.com can help write articles and books to get your ideas noticed. Larry Chambers offers Attraction Marketing Academy, a boot camp that will take you through the process. His boot camp includes a workbook, *Attraction Marketing: Shifting from Pursuit to Pursued.* It is well worth the money.

 ## So, What's the Story?

In the future, the need for marketing and public relations will become much more important as the competition for clients becomes fiercer. You won't have the luxury of making mistakes, so carefully plan your approach, track your progress, decide what's working for you, and keep at it.

If a man smiles all the time, he's probably selling
something that doesn't work.
—George Carlin, comedian

Your brochure is one of your first opportunities to let people know about you and to qualify them at the same time. You have a couple of choices for an initial information brochure. You can get a big, slick, professionally printed one, or you could create your own with desktop publishing, printing only what you need, when you need it.

 The Big Brochure

Many advisers produce a slick brochure with information and pictures of the principals and key personnel. These can be very impressive, but there are a few things you must think about before deciding to make this commitment. Budros, Ruhlin & Roe in Columbus, Ohio, have gone this route. Peggy Ruhlin advises:

- Get a professional. Unless you have talent in this area, hire a professional to design your image, including the logo, then lay out the brochure to speak to your target market. Peggy says their target is high-net-worth individuals, so they wanted a "rich" look.

- Be sure the copy speaks in your voice. A copywriter will probably do the work, but you will need to inspect it carefully to be sure that it is in keeping with your personality and style. Peggy advises that it is not necessary to use a professional who has done other financial brochures. In fact, sometimes a fresh new look emerges from someone who has not.

- Get ideas from clients (a client advisory board, perhaps) about the content. For example, you may interview several clients and ask what issues about your relationship and services are important to them.

- Consider the costs of the design you choose. Peggy notes that the costs of printing their big brochure were "astronomical." This was in addition to the costs for the design. She and her partner, Jim Budros, decided to order thousands of copies to get a price break. "Unfortunately," reports Peggy, "we have new partners in the firm who are not even in the brochure. We handle this by including bios on all of us when we send it out." She suggests that in the future they might consider one with "moving parts" so that they can update pieces periodically.

RTD Financial Advisors also has a professional brochure. Roy Diliberto, the firm's president, decided to hire a financial writer to design and pen the copy for the brochure. As a result, Roy feels that the depth of knowledge from someone who knows the business well can add a great deal to the content.

Simpler Brochure Options

There are alternatives to making the expensive leap Peggy made. Ron Tamayo, Dan Moisand, and Charlie Fitzgerald of Moisand Fitzgerald Tamayo, LLC in Maitland, Florida, have written a snappy brochure using Microsoft Word. When it needs updating, they simply revise the document and reprint it. To give it a little distinction, they use a heavy, more polished-looking paper stock. Ron's suggestions for producing the brochure include the following:

- Keep it simple. Don't try for fancy graphics or pictures. Unless you use a pro, it will probably look homemade.

- Include a page on your company philosophy. A clear explanation of your mission avoids misunderstandings later.

- List the principals. Give partners' background and education as part of the material.

- Keep it businesslike, not gimmicky. Cartoon characters and stick figures may show off your sense of humor but don't make a serious impression.

- Include explicit descriptions of your services and fees.

Ron, Charlie, and Dan have shared their five-page Word document for your use as a model to customize (see **Figure 5.1**, p. 74). I like their format because, although the style is simple, it's classic-looking and covers all the material that I think you should impart to prospective clients. Notice how the information goes from broad to specific. That is, they talk about their firm and their philosophy, then lead in to specific details like indexing and tax planning. Then they discuss the planning process and the fees. Finally, they introduce you to the players—a section with short bios to impress the prospects with their experience and credentials.

Greenbaum and Orecchio in northern New Jersey once had nice preprinted brochures but have since elected to desktop publish their own on demand. "For one thing," reports Tom Orecchio, "we like to make our informational packages more customized to the client's interests and the type of work he wants us to do." Tom credits their flexible design and high-end color printer with making the package look more professional. "You can have the best-written material in the world, but the design and print quality make a big difference in the presentation." Tom also advises not to make the informational package too technical. "Our old brochure even had pictures of the efficient frontier." Along with a warmer style, their new format includes a client profile sheet. This can be found in **Figure 5.2**. Tom and his partner Gary Greenbaum decided that prospects would be more comfortable with them as advisers if they could identify with other clients of the firm. This is a great idea because my experience has shown that prospects will usually ask what types of clients we have. This preempts the question.

Introduction

CLIENT PROFILES

Greenbaum and Orecchio, Inc. provides wealth management services to a wide variety of high-net-worth individuals, trusts, foundations, and endowments. All client information is held in the strictest confidence. Presented below are a number of Greenbaum and Orecchio client profiles that fairly represent the wide variety of clients that the firm serves. We currently represent seventy-four clients with total assets under management of nearly $125 million.

Executives
- Total number of clients: 19
- Average age: 51, ranging from 38 to 66
- Assets under management: $55,000,000
- Current client status: 12 working, 7 retired

Widows
- Total number of clients: 6
- Average age: 69, ranging from 58 to 86
- Assets under management: $10,000,000
- Current status: 1 working, 5 retired

Business Owners
- Total number of clients: 16
- Average age: 51, ranging from 41 to 66
- Assets under management: $16,000,000
- Current client status: 11 working, 5 retired

Consultants
- Total number of clients: 7
- Average age: 65, ranging from 55 to 78
- Assets under management: $5,000,000
- Current status: 2 working, 5 retired

Professionals
- Total number of clients: 8
- Average age: 57, ranging from 44 to 67
- Assets under management: $13,000,000
- Current status: 5 working, 3 retired

Corporate Employees
- Total number of clients: 7
- Average age: 59, ranging from 47 to 70
- Assets under management: $4,000,000
- Current status: 2 working, 5 retired

Trusts & Foundations
- Total number of clients: 11
- Assets under management: $19,000,000

FIGURE 5.2 Client Profiles *Source: Greenbaum and Orecchio*

Among the other materials that Greenbaum and Orecchio provide in their initial package is a one-page description of services (**Figure 5.3**). This page outlines the services available and explains whether each is a one-time matter or an ongoing function. The at-a-glance format makes it easy for the prospect to grasp whether the services are what he is looking for.

Brochure Supplements and Alternatives

Along with the material in our prospect package, we include a rather detailed philosophy statement (see **Figure 5.4**, p. 79). We also use it separately for reinforcement during the client relationship. We include detailed information about investment theory, client-related concepts, and implementation. I am positive that most clients do not read our statement when we send it out initially, but we always walk new clients through it during our education process.

Introduction
DESCRIPTION OF SERVICES

Features and Benefits of Our Services	Consulting	Investment Counsel	Wealth Management
Define how we will work together with you	One time	Ongoing	Ongoing
You will get full disclosure of risks and fees so that by understanding how we work together, you avoid unpleasant surprises.			
Learn about you and your goals and answer your questions	One time	Ongoing	Ongoing
We learn about you, your goals, and your constraints so we both understand where you are starting from and where you want to go.			
Analyze financial planning strategies to help you make informed decisions	One time	----------	Ongoing
We evaluate alternative solutions and make specific written recommendations so you can understand how to best achieve your goals.			
Analyze investment choices and allocation strategies to help you make informed decisions	One time	One time	Ongoing
We evaluate investment options and different allocation choices with you so that you understand the risks you are about to take and the risks you can expect.			
Implement the financial planning strategies that best achieve your goals	-----------	Ongoing	Ongoing
We help you to implement the written recommendations we present to you, and we consult your other advisors so that we work toward a coordinated, comprehensive strategy for you.			
Measure, manage, and report to you your progress toward your financial planning goals	-----------	-----------	Ongoing
Quarterly, you receive a financial goals report that details your progress toward those goals.			
Measure, manage, and report to you your progress toward your investment goals	-----------	Ongoing	Ongoing
You get ongoing investment management and communications. Quarterly, you receive a performance report that monitors your progress toward achieving your investment goals. We rebalance your portfolio periodically so that you stay on track and earn what you need to achieve your goals. This strategy causes you to systematically buy low and sell high.			
Update your financial plan to accommodate changes	-----------	-----------	Ongoing
During our comprehensive review we answer any new questions you may have, we integrate new research, products, and tax law, and we learn about your updated goals. We do this so that you can continue to make informed decisions and we can update your strategy so that it stays optimized, prudent, low cost, and tax smart.			
Update your investment strategy to accommodate changes	-----------	Ongoing	Ongoing
During our comprehensive review we answer any new questions you may have, we integrate new research, products, and tax law, and we learn about your updated goals. We do this so that you can continue to make informed decisions and we can update your strategy so that it stays optimized, prudent, low cost, and tax smart.			

FIGURE 5.3 Features and Benefits *Source: Greenbaum and Orecchio*

We also may include a reprint of an article or two that gives us some credibility. We choose an article that either describes our services well or is a current quote from a national source, such as the *Wall Street Journal* or the *New York Times*. Generally, if we know what interests the prospect has, we will include a pertinent article as well. Since I have covered public relations in Chapter 4, I won't go into any other detail here. The entire package is placed in a linen-type, colored folder with our name embossed on the front. You can purchase these from a local office supply store, or alternatively try www.paperdirect.com for some very nice specialized paper for stationery, folders, and envelopes. We do our own embossing, but a local instant printing office can probably do it as well. As a courtesy to the prospect, we also include a detailed map of Coral Gables to assist in locating our office. MapQuest (www.mapquest.com) is a great website to use in making highly customized maps and directions.

Along with the package, we include the following simple prospect letter explaining what we've sent and indicating that we will contact the prospects later to see if they have questions or want to make an appointment. The whole experience is very low key, which is our style, but many advisers are much more proactive in attempting to set an appointment.

Dear PROSPECT:

It was a pleasure speaking to you regarding our services. As I mentioned, I have prepared a packet of information describing the nature of our firm's practice and our philosophy.

Once you've had the opportunity to review our material and would like to consider establishing a relationship with us, please fill out the enclosed data-gathering booklet, and return it in the self-addressed envelope. This information will help us better understand your needs so that we can make our preliminary meeting more productive. I will call you in about one week to see if you have any questions and to schedule an appointment at your convenience.

Should you have any questions in the interim, please call me at 305-448-8882.

Cordially yours,

Financial Planner

A few years ago we became a bit frustrated with the cost of sending our expensive brochures to anyone who happened to find our phone number, so we developed what I call the "tire-kicker" brochure (see **Figure 5.5**). It folds to business-envelope size and has the "quick-and-dirty" information about us, including lists of services, fees, and philosophy. We use it for people we think are not yet serious about our services. It has saved us time and money over the years. I have reproduced it here for you, so you can customize one for yourself.

The Targeted Brochure

The late David Norton of Norton Partners in the United Kingdom designed a brochure aimed at entrepreneurs. The first page reads like this: "You're an entrepreneur. Do you run your personal finances as if you were a business? In your business, you'll seek to increase your income, spend and invest effectively, protect yourself from disaster, and plan for the future. We'll help you do the same for yourself personally. Read on to see how the Entrepreneur as a Business Program can meet your needs." David then gave a list of problems a target market might have:

- My accountant advises the business, but I'd like someone who specializes in advising directors to assist me personally.
- I'd like to increase my after-tax income.

FIGURE 5.5 Summary of Services: Tire-Kicker Brochure

Evensky & Katz

Evensky & Katz is nationally known for its skill in wealth management and financial planning. The firm provides its clients with traditional wealth management service as well as comprehensive tax, insurance, and estate planning services; generational wealth transfer and charitable planning advice. Taking responsibility for providing and/or supervising all aspects of the members' financial planning needs enables the firm to provide its clients with cost-effective, "one-stop," hassle-free personal financial planning and management.

Implement and Monitoring

The Company's strategy for providing many services is to enter into alliances with established service firms and outsource providers (for example, attorneys, accountants, banks, trust companies, insurance firms, mortgage financing, auto leasing, bill paying, college planning) to seamlessly provide products and service to clients.

Evensky & Katz
2333 Ponce De Leon Boulevard
Penthouse Suite 1100
Coral Gables, FL 33134
(800) 448-5435
(305) 448-1326 fax
www.evensky.com

Planning to Live Well

Private Family Office. We developed our Private Family Office to offer our clients comprehensive solutions to their financial and related personal needs. Evensky & Katz Private Family Office provides an exceptional experience and a level of sophistication and service that, until now, has been impossible to obtain for individual investment portfolios of less than $50 million.

A Private Family Office . . .

Evaluates

▲ Client Objectives
▲ Investment Issues
▲ Risk Management
▲ Tax Issues
▲ Estate and Gifting
▲ Income Needs
▲ Other Financial Issues

Plan Design

▲ Investment Planning
▲ Risk Management
▲ Tax Planning
▲ Estate Planning

FIGURE 5.5 Summary of Services: Tire-Kicker Brochure (*Continued*)

Custody of Funds Managed by E&K. When appropriate, we recommend that Fidelity Institutional of SEI Trust be selected as custodian for your accounts. Fidelity accounts are insured to $100 million per account. There is no charge for opening or closing an account. All checks for your investments will be made payable directly to an independent brokerage firm or trust company. All accounts are held in your name. E&K acts solely as your independent investment advisor.

E&K Professionals. All Evensky & Katz advisors are required to become Certified Financial Planner certificants within a reasonable amount of time. Our advisors are also required to meet minimum annual CFP Board educational requirements plus additional hours in a specialization such as retirement, pension, trusts, estate, and investment planning.

The company has developed a team-oriented Service Delivery System for providing high-level, one-to-one customized services. The team structure flows through all levels of the service model: sales, member relationship, and planning.

Advantages of working with Evensky & Katz. We are committed to providing planning and investment management guidance for individuals, families, pension funds, trusts, and institutions. In addition to providing the same level of expertise and service formerly available only to large institutional clients, we offer:

▲ Absolute confidentiality
▲ Qualified, experienced, and credentialed professionals
▲ "Best of Breed" solutions
▲ Unbiased advice and judgment

Advisory Fees. Fees are based on the firm's evaluation of the client's service and advice needs and are designed to insure that the client receives superior value. Fees are billed quarterly, in advance. There are no entrance or exit fees.

**EVENSKY & KATZ
PRIVATE FAMILY OFFICE**

Summary of Services and Fees

■ Initial Data Gathering
■ Risk Tolerance Questionnaire
■ Analysis and Evaluation of Investments
■ Capital Need Analysis
■ Investment Policy Design
■ Financial Planning Review and Issue Identification

Minimum Fee: $2,500

Private Family Office Services

■ Investment Planning and Management
■ Tax and Estate Planning
■ Risk Management Planning
■ Other Personal Financial and Related Services

Minimum Fee: $10,000

Harold R. Evensky, CFP
Deena B. Katz, CFP · Lane M. Jones, CFP
Matt McGrath, CFP · Deana L. Kelly, CFP
Brett Horowitz, CFP · Charles Sachs, CFP
Taylor M. Gang, AIF · Charles Sachs, CFA

- My financial affairs could be better organized.
- I want to run my business and leave personal finance to someone who knows what he is doing.
- I'm not sure how my pension schemes work or what they are worth.
- I'd like to plan how I'll exit from my company.
- If I die tomorrow, I don't know how secure my family would be.
- I wish I had more time.
- I wonder what my company is worth.
- I haven't got anyone I can really talk to about my finances.
- I'd love to do something different, but I don't know if I can afford it.
- I'd love to find a financial adviser I can trust.

If a prospect identified with any of the problems, he suggested they see if they qualify for the Entrepreneur as a Business Program.

David reported that he had good success with this brochure because it was customized to the prospects he was seeking. They could immediately identify with the material, and David was sure that those people he wanted to see had gotten the message he wanted them to get.

 ## Video and Audio Brochures

I have seen audio and video "brochures" used as different approaches to telling clients about you and your services. Some advisers have had great success with these, so you might want to investigate yourself. Just google "video business cards" on the Internet. There are plenty to view. For a real change, try putting a "talking head" on your website to explain your services. A short video clip of you or other key personnel in your office may be a unique way to personalize your Internet impression.

 ## Going Brochureless

Many advisers are telling me that they are not investing much in brochures these days, but letting their website be the entrée to their services. The Web is so widely used now that it's possible to just direct your prospect to your website to get background information and become familiar with you and your company. In our experience, prospects visit our site before they even give us a call. The right website vendor provides you the ability to track visitors to your site and connect with them through your site. (Check out www.advisorsites.com.) Don't discount the value of a good website to support your marketing efforts.

The Second Impression

There is no question that the material you provide to a prospect makes the second impression. (The first, I maintain, is in the voice of the person who attends to the call when the initial contact is made.) If your material is haphazard and disorganized, or if it looks amateurish, it will affect what the clients feel they can expect from you. If it makes a good impression from the day they receive it, you'll be managing their expectations of an excellent experience with you.

■ | **FIGURE 5.1** Public Relations Material

MOISAND FITZGERALD TAMAYO, LLC FINANCIAL PLANNING & WEALTH MANAGEMENT

OUR FIRM provides comprehensive fee-based wealth management services to corporate executives, professionals, business owners, and other affluent clients. We use a team approach in analyzing and planning a client's investment portfolio, estate plan, cash flow, income taxes, and retirement. Recommendations are based solely on your specific needs, circumstances, and goals. The firm and its partners are registered with the U.S. Securities and Exchange Commission. The partners are Certified Financial Planner licensees with more than thirty years planning and investing experience. All are active members of the Financial Planning Association, the Central Florida Estate Planning Council, and other professional organizations.

OUR MISSION is to partner with clients to establish and achieve financial goals through objective planning and management of investment assets. Our purpose is to help build, manage, and preserve your wealth. We put our client's interest first, act with integrity and honesty, and strive for excellence in every facet of our practice. Our success is not measured by performance statistics but rather by our clients' success in achieving their goals.

OUR CLIENTS share in the realization that by coordinating and managing today's financial decisions they can achieve their goals for tomorrow. They are individuals and businesses who expect excellence and have made a firm commitment to achieving it themselves. Our clients usually have no desire to manage their financial affairs on a daily basis, want to simplify their lives, and are willing to enter into a long-term relationship that is mutually beneficial. They are highly motivated to work with a professional adviser, not a sales representative.

OUR PHILOSOPHY is to provide our clients with the highest level of service and technical expertise in the management and preservation of wealth. The entire staff of Moisand Fitzgerald Tamayo is firmly committed to this philosophy.

(continued)

■ | **FIGURE 5.1** Public Relations Material (*Continued*)

PHILOSOPHY

MOISAND FITZGERALD TAMAYO seeks to build and preserve your wealth. Through client-specific financial analysis and investment research, our services are designed to secure your financial well-being for the long term. As your investment manager, we are dedicated to delivering advice in a manner that is both confidential and consistent with your needs.

A SERVICE ORIENTATION

Service and personal attention are the hallmark of Moisand Fitzgerald Tamayo. It is the defining quality that sets us apart from our competition. The personal relationship that we develop with each of our clients starts with an initial meeting that identifies your needs, objectives, and risk tolerances. Thereafter, we develop a plan and illustrate our investment process, philosophy, and portfolio design. Once we have agreed upon an appropriate portfolio, we implement our portfolio recommendations. Every three months you will receive a written portfolio performance report, which gives you a clear picture of your account performance. We are available to meet with you to review your performance report each quarter, as well as for periodic reviews.

In short, Moisand Fitzgerald Tamayo is service oriented—not sales oriented. Our ongoing attention to the composition and performance of your portfolio, and our frequent communication with each of our clients, distinguishes Moisand Fitzgerald Tamayo as a truly client-focused firm.

FINANCIAL PLANNING

We believe in the financial planning process. This is the process of identifying goals, gathering and reviewing financial data, and designing and implementing a plan to help you reach your goals. It is a lifelong process. Once the plan is in place, it needs to be monitored, reviewed, and updated to meet dynamic circumstances. Not everyone needs to have a written comprehensive financial plan. Everyone, however, can benefit from the financial planning process.

OBJECTIVES

There is no one particular investment portfolio that is appropriate for all individual investors. The optimal portfolio will depend on the amount and timing of cash flow needs, tax considerations, and market conditions. Investment decisions should be based, therefore, on the client's objectives. Through that objective-driven process, crucial factors such as appropriate levels of risk and return are derived and optimized to achieve those objectives.

(*continued*)

■ | **FIGURE 5.1** Public Relations Material (*Continued*)

INVESTMENT PLANNING

Investing is only one component of financial planning, though certainly an important one. We believe that an investment policy and asset allocation can be designed only after the initial financial planning process is complete and a target return is established. We allocate assets among the major classes of cash, stocks, bonds, and real estate. Stocks are divided between domestic and foreign and large and small capitalization. We further divide domestic stocks into growth and value styles. Bonds are divided by short, intermediate, and long-term duration. We use real estate investment trusts (REITs) for the real estate component of a plan.

INVESTMENT POLICY

We believe in developing client-specific investment strategies that emphasize diversified asset allocation. Each client has a personalized Investment Policy Statement, which outlines the strategy just right for that individual.

TAX SENSITIVITY

Taxes represent a significant consideration for every long-term investor. By minimizing income taxes, investors retain more wealth to help meet their goals. We exercise care in the appropriate placement of investments within taxable and tax-deferred accounts. For example, we generally place index and tax-managed vehicles in taxable accounts and higher-turnover mutual funds in tax-deferred accounts. However, tax considerations do not dominate our portfolio management process.

INDEXING

We use index investments predominantly with domestic large-cap stocks and domestic bonds. Index mutual funds and exchange-traded funds offer lower transaction costs, minimal asset class drift, and greater tax efficiency. However, we also use actively managed funds to overweight the growth or value portion of the domestic equity allocation.

(*continued*)

■ | **FIGURE 5.1** Public Relations Material (*Continued*)

FINANCIAL PLANNING

These services are oriented toward developing written strategic plans for solving specific problems and/or reaching specific goals depending on family needs. There is a one-time fee charged for this initial plan development. Fees may be between $900 and $4,000 depending upon the complexity of the plan. Available individually or as part of a comprehensive plan that often includes:

- Retirement Income and Capital Needs Analysis
- Investment Analysis and Strategies
- Estate Planning and Tax Minimization
- Charitable Giving Strategies

WEALTH MANAGEMENT SERVICES

Our wealth management services provide a comprehensive level of planning and investment management in two phases. The first phase of our wealth management services includes development of a financial plan and portfolio design. There is a one-time fee charged for this initial plan development as outlined above.

The second phase of these services is ongoing management and financial planning services fees. Included with this phase are quarterly reports on the client's investment portfolio, target allocation, and related performance. This includes a tracking of portfolio holdings, interest and dividend payments, capital gains, overall portfolio performance, and so forth. Periodic meetings are held with the client to review his or her current situation and investment portfolio. These services are limited to those with a minimum of $_____ to place under management. Fees are calculated as a percentage of assets under management and include ongoing financial planning services. The schedule is as follows:

- The first $XX is billed XX% per quarter;
- The next $XXX is billed XX% per quarter;
- Amounts over $XXX are billed XX% per quarter.

INVESTMENT ADVISORY SERVICES

These services begin with the establishment of an Investment Policy Statement developed from the portfolio optimization process. We will implement, manage, and reevaluate your portfolio on a regular, ongoing basis. The fees for these services are the same as for our wealth management services with the exception of the initial plan development fee. Once an asset allocation strategy has been determined for a pool of capital through the optimization process, specific investment decisions must be made. A carefully selected group of no-load mutual funds is typically used for most portfolios under $500,000. Larger portfolios may be appropriate for our private account management service. Assets are custodied at either Charles Schwab & Co., Inc., or Fidelity Investments. These reputable institutions assure our clients of reliable execution and reporting.

(continued)

■ **FIGURE 5.1** Public Relations Material (*Continued*)

DANIEL B. MOISAND, CFP

Dan is a principal of the firm. He specializes in retiree cash-flow planning, trust planning, planning for new wealth, estate planning, and portfolio management. He is a member of the Financial Planning Association (serving as its national chairman in 2007), Brevard County Estate Planning Council, the National Association of Personal Financial Advisors, and the Society of Financial Service Professionals. Dan is an active writer and is the only two-time winner of the *Journal of Financial Planning's* national Call for Papers competition. His writings have also appeared in publications such as *Financial Advisor, Financial Planning, Investment Advisor*, and *Wealth Manager*. He is frequently quoted by a variety of media, including *Business Week*, ABCNews.com, CBS *Market Watch, Forbes, USA Today*, and the *Wall Street Journal*. Dan holds a bachelor of science degree in finance from Florida State University.

CHARLES E. FITZGERALD, III, CFP

Charlie is a principal and founding member of the firm. He specializes in retirement planning and investment services to corporate employees, business owners, and retirees. Charlie is a member of the Financial Planning Association (FPA), the FPA of Central Florida, and the Central Florida Estate Planning Council. His planning advice has been featured on NBC Channel 2, in the *Orlando Sentinel,* and as a frequent cohost on AM 580 WDBO. Charlie was a financial manager at AT&T Corporation for thirteen years and is an honors graduate in business administration and finance from the University of Florida.

RONALD TAMAYO, CFP

Ron is a principal and founding member of the firm. He specializes in portfolio analysis and design and estate planning with the goal of protecting and enhancing retirement assets and estates. He has more than fourteen years of financial planning and tax consulting experience. He is also a registered investment adviser affiliate of the firm. Ron has appeared as the featured planner, and his expertise has been written about, in *Morningstar 5 Star Investor*, a national publication for individual investors. He is an active member of the Financial Planning Association (FPA) and the Central Florida Estate Planning Council. He is a board member of the Financial Planning Association of Central Florida. Ron earned a bachelor's degree in accounting from Orlando College and is an adjunct instructor of financial planning and investments for the University of Central Florida.

Source: Moisand Fitzgerald Tamayo

■ | FIGURE 5.4 Investment Philosophy

INVESTMENT PHILOSOPHY

The following summarizes our firm's core beliefs. These provide the basis for your Investment Policy. The entire staff of Evensky & Katz participates, at different levels, in the development of our philosophy. All members of the firm are committed to its consistent implementation. Policy design, implementation, continuous monitoring and, as necessary, modification, are integral parts of the wealth management process. Our success is measured not by performance statistics but rather by our clients' success in achieving their goals.

CLIENT-RELATED ISSUES

Goal Setting
We believe that clients must set their own goals. It is our responsibility to educate them in the process and to assist them in defining, quantifying, and prioritizing their goals.

Cash Flow
We believe that clients need total return, not dividends or interest. The traditional concept of an "income" portfolio is archaic and places unnecessary and inappropriate restrictions on portfolio design.

Expectations
We believe that "conservative" assumptions are a dangerous myth. Return requirements should be based on real rates of return. An investment policy should not be prepared based on a client's unrealistic expectations. If necessary, we will refuse the engagement.

Risk Tolerance
We believe that a client's risk tolerance is a significant constraint in the wealth management process. Success can be measured by our clients' ability to sleep well during turbulent markets.

Tax Constraints
We believe that tax considerations must be considered. However, the goal of tax planning should be to maximize after-tax returns, not to minimize taxes. Neither reported turnover nor holding period calculated from reported turnover is a useful measure of tax efficiency. Annuities should generally only be considered when asset protection is an issue (in those states where the law protects annuity assets).

(continued)

■ | **FIGURE 5.4** Investment Philosophy (*Continued*)

INVESTMENT PHILOSOPHY

INVESTMENT THEORY

Risk and Return Measures
We believe in the use of appropriate mathematical measures of risk and return. The primary measure of risk should be standard deviation. The primary measure of risk-adjusted return is the Sharpe ratio. Duration, not maturity, is the appropriate measure of a bond's exposure to interest rate risk (within narrow rate changes). Convexity is an important measure of a bond's sensitivity to large changes in rates.

Efficient Market Hypothesis (EMH)
We believe in the weak form of the EMH. We reject the use of classic technical analysis and market timing.

Growth Versus Value
We believe in the conclusion of the Fama/French research that, over time, value equity portfolios will provide superior performance. However, we also believe that eliminating growth allocations will result in interim divergence from the broad markets that our clients would find unacceptable. We believe a 2/3 weighting for value and 1/3 for growth is the most appropriate weighting to balance these conflicting issues.

Active Versus Passive
We believe that the choice between active and passive management is not either/or. We use both. In general, we believe that our value portfolios should be passively managed and our growth portfolios actively managed.

Asset Allocation
We believe that the portfolio policy is a significant determinant of long-term portfolio performance. Because we believe in the overriding importance of the strategic allocation, we reject managers who do not have clearly defined philosophies or who diverge from their stated policies. Because we do not believe in market timing, we reject sector managers.

We believe in maintaining a strategic allocation and only infrequently revise that allocation. We believe in rebalancing to the strategic allocation. However, the influence of taxes and transaction costs leads us to conclude that contingent rebalancing with fairly wide bands is the most appropriate solution. We do not currently implement a tactical allocation overlay. However, we believe it is an appropriate strategy.

INVESTMENT PHILOSOPHY

Optimization

We believe that mathematical optimization is the appropriate method for designing a strategic asset allocation model. We also believe that an optimizer is simply a tool to be used by a knowledgeable wealth manager. The primary controls over the optimizer are the development of logical input data (expected returns should not be historical projections), an awareness of the optimizer's sensitivities to the input, and other appropriate constraints. The final recommendations should not be based on the optimizer's unconstrained optimal solution but rather the optimal, suboptimal solution.

Time Diversification

We believe that the relative risk of increasing equity exposure decreases as the time horizon of the goal increases. We do not believe that any investment should be made for a goal with less than a five-year time horizon. Funds required in fewer than five years should be placed in money markets or fixed-income securities (e.g., CDs, Treasuries) with maturity dates equal to or less than the goals' time horizons.

IMPLEMENTATION

Managers

We believe that professional money managers will generate results far superior to a client's or wealth manager's direct security selection and management. With rare exception, separate account management (including wrap accounts) is inefficient and expensive. The universe of public and institutional funds offers the best alternative for the superior management of multiple-asset-class portfolios.

We believe that managers should be selected and evaluated based on their philosophies, processes, and people. Once selected, a manager should be allowed periods of poor performance if he remains consistent with his philosophy and process. He or she should be replaced immediately if his or her implementation strays significantly from the stated philosophy or process.

Evaluation of managers should entail a detailed review of all available pertinent information, including both fundamental qualitative and return factor analyses. However, the ultimate decision to hire or fire should be based on fundamental data. Performance measurement should be against appropriate benchmarks, not broad market indexes.

Ongoing Management

We believe that there should be regular review of a client's situation to determine if he is continuing to move in the direction of achieving his goals. This includes revisions in strategic allocations as a result of revised assumptions or changing client circumstances or goals. We should continue to educate our clients, always remaining sensitive to the volatility of each one's expectations. Our responsibility is to assure that our client "stays the course" and does so with a minimum of emotional pain. The focus should always be the client and the achievement of his goals, not the performance of the portfolio.

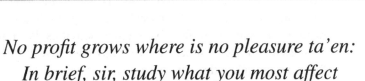

Profitability and Optimizing

6

No profit grows where is no pleasure ta'en:
In brief, sir, study what you most affect
—William Shakespeare, *Taming of the Shrew*, Act 1, Scene 1

Twenty years ago, I sat in a session that Mark Tibergien, then of Moss Adams (now at Pershing), gave at an International Association for Financial Planning (IAFP)—now the Financial Planning Association (FPA)—Registry Conference in Washington, DC. Mark talked about how each of us needs to treat our practice like a business. He talked about the difference between revenue and profit and what metrics to use to measure our profitability. For most of us, this was new territory. We knew what profits were—it was everything that was left over after we paid the bills. That was our salary, too.

A few weeks ago I had the pleasure of hearing Mark again. Once more, he talked about how we need to treat our practice like a business. He talked about how to measure our profitability. He talked about revenue and profits. Sure, there were new faces in the crowd, but plenty of seasoned ones who probably needed to hear it again. In the past, we didn't need to pay too much attention to the mechanics of the business, or at least *we* thought we didn't.

Today, there are plenty of good reasons to pay more attention to your business. The FPA Moss Adams studies have been showing for years that well-managed firms are more profitable. Competition has supercharged the landscape, margins have been squeezed, and you need to stay focused to stay in business. More important, you can't tell how you are doing unless you are keeping track. Knowing metrics such as the number of clients per professional helps you decide when you need to add staff. Revenue per client helps demonstrate the wallet share and pricing of a fee-based practice. These are the metrics that help shape and improve your bottom line.

But, for many advisers, it's difficult to see that impact, unless you have been paying close attention to your business and know what a profitable activity is, and what it isn't. And it's easy to ignore because you are undoubtedly busy with your clients, and ultimately, that's what makes you a success. However, if you want your practice to rise to the next level, you will want to spend some time managing the business, too.

One of the first steps is to get your arms around your current client costs and capacity—the first step toward improving profitability. First, let's agree that your time is a limited commodity. Let's also agree that your time is a valuable resource and represents the majority of your costs in servicing a client. If you have not already done so, try to determine what your time is worth on an hourly basis. You can do this easily by backing into this number using a revenue target. Then determine how many hours you

83

spend working. Let's say you work fifty hours a week, fifty weeks per year. That would be twenty-five hundred hours. These are the total hours so, if you believe that you work more hours per week than fifty, use that number. Now look at how many hours you spend directly on client activities. For purposes of this example, let's assume 60 percent because you may have investment activities or marketing that does not relate directly to a client.

So, of the twenty-five hundred hours you work, fifteen hundred could theoretically be billed to different clients for work directly for them. Now, let's say you have a revenue target of $500,000; your hourly rate would be $330. You've learned in every marketing course you've had that *time is money*. Now, you know just how much *money* your time is worth. Notice that when you translate your time into a dollar amount, you can begin to see which clients are profitable, and which are not. You can begin to be more cognizant of the time you put into each part of your relationship with them. The form provided by Moss Adams in **Figure 6.1** will help you establish the cost of service to each client.

Next, think about all the time you spend on a client relationship. This includes the initial preparation, analysis, implementation, monitoring and rebalancing, update meetings, and reviews—whatever time that you could bill directly to a client if you were billing. If you have administrative or planning staff working on client activities, you could include that but with a lower hourly billing rate. You could also include your overhead in the calculations—technology costs, office space, and other expenditures, but, we're keeping it simple here; you just want to get at what a client costs *you* in time.

You also want to include start-up costs, or costs you incur in taking on a new client who you might not have on an ongoing basis. Amortize those first-year costs over five years (because you don't have the initial start-up time every year), and say you reach a minimum client revenue number of $5,200. So, let's assume that you need $5,200 from every client you work with, or you lose money.

Now, let's assume that your practice is a big dining room table. You have one hundred chairs around this table. If you are to reach your revenue goal of $500,000—each person occupying a chair must give you $5,000. But, suppose you have people sitting in chairs that are only giving you $3,000 annually. You can't get any more chairs around the table so the only way for you to make more revenue is to (1) hope somebody falls out of a chair, (2) push somebody out of a chair, or (3) hope someone leaves a chair on his own so you can replace him with someone who will pay the $5,000.

One of the biggest traps we advisers fall into is ignoring capacity. We say, "Well, I'll take this client, even though he does not fit my profile, even though he does not meet my revenue requirements, because I really have no additional costs to service this client—so the revenue he generates will just be profit." Keep in mind, he still occupies a chair—he takes up capacity—and you can only handle so many clients, so why shouldn't they be profitable?

Once you know what your cost per client is, you can be more selective of the clients you want to take. That doesn't mean you can't take on a new client who'll pay you less, but consciously know why you are doing it. Remember, opportunity clients cost you, too, so be certain that you're not filling up chairs with expectations instead of with paying clients.

FIGURE 6.1 Establishing Client Viability

Example: Establishing Client Viability

The viability of a client is really a function of the cost of the service you deliver. If the cost of service is $2,000, then you can service any client who generates revenue greater than $2,000. The real issue is how to establish the cost of service. The first step is to estimate the cost of your time since your time is the most valuable resource and represents the majority of the service cost.

Estimating the cost of your time (example only). Let's make the following assumptions about how you spend your time:

a. Total Hours Worked	2,500
b. Percent Spent with Clients (billable)	60%
c. Client Hours (a × b)	1,500
d. Revenue Target	$500,000
e. Revenue Target per Hour (d ÷ e)	$330

Next we need to look at how much time you expect to spend with clients.

f. Time Spent with a Client (example only)

- Initial Data Collection	5 hours
- Initial Strategy and Plan Design	8 hours
- Plan Discussion/Approval	2 hours
- Implementation/Paperwork	8 hours
- Ongoing Monitoring/Rebalancing	2 hours/quarter
- Yearly Update Meeting	3 hours

Totals:
- 23 hours in the first year
- 11 hours ongoing

g. 23 hours in the first year × $330 =	$7,590
11 hours ongoing × $330 =	$3,630
h. Amortize first-year costs over 5-year relationship	$1,518
Ongoing costs	$3,630

Minimum client revenue necessary to meet revenue target: $5,200/year

The above example shows a process for determining client viability. You should go through the same process in the space provided on the next page.

(continued)

■ | **FIGURE 6.1** Establishing Client Viability (*Continued*)

Exercise

Productivity (example only)

    a. Total Hours Worked   _____

    b. Percent Spent with Clients (billable)   _____

    c. Client Hours (a × b)   _____

    d. Revenue Target   _____

    e. Revenue Target per Hour (d ÷ e)   _____

Viability

    f. Time Spent with a Client (example only)
      - Initial Data Collection   _____
      - Initial Strategy and Plan Design   _____
      - Plan Discussion/Approval   _____
      - Implementation/Paperwork   _____
      - Ongoing Monitoring/Rebalancing   _____
      - Yearly Update Meeting   _____
      - Other (list)

           _____   _____
           _____   _____
           _____   _____

    Totals:
           - First year (hours)   _____
           - Ongoing (hours)   _____

    g. _____ hours in the first year × _____ per hour (e) = _____
       _____ hours ongoing × _____ per hour (e) =   _____

    h. Amortize first-year costs over 5-year relationship   _____
       Ongoing costs   _____
Minimum client revenue necessary to meet revenue target: _____

If this seems too expensive, the only way to decrease your target revenue per hour is to modify the model in the following areas:

- Hours per year (a); work more hours per year to reach your revenue target.
- Spend more time on clients (b); spend less time managing the practice and more with your clients.
- Lower your revenue target (d).
- Spend less time with the client (f); decrease client interaction either up front or ongoing.

Source: Moss Adams

Knowing your cost per client helps you determine if fees are appropriate, but the process of determining that cost will help you see how you can leverage your time, when you are at capacity, and when you need to add staff. This is the first step in turning your practice into a business. Those who have transformed theirs will tell you that means improved profitability and growth with purpose. You may love what you do, but it really is a lot more fun when you make money at it.

Again, I highly recommend that you purchase a copy of *Practice Made Perfect* by Mark Tibergien and Rebecca Pomering.[1] This book will help you get your arms around your profitability and help you to benchmark your progress with appropriate matrixes.

Companies are a lot like people. They go through different stages throughout their lives. Businesses, however, do not automatically move forward toward the next level just because they celebrate another birthday.

—Jim Wood, director of entrepreneurial consulting services at Ernst & Young

Successful planners can expect to address one of two scenarios likely to appear in maturing firms. One involves shifting the compensation structure from commission-only to fee and commission, and from fee and commission to fee-only. The second one involves converting an existing fee practice, in a related profession, such as accounting or law, to an advisory practice with asset management.

First, let's look at why some planners suggest that you may want to consider moving to fees. Ron Tamayo has been a fee-only planner since 1992. He worked with a regional planning firm that accommodated not only fee planners, but also commission-only and fee and commission combination advisers. In 1998, Ron formed a new practice with two commission-based planners, Susan Spraker and Charlie Fitzgerald, with the express purpose of becoming a fee business. During eleven of fourteen years in practice, Susan was commission-only, and then began to take larger clients on a fee basis. Charlie had been commission-only since the day he began. All three felt a commitment to change the way they did business.

"When Ron and Susan told me they wanted to go out on their own and invited me to join them, I did a lot of soul-searching," said Charlie. "Probably the defining moment was when I looked at my $1.5 million life insurance policy and asked myself who I would want to advise my wife and children if I died. Truthfully, I'd choose a fee-only planner. I'd want that guy to be on the line, responsible for helping her achieve her goals for the rest of her life." Charlie feels that the nature of commission business and the need to be a "perpetual marketing machine" may prevent the close counseling relationship necessary for working with the clients he wants. "Commission work is like the quarterback suiting up for the football game, calling the first play, and then walking off the field. I want that player to be in the game until the end. If I'm paying a fee, I am assured that he will be."

Because they were forming a new business entity as well as shifting to fees, Ron, Susan, and Charlie had a potpourri of complex issues to deal with. The business entity issues were discussed earlier in Chapter 2. The issues involved in converting to a fee practice include the following:

Potentials

- Create a dependable source of income.
- Provide independence from a broker-dealer relationship.
- Position the practice favorably in the eyes of the media.
- Allow flexibility in the selection of investment vehicles and reporting.

Perils

- Less income (at least initially). Consider that in a commission practice an investment of $100,000 will generate a commission, paid up front, of about $4,000. In a fee-only practice with a base fee of 1 percent and a quarterly billing cycle, the initial income would be $250. That's a *big* difference when you're planning your cash flow. "There is no question, you can make more money on a transaction basis," said Susan, "but with fees you develop different relationships and get paid for them over a longer period of time."

- More accountability. Clients are more aware of what is happening with their accounts. They receive statements from everyone, including you. You wave account performance under their noses every quarter. Fees are also much more obvious than commissions.

- More service required of you. You may be incorporating more offerings and amenities into your practice. You will probably be communicating more with your clients as well.

 ## Compensation Models, Licensing, and Registration

Your compensation model will dictate where you will need to be licensed and registered. If you will be receiving commissions on securities, you will need to be licensed with the Financial Industry Regulatory Authority (FINRA, formerly the National Association of Securities Dealers—NASD).

If you provide advice for a fee, you will need to be registered as an investment adviser, either by your state securities department (under $25 million under management) or the Securities and Exchange Commission (SEC) ($25 million or more under management).

You must file an ADV Part I and Part II. ADV Part I must be completed in electronic format and filed with the Investment Adviser Registration Depository (IARD). ADV Part II must be completed and filed in paper format.

In most states if you file with the SEC, you must also file with the state or states that you plan to do business in. Registration with both the state securities agency and the SEC must be renewed yearly.

You can also be dually registered, that is, carry a securities license under FINRA and be registered as a registered investment adviser (RIA) under the SEC (or the state securities department, whichever applies). For this arrangement, you will need to have the blessing of your broker-dealer because technically it is still responsible for your activities as long as it holds your securities license. Some broker-dealers have fee arrangements available; some will not allow you to do this. If you are transitioning to fees, this can be a good way to retain your current client base and still do some business while you are transitioning old clients or attracting new clients to your new fee structure.

The following are examples of the types of questions you will be expected to answer in completing your SEC application:

- Advisory services: how much of your activities are supervisory and whether or not you use market timing

- Fees: how they're calculated, when they're payable, and how a client may terminate and get a refund

- Types of clients: individuals, families, pension plans, endowments

- Types of investments you will recommend and give advice about

- Methods of analysis: fundamental, charting, cyclical

- Sources of research information: annual reports, newspapers, newsletters, online sites

- Investment strategies used to implement advice

- Reviews: how often you will provide reports and meet with clients

 ## Fees and Minimums

You can charge by the hour, by the project, for assets under management, by some calculation of net worth, or any combination of those. Most fee advisers use a combination of a project fee for the initial planning work, then a percentage of the assets they manage.

If you elect to use an asset-based fee, you will need to be clear about the minimum dollar investment you will accept under your fee arrangement. As I did earlier, do the math. If your client has $100,000 to invest and you use load funds, your commission may be 4 or 5 percent. If you are charging fees, let's say 1 percent, you make $1,000 annually. If you charge on a quarterly basis, that is $250 per quarter. How much work can you afford to do for your client?

As I mentioned in earlier chapters, we originally set our minimums at $100,000 investable assets, with no rationale whatsoever. Later, when we decided to analyze our client base, it was with the declared purpose of establishing minimums based upon intelligent thinking. I decided on a cost analysis first. I determined that in consideration of our space, reporting costs, operating costs, including reasonable owner salaries, we needed $3,000 per year to maintain a client relationship. A 1 percent annual fee would suggest a $300,000 minimum.

In the calculation, it is important to include reasonable owner salaries, representing the time you need to spend on the client relationship on an ongoing basis. Many years ago I attended a business-planning seminar for the IAFP presented by Mark Tibergien. As a requirement for the session, attendees had to complete a questionnaire about their businesses. One section asked about overhead costs.

Almost everyone in the room wrote down staff salaries, but neglected to include salaries for the owners. When Mark asked how we got paid, we admitted that we thought owner salaries were a function of the profit the company generated. "My God," Tibergien barked at us, "isn't your time worth anything?"

Again, I recommend picking up a copy of Mark's book, written with Rebecca Pomering, *Practice Makes Perfect.*[1] In the book, Mark outlines how you should set up your books so that you can separate your reward for labor (compensation) from your reward for ownership (profit). By doing this, you can also benchmark your progress by looking at certain ratios, for example, revenue per professional or revenue per staff member.

There is controversy about how practices set their fees. Our practice determines fees by the amount of the assets that we manage. I consider the fees paid a retainer and refer to it that way in our practice.

Some advisers charge based on net worth. Planners who have done this admit that there is often resistance from clients who have a significant net worth. These clients balk at paying a fee based on a net worth that the adviser had no role in creating. On the other hand, it does focus the adviser's services away from performance. Joe Kopczynski of Universal Advisory Services admits that when he began to charge based on net worth, he had some clients who did not feel comfortable with the arrangement, but eventually they agreed. "Now it's not hard for my clients to see our value, separate and apart from the asset management, when I charge this way."

When I presented my partners with the $3,000 minimum fee proposal, both froze at the thought of turning business away. Harold stuttered, and Peter said he simply could not do it. I persisted. It was a necessity for our business plan. To make it easier, we redesigned our brochure, screened prospects more carefully, and wrote a letter to existing clients outlining our minimums for new clients. We all took a leap of faith and actually declined business, and as you'll recall from Chapter 1, we started getting more business.

I have covered fees and pricing in Chapter 6, but if you are considering transitioning to fees, you will need to think about budgeting the transfer. While you are spending time converting your client base, you will not be bringing in new business, and getting through that will take some planning. In Chapter 1, I spoke about the viability of a client relationship. In considering transitioning, you will need to assess each current client with regard to fees, pricing, and profitability.

Philip Palaveev of Moss Adams has devised a short worksheet to help you through this process. First, you will need to know what it costs you in time to service your client. If you have completed the exercise in Chapter 6, you will have determined a number of hours that it takes to provide initial, and then ongoing, service. Our example in Chapter 6, assumed twenty-three hours to bring on a new client and eleven ongoing per year. At twenty-three hours per new client, realistically how many can you handle in a year? For purposes of our exercise, let's assume one hundred. Now, using Philip's worksheet (see Figure 6.1), determine how much you expect you can make in revenue. For purposes of this example, let's assume $500,000. That means roughly one hundred people must pay you $5,000 each for you to make this goal.

Before you make this leap, you will want to understand your current client base and how many of your current clients you will be converting to the new fee arrangements. I have provided a budget form to help you through this thinking process (see **Figure 7.1**).

Budgeting the Transition

Budgeting the Transition

For a typical client, estimate transition time:

a. Initial meeting, explaining concept _____
b. Developing investment strategy _____
c. Deliver/explain proposal _____
d. Account setup/compliance paperwork _____
e. Implementation of strategy _____
f. Total transition time per client (sum a through e) _____
g. Target number of transitioned clients _____
h. Total estimated hours (f × g) _____
i. Estimated hourly rate (from Section 2) _____
j. Estimated opportunity cost (h × i) _____

Estimate one-time out-of-pocket expenses:

k. Staff overtime _____
l. Investment software _____
m. Research _____
n. Continuing professional education _____
o. New hardware _____
p. Client fees, paid by adviser _____
q. IT consultants _____
r. Marketing and collateral (brochures, website, etc.) _____
s. Licensing, registration fees _____
t. Other _____
u. Total (sum of k through t) _____

Estimate Ongoing Transition Expenses

v. Report production/mailing _____
w. Software upgrades/support _____
x. Research/subscriptions _____
y. Fees and licenses _____
z. Office expenses _____
aa. Other _____
bb. Total Ongoing Expenses (sum of u through aa) _____

FIGURE 7.1 Budgeting the Transition

 Investment Selection

The common belief is that becoming an independent fee adviser will give you more investment flexibility. In fact, although your selections will be different, you will have fewer options, not more. There is greater flexibility to a portfolio designed around no-load funds, in that you can rebalance when necessary with little concern for penalties or loads. On the other hand, there are limited annuity and insurance choices in the no-load area, particularly if you are intent on becoming totally fee-only and will not maintain licenses to sell product.

Investment Planning

Designing your investment policy, optimizing portfolios, devising investment criteria, and selecting funds are clearly outside the scope of this book. Nearly every adviser I interviewed suggested four books for advice and support in this area: Roger Gibson's *Asset Allocation*,[2] Harold Evensky's *Wealth Management*,[3] Charles Ellis's *Investment Policy: How to Win the Loser's Game*,[4] and Don Trone's *The Management of Investment Decisions*.[5] However, you will want to look at Norm Boone and Linda Lubitz Boone's IPS AdvisorPro (www.ipsadvisorpro .com), good software for building investment policy statements.

 ## Select a Custodial Partner

You will need to select a custodian to handle client assets on a fee basis. The three largest players are Schwab, Fidelity, and TD Ameritrade. Schwab has been supporting independent advisers for ten years and commands a whopping 80 percent of the marketplace.

Think carefully before you make a decision. Poor back-office operations can destroy a client's trust in you and your organization. Before you make your choice, you will want to consider these issues.

- How easy is it to open accounts? How long does it take? Can you get forms and supplies online?

- How well do they manage distributions? If your client needs a check, how difficult is it for you to get it to him?

- What are the procedures for transferring assets? Do they estimate the time and work involved and keep you well informed of the progress?

- How is data transferred to you? Most of these companies have their own proprietary software that links to some of the major portfolio management software. Does it tie into what you are currently using? Is it reliable and easy to use?

- How are trades executed? Can you do the bulk of them electronically?

- What are the fees and transaction costs?

- What other support systems do they have available? Some have referral, business development, or marketing programs you can participate in. Some have human resource support or materials that you can use to manage and grow your practice.

- Do they carry all the investments in your recommended universe? Ask them what their policy is for adding new funds.

- If you use individual securities, what is the background and education of their staff at the trading desks?

- How effectively do they protect their institutional clients from the retail market? (Are they farming your market or are they likely to farm your clients?)

- How do you fit in their target institutional market? Do they want you for a client?

If you are transitioning from commission to fees, all of the custodial firms have some form of support to help you make the leap. Pershing, who has provided broker-dealer support for most of the BD firms in the country, has now developed a fee platform for advisors. If you are transitioning your practice, their solution may be ideal since they have a technology dashboard available that will allow you to see your commission business and fee business simultaneously.

For More Information on Custodians

Fidelity	fiws.fidelity.com
Pershing	www.pershing.com
Schwab	www.schwabinstitutional.com
TD Ameritrade	www.ameritradeinstitutional.com

 Manage Client Conversion

Anticipate some attrition in your client base once you have made the decision to shift to fees. Some of your clients will not be appropriate for conversion, while others will just be uncomfortable with the new fee program.

When I was in the real estate business in Chicago, if we wanted to rehabilitate a building, we devised a progressive program. We allowed one-third of the leases to lapse and began our work on that one-third of the building. The other two-thirds generated some income so we could eat. When the first third was complete, we leased that space, then began working on the second third. This is the approach I recommend for your own conversion to fees.

Susan Spraker started meeting with her larger clients individually, reviewing their goals, objectives, and portfolio, then explained that henceforth she would be working on a different compensation arrangement. "This seemed to work well," she says. "Clients usually end the conversation with, 'What do I have to do to stay with you?'" Meanwhile, the clients she still worked with on a commission basis were undisturbed.

If you plan to migrate to entirely fee-only, during this period you should identify which clients will be inappropriate for the transition. You will need to decide if you will be able to maintain the relationship on an hourly or project fee basis. In any case, have a list of advisers you'd recommend to take on your clients who don't make the transition.

 Straddling the Fence

As I discussed earlier, you need to be aware that if you elect to maintain relationships with both a broker-dealer and an institutional custodial partner, you will need to discuss the arrangement with the broker-dealer. There are regulatory constraints. For example, your broker-dealer may want a percentage of your fee business since it is still responsible for you whether you work for commissions or fees. Be sure that you understand the requirements before you get too far in your planning.

☐ JERRY NEILL'S STORY

"When I decided to go to fees, I sat down with one of my biggest clients, explained that I had elected to change my compensation structure, and told him what the new fees would be," says Jerry Neill. "He blanched at the $16,000 fee, when with the commission arrangement, he felt like he was paying nothing. It was the toughest sale I'd ever made. Next time I sat down to convert a client, I first told him of my decision to add services to my practice and outlined them in detail. I explained how these new services would benefit my client. I then calculated the commissions I had reaped and compared that to the fee I would be charging. That went over much better. One thing I learned, though, not every client will want to make the change. Just be prepared to let them go."

 ## Invest in You

Use the opportunity to create a new corporate image or consider a new name, with new brochures and stationery. Like it or not, many of your clients have seen you in a salesman's role, rather than that of counselor or planner. New marketing material and letterhead will help to reposition you in their minds.

 ## Related Professional Practice Changes

The discussion so far has been about an existing financial advisory firm's moving to a different business style and compensation method. Plenty of other professionals with overlapping skills are eyeing planning these days. It is reported that thousands of CPAs will be entering the financial planning and asset management business within the next few years. In a 1996 survey completed by *Accounting Today* magazine, 58 percent of the respondents indicated they were already involved in personal financial planning. Not surprisingly, CPAs generally have strong relationships with the clients for whom they provide tax-planning advice. It seemed appropriate that they would gravitate to financial planning and investment advisory work. CPAs have their own designation to identify planners, the PFS (personal financial specialist), although many have embraced the CFP (certified financial planner) mark.

"The accounting profession is changing," reports Randi Grant, CPA, PFS, CFP, at Berkowitz Dick Pollack & Brant in Miami, Florida. "CPAs are looking for new sources of revenue. Many want to provide more support to their current clients. CPAs have the public trust."

Initially, after a career of taking fees, many CPAs are scrambled into the commission business. Shaky markets and volatile returns have led many back to the fee world in recent years, though.

One of the biggest hurdles is making the commitment. "This is not a part-time job," said Mark Ritter of Maxwell Locke & Ritter, a CPA firm in Austin, Texas. "We assigned two of our partners to the financial planning and investment advisory division. They are no longer responsible for conventional accounting activities."

Randi Grant agreed. "The planning CPAs must be relieved from preparing 1040s, for example. We not only need the time to spend with financial planning clients, but we need time to educate our own partners so they are comfortable with the work we are capable of handling now as well."

That's great advice if you have a big practice behind you. You can parcel out the responsibilities and still handle all the accounting activities as well. If you are a sole practitioner, warns Ben Tobias of Tobias Financial Advisors in Plantation, Florida, you will have to decide what hat you will wear. "I always did a limited amount of financial planning with my clients. If you are doing individual tax returns, you generally do. When I began to offer investment advice to my current clients, it worked for a while, but it's not easy to keep up with both worlds."

Many CPAs see this kind of functional shifting of their practices as a slam dunk. "Farming our current clients can keep us busy virtually forever," said Randi. "But," she cautions, "you need to handle this with care. There's a lot on the line if you don't handle the relationship well; you not only lose the planning and investment business, but the tax business too."

If you're planning to make this jump, here are some valuable tips from folks who've done it:

- Investigate your options carefully. CPAs are in big demand now. Every broker-dealer and asset manager would like your business.

- Decide what form of compensation will be most comfortable for you. If you have been charging fees for your entire professional life, you may be uncomfortable positioning yourself with your clients once you begin charging commissions.

- Educate your partners. A lack of knowledge and fear of the unknown may prevent them from committing to the change.

- Restructure current relationships and delegate work to colleagues, so that you will be able to handle the time commitment.

- If you do not have education and training in financial planning, work with someone who does. You cannot be an expert in everything. (The American Institute of Certified Public Accountants [AICPA] offers a professional designation for planning, the CPA/PFS.)

When you're restructuring your practice, use local resources as much as possible. Roger Smothers, a certified financial planner from Binghamton, New York, who is also a practicing psychologist, has found his local study group extremely helpful as a source of information, as well as a good sounding board. "We are at all different levels of transition. We really can offer substantive advice to each other." Whether you have an existing practice in planning or any other professionally related field, the best advice is to network. Go to the planning industry conferences and conventions and ask questions. The planning and investment community is quite generous with time and information.

THE STAFF

One of the problems with managing a practice is the need for competent assistance. Forming a great staff is extremely difficult. As the practice matures, many advisers consider taking on partners, and new staffing is required. Who you need to hire depends upon how you want to grow. Working out scenarios in advance avoids wasted time, money, and energy. This section discusses the value of strategic planning for selecting a partner plus the hiring and retention of good staff.

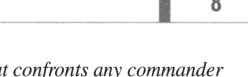

One of the most difficult problems that confronts any commander who has committed his forces in accordance with a well-developed plan is to alter this in the light of changing circumstances.
—Sun Tzu, author of *The Art of War*

I t's the shoemaker's children, they say, who go barefoot. Most advisers avoid thinking about retirement, death, or the chance that they or their partner will become disabled. Struggling to acquire and retain clients always seems to take precedence. I am going to cover some management succession planning techniques in this chapter. Management succession is wholly different from business succession, and you'll see why a bit later. I also want to explore the effect of a traumatic personal event on your practice and clients and to suggest how to make some practice contingency plans to be implemented in times of crisis. First, I'd like to share with you the experience of a few friends who have actually faced these issues.

Crisis Planning for Death

I met Andrew Wray about ten years ago at the then Institute of Certified Financial Planners (ICFP) retreat. At the time, Andrew was a planner in Memphis with a small successful practice and one partner, Bill Howard. Andrew and Bill met when they were taking courses for the CFP exam and had practiced together since 1985. They were best friends. Their clients were all considered clients of the firm, but they primarily had a relationship with either Andrew or Bill. One Saturday evening, while working late, Andrew, then only forty-nine, suffered a heart attack and died at his desk. Andrew's son discovered his body when he went to the office because his dad had not returned home or responded to his worried family's phone calls. By Saturday morning, Andrew's death had affected not only his family but Bill's life, and the lives of all their clients.

All of us in the planning community were stunned. Andrew was young. Andrew was presumably in good health. Andrew was gone. My partner Harold and I, along with many other advisers, offered help to Bill. Unfortunately, we did not know how we could be of assistance.

Bill, shocked and grieving, recognized immediately that Andrew's clients would also feel the tremendous loss. He began to make phone calls to each of them. He felt it was imperative to inform them of Andrew's death before they heard it anywhere else. So while Andrew's family was making preparations for the funeral, Bill was talking with Andrew's clients, assuring them of the business continuity and ongoing professional support. In the subsequent weeks, Bill met with each of Andrew's clients. He was pleased to find that for the most part, they were not concerned about the company's stability. Naturally, they were upset. In many cases, the grief for the loss of Andrew helped forge stronger relationships with Bill.

As Bill provided care for Andrew's clients, he was personally grieving for his friend and partner. He was also personally worried about his responsibilities to the staff. He and Andrew had just signed a new five-year lease and hired four additional staff people. Andrew had carried the primary responsibility for running the office. Bill had never been interested in that aspect of the practice. Now he had to take over under the worst circumstances. Bill had to keep the staff together, make the clients feel comfortable and confident, and finally, try to take care of himself.

The firm's staff was also suffering from grief and shock. Within one year, three left, compounding the chaos. Bill confides that systemization, coupled with his own tenacity, kept the business going. Two years after Andrew's death, Bill changed the name of the company. He felt this was necessary in order to focus on the future and keep the business growing. In hindsight, Bill said he probably should have done that sooner, but didn't want to seem disrespectful to Andrew's memory.

Even though plans had not been made to address the future, Bill was able to work through many issues with his clients, and today he has a successful, vibrant practice, fully recovered more than ten years later from the consequences of Andrew's passing.

If you do not have a partner, you will want to address what happens to your practice, your staff, and your clients in the event of your passing. I spoke with an adviser a few months ago who assured me that his planning was in place. "My firm goes into a trust," he informed me. "My three children are beneficiaries of the trust and will make all the decisions concerning the firm. None of the children work in the firm, so I have hired a fine young man who manages the firm and maintains the client relationships. He is just an employee. It's important that he just wants to be an employee because I do not want him to attempt to take the client relationships and leave when I am gone." As I tried to envision the children directing the firm, and the young man with no ambition managing his own client relationships, it occurred to me that clients want a trusted relationship, not a relationship with a trust.

There are much better ways to solve your succession problems. One is to look for a key employee with leadership skills and an ability to work well with you in the firm presently. Chapters 9 and 10 will discuss how to select good staff and potential partners and successors.

Disability Crisis

It's prudent to consider the possibilities of a partner dying. It is also important to consider the possibility of a partner suffering a disability or illness that might keep him or her from working for many months or years. This requires an entirely different type of contingency planning, because at some point you expect the partner to return. Consequently, it is necessary to also consider what that reentry might be like.

A few years ago, John Ueleke of Legacy Wealth Management in Memphis, Tennessee, was diagnosed with a rare cancer. As part of his treatment plan, he had to move to Houston for several months. John told me, "When your practice gets large enough and your staff consists of more than just you and a couple of support people, you have to think not only of your clients, but also of the employees who rely upon you for their livelihood. I realized that I had to make plans not just for my clients, but for the management of the business, too. I needed to do this so I could focus on myself and getting better."

In the few days before John had to leave for Houston, he and his partners worked out a new business plan. They used this as an opportunity to restructure their practice, making some changes they'd been thinking about in the past few months anyway. They began by developing a client strategy delivery worksheet, listing who was currently responsible for delivery of services to each client. They also reviewed the nature of their relationship with all their clients. They listed client personality traits and familiarized each other with the nature of the engagement and the client's personal circumstances. Based on this information and the knowledge of their own personality styles, they then assigned a primary partner, a primary assistant, and a backup partner.

They also felt it was important to be up front with the clients about John's illness. Together they wrote a letter, explaining what they knew about John's condition and how they planned to redistribute the workload. John explains, "This brought an additional benefit. I was able to elicit support from my clients. Through this experience, I have learned that we rely on our clients not only for financial sustenance, but for personal and spiritual support as well."

In preparation for this book, I discussed contingency plans with many successful planners, including Bill Howard and John Ueleke. I've divided their suggestions into three parts: an action plan for now, a contingency plan for during a crisis, and one for after a crisis.

Action Plan for Now

There are several items that you should make sure are in order in case of a crisis involving your firm specifically, such as the death or disability of an employee. Planning that is done prior to the crisis will directly influence the capabilities of your employees and firm to weather the storm.

- Draft a buy-sell agreement and fund it if required. Many planners told me that in the early years, there seemed no reason to have a buy-sell agreement. The company wasn't worth much and was often burdened with debt from the start-up costs. Unfortunately, those same planners told me that by the time the company was making a nice profit, the partners were so preoccupied with growth, they never got around to revisiting the need for that agreement.

- Get your business-insurance planning in order. Maintain and continually update all pertinent information including types and amounts of coverage, beneficiary designations, deductibles and exclusions, premium payments, renewal dates and contact phone numbers, plus mail and e-mail addresses.

- Get your personal risk-management planning in order. This includes disability and life insurance as well as property and casualty coverage. For example, when Hurricane Andrew devastated much of South Florida in 1992, my partners and I were able to concentrate on the problems caused to our business (for example, property damage and long-term power disruptions) and the problems faced by our clients, because our own personal insurance was adequate to cover the costs of quickly repairing the damage to our own property. There were a few less-prepared planners who suffered significant business disruption because they had to spend so much time resolving their personal recovery problems.

- Get your personal estate planning documents in order. The quality of your personal estate planning will have a significant impact on your partner(s) and staff should you die while still active in the business.

- Discuss your business arrangements with your partner's family. If the family does not understand the business arrangements you and your partner have devised, they may have unrealistic expectations about the amount due them. You and your partner should consider discussing the rationale of your arrangement with those who may be beneficiaries. If you are not comfortable having the discussions prior to a crisis, consider writing a letter or making a videotape explaining your decisions, so that it will be available when needed.

- Develop and document a contingency plan for keeping your staff, your clients, and your partner's family informed of important activities and practice changes during the period of crisis.

- Systematize your office activities and, based on this, prepare a crisis action plan. No matter what the crisis, certain activities must be completed. If your contingency planning indicates that you will be required to bring in outside help (for example, accounting support, computer consultation, personal counseling), determine and document in advance the type and sources of this assistance. Maintain a list of time-sensitive activities and a list of who will handle these activities during a crisis.

- Maintain a comprehensive inventory of important documents (for example, property and casualty insurance policies, corporate records) and where to find them.

- Establish a comprehensive computer backup system. List where backups are stored and who has responsibility for the archiving system.

- In addition to your client list, maintain a comprehensive and continually updated list of other important contacts, such as your attorneys, bankers, and accountants and property, casualty, and health insurers, etc. Include a notation of when and how they should be contacted (phone, letter, or e-mail) and who will be responsible for the contact.

- Clearly define the managing partner's responsibilities and plan for short-term coverage of these responsibilities in the event of his or her absence.

- Prepare a reentry plan in cases in which a partner may return after a prolonged absence. Include how responsibilities will be redistributed and how long this assimilation will take.

All of these recommendations pertain to those of you who have partners. If you are a sole practitioner, you will need to consider other avenues. Later in this chapter, we will consider selecting key personnel and other staff to support your planning efforts.

 ## What To Do During a Crisis

- Implement the action plan. This is not the time to rethink your strategies. Follow the plan.

- Immediately contact clients personally and assure them that you and your partner(s) had developed a comprehensive contingency plan and it is being implemented.

- Take care of yourself emotionally. Do not assume that you are Superman or Wonder Woman. You are human. Go to a counselor or therapist for help working through the emotional trauma you are experiencing.

- Take care of your employees. Consider counseling for your key employees.

- Implement the contingency plan strategy for keeping staff, clients, and your partner's family informed.

 ## What To Do After the Crisis

- Review with your staff, clients, and personal advisers how well your crisis plan worked. Make adjustments and document them.

- If the crisis was due to the death of a key person or partner, review the business plan to establish new goals and objectives for the business.

- Revisit all legal documents to ensure that they reflect the nature and intention of the current owners or partners.

John Ueleke summed up your responsibilities to your company best: "When your business gets to a certain size, you realize that many people are depending upon its continuance. Never forget that you are not in this alone. You owe it to your clients, your staff, and your partners to see that your company will survive."

 ## Disaster Plan

If you are a registered investment adviser (RIA), the Securities and Exchange Commission (SEC) has now made it mandatory for you to make disaster plans to include what will happen if your office can't open. Instances of disaster would include natural disasters, terrorist attacks, large power outages, etc. Since our practice is in Florida, our disaster plan for hurricanes has been tested many times.

A couple of months ago our office had our annual disaster-planning retreat. Each person in our office was given a personal notebook, called "Keeping the Light On," that describes our disaster plan and what responsibilities he or she has, before, during, and after a crisis. At the retreat, we reviewed our plans and refined them as necessary. Every staff member left the retreat with his own personal directives in the event of an emergency.

Long before the SEC required that investment advisory firms have formalized disaster plans, we starting holding our retreats. In fact, we have had one every year since 1992 when Hurricane Andrew swept through South Florida, destroying homes, families, and businesses.

Although the SEC has some guidelines for preparing disaster plans, they are generic. It occurred to us that many firms don't spend time customizing their plan for the unique environment of their office and community. They neither familiarize staff with the firm's plan, nor run through drills to ensure that everyone knows exactly what to do when the plan is activated. Our chief compliance officer, Mena Bielow, spends an extraordinary amount of time thinking through our plan and reviews the details before she facilitates our retreat.

When asked about the genesis of her planning notebook, she said, "When I created the disaster-planning book for the first time, my inspiration came from another binder which I put together when we moved our office from its Sevilla address to our current Colonnade office. At the time of the move, there were a thousand and one details to take care of, from the new furniture to the wiring for computers and telephones to arrangements with the moving company, etc. For each company I dealt with, I had notes and a person's (or more than one) name and telephone numbers. Because everything was interrelated (I had to move the copier and the coffeemaker the same day the furniture went out—but the copier and coffee machine were handled by other companies), not only was it not practical to have my files on a computer with different classifications, I knew that during the move I wouldn't have access to our computer database. It was also a lot quicker and easier to have all the information at my fingertips and on my lap. The day we moved, although I had no computer to get my information from, I had to call several people. My "moving" binder was my biggest help for sanity and a job done well. So, I approached the disaster-planning book the same way: What am I going to need or want to know, when I am not in the office and have no computer?"

The book is actually a combination of scenarios: What's the plan in case of an approaching storm? How do we handle the countdown to the storm getting closer? What's the plan should the storm hit (when there is no electricity and no access to computers)?

When a storm is headed our way, employees want to know "When will you tell me to pack up and go home?" That's why we have a 48-36-24-hour countdown. When employees are told to get ready to go home, tension and the worry level is high. Most need reminders on what to do (cover your computer, put papers away, etc.) and reminders on what to do for themselves (get cash, get gas, take your keys). Mena believes that half the employees, without instructions, will go out the door leaving the windows open behind them, in the hurry to go home. This is why we have specific instructions on what "to do now" and what "we will do" before leaving.

As a result, our staff action list is a compilation of what must be done before we close the office doors. Naturally, this depends upon how much notice we have before an impending disaster. This list is prioritized so that printing a new master client list for contacting and calling our custodians and providers is at the top of the list.

Naturally, with a hurricane, we often have more time to prepare for the event than we might have with other types of disasters, so we thought it would be helpful to include Mena's "Table of Contents" so that you can quickly see what is in the notebook and how you might customize a plan for your company in your area.

1. Preparation and Plan: Identifying the Disasters We May Face
2. Action Plan: 48-36-24 Hours Out
3. Scenarios: What If This Happens?
4. Computer Systems: Backup and Storage
5. Alternate Work Locations
6. Staff Cell Phone Numbers
7. Employee Data Sheet Declarations
8. Client Contact List by Staff Member
9. Staff Action List
10. Emergency Phone Numbers

We learned from the experience of those evacuating New Orleans and the Gulf coast after Katrina that having a cell phone is useless if the cell phone towers are out. So, two years ago Mena bought our advisers disposable, prepaid cell phones with a Memphis area code. During our last disaster, those phones were the only ones that worked.

Everyone is provided a list of emergency address and phone numbers for utilities, emergency medical services, hospitals, and other important information. This can help us get assistance to our clients as well as our staff postdisaster.

Staff members are divided into teams of three or four and given a list of client contact information. After the disaster, the teams will begin calling clients to see if they are safe and whether they need help. Since we have online vaulting capabilities through our Web provider LightPort, we know that our clients should be able to access important documents such as insurance policies, pictures of their home and valuables (for insurance claims), wills, trusts, birth certificates, and the like.

We obviously also care about our staff's personal safety. So, each employee must fill out a form stating what he or she intends to do and where he or she intends to be in the event of a disaster. Names of close family and friends are also included on that list, so we have a chance of finding our people if they are unable to check in with us after the event. This information is included in everyone's notebook.

Of course our notebook is a work in progress since new experiences help refine our information and address new issues. As Mena tells it, "The book improves a little every year because we get to use it! Simple things: For example, after Hurricane Wilma in 2005, I discovered that I wanted all cell numbers on one page because most people did not answer their home phone, and I also did not want to flip through the eighteen individual employee pages looking for each person's unique phone number. I did get to use the instructions on how to forward the phones through BellSouth over and over again; I am glad I had those instructions."

We've learned over the years that it is not enough to have a plan in place to please the SEC. We need a plan that works for us and our clients. It's important to know that all your staff is aware of how to react, how to help, and what will need to happen so you can reopen your doors. Our disaster notebook and retreat keeps everyone current and prepared.

Management Succession

It's important that you understand, as you think about the growth and direction of your business, the difference between management succession and business succession. One of my adviser friends told me he is not retiring, ever. "I don't need an exit strategy," he says, "I will do this until I die." He's in his fifties and has a fair-sized business with one young adviser working with him. He is about to hire his second. "I just want someone who will be a good employee," he goes on. I think about this for a minute. "Will you always run your company?" I ask. "Well," he hedges, "I think in ten years or so I will probably want to live in California part-time. But I can still handle my clients." "Who will handle the office?" I continue. He looks at me puzzled. He obviously doesn't have an answer for this yet. It's then that it occurs to me why advisers really need to know the difference between management succession and business succession.

You may never want to sell your company, but it is likely that if you want to enjoy extended time away from your office and your staff, you will want to pass the management to someone who can take responsibility for the human capital, financial matters, and day-to-day decisions. You will want key staff with management and leadership qualities. This may or may not be a planner.

Many larger firms are hiring chief operating officers (COOs) to manage the business while they continue the practice of planning. Most smaller firms cannot afford this luxury and rather short-sightedly decide that they will simply continue to manage the practice as they have always done—forever. If you just look at the increase in compliance regulations, you can see that it is unlikely that even smaller firms can expect that the business of managing the business will be static.

Although the size of your firm will probably dictate your options, it is still wise to do some strategic planning. Answering a few questions about where you see your future will help you decide what human capital you need and how you can plan to transition your practice over time. Mark Tibergien of Pershing always asks advisers to start by describing their personal definition of success. "It's important to know what motivates you," Mark says. "Some people feel successful if they are making a certain amount of money by a certain age. Others set personal fulfillment expectations." Determine your motivator and what drives you to personal satisfaction by answering the questions below. This is the first step to making plans for the future of your practice, and for your life for that matter.

 ## Personal Definition of Success

- Where do you see yourself in five years? Ten years?
- What is an optimal size for your practice, both in clients and staff?
- What will be your ideal lifestyle in five years? Ten years?
- What responsibilities will you have to family and staff that are short term? Long term?

We have included a "Personal Definition of Success" form that Moss Adams provided for your use (see **Figure 8.1**).

FIGURE 8.1 Personal Definition of Success

Personal Definition of Success (PDS)

Step 1 - Clarify your personal goals
Step 2 - Summarize your PDS
Step 3 - Discuss your PDS with your executive team
Step 4 - Draw preliminary conclusions about how your PDS will have an impact on the strategic direction of YOUR COMPANY

Step 1

1. How old will you be five years from now?_____
2. At what stage in your career do you expect/want to be?
   _____
   _____
   _____
   _____

3. What do you want your role to be in the firm five years from now?
   _____
   _____
   _____
   _____

4. What will your ideal lifestyle be in five years?
   _____
   _____
   _____
   _____

5. How many hours will you be working, and who will you be working with in 2006?_____
   _____

6. Will you be working from home, office, or another location?
   _____
   _____
   _____

7. What will your responsibility be to your family (spouse, children, parents)?
   _____
   _____
   _____
   _____

8. Where do you expect/want to get your income?
   _____
   _____
   _____

9. How much will you need to be earning?
   _____
   _____

(continued)

■ | **FIGURE 8.1** Personal Definition of Success (*Continued*)

10. What will your role in the community be?

_____

_____

_____

11. How will you spend your leisure time?

_____

_____

_____

12. From what will you receive your greatest satisfaction?

_____

_____

_____

13. What are the values* that you want to use when choosing a business strategy?_____

_____

_____

14. What part of your work will be most personally satisfying to you in five years?_____

_____

_____

15. How will you know that you are personally successful in five years from now?

_____

_____

_____

_____

_____

_____

_____

_____

_____

_____

*How values fit into the decision-making process.
An important aspect to understand is that for most of us values are non-negotiable. Values affect every facet of our lives. Most people find it hard to be motivated if their work violates their values. For instance, if your values include a respect for the natural environment, you would not want to be personally involved in a financial enterprise that was not environmentally responsible. You may find it helpful to list your personal values in order to establish your business values. You can then use your personal values as a part of your decision-making criteria, as well as a final checkpoint to ensure that you have not selected a business strategy that is in conflict with those stated values.

Source: Moss Adams

As you formulate your future plans, envision realistically how much time you will expect to spend in your office. Think about the details that you handle today. Will you want to have responsibility for those activities in the future?

Planning for management succession ensures that you, as the business owner, have top people in place to continue your business whether you are there or not. It is unrealistic to think that you will not want to off-load some responsibilities so that you can enjoy another phase of your life. Management succession strategies ensure that those you have placed in management roles will stay with your company and your clients when you are not there. It's not unreasonable to think that at some point you will want to be certain that your clients are handled by well-qualified, caring professionals of your choosing. You may decide that you're going to die in front of your computer. Let's just be sure it's a laptop and you're on the beach somewhere.

Business Succession

As planning practices mature, the decision of whether you want your business to outlive you becomes more pressing. To me, this decision differentiates a practice from a business. A practice is based on a personality. If that personality leaves, the practice dissolves. A business is dependent on structure, philosophy, and continuity; it does not rely upon any one personality.

The Loyola University American Family Business Survey of 2002 on small business succession revealed that nearly 40 percent of all CEOs are within five years of retirement or semiretirement. Furthermore, over 40 percent had not yet identified a successor.

Many advisers have prepared for their succession by grooming younger people to move into key positions. This takes considerable time and training, but ensures continuity with clients. For example, the partners and planners at RegentAtlantic Capital in New Jersey work as a team to meet their clients' needs. Using client service teams will help you leverage your time in the practice, as well as provide a means for transferring client relationships. Having teams means that you may need to decide to become somewhat dispensable within the client relationships. That decision is bittersweet. After my decision to move clients to our team, one of my favorite clients called and I picked up. After a few moments of small talk, the client explained that he had actually called for my associate, Matt. "I need some advice," he said. "I can just talk it over with Matt." Although that's the idea, I didn't feel particularly wanted or needed.

It's a good idea to consider your own plans for retirement before you commit to an exit strategy. Judy Lau, CFP, of Lau Associates in Wilmington, Delaware, is a sole practitioner. Judy always thought that she'd sell her company to another planner one day and just retire. Recently she began to reconsider the ultimate disposition of her business. "If I retired, I would only want to play 50 percent of the time. I would need something else to do, so I probably would do volunteer work. The more I thought about this, the crazier it seemed. Let's see, I am going to stop doing something that I really love, and for which I am very well paid, so that I can play half the time. In my spare time, I will work for a volunteer organization where I will have no control, no respect, no pay, and no appreciation. What's wrong with this picture?" Judy finally decided that she would hire someone with a high level of skills to work with her now to share the workload. This will allow her to take more time away from her office. Eventually her younger partner will assume ownership.

Outright Sale

If you are not planning to groom a successor, you may be thinking of an outright sale to someone already in the business. Loyola University's business survey found that only 45 percent of owners had regularly determined the value of their businesses. If your business were a major asset, wouldn't you want to be aware of its worth so you could know how it would fit with your future plans?

In preparation for this book, I spoke with Mark Tibergien. Mark's expertise is valuing and facilitating the transfer of financial service companies. I asked Mark for some hints for financial advisers planning a sale as their exit strategy. Here is his dos-and-don'ts list:

- Don't overestimate the value of your practice. It's a buyer's market. You know what that can do to the price.

- Do consider other issues besides price. Mark reports that in his experience only 30 percent of the deals are consummated. The failure of the rest is due to the terms, contrary cultures, or differences in philosophy.

- Do get a professional valuation. If you are counting on the sale of your business for retirement, you definitely need a valuation to incorporate into your capital needs calculation. "Ask yourself, 'Can I afford to retire without including the value of my business?' You must perform the same analysis for yourself that you'd do for any financial planning client. As a rule, you shouldn't count on your business as a retirement bailout, merely your bonus," says Mark.

- Don't overestimate the goodwill aspect of your business. There is no correlation between goodwill and the number of years you have been in this business. Goodwill is that intangible that keeps clients coming to you. Your participation (or lack of it) in the new business may have a significant impact on the goodwill factor.

- Do start your planning early. Know the elements of valuation, and manage your practice with that in mind.

- Don't compare your business to others and anticipate the same terms. Businesses are unique, valuations are unique, transfers are unique.

It is important to remember that the value of your business is realized every day in the form of high income. The more your practice is dependent upon you, the less attractive it is to a buyer. The more closely your company resembles a commercial enterprise, the more likely you will have something to transfer. A prospective buyer will be interested in your client demographics, your philosophy with regard to investments, and the nature of the income (for example, if the income is largely dependent upon investment performance and market performance). He will also be interested in the level of service, operations, and the standardization you've instituted in your business.

Consolidation

Advisers today can't ignore the very real trend toward consolidation of practices. In the past several years, many advisers have sold to consolidators who invest in firms either as a long-term investment or as a roll-up to ultimately go public. While these deals vary widely, the good news for advisers is that they have the ability to diversify their equity, maintain some control over the management, and ultimately have an exit strategy designed for them.

 ## Valuation

Naturally, it is possible that you might consider the sale of your practice to someone who is not in this profession. This may be a much more difficult hurdle. During my interview with Mark, he walked me through an important reality check that I want to share with you.

There are two popular methods for valuing a company. One uses a multiple of the gross; the other uses a multiple of the net profit. The problem with using the gross figure is that the cost of realizing that income is not factored in. Mark suggests that planners thinking in terms of gross numbers may be living in a world of unrealistic expectations.

Bottom line—to increase the value of your business, follow these four tenets from Mark Tibergien:

1. Maximize cash flow. Pay yourself a reasonable salary, and watch your expenses.

2. Minimize risk. Ensure the operation of your business is not entirely dependent upon you.

3. Manage growth. Prepare for growth; don't let it surprise you.

4. Enhance transferability. Systematize your operations.

 ## Don't Wait—Plan Now

Stan Corey of Great Falls Financial Services in Great Falls, Virginia, has been concerned with succession planning for some time now. "I am a sole practitioner. I have long dialogues with my clients about their own future plans, but I haven't had much to say to them about mine. Recently, I have discussed this with other planners in my area. We have agreed to formulate some succession plans among us. We will agree in advance on who is willing to pay for our clients if we retire or die."

Whether you are planning for management succession or an exit strategy, the preparation for your practice is much the same. There are three keys for planning for succession:

1. Philosophy: Build your mission, vision, and core values to ensure that all staff share the same company philosophy.

2. Process: Automate, systematize, and refine processes to ensure consistent and quality execution and assured profitability.

3. People: Deliberately and consistently present your firm—and not you—so you can turn your practice into a business and your business into an asset.

Schwab has an arrangement for buyers and sellers on its website. If you are a Schwab adviser, you can hook up and explore a transaction. It allows you to list your firm as a buyer or seller, search for acquisition and merger candidates, and get in contact with other firms (www.schwabadvisortransition.com).

The Financial Planning Association (FPA) website also has material available on business succession strategies; go to www.fpanet.org/FPAStore to see what's available.

It is clear that no matter what size business it is, you must think about its future, and yours. When you review a client's financial activities, you don't hesitate to discuss gaps in his risk exposures, for example, no disability, no life insurance, no estate plan. Yet, many of the advisers I've interviewed in the past months have neglected to follow their own advice. Don't procrastinate. As your business grows, you will have less time to devote to your own planning. Do it now.

I choose to work with every single person I work with. That ends up being the most important factor. I don't interact with people I don't like or admire. That's the key. It's like marrying.
—Warren Buffett, chairman of Berkshire Hathaway

A young planner stopped me a few years ago at the International Association for Financial Planning (IAFP) Success Forum in Minneapolis and told me he was thinking about going on his own. He had spent the past five years working with a medium-sized regional planning practice but now wanted ownership and more flexibility. He also wanted a partner. When I asked him why, he replied that he was nervous about making this leap and wanted someone who could share the responsibilities and workload. "I think I found him," he said. "He's a broker and has a pretty good business going, too, but he really doesn't do planning. He told me that although he's not interested in financial planning, he wouldn't mind having a partner who was."

At some point in their careers, many practitioners entertain the idea of taking on a partner. As with my friend in Minneapolis, this thought may crop up when considering a redefinition of your practice, or it may occur during a growth spurt when it seems impossible to keep up with new business and still maintain old relationships. Taking on additional personnel propels you into managing staff and focusing your attention away from clients. "If only I had a partner," you think. What you probably have in mind is cloning yourself.

Dr. Meredith Belbin, a British expert in management, spent nine years researching the effectiveness of management teams. His book, *Management Teams,*[1] offers some invaluable advice for building partnerships. Dr. Belbin's research dealt with the formation of high-powered management teams, known as "Apollo teams." Based on the assumption that the most effective team would be one composed of the most effective people, he established all-star partnerships, made up of clever, critical-thinking individuals. Contrary to expectations, the Apollo teams performed their tasks much less successfully than teams composed of less extraordinary but more complementary members. The problem was that the Apollo individuals all had the same aspirations and wanted to perform the same functions within the organization. They spent most of the time trying to persuade their partners to adopt their ideas. They were miserably ineffective teams. So much for cloning yourself.

Why a Partnership?

It is important to determine why you really want a partner. I suspect my friend in Minneapolis was insecure about going on his own. The idea of having a partner seemed to fortify him. Unfortunately, a teddy bear is a better solution for insecurity and a lot less expensive. Be sure you know why you want a partner. Ask yourself these key questions:

- What can I contribute to a partnership? Remember the old Groucho Marx story? He said he wouldn't want to belong to any club that would have him as a member. Why would someone want to partner with you? What strengths do you have that would enhance those of a partner? Both of you should see the collaboration in your mutual interests.

- What are the talents missing in my practice that can be best provided by another individual? Ross Levin of Accredited Investors in Minneapolis admits that he is no administrator and is thankful to have a partner who is not only an excellent administrator but who also enjoys administration as much as Ross loves planning.

- Do I really need to share ownership, or can I accomplish my goal by delegating authority to key employees? Don't assume that a partnership is the only answer to your problems. New senior staff may add the necessary depth to your practice, without the added burden that a partner may bring.

- Would an affiliation with another practitioner, sharing overhead and resources, be a better alternative? To some, this may be the best of all worlds; your business remains autonomous, but you have access to resources and support when you need them. There are, however, some not-so-obvious drawbacks to an affiliation. If you operate as separate corporations but under one trade name, you run the risk of accepting liability for the actions of your affiliate. The world sees you as partners, and that is a risk you should not accept lightly.

- How will work responsibilities be divided? Probably one of the best partnerships I know is that of Jim Budros, Peggy Ruhlin, and Dan Roe of Budros, Ruhlin & Roe, in Columbus, Ohio. All their clients are clients of the firm and meet with the partners interchangeably. Peggy explains that she and Jim have very different work styles and specialties. This enhances the client relationship because they each have a different emphasis or focus when they meet with clients. Peggy usually handles the administrative activities, although Jim covered seamlessly for Peggy while she committed much of her time to meeting her responsibilities as president of the IAFP (now the Financial Planning Association [FPA]).

- What new ideas or activities would the partnership bring to this practice? Do the advantages outweigh the disadvantages? Is the relationship in both your interests? If you are joining forces with an experienced adviser, most likely he or she will be bringing a mature skill set to the mix. It may appear wonderful on the surface, but be sure that those skills are ones you want to bring into the practice. One adviser I know merged his practice with another planner who provided tax preparation as part of her practice. It was decided that the tax work would be integrated into the new entity and offered to all clients. My friend did not realize the impact that offering tax preparation would have on the business. It was a time-consuming activity, one that he felt they were not sufficiently paid for. More importantly, this new service caused some ill will among his existing referral sources, who were largely CPAs.

- Would bringing in a partner improve your bottom line or just expand the workload? Paul Brady of Australia suggests that it is necessary to analyze the impact of one or even two or three partners with respect to the expected profit. Oftentimes it looks good on paper, but doesn't translate well in practice.

Address the Personalities First

Every adviser I know who is in a partnership used the same words when discussing the relationship: It's like marriage. As a person who is married to her partner, I can reinforce that. In fact, it can be better or worse than marriage. For me, both relationships rely on successful teamwork. If we can just know how to construct the perfect teams, we've got it made.

Identify Successful Teams

Dr. Belbin found that the most successful teams were those composed of individuals who complemented each other's talents. When complementary personalities were paired within the team, they were unbeatable. He determined that defining the key personalities and their functions is a good starting point when looking for a partner.

Begin by identifying the attributes of a personality that will complement you. In order to identify your potential partner's characteristics, you'll need to have a clear sense of your own personality and style. Dr. Belbin defines four broad personality types that may be used for classifying yourself. These types are identified, as follows, on Belbin's extrovert-introvert versus stability-anxiety scale:

- Stable extroverts are individuals who work best in cooperative or liaison relationships. They tend to be easygoing and well received by other personality types and may make great salespeople.

- Anxious extroverts like to work at a fast pace and enjoy positions that allow them to motivate and influence others. They are good at seizing opportunities and respond well to rapidly changing situations. Anxious extroverts make great sales managers.

- Stable introverts work well with smaller groups, maintaining relationships for extended periods of time. They are strong in details, organizational skills, and planning. They make good administrators.

- Anxious introverts are self-directed and persistent. They work best on their own and are not particularly team-oriented.

If it is difficult for you to identify yourself within these brief descriptions, list the activities in your business that you enjoy most. Is it the rainmaking, the client meetings, or the number crunching? Which do you avoid or tackle last? Do many of your ideas fall away because you just don't have the time, opportunity, or personnel to carry them out?

Belbin also identified eight distinct team roles that can be useful in identifying personality characteristics for possible partnerships.

Partnership design is analogous to portfolio design. The focus should be on the portfolio (that is, the partnership) and not the security (that is, the partner). Partnership is about balance. What is needed is not well-balanced individuals, but individuals who possess characteristics that complement and balance one another.

Assess Yourself as a Team Member

Belbin's theories may help you identify personality types. However, you'll also want to explore work style preferences when considering partners or teams. Dr. William Taggart (with Barbara Taggart-Hausladen) of Santa Cruz, California, has developed a Personal Style Inventory (PSI). Dr. Taggart's research suggests that there are six personal style modes that identify an individual's preferred behavior. The style modes—planning, vision, analysis, insight, control, and sharing—dictate how you will react in approaching your work, solving problems, and preparing for the future.

Taggart has been studying personality and the way in which we process information. In addition to the style modes, his research suggests that there are two possible dominant preferences (rational and intuitive) that can be measured by six style dimensions. Based on these conclusions, he has designed the PSI to assist individuals in developing a picture of their rational or intuitive preference. In his terminology, an individual with a rational preference will prepare for the future by planning, solve problems with analysis, and approach work with procedures and control. An individual with an intuitive preference, will prepare for the future with vision, solve problems with insight, and use a sharing (people-oriented) approach to work. Although Taggart's survey is much more comprehensive (booklets summarizing the PSI Approach to rational/intuitive flexibility can be obtained by calling Psychological Assessment Resources, at 800-331-8378), the following "quick and dirty" questionnaire he devised as a teaser will give you an idea of its application.

Each of the four statements below describes a behavior, a belief, or a preference that relates to a common work or life experience. Respond to each statement by rating it according to the answer that best describes you.

Response	Score
Never	1
Once in a while	2
Sometimes	3
Quite often	4
Frequently, but not always	5
Always	6

1. When I have a special job to do, I like to organize it carefully from the start.

2. I feel that a prescribed, step-by-step method is best for solving problems.

3. I prefer people who are imaginative to those who are not.

4. I look at a problem as a whole, approaching it from all sides.

First, add up the score for the first two questions. For example, if your response to the first two questions is 5 and 3, respectively, your total score for the first two questions is 8. Then calculate the score for the last two questions. For example, if the responses are 6 and 6, your total is 12. Finally, subtract the score for the second calculation (12) from the first one (8). In this example, the answer is –4. Look at the following scale:

If your answer is a positive number, you have a dominant rational preference and will use rational rules to make a decision. If your score is negative, your dominant preference is intuition. If you are in the middle, you have a nice balance between the rational and the intuitive, and can draw from both as necessary in your working environment.

Carl Jung, the first to identify intuition as part of the personality, suggests that some individuals have an innate sense of perception and process information in the unconscious. Rational individuals take a more analytical approach, emphasizing process and planning. In application, it is appropriate to be cognizant of your dominant preferences, but it is not necessary to search for a partner who is your complete opposite. Taggart and his associate, Dr. Anisya Thomas of Florida International University, conclude that "to succeed, most organizations must balance creativity and efficiency to nurture intuition in some parts while simultaneously promoting rationality in others. Our experience suggests that heterogeneous management teams that reflect a balance of reason and intuition are best suited to the task (of succeeding)." Partnerships can work only if you recognize, respect, and use these differences.

Successful Teams in Practice

I asked Dr. Taggart to participate in one of our company retreats. It was magnificent. Through his survey of our partners and staff, we were able to identify those of us who could work well together. More important, we knew why we could accomplish more if we adjusted work responsibilities and teams. One of my staff members told me after the retreat that she had always had problems working closely with another member of the staff. "This was so revealing. I realize now that we have completely different work styles. I was relying on her to accomplish her tasks the same way I always do. Now that I know her personal style, my expectations for her will be different and I will be less frustrated."

Probably the most dramatic demonstration of how an understanding of differences in work styles can help an existing team was the work Dr. Taggart did for our Alpha Group. The Alpha Group is a study group of thirteen members from nine firms around the country. We began as an informal study group in 1990. We also had a cause to champion. Portfolio managers of mutual funds were not providing much information. We felt that it was important for us to know much more about their style, process, and thinking than could ever possibly be shared through a prospectus. As a group, we could approach various fund managers, ask for information, and even request phone calls with them. Collectively, we represented over a billion dollars in assets, so we were worth their time.

We developed our monthly manager calls. Each month we invited a different manager to conduct a phone conference with us. Soon, this idea caught on and managers began conducting their own calls, inviting any advisers to participate. There was no need for us to request our own calls any longer. Within two years, it was clear that on any one day you could participate in any of at least five different calls with various managers. We thought we needed another cause.

As time went on, at our periodic meetings, we would devise wonderful projects and white papers. We would leave our meetings energized and excited. By the next meeting, none of us had carried out the things we intended to do. We simply could not figure out why we were not more productive. That's when we asked Dr. Taggart to give us the work style assessment. "It's amazing," he told me. "You all have an intuitive work style in the extreme. There isn't a planner in the bunch." This was a pretty big surprise to us, since we all considered ourselves top-notch financial planners. Taggart went on to explain that we would probably make a better industry think tank by arranging to hand off projects we design to those planners who enjoy carrying out the tasks. This was an amazing, liberating realization. Since that time we have pulled together ideas, then shared them with others in the industry who have acted on them.

The Myers-Briggs Type Indicator (CPP and Davies-Black Publishing; 1055 Joaquin Road, 2nd Floor, Mountain View, CA 94043; 800-624-1765; www.cpp .com) is possibly the most well-known personality indicator. It is based on Carl Jung's theory of psychological types. The instrument divides personalities into sixteen types, each possessing certain distinct personality characteristics. Answers to ninety-three questions place the personality on four different scales:

1. Introvert or Extrovert
2. Sensing or Intuition
3. Thinking or Feeling
4. Perceiving or Judging

Because this is a fairly popular personality exercise, I won't go into detail. I have however referenced its availability (above), as we've used the Myers-Briggs during our retreats and found it most useful. You may find it an effective method for identifying complementary personality traits in potential partners.

 ## Collective Vision

Once you have identified personality types, you must ensure that you and your potential partner share the same vision for the future of the business and the same ethical standards. There must be mutual respect and a comfortable working relationship before you establish a partnership, which cannot be formed overnight. Most married couples have had some kind of courtship before the wedding. Prior to formalizing a transfer of ownership, establish a formal courting relationship.

You can do this by keeping the relationship temporary or on a trial basis for a period of time, or you may structure a buy-in over a longer period of time. Whatever strategy you use, be sure that each participant has an equitable way out of the partnership if it does not appear to be working. Schedule frequent evaluations during the trial period, and keep the communication flowing.

 ## Threatening the Marriage

More and more established advisers are considering bringing in younger partners to absorb the work overflow and/or participate in the succession plan. Unfortunately, it may disturb relationships that exist between the older partners. Peggy Ruhlin refers to this as "threatening the marriage."

A friend confided to me that he and his partner in an established fee-only practice had been approached by another planner in their town who suggested that they combine their businesses. This planner was a broker with a substantial commission-based clientele. He was willing to share his revenues for a percentage of the combined practice and a substantial, dependable salary. He was a good marketer and felt he could attract substantial business to the firm. They settled on a 15 percent share of the practice and a $75,000 base salary for the new partner.

There were several unpleasant surprises not anticipated by any of the partners. Much of the business the broker expected to bring did not come with him. His existing clients, comfortable with paying commissions, were not happy with the fee-only philosophy of the new firm. The idea of paying an annual fee was not attractive. The minority partner was indeed a good marketer, but even the new clients he attracted did not match the new firm's client base, and as a result, they did not remain clients very long. Unfortunately, in all their planning, none of the three had considered an exit strategy. After four years, my friend and his original partner are exploring ways to buy out the minority partner. In hindsight, it would have been better to form an affiliation and cement or sever it at a later date.

Find Common Ground

Once you have agreed to take on a new partner, recraft your positioning and vision statements to ensure that you are both/all in agreement with your business plans and purpose. Eleanor Blayney, formerly of Sullivan, Bruyette, Speros & Blayney, suggests that the hardest thing to overcome in any business relationship is each partner's different sense of priorities. The more partners, the more varied the range and intensity of these perspectives. Clearly defined core values and a common investment philosophy help.

As you ponder the commonalties of your business styles, consider whether you and your partner share the same vision of growth for the firm. Ross Levin, of Accredited Investors, says that after having increased his client base manyfold, he and his partner agreed that taking on more clients did not match their vision of growth. They would prefer to spend more time with fewer people than progressively less time with more people. As a result, they mutually agreed to "grow down."

Then consider the practical issues. What will your work products look like? What investments will you use? For example, do you both agree on the efficacy of active money management? Are you both committed to the exclusive use of mutual funds, or will you also use separate accounts, or individual stocks and bonds? A successful partnership requires members who are flexible, adaptable, and possess an ability to communicate and compromise.

Finding the right partner is as important as deciding you want one. It is imperative that you both have a clear vision of how that relationship should work and what you expect from it. By carefully listing and analyzing the reasons for having a partner, you may decide that all you really need is a good administrator to run the practice while you concentrate on gathering new business. Perhaps a good salesperson will free up your time so it can be devoted to existing clients. Partnerships still risk failure, even if you have thoughtfully analyzed your requirements, determined that you need a partner, and selected someone to complement your personality. So plan carefully and consider an engagement first.

Who's in Charge?

Once you have constructed your partnership arrangement, you and your potential partner must choose a managing partner. It is unrealistic to believe that more than one person can stand at the helm and steer the boat. The managing partner should be the person with the best management and organizational skills. All staff management and day-to-day business decisions should be the responsibility of the managing partner. Be honest and realistic. If managing people is not your forte, admit it and be prepared to let your partner take the helm. Then stay out of his way. Each of you has different responsibilities within the organization and respects the other for contributions to the company as a whole.

Periodic Evaluation and Review

As a practitioner, you use benchmarks to gauge your client's progress. Similarly, you and your partner(s) need to establish benchmarks and periodically review your progress. Set both short-term (for example, three- to twelve-month goals) and long-term (for example, three years) benchmarks. Include business goals, such as the number of new clients per quarter, and organizational goals, such as additional staff or the purchase of software. Finally, list personal goals. Quite often business and personal goals are inextricably linked, and it is wise to share these goals with your partners as well. Evaluate your process and your results. The following is our partner evaluation form:

Partner Self-Assessment

1. Did you accomplish your personal goals from last year? Describe your successes and failures.

2. What would you like to accomplish personally during the next three months? Six months? Nine months?

3. Are you satisfied with your performance as a partner? If not, where would you like to make some improvements?

4. What are your expectations for this company in the next year? Two to five years?

5. Where do you want to be at this time next year?

    a. Personally

    b. Professionally

    c. With regard to family

    d. With regard to friends

    e. Financially

6. Where would you like the business to be at this time next year?

    a. Number of clients

    b. Assets under management

    c. Number of employees

    d. Your salary and company profit

Regular Partner Retreats

Five years ago, my partners and I began having formal, scheduled partner retreats. These are separate from our company retreats, which everyone attends. We always meet away from the office, either at my home or a hotel. We believe it is important to meet outside the office. There are no distractions or interruptions, and often the new venue stimulates new thoughts and visions.

We begin the day with my "State of the Business" report, which includes detailed financial reports, staff evaluations, and growth projections. We continue with our benchmark and personal evaluations, and end the day with our strategic planning. We always review our mission and vision statements, making sure that our new objectives for the upcoming year are in keeping with them.

 ## Partner Compensation

Since you and your partner(s) presumably have different work responsibilities, you will need to address the partnership compensation structures. It should seem fair to everyone involved, and all partners should be satisfied with their share. In my experience, it is not wise to keep revisiting this issue unless something substantive in the relationship changes.

Of the firms I have interviewed, all have a partner compensation structure that considers the individual's contribution to the company. Every partner receives the same base salary, but bonuses are based on the income generated by each person.

The partners of a firm I've been advising recently discussed their compensation structure for a new partner who would function purely as a back-office person. It was not expected he would be directly responsible for new business. The other two partners had been together for seven years. They proposed a base compensation, plus a percentage of new business for the new partner. I challenged this rationale since only the original two partners would be bringing in new business. There seemed to be an eventual opportunity for resentment since the third partner's bonus would be based upon new business that he did not bring into the firm. I pointed out that their new partner influences client retention and suggested a compensation structure for him that was based upon client retention rather than client acquisition. Compensation should be linked to some measure of the partner's value to the company.

If you want some guidance with compensation, get a copy of the "2007 Moss Adams Compensation and Staffing Study of Advisory Firms." Moss Adams completes this study every other year, and you can get it through Moss Adams Business Consulting Group at www.mossadams.com/services/bizconsulting/default. aspx. It will not only help you with partner compensation, but will give you guidance on staff positions as well.

 ## Granting Ownership to Associates

A great deal of controversy exists over granting minority partnership interests for career path personnel. Many CPA and law firms use this structure to encourage excellent professionals to remain with the practice. I have some objections to this, as do some other advisers I've interviewed. Many of the objections center on the lack of well-formed succession plans. Most of us have not yet decided how we will transfer our businesses and are reluctant to grant ownership until the succession issues are clear. On the other hand, granting ownership seems to be working well for some others, and is, in fact, an integral part of their succession plans.

Jerry Neill, formerly of Neill & Associates in Kansas City, Missouri, started as a sole practitioner. As his business grew, he added young planners. These new members proved so productive that Jerry felt he would not be able to keep them unless he provided some incentives. He believed that good salary, bonuses, and benefits are not enough to retain good people. He arranged for his key employees to purchase minority interests in his company. "It made a world of difference," he confided. "They have a stake in this company and they treat their responsibilities differently." Jerry thought about an Employee Stock Ownership Plan (ESOP) for future incentives. "Frankly, these people are my exit strategy."

Conversely, Peggy Ruhlin did not want to dilute her company Budros, Ruhlin & Roe with minority interests. "When we took on our new partner, it was for the full one-third. We would much rather consider a phantom stock arrangement as an incentive for employees." Phantom stock arrangements do in fact avoid the time-consuming administrative detail that accompanies actual stock transfer, since actual shares of stock are not issued. The company pays additional compensation to the employees, which is translated into shares, based on the number that could be purchased with that amount of compensation. Naturally, some fair valuation of the company is made periodically. Shares are valued at some date in the future—

that is, the date of separation, death, or disability—and compensation is made. They provide incentive by having employees participate in the growth of the company, but the cash required for these incentives is deferred.

Plan Your Future Before You Plan Your Clients'

As an adviser, you spend your career guiding individuals in attaining their financial objectives. It is virtually impossible for you to continue giving good advice when you've spent relatively little time developing your own future. Whether you choose a solo practice, an affiliation, or a partnership, planning your practice deserves as much thought as you'd give to planning your clients' investments. After all, their future depends upon how well you've planned for yours.

*We desperately need meaning in our lives and will sacrifice a
great deal to institutions that will provide meaning for us. We
simultaneously need independence, to feel as though we are in charge
of our destinies, and to have the ability to stick out.*
—Tom Peters, author of *In Search of Excellence*

I t is virtually impossible for you to meet all your clients' needs without the help of
a good support staff. As your practice grows, delegating to key people is crucial to
your growth and success. Yet nearly every adviser I know has experienced difficulty
finding the right people, hiring them, and keeping them. The larger the practice, the
more difficult that job gets.

There are many proven ways to attract good personnel, but the only way to keep
them is through quality training, good compensation and benefits, and a nurturing,
stimulating, challenging work environment. The success of your practice depends on
the people who interact with your clients every day. In fact, long-term clients are comfortable and secure with long-term employees.

You've probably spent significant time figuring out how to manage your clients' expectations. It's worth the effort to figure out how to manage your staff's expectations
as well. Just remember, where clients are concerned, there is no way to compensate
for lousy support staff.

 Hiring, Mentoring, and Internships

We've devoted a great deal of time in our practice to finding the most effective approach
to hiring and retaining good people. We prefer the mentor-apprenticeship method of
staffing. We search for people with good education and pleasant personalities who
demonstrate the most flexibility in terms of their work style. When someone meets
these requirements, we can generally integrate him into our workplace by training him
in our philosophy and methods. One of our favorite sources for new staff is through internships. Internships provide a "free look" at potential employees, and many interns
are offered positions with the same firm when they graduate. On the downside, this
requires a two- to three-year training period, and a considerable corporate investment
of time and money.

We nearly always promote from within and seldom hire someone who will "hit the
ground running." This gives us ample familiarity with an employee's work style and
capabilities, as well as how he or she will integrate with other staff members.

Currently, there are more than two hundred academic programs at colleges and universities nationwide that offer financial planning programs registered with the Certified Financial Planner (CFP) Board of Standards. Some are degree programs, but most are certification programs that simply prepare the students to take the comprehensive CFP certification exam. Degree program graduates will actually receive a degree in financial planning. The programs may be delivered at the undergraduate or graduate level.

The University of Miami offers the CFP program as part of its master's in accounting and personal finance. We approached the director of the program and expressed an interest in working with the school to provide business experience for interns. As a result, we've had some great intern relationships that have blossomed into permanent employment.

Texas Tech University in Lubbock, Texas, has the oldest, most comprehensive and robust academic program in the country, offering undergraduate and graduate degrees, as well as the only CFP Board–registered financial planning PhD degree program in the country. They have a very impressive internship program, and all undergraduates are required to complete an internship in financial services prior to graduation. Dr. Vickie Hampton is the director of the academic program. Her students are bright, capable, and well educated, as well as eager and passionate about the planning profession. The semester prior to their internship experience, the students take a professional practices course, learning about different financial services opportunities and business models. They also learn to prepare a business plan and a marketing plan so they can assist in some practical ways when they serve as an intern. Texas Tech also provides extensive software training in financial planning, portfolio management, client relationship management, as well as portfolio software, such as Morningstar Principia, MoneyGuidePro, NaviPlan, SunGard, Money Tree, and iRebal. Since the students volunteer as support staff for the Financial Planning Association (FPA) Forum each year, this offers a good opportunity to connect with possible candidates for your office.

The Personal Financial Planning (PFP) program at Texas Tech also offers an event, Opportunity Days, each year, with a designated career day and banquet to give you an opportunity to interview for potential interns and job applicants. For more information, you can view their website at www.pfp.ttu.edu.

Other programs you might consider are at the University of Georgia (www.terry.uga.edu/exec_ed/cfp/), Kansas State University (www.ipfp.k-state.edu/), and University of Missouri (http://pfp.missouri.edu/index.htm).

Cindy Conger of Cynthia L. Conger, CPA PA, says that technology has replaced lower-level positions in her practice. Nowadays, even assembling their files requires some financial knowledge. They use interns to help in all aspects of the business, particularly in assisting the planners. "It's a matter of attitude," says Cindy. "I can ask a file clerk to prepare our client files in a certain way, but that file clerk sees that job as menial. When our intern prepares those files, he knows it is vital to the operation of the practice. His attitude toward the job is different, so his end work product is different." Interns are young, eager to learn, enthusiastic, grateful for the work, and they can always teach you something.

In the early years of our practice, we called our professional support staff "paraplanners," and then "associate advisers." We discovered that clients tend to identify the term *associate adviser* with junior people. Since we are attempting to encourage closer relationships between our clients and these professionals, we need to make sure that they are professionally elevated and presented as seasoned staff. Therefore, these days, we use the term *adviser* to describe the professional staff who work directly with clients. All our advisers are CFP certificants or are working toward that designation. To differentiate, we now refer to the firm's principals as the "partners," rather than the "advisers."

Naturally, as soon as you bring other advisers into your practice, you will want to have a formalized agreement about whether clients are considered to be company contacts or personal contacts and how situations will be handled if you agree to part company with the advisers. We request that our advisers sign nonsolicitation agreements. It is wise to have an attorney prepare one for you. There is a difference between "nonsolicitation" and "noncompete," and although you have a better chance of protecting your clients with a nonsolicitation agreement, neither has held up very well in court cases.

A nonsolicitation document states that clients are clients of the firm. In essence, this precludes advisers from soliciting clients for business if they leave the firm. As your practice becomes less dependent upon you and more dependent upon others on your team, a noncompete document is vital. Additionally, if you are planning for the transfer of your practice sometime in the future, you will want these agreements, to ensure that key personnel will remain with the firm, even if you don't.

Selecting and Retaining Good Staff

One of the biggest challenges we have as advisers is staffing. Most of us started out as sole practitioners and began to hire support staff to help us manage relationships. As we grew, the need for support staff in the traditional sense diminished as we recognized that we needed highly skilled and educated professional staff to be able to leverage our efforts. Our experience in hiring was limited to bringing in young people with no experience and "training them up." Our lack of experience at incorporating professionals, coupled with our lack of knowledge of the best human resource practices, made it difficult to fulfill our staffing needs adequately.

Before you hire, be sure that you have a complete job description written so that you search for a person to fill the exact position that you require. Be specific about the responsibilities and career path. New entrants in today's financial profession want to know what their future opportunities will be.

Next, you will want to advertise your position to get the best possible responses. The FPA (www.fpanet.org), the National Association of Personal Financial Advisors (NAPFA—www.napfa.org), and Schwab Institutional (www.schwabinstitutional.com) have employment opportunities on their websites. Texas Tech also has an employment opportunity program for current students and will even contact their alumni with information as well.

What to Look For in a Résumé

The résumé is the first impression you have of a potential employee. The résumé should have enough information to pique your interest and should only give you a good basis for asking lots of questions during an interview. At a minimum, here are some things I like to see in a good résumé:

- No errors—You would be surprised at how many I have seen with obvious grammatical and spelling errors.

- Good organization—The résumé should be visually appealing, well constructed, and well thought out.

- Relevant education, experience, and community service—You want to see education and experience that reflect an ability to handle the position you want to fill. It would also be good to see other interests, such as community service or other involvement outside a work environment, which may indicate more developed social skills.

Testing

I recommend that you invest a few dollars in testing your potential candidates. There are some great tests available that will help you make good choices. It is far too expensive in time and money to bring on someone because you "think it might work." It is far better to get some help with your decision-making. I recommend the following:

- Myers & Briggs (www.myersbriggs.org) offers a personality test, to help you understand the personality characteristics that will best fit with your current practice and your future plans. The Myers-Briggs test identifies sixteen personality types. (See also Chapter 9.)

- Kolbe Indexes (www.kolbe.com) are work-style assessments, to help you gain knowledge about how a candidate will work with you, other staff, and clients. Kolbe tests help uncover natural instincts and innate abilities.

- Wonderlic Personnel Test (www.wonderlic.com) measures general intelligence or cognitive ability to help you determine if your candidate has the ability to perform well on the job.

- Financial DNA Profiles (www.financialdna.com) determine how your staff make financial decisions at their most basic, visceral level. It will also provide communication keys to facilitate the best communication between you, staff, and clients.

Interviewing

Tests alone will not give you the comfort of bringing the best people into your firm. Develop some situational questions for young, new hires that will test critical thinking skills and leadership or management capabilities. Try some of these:

1. You are a first-year financial planner. You have been asked to sit in on a planning meeting with clients. Before the meeting, you have familiarized yourself with the client's situation by reading the "client diary," and you

have also worked on the update of his or her financial plan. In the meeting, the senior planner makes a statement that is clearly not factual. You assume that this is unintentional. What do you do, and why?

2. You have been working for the same fee-based firm for two years. One of the firm's clients asks if you will take his children (ages twenty-three and twenty-seven) as clients. The children's assets do not meet the firm's minimums. How do you handle this situation?

3. You have a well-qualified prospect who says that she is prepared to take reasonable risk, but that she is expecting a return in the 12 to 15 percent range annually. What do you tell this prospect, and why?

Don't ask belt-roller questions!

- "If I go into any drawer in your house, what will I find?" If they tell you they roll their belts, you'll conclude they are well organized. Any idiot can figure out what you'd like them to answer. Well, let's put it this way, if they can't, you wouldn't want them anyway.

- "Besides the TV show, are you familiar with the term *OC*?" You may think you want an obsessive-compulsive personality, but I promise you, you don't.

- "Are you organized?" Realistically, how do you think a smart person would answer this? Stick to Socratic questions (open-ended) that will allow your prospective candidate to think and talk. Here are some questions you might consider:

  1. What kinds of projects have you worked on?
  2. What is your personal definition of success?
  3. What motivates you?
  4. Tell me about yourself.
  5. What do you think you can contribute to our practice?
  6. What are your strengths and struggles?
  7. What goals have you set for yourself for the next five years? Ten years?
  8. Have you ever had a conflict with someone at work? How was that resolved?
  9. Do you have plans for further education?
  10. Would you rather work with information or with people?

Some questions are taboo under any circumstances, so don't ask a woman if she is pregnant or plans to be. Don't ask if someone has ever declared bankruptcy, served in the military, or is gay. Stay away from questions of nationality, sex, weight, or religion.

It's a good idea to interview your prospective employees more than once, giving them different opportunities to impress you. It is also a good idea to have your key personnel interview them as well. Prospective employees will often become more relaxed around your other staff and will make a different impression on them.

Be prepared to discuss salary and benefits with serious prospects. To see if you are in the ballpark, you might ask, "What are your salary requirements?" Your compensation structure should be well defined, industry-competitive, and incorporated into your career path structure. I will discuss compensation and career path structures next.

Lastly, don't spend your interview time talking about what you want. You won't gain any new information by listening to yourself. Let your prospective hire ask you about the job and responsibilities.

Taking Care of Your Most Valuable Asset: Your Staff

Let's assume that you find a candidate that you really want to hire. First, I suggest that you provide that individual an offer letter, stating that you are formally offering her a position, what the position is, and what salary and benefits you are providing. Extending your offer in writing formalizes your intention and guards against any misunderstanding.

Your staff members are the people who make the very first impression on your prospects and can enhance or destroy relationships with existing clients. If you want to attract great clients, hire great staff, train them, and then empower them. You must give them a sense of self-worth beyond their value as employees, and then compensate them accordingly. Just as you would with your best clients, find out what they expect from this relationship and manage their expectations. We want our staff to know how important they are to our business, so we spend significant time demonstrating how much we value them.

Money Plus

In 1998, Princeton Research found that workers aged eighteen to twenty-nine felt that advancement, opportunity, and benefits (health coverage, vacations, flextime) were more important than money or number of working hours. Seventy percent of our employees are under age thirty. It is very clear that our staff wants flexibility, benefit choices, respect, personal and professional challenge, plus money. Money is essential, yet money by itself is not enough.

Jerry Neill told me years ago that several of his employees abruptly quit. He conducted exit interviews to ask what some of the problems were. Among other things, they all said it wasn't "a fun place to work." "I just didn't understand that," Jerry told me. "This is not the kind of business I grew up in. Work is work." So Jerry hired a business consultant who made some simple suggestions to keep the troops happy. "These people would have killed for a casual-dress Friday. How did I know?" Jerry's consultant suggested they have more family-centered activities such as a company picnic and holiday party. Of course, now casual Fridays in his office are a must. Jerry and his partners hired an office manager who, along with other key personnel, has completely rewritten the employee manual. The office manager is closer in age to their under-thirty employees, and the change in the office has been remarkable.

Ross Levin, of Accredited Investors in Minnesota, explains that he and his staff go out together about once a quarter, usually to celebrate something, like tax day or some bogus event that requires a celebration. "Everyone loves this. We have a good time and enjoy each other's company." Ross's firm also participates together in community activities such as Habitat for Humanity. This not only promotes bonding but also gives back to the community in very useful ways. There is a trend among established advisers toward creating office-family activities with opportunities for employee bonding with philanthropic or community-based intent. Martha Boudos of Morningstar told me that she is amazed at the number of new hires she has who ask what opportunity they will have to give back to the community in some way through events created by Morningstar. This "doing good by doing good" mentally helps staff develop strong relationships over the years.

But employee bonding and creating the right environment is only one aspect of your relationship with your employees. The career path and the compensation you provide will keep your employees happy and satisfied. Rebecca Pomering of Moss Adams in Seattle explains the compensation issues this way: "Your employee should be able to say, 'If I do more of X, then I will get Y.' That includes salary, incentive compensation, and career paths."

Eleanor Blayney (formerly of Sullivan, Bruyette, Speros & Blayney) and I have had numerous discussions about managing and compensating staff. This is a huge topic among planners who started their careers as sole practitioners and wound up growing into larger firms with numerous personnel. Eleanor considers her staff members valuable assets, but she has also compared them to capitalizing a business. "If you wanted to capitalize a new business, you would probably have some bondholders and some stockholders. In staffing, the bondholders are the steady, loyal employees who are not particularly looking for advancement, but enjoy what they do and fully intend to do it as long as they work. They would like to be well paid for their efforts but are not generally motivated by entrepreneurial career path incentives. Bondholder staff want security and income. Conversely, the stockholders on a career path want incentives, challenges, and opportunity." Eleanor believes that these two "asset classes" should be treated differently and offered different remuneration and benefit packages.

Compensation

We have designed our staff compensation based upon the career path the individual has chosen. We want to ensure that they remain successful, satisfied members of the staff, so our career paths are not written in stone. One of our advisers began working in back-office operations. Each year for several years, we met and discussed his plans for the future. Every year, he told us he was happy in operations and had no plans to do anything else. Then one year, because of personnel changes, we asked him to sit in on some client meetings until we hired someone new. Within the month, he declared an intention to take CFP courses and accept the responsibilities of an adviser. He has now completed his CFA and has become the COO of our company, taking over many of the roles and responsibilities that I previously held.

A few years ago, we hired Moss Adams up to do a compensation study for us. This is one of the most important analyses you can do for your company because you will want to be sure that your staff is not only fairly compensated, but that they fully understand *how* they are compensated as well. As I mentioned earlier, Moss Adams prepares a compensation and staffing study every other year that will give you great information and benchmarks on the advisory industry. You can get a copy of the 2007 version through Moss Adams in Seattle, Washington. Information from this study, as well as in places like www.salary .com, will help you design and develop your compensation strategies on your own.

Compensation is composed of base salary, benefits, and incentive compensation. Compensation and benefits are less complicated to construct, but you should give careful consideration to the incentives you put in place. Consider incentivizing to encourage the behavior that you are trying to reinforce. For example, employees responsible for client acquisition could get bonuses based on the new clients they bring to the table. Employees responsible for retention could get bonuses based on the clients who stay with you from year to year.

I've required our adviser employees to investigate benefit options to help us structure them for the advantage of all of us. I have discussed the dollars we have available for benefits, and I have let them decide how to put this package together. They present their findings to all of us at a weekly staff meeting. A staff committee also designed our investment policy and manages our profit sharing plan.

Aside from the usual benefits, we have also instituted a Personal and Professional Development Fund in our firm. Employees may spend up to $3,000 per year for courses or seminars to further their professional or personal development. In past years, staff have taken courses from the Dale Carnegie Leadership Training Institute, Evelyn Wood Reading Dynamics speed-reading classes, advanced computer courses, neurolinguistic programming classes, and seminars for executive assistants and middle managers.

Naturally, we subsidize anyone who wants to pursue the CFP certification, and it is a requirement for those who will work directly with clients. Interested employees are required to pay for the first course. If they decide to continue, we pay for the remaining courses and examinations, and we reimburse them for the first one upon successful completion of the program.

It is important for young advisers to get well entrenched in our profession by becoming involved. We encourage our staff to attend local and national FPA meetings, NAPFA meetings, and other professional meetings. They are great networking and professional development opportunities, and well worth the time staff are away from the office. Many of our staff have created their own study groups from these relationships. This can only benefit everyone, just as my generation benefited from creating our own study group, the Alpha Group.

Peggy Ruhlin explains that Budros, Ruhlin & Roe has a "growth sharing" arrangement for providing bonuses for its advisers. Each year a percentage of the firm's gross is deposited into an account to be shared by the employees based on a point system. Peggy said they elected to base these bonuses on the gross, rather than the net profits so that the advisers will be assured of some extra compensation even if the company has no profit for the year. The staff members are given points for longevity, client retention, support for new business, achieving a new professional designation, and completing continuing education courses. They receive bonuses annually based on the number of points acquired throughout the year.

To design your compensation program, consider:

- New business

- Experience

- Performance

- Designations

- Base salary

- Bonus structure

- Professional development

Truthfully, people entering the profession today, especially from academic programs, will want to see some equity in their future. Older planners have resisted this. One adviser told me, "It took time and great effort, working a hundred hours a week for years to build my practice; I'm not just handing if off to some ninety-day wonder." In the February 2005 issue of *Investment Advisor*, consultant Angie Herbers discussed the problem of the expectations of new advisers versus the older, more experienced ones. She explained that young advisers were graduating with degrees in planning and no real career track. One young planner complained, "I am a new CFP and know that I'm going to start off at the bottom, but the long-term benefits and opportunities to move up within the company are going to ultimately be the deciding factor for me. I don't want to work at a job for three years and leave, but I can't work a job for five years with zero chance for income growth or meaningful ownership." They wanted equity and older advisers were "in denial" about the capabilities and expertise of these newer planners.

A misunderstanding seems to exist on both sides. As an older planner, I believe we need young, enthusiastic, well-educated people to join us in our efforts, particularly if we are thinking about management succession and exit strategies. On the other hand, these people who want to succeed us will need to demonstrate leadership abilities and entrepreneurial qualities to earn the right to purchase equity. As I see it, equity is not a gift for working five years. Plenty of business models, including those for law and accounting firms, seem to have successful models for integrating new people into practices and providing equity.

In any case, advisers, young and old, need each other.

Recently, I needed to see a doctor, but I was in my Texas home where I have not established new medical relationships. My old family doctor is in Florida where I also have a home, but this wouldn't wait. So, I took myself to a local clinic that immediately allowed me to see the doctor, a young man in his mid-to-late thirties. He greeted me warmly, and then turned to the computer terminal attached to the wall in the examining room. After unsuccessfully connecting to the system, he opened the door to the hall and yelled, "Sarah! Is there something wrong with the computer system? I can't connect and I can't do anything in here without it. Get Daniel on it right now!" Despite the pain I was in, I cracked up. My old doctor would have been poking and prodding by now and probably formulating a diagnosis already. Truth is, this young doctor was very good and, from the half-dozen questions he asked, ordered tests that confirmed my condition.

This incident only confirmed what I suspected; it takes an old doctor and a new physician to provide good patient care. Think about it, the old doctor:

- Has taken care of some patients for decades, developing tight, loyal relationships
- Has learned from an older set of principles
- Prefers paper charts, prescriptions, and textbooks
- Is a good diagnostician, using tests to confirm
- Relies on standard medications

The new physician, on the other hand:

- Has not had long-term patients
- Is well versed in the newest tests and drugs
- Was trained with computerized medical records and cyber literature
- Uses tests to diagnose
- Explores newer medications and tests frequently

Now think of this analogy in terms of a financial planning practice. Together older and newer advisers can bring the newest thinking and the best relationships together to benefit all clients. The ability of more experienced advisers to mentor and guide newer planners and the ability of younger planners to bring new, fresh ideas and techniques to the table are invaluable.

Career Paths

Employees you hire today, especially when they have come from an academic program, will want to have a clearly stated career path as they begin their employment experience. Lou Stanasolovich at Legend Financial Advisors in Pittsburgh has an extraordinarily detailed program, beginning with the use of interns in various critical phases of his company. Legend has hired many of these interns postgraduation. The integration is seamless since many have been working with Legend since their sophomore year of college. The key to Lou's success with interns is that he gives them jobs and responsibilities, trains them well, and expects them to work hard and take advantage of the opportunity he has given them.

Empowerment

We devised a staffing philosophy in much the same way as we designed a business and investment policy. There are several components that are key to this philosophy: worker empowerment, a warm working environment, nonaccusatory attitudes toward errors, and continuing education. We use cross-training and team-building to help facilitate our philosophy. Last year, for example, our employees divided themselves into teams, addressing our prospect and client delivery systems, such as brochures, data-gathering questionnaires, and review documents. At a company staff meeting, each team presented recommendations for improving or redesigning our systems. We are still in the process of implementing their recommendations.

Our employees are given titles commensurate with their responsibilities. Further, they are empowered with the authority to make a situation right for the client. Staff are trained to accept responsibility for errors, even if they are not ours. We never argue with a client or make him feel uncomfortable about a situation. We call this empowerment "Nordstrom Authority."

If you've ever been to San Francisco, you may have been to the original Nordstrom department store. It is nationally known for its superior service. During my first visit, I bought a suit that needed a minor alteration. When I went to pick it up later that day, it was not ready. I reminded the clerk that I was going home early the following day. After a profuse apology, the saleswoman reassured me, "Don't worry, the suit will be ready at 7:00 this evening. I will have it delivered to your hotel by 7:30 p.m." It was. She did not have to obtain permission from anyone else.

The first time one of our advisers used his Nordstrom Authority, a new client had just complained that during a transfer of funds, one security was liquidated when it should have been transferred in kind. The result was a loss of about $650 to the client. Although the transferring firm caused the error, our advisers told the client, "You are absolutely right. I will immediately call to have it rectified. Don't worry." He went on to say, "I will make your position whole as though the transfer had been made correctly." Later that afternoon the new client called once again, this time concerned that the adviser would be "eating the mistake himself." The adviser told the client he appreciated his calling but that he need not be concerned. It is the policy of the firm to stand behind the client and the adviser.

Realizing Potential

Adviser Karen Spero, now successfully retired, felt that it was her responsibility to help her staff realize their own potential. To that end, she devised a self-assessment form that all staff members completed at the beginning of each year. Self-assessments can help guide the upcoming year's activities, and from an analysis of these responses, you may discover that your people have interests in areas of which you were unaware.

For example, the first two questions focus on goal setting and reviewing accomplishments in light of those goals.

1. What do you regard as your most significant accomplishment last year and why?

2. What do you most want to accomplish this year? Describe at least three goals and how you plan to achieve them. Please be as specific as possible.

Karen confided to me that from responses to these two questions she learned that one of her employees had a strong interest in spending more time with clients rather than in the back office. "Frankly," said Karen, "she was hired for her analytic expertise. I never really thought she was interested in client communications. Naturally, we were delighted to shift responsibilities to give her new opportunities."

Thanks to Karen, I've used these questions not only in our practice, but also as part of consulting for other firms. One response I received from a particular employee surprised me. The respondent prefaced his remarks by thanking me for asking. It seems that he had been given a work responsibility because the last employee to handle it left the practice. He was told that he would have this responsibility until a new employee was hired. New employees were hired, but no one ever revisited this work responsibility, and by default, after two years, he still had it. "I was not trained to do this and I really feel I am not doing the best job. I am certain that someone else would handle it better." When I asked him why he did not bring this up with his boss, he said, "He's not interested in how the work gets done, he just wants us to 'Make It So.'" By not encouraging his employees to provide feedback, the employer guaranteed that his staff would "Make It So-So" inefficiently.

It is vitally important to ask staff what resources or support systems they need to work more effectively. You might be surprised at some of the answers you receive to the next two questions.

3. What resources/support would make you more efficient in your job?

4. How much and what type of supervisory input do you feel you require to accomplish your job?

My chief financial officer presented me with a list of answers to the resources question. "Our director of concierge services needs her own credit card to purchase gifts and make arrangements for special events for clients. She should need authorization only for purchases in excess of $500. You should get our intern permission to use the law library at the University of Miami so he can have more flexibility in his research. He should be allowed to set his own schedule. He can just check in to see that we don't have anything more pressing for him here at the office. And," she added with authority, "put a waterfall in the conference room. It will be very soothing to clients and will be a good retreat for us when we feel overwhelmed." She does, he does, I did, and we do.

The next four questions were helpful in creating our work teams. We were able to encourage people who complemented each other to work together on projects.

5. What three skills/abilities do you see as your strengths? What three skills/abilities do you see as weaknesses?

6. How would you further develop your strengths?

7. What aspects of your job are most appealing?

8. What aspects are least appealing?

Several of Karen Spero's employees answered number 5 stating that they felt they lacked the skills necessary for communicating well with clients. As a result, Karen arranged for her staff to attend seminars on improving communication abilities.

The last three questions will help get a sense of the vision and goals each person has in the workplace.

9. Please write a description of your job as it now exists. (Be as brief as possible; bullet points are okay.)

10. Please write a job description of what you would like your job to be. (Be as brief as possible; bullet points are okay.)

11. Now describe your job in five years.

I particularly like this last question. On a consulting job, one employee told me that she pictured herself retired in two to three years. From this, I fully understood her demonstrable lack of energy and enthusiasm for her job. She was coasting until retirement. With an understanding of her personal goal, I was able to arrange for her early retirement over the next year, during which time she enthusiastically trained her replacement.

I have included this self-assessment form for your use (**Figure 10.1**). It is helpful to have everyone in your office complete this form periodically to ensure that they are moving on a career path that will meet their own expectations.

My sister owned her own business for twenty years. On the wall in her office hung a poster with the following line: "If you aim at nothing, you're sure to hit it." Karen's self-assessment survey encourages everyone to set goals and measure progress.

Food, Comfort, and Other Care

My former partner Peter Brown remarked that we have one of the few cafeteria benefits programs in this country that actually involve food. Our office kitchen has become the center of our office activities and our home hearth, so to speak. I hadn't thought much about the impact this lunchroom has had on everyone until I sauntered in one day for my own coffee and found a couple of clients sitting at our lunch table, sharing sodas and jokes with two of our advisers. Everyone feels at home. It's what we had in mind.

Our food fetish started with an Alpha Group visit to Advent Software in San Francisco. As we were shown around the programmer floors, I noticed trays of fresh fruit and baked goods at various locations around the work areas. Advent's president, Stephanie DeMarco, told me that the trays are delivered each morning for staff to nosh on all day. She also has fresh flowers delivered once a week. The programmers told me it makes a comfortable environment, facilitating thought and creativity.

We grabbed the idea and expanded it. Rather than the same fruit and pastry plate every day, staff decides what they will order on a weekly basis. Mornings we all meet around the big table for morning coffee, breakfast treats, and vitamins. Yes, vitamins. A few years ago our office manager, Mena Bielow, decided that we were passing around colds and flu too frequently. She brought in a bottle of vitamin C and insisted that everyone take one 1,000 mg tablet each morning. After a few weeks, we all felt better and had fewer illnesses among us. Now, the company provides a selection of multivitamins, and Mena monitors our intake. Mena also ensures that everyone has a company-paid annual physical and flu shot.

Often our morning coffee moments turn into brief, informal coordinating sessions with everyone discussing his or her planned activities for the day. Lunches

Self-Evaluation

1. What do you regard as your most significant accomplishment last year and why?

2. What do you most want to accomplish this year?

3. What resources/support would make you more efficient in your job?

4. How much and what type of supervisory input do you feel you require to accomplish your job?

5. What three skills/abilities do you see as your strengths? What three/skills abilities do you see as your struggles?

6. How would you further develop your strengths?

7. What aspects of your job are most appealing?

8. What aspects are least appealing?

9. Write a description of your job as it now exists.

10. Write a description of what you would like your job to be.

11. Now describe your job in five years.

■ FIGURE 10.1 Self-Assessment Form

are usually enjoyed together at the big table in our great room. At any time during the day there are pastries, fruit, cookies, and hot and cold drinks. For the staff meetings each week, the company provides a full breakfast, and Fridays are generally company-catered pizza lunches. This environment facilitates personal as well as business discussions.

Birthdays and anniversaries with the company are excuses to get together for conversation and cake. Our comptroller always assigns someone to choose a small gift and card that everyone personally signs. Often if clients are visiting, they join in the festivities. Everyone loves the special attention.

Owning Up to Mistakes

Back in the 1970s I read a book on transactional analysis, *I'm OK—You're OK*, by Thomas A. Harris. One silly vignette stayed with me. Since then, I've used the concept numerous times in working with staff. Here's the scene: Your spouse is fixing breakfast and inadvertently burns the toast. You know it's inadvertent because nobody gets up one morning and says, "I think I will burn the toast this morning so it's inedible." You come down to breakfast and see the burnt toast. You could say, "How could you be so stupid to burn this toast?" or, "This toast is burnt; I won't eat it." Now, you know that your spouse already knows the toast is burnt, and that mentioning something he or she already knows is unproductive. Your spouse probably already feels bad about the toast. A transactionally aware person says, "You must be having a bad morning. What can I do to help?"

When a staff member makes a mistake, it is rarely intentional. It is usually for one of three reasons: Our system isn't working, someone made a bad judgment call, or someone inadvertently did something stupid. Since staff are empowered to make judgment calls, there will be times when they will be wrong. If the mistake recurs, it's probably the system. If it's just plain stupidity, even the best of us does something stupid from time to time that's forgivable. If it's terminal stupidity, that's probably an indication that it's time to free up someone's future.

I believe in fixing the problem, not the blame. To encourage people to admit mistakes, I devised the Turkey Award. The Turkey is a goofy-looking stuffed animal suspended from a gold cord. At each Friday meeting, we discuss our mistakes for the week. The person who made the stupidest, craziest, most unbelievable mistake gets the turkey for the week. He or she is saluted with the Turkey "gobble," and the stuffed Turkey sits on his or her desk for the week. We have given the Turkey for cutting off a tie in the shredder, trying to send a fax to our own fax number, confusing two clients with similar last names, and preparing a rebalancing proposal using the wrong portfolio policy. Despite the array of available scenarios, these days we are hard pressed to give the Turkey away. For all mistakes, I always ask, "Did this happen because the system is bad?" If that's the case, we revise the system.

As I've noted earlier, each staff member has the power to do what must be done to make it right for the client. That means eating transaction charges when we've made a trading error, sending an apology gift to a client for a mistake, or accepting the blame for a situation even though we know we weren't responsible for it. I support my staff and any of their decisions to make a situation right for the client. I only ask to be informed as soon as the problem arises. Most of the time, a staff member tells me the problem and the solution simultaneously.

Ross Levin tells the story of a huge trading mistake made in his office at Accredited Investors last year. One of his staff members thought he was buying one fund, when he actually purchased another. By the time the trader discovered the error two months later, the fund they actually bought was down $13,000. "We believe in owning up to mistakes immediately. This is a client who would probably have never known we'd made this mistake. Of course, we brought it to his attention and we made it right, which means we ate the $13,000. We were honest, no matter how painful. Now, we have a client for life."

Appreciation

I have been talking about appreciation that we as employers have for our staff and the ways we demonstrate it. We also provide opportunities for staff to show their appreciation for each other. The companion to our Turkey is the Star, a stuffed gold star with multicolored streamers hanging from a long ribbon. The Star of the Week is nominated at our weekly staff meetings, right after we declare the Turkey. We have awarded a star for chasing down the mail carrier when we inadvertently mailed one hundred letters without postage. We've given stars for fixing the stapler, for volunteering to stay late and help an associate get out an important mailing, and for discovering an error on a client's death certificate that saved us and his attorney a great deal of aggravation. The Platypus Award is given to a deserving employee who has received both a star and a turkey during the same week. It is rare, but it has happened.

I particularly like Greg Sullivan's (of Harris SBSB) appreciation strategy. Years ago he started buying a batch of lunch coupons to the local deli in his building. He gave everyone ten five-dollar coupons to give away to thank a coworker for appreciation for something special. The only requirement was that if you give one away, you must inform a principal and report why. Any demonstrative appreciation just enhances any office environment.

 Employee Reviews

Jeffrey Pfeffer, the Thomas D. Dee professor of organizational behavior at the Stanford Graduate School of Business, said that many business people compare annual employee reviews with "filling out your income tax form. It's not a process that anybody likes, but you've got to do it."[1] It does have to be done, but it doesn't have to be painful. Before my reviews, I talk with my partners and my office manager. Together we compare notes about each staff member. Using these discussions and my own observations, I formulate a list of strengths and weaknesses for each person. That list becomes the basis for my reviews. I used to use Employee Appraiser software (SuccessFactors, formerly Austin-Hayne), which I thought was fairly good. But I found the framework only made my discussions stilted since they were not formulated by me or directed by the self-assessments.

I also use this review time to elicit staff member recommendations; in essence, they are judging me as a leader. This has been helpful to me personally, and I welcome their thoughts. From time to time when I have fallen behind in giving out my reviews, staff have asked me for them.

It is wise to have annual expectations planned for each employee. If you have a career path in place, you probably have a list of accomplishments that you expect as they move along their advancement pathway, but I find it useful to have each employee make his or her own list for each year.

I usually conduct my reviews based on the self-assessment document that staff members complete. (See Figure 10.1.) There are a few items to keep in mind when you conduct a review.

- Keep the review private.
- Focus on the employee. Do not make comparisons to others.

- Ask staff members how they think they are doing. You'll be surprised at how candid people can be about their own work.

- If you have tough criticisms, cover those first. Always end with something positive, encouraging, and upbeat.

- Give them an opportunity to make open and honest observations about anything, with no recriminations. Be sure to tell them that the comments will not leave the room, and mean it.

- Ask them how they think you can be a better leader.

- Take notes on what you have discussed and file them in a permanent employee file.

Many companies conduct upstream and downstream reviews, so while you are assessing your staff, they can also be giving you constructive criticism on your performance as a leader.

 ## Little Things

The bottom line is that we treat our staff the way we would like them to treat our clients: with Intensive Customer Care. We surprise them from time to time with an impromptu party after a particularly grueling week. When we travel, we always bring them small mementos of the places we've visited, so they know we're thinking about them, and they return the favor. We have arranged to have the local dry cleaners pick up their laundry at the office each week if they like. We have an annual company picnic to which families and friends are invited. We have even sent interested staff to a local nutritionist for counseling and menus. (With our food fetishes, is it any wonder?)

Our holiday party includes spouses and significant others. We choose a fine restaurant for dinner then retreat to my house for "The Rookie Show." For the past five years, we were hiring new people so fast that each time we got together for the annual holiday party, there were so many new faces that we practically had to wear nametags. My former partner, Peter, decided we needed some sort of icebreaker and initiation rite, so he created the Rookie Show. At each holiday party, anyone who is new to the firm in the past year must perform for the rest of us. They can sing, dance, tell a joke—whatever they want to do. It's a great deal of fun and a wonderful bonding mechanism.

All these little things demonstrate our support and interest in staff members as individuals, not just as employees. They show their support and interest in us by taking very good care of our clients.

 ## If It Ain't Fixable, Break It Off ASAP

I have spent the better part of this chapter discussing getting and keeping good staff and promoting good teamwork. However, it would not be complete without a discussion of terminating staff. This is not an easy task. Most of us have never been trained as human resource professionals. Advisers don't like confrontation;

we want everyone to like us. If the salesman's curse is to close the sale, then the planner's curse is the need for everyone to like us.

During the ten years that *Murphy Brown* was on television, she fired no fewer than ninety-two secretaries. They ran the gamut from bizarre, unskilled, or bossy, to timid, overqualified, or certifiably insane. This was great comedy, but it's not so funny when it sits outside your office. My former partner Peter loves to tell the story of the time he had to fire Harold's secretary because Harold stopped coming to work in order to avoid her. He couldn't work well with her, but he just couldn't let her go. Peter didn't want to fire her either, but it was that, or let Harold work from home for the rest of his life.

Over the past twenty-three years in business, I have formed several hard-and-fast rules about firing employees.

- If it's not working out, fire sooner rather than later. Don't wait for things to get better. They won't. "We had a very toxic person in our office once," Ross Levin told me. "It really affected morale. We should have terminated that relationship six months before we did. Today, we're happier and more efficient."

- Keep copious notes on employees, including personal discussions and your observations, as well as observations from others. You never know if you may need them later.

- If someone quits, then later asks you to rehire, don't. Office environments are dynamic. Although he may have been the right person for the job before he left, it does not necessarily follow that he will be the right person now.

- Be certain that you have documents and procedures in place for letting someone go. For example, I recommend that when you "free up someone's future," you give them a severance package, according to plan, and make that their last day. I have heard of advisers giving notice and actually letting employees work beyond the notice.

- Allow a limited time for two employees to solve their own conflicts. Allow a limited time for you to mediate. When all else fails, terminate one or both of them. Forcing warring employees to work together can threaten the success of your company.

People Management Is the Key

Happy, efficient, hard-working staff members are critical to your business. Learn how to manage them, or immediately pass the responsibility to a partner who can. If you don't have a partner, or neither of you have the skills to successfully manage people, hire someone to do it for you.

You may be able to solve your management problems by hiring an office manager, someone who is capable of directing the daily activities of the practice. Your office manager can hire and fire, supervise personnel, and manage daily work responsibilities. Decisions about marketing, budgeting, and long-range planning still fall to you.

If you feel you need a higher level of expertise, you may consider hiring someone with the skills necessary to take over the management of the entire business.

If your company is large enough, you will be able to hire a chief operating officer to manage while you assume the adviser or rainmaker role in your company. Many midsized financial planning firms have not opted for COO management. One real success story is Jim Isaacs at Legacy Wealth Management in Memphis, Tennessee. Jim has taken the management responsibility from John Ueleke, the firm's founder, allowing John to do what he does best: attract new clients. The firm has grown substantially since Jim came on board. If you are a smaller firm, consider taking on a partner who has administrative skills that will complement your own skill set.

THE CLIENT

I've spoken with advisers all over the world who tell me that attracting and retaining good clients is a major challenge. This is an issue that potentially presents many heartaches as well as joys and rewards.

This section is concerned with building your clients' trust by educating them, understanding their needs, and by managing expectations through superior service and continual communication. If you do this well, you will never have to explain your value to clients; they will already understand it.

Do it now. The business obituary pages are filled with planners who waited.
—Harry Beckwith, author of *Selling the Invisible*[1]

Entrepreneurs are visionaries and dreamers, but most of all, risk takers. Considering that the financial advisory profession has been largely entrepreneurial, it is interesting to discover areas where advisers balk at taking risks. Sacred cows—"we do it this way because we've always done it this way"—are akin to Linus's security blanket. They provide a false sense of safety.

Reverence for sacred cows seems to be an endemic problem in planning firms. I find it most often when I talk to advisers about committing to minimums or limiting practices to a finite and narrow client base. Some of this risk avoidance may stem from many of us having started out in the product business. We learned sales techniques. We took courses in it. The goal was to make the sale, any sale. All sales were good sales.

Once I took a "closing" seminar. I walked out with no less than 112 one-liners to "close the client." "Don't let the prospect get out the door," they told us. Never ask, "Would you like to buy this one?" Ask, "Which one of these are you buying?" This emphasis on closings may account for our need to capture every prospect that walks in the door. I have a good friend, an adviser who tracks his monthly and annual closings. He keeps these statistics at hand, impressing everyone in our business with his 80 percent conversion ratio. Meanwhile, he complains that he is overworked and his staff is overwhelmed. I talked with his planning director about this. "We do comprehensive plans here, but many of the people we take don't fit our profile. We really don't get paid for all the work we do on the plans." It's not that his firm doesn't have specific client profiles and minimum criteria. My friend simply ignores his own standards because a prospect turns up and he loves the challenge of "closing" him.

 ## The Sacred Cows

If You're Breathing, You Can Be My Client

I loved the Julia Roberts and Richard Gere movie, *Pretty Woman*. The heart-of-gold-hooker, rags-to-riches theme is appealing to nearly everyone. In the film, these lovable streetwalkers always leave each other with the salutation, "Take care 'a you." This is my advice to all you planners out there. I use it to mean "don't take troublesome clients." (I cleaned that up.)

Stewart Welch, founder of the Welch Group, in Birmingham, Alabama, told me that once he decided to grow his practice, he set a dollar amount goal for each month. Quite often he agreed to take inappropriate clients or difficult relationships because it added to the bottom line and helped him reach his monthly goal. In Stewart's office, he is the rainmaker. But once he establishes the relationship, his director of planning maintains the relationship. It finally dawned on Stewart that he was not committing himself to these difficult relationships; he was committing his staff. "It's kind of like the movie *Jeremiah Johnson*," Stewart says. "Two hunters have been stalking a huge bear for days. One day, one of the hunters is sitting in the cabin, cleaning his gun. The second man rushes through the door, the bear chasing close behind. 'I caught 'im,' the man yells breathlessly, 'now you skin 'im!'"

If you are the rainmaker for your firm, resist the temptation to close each prospect. Rather than tracking "closings," track the "openings"—those people who fit your criteria and with whom you'd enjoy an ongoing relationship.

I Need Low Minimums to Attract Clients

Some controversy exists about creating minimum criteria for your practice. Note that "minimum criteria" do not necessarily have to translate into a dollar figure. It is good business practice to restrict your advice to those clients with whom you have an affinity and whose problems you're interested in solving. You shouldn't try to be all things to all people. At the very least, you should like the people you take on as clients. Diana Kahn, at The Financial Pharmacist in Miami, has the following minimum criteria for the clients with whom she will work. None of these criteria involves minimum investable assets:

- They want to do the planning themselves.
- They nevertheless recognize that they need help.
- They're willing to be guided and educated.

When planning the future of your practice, it is necessary to address the use of minimums. For example, you may wish to increase your practice by increasing the number of clients and would consequently set a low minimum portfolio size. We elected to expand our practice by attracting fewer, but higher-net-worth, clients. We set our first minimum at $100,000 investable assets, but we still took anyone who walked in the door or in any way expressed interest in becoming a client. A year later, I proposed we move the minimum to $300,000. Both of my partners choked. Yet each time we raised minimums, and actually stuck to them, more business came in the door. When we decided to join Schwab Institutional Advisor Network, they tried to discourage us from using a million-dollar minimum, but we did anyway. Schwab was sure that we'd get no referrals. On the contrary, we got quality referrals that we turned into great client relationships.

Last year at our annual retreat, our staff requested that our minimums be increased to $2 million. Let's think about this for a minute. This is not a leap of faith here. It just makes good sense. From whom do you get your referrals? Existing clients? Existing clients tend to refer friends who are in the same financial situation. It is rare that someone with a half million in investable assets will pal around with someone who has four times that much. Do you really think that the CEO of a major corporation will want to use the same financial planner that his secretary uses? The success of this philosophy has been proven to us time and again.

Two years ago a woman called us for an appointment. We agreed that she did not fit our client profile. It is our policy and commitment to prospects that we will help them find the appropriate planner, so we gave her the names of two advisers in our area. We think highly of them and they have lower minimums. The following year, the woman's father called us, at her suggestion, because he had substantial assets and was not happy with his adviser. Although the daughter was still working with her adviser, she did not recommend him because his client base consisted of people with fewer dollars and she did not think that he would be appropriate for someone with her dad's significant net worth.

Maybe They Know Someone Rich

The example above is a first cousin to what I call "opportunity" clients. You know, these are the people who are not particularly desirable clients but who may lead to an opportunity. I fell for that sacred cow and played that game for years. None of these people proved to be a great referral source for my target market. They required time and attention and often had different needs than my regular client base. Often I felt I was shortchanging my opportunity clients because they needed services that I didn't have or want to provide.

For example, for my target clients, planning their cash flow needs did not involve budgeting or entail preparing a cash flow statement to help them identify discretionary income to accomplish goals. It usually concerned planning techniques for retirement distributions, or for maximizing their estate transfer. It is far easier, and more profitable, to offer to find a new and appropriate planning relationship for opportunity clients than to attempt to do something that you are not really prepared to do.

If You Ask, I Will Stand on My Head

This is another compromise we make early on in our practices when we don't have many clients and customized, irregular services don't cost us much. If you're new to this business, don't start it. If you've got a seasoned practice and you are still doing it, cut it out.

Jack Firestone of Firestone Capital Management in Miami shared this story with me. He had been working with a particular client since 1991. Suddenly, during the great bull market beginning in 1996, this client asked him to change his reviews to the calendar quarter so that he could compare his returns to Standard & Poor's 500 Index. Jack explained that this was an inappropriate benchmark, since less than 20 percent of the client's assets were in large company stocks. The client insisted. After all, he said, "that's what's in the news every day."

Jack began to review his relationship with this client. Over the prior five years, the client spent more time on the phone with Jack looking for more reassurance than any other client he had. In 1994 when the market ended relatively flat for the year, the client was unhappy that he did not get a better return. When 1995 began an amazing run in the domestic large company market, his client was upset because he wasn't getting those returns in his portfolio.

Jack could do one of two things. He could do what the client requested, or he could do what he knew was right. I related my similar circumstance to Jack. I asked a client of mine, "Just what do you pay me for?" "I pay you for advice," he answered. "Then why don't you take it?" I responded. I explained that I did not feel it was in his best interest to compare his returns to the S&P 500. I then offered to recommend another adviser. The client asked to stay. He's still my client. Jack still has his, too.

Presumably clients come to you for your expertise and advice, not for the frequency of reporting, the format of the reports, or the additional material you have to include in each different report. If the suggestions you receive from clients are good and worth implementing, then offer them for everyone. If it's not appropriate, yet your client insists on extraordinary special requests, introduce your client to another planner. Life is too short. Furthermore, if you want a profitable, efficient, and marketable practice, you'll want to systemize as much as possible, without losing the uniqueness of your service relationship.

You Must Meet with Clients Quarterly

Roy Diliberto, of RTD Financial Advisors, maintains that it took him "only several years" to realize that quarterly meetings were not essential to client retention. When a client asks, "How often will we meet?" Roy asks, "How often do you want to meet?" Every year he completes a questionnaire with the client to note if anything substantive has changed. Some clients talk with him two or three times per week; others two or three times a year, their choice.

Paul Brady of Brady & Associates of Sydney, Australia, says he does not have regular quarterly appointments. He does have what he terms "cluster meetings" for his clients, however. At least once a year he invites a select group of clients and a top-notch speaker from the financial services field to a private room in a luxury hotel in downtown Sydney. Clients are encouraged to bring friends. This becomes not only a client information meeting, but also a good source for referrals.

I'll Be Right Over

My first clients were little old ladies in the Chicagoland area. I didn't have many clients, so we both had plenty of time. It seemed logical to go to their homes to discuss their financial plans over tea and cookies. After all, I was in the service business, wasn't I? They showed me pictures of their grandchildren and we planned their futures, too. Many of us in this industry started that way.

In the early days of planning, we were considered salespeople, not professionals. We traveled to make the sale. With my new partners, we agreed that we would not visit clients, except under extraordinary circumstances. Early on, this wasn't a hard-and-fast rule and many times we traveled, rationalizing that our high-net-worth clients wanted superior service, which included accommodating their schedules. Most of the time we found that the more accommodating we were, the more we were treated like salespeople, not professionals.

Today, it is very rare that someone will ask us to leave our offices for meetings. We generally refuse if they do. We consider ourselves professionals. Doctors and attorneys expect to conduct business in their offices. So do we. Clients come to see us from all over the country. (I'll admit that it doesn't hurt that we are in South Florida.) This is one choice that has never cost us a relationship. In fact, prospects and clients appreciate that we take the use of our time seriously.

If You Feed Them, They Will Come

In Miami you can hold a seminar every day in the high-rise condominiums on the beach. You can usually get about fifty to sixty people to attend depending upon the weather and what you serve. If it's a sunny day and you serve only orange juice and doughnuts, you'll get a handful of attendees. Rain and brunch yields tons of warm bodies; most of whom won't fit your client base or already have more financial advisory relationships than they can handle. Unfortunately, rain or shine, none of these people are particularly interested in what you have to say, but they are interested in what you have to serve. They're bored and you are the entertainment. Better yet, you're paying for lunch.

Small-scale, exclusive seminars have worked well for many advisers. When Robert Levitt, of Levitt Capital Management, wanted to generate new business in his firm's location of Boca Raton, Florida, he put an ad in the paper, advertising a seminar on selecting mutual funds. The ad specified that space was limited. When ten people signed up for the seminar, he told the rest of the callers that the seminar was filled, offering to sign them up for the following week. It worked. People liked the exclusivity and took the seminars seriously. He gave these seminars every week for a month.

This isn't really a book dedicated to marketing, so I won't go into detail about what will work and what won't work for you. Just remember, whatever you select as a marketing strategy, don't pander.

If I Don't Take Them, the Sharks Will Eat Them Alive

You can argue with me all you want, but it is my personal belief that most financial planners are closet social workers. We love getting into a case, coaching, counseling, and giving substantive advice that really affects lives. We go home each evening feeling renewed, energized, and full of self-worth.

Things go along pretty well, then one day a little old lady steps into our office, has limited investable assets, a ton of personal problems beginning with the facts that her husband has just died, her daughter is on drugs, and she knows absolutely nothing about finances. You know that if you don't take this one, she will get lousy advice from someone else, lose all the money her hardworking husband left her, and wind up living on the streets within five years. She doesn't fit your profile, probably can't even afford your fees but, if you help her, by the time you're finished, you could probably get her daughter into drug rehab and double her money, while improving her quality of life. It won't take much time, either. Get real!

Truthfully, I still do so much pro bono work in my professional career that I often think I work for a nonprofit organization. It is perfectly okay for you to get paid for the work that you do. But remember, it is perfectly okay for you to take clients that you want to take. Just be sure you know why you are taking them.

Dorothy Bossung, formerly of Ernst & Young, told me that she would suggest that all planners work for a big accounting firm, logging in hours and billing hourly for their time before they try to work on their own. "Billing for time really helps you put time management, and the selection of the clients you will work with, in perspective."

Performance Is Paramount

We always provided quarterly and year-to-date performance returns in our reviews. Everyone does. One day we asked ourselves what message we were sending our clients by listing short-term performance, when we are constantly preaching the need for a portfolio with a long-term time horizon. It really made no sense, but of course peer pressure is mighty. We argued over including the short-term performance numbers for months until we took Nike's advice to "Just Do It." We did. We waited for the barrage of calls, questioning us about the absence of short-term performance numbers. We received three calls, all of them just asking if we had forgotten a line in the review. When we explained why the line was missing, all agreed it wasn't necessary.

We took the same tack when we omitted the page of index returns in our quarterly reviews. One day we just agreed that comparing managers to their benchmarks was a function of our job, not the clients'. Although we were perfectly willing and prepared to discuss it with any clients who asked, no one called.

Clients Need a Full Understanding of Modern Portfolio Theory (MPT)

Roy Diliberto admits that at his firm RTD Financial Advisors used to beat clients over the head with education on MPT. They'd explain Sharpe ratios, alphas, betas. They would, in fact, have a lengthy discussion of whether beta was dead. Most people didn't know what beta was, let alone whether it was dead or not. Furthermore, they didn't care. "We finally shot this cow," said Roy. "Clients only want to know two things: (1) Are you competent? and (2) Do you put their interests first?"

She's Too Old to Surf the Net

My Aunt Ruth, who passed away last year at age ninety-five, sent me e-mails up until four months before she died. She told me she knew how to do only one thing on the Internet—send and receive mail. However, weekends her son was training her to "surf the Net." Monthly, Aunt Ruth sent me electronic, musical, animated Care Bears cards with cute, "Thinking of you," notes that she'd composed herself.

Last week my partner's eighty-three-year-old cousin e-mailed him to get his parents' (also in their eighties) e-mail address. They were developing an e-mail list of all their friends and family.

I assumed we could not communicate by e-mail to our over-seventy-five age group. We sent Flash Faxes and e-mail notes to many clients, but just assumed that at a certain age, technology would be beyond them. How wrong I was. Our over-age-seventy-five clients are the group that is the most active online with me. Go figure. They find something that piques their interest and write me to ask what I think about it. They suggest websites for me to visit; they download their positions into files they keep current themselves.

I Don't Have Any Sacred Cows

I was amazed at the number of planners I interviewed who emphatically stated that they did not have any sacred cows. I have been in business over twenty years and from my experience and perspective, these people are in denial. It is virtually impossible to resist complacency, especially when you are preoccupied with other issues like increasing your practice. Keep this in mind: just because something works, that doesn't mean it is working well.

I use the "T" account principle to locate hidden sacred cows and review any changes I may contemplate within the practice. To do this, draw a *T*. As you review your procedures, systems, and philosophies, put the positive attributes on the left, the negative ones on the right. This will allow you to visualize the impact these various decisions can have on your business. Consider:

- Why do we do it this way?
- If we change it, will it have a substantive effect (positive or negative) on our clients, our office, or our company?
- What could be the worst-case outcome?
- What could be the best-case outcome?

Although you may feel a sense of accomplishment and security in getting your business organized and humming, challenging your current practices periodically and exploring new solutions and systems will make your business dynamic, successful, and profitable.

Finally, One Sacred Cow to Keep . . .

Remember your roots. Just what brought you to this business, anyway? For most of the advisers I know, it was not the money. I'm not downplaying the money, but I think we all appreciate that we have a unique opportunity to affect lives. I like Charlie Haines's mission statement at Charles D. Haines, LLC, ". . . to improve the quality of our client's lives." Notice he doesn't say, "improve the quality of their *financial* lives." If you think you've moved away from managing the client to managing the portfolio, I suggest a return to your roots.

The best argument is that which seems merely an explanation.
—Dale Carnegie, author of *How to Win Friends and Influence People*

I used to work for a realty group that syndicated commercial residential properties in the Chicago area. We also managed the properties after they were syndicated. Each quarter, we provided reviews on the properties' performance to our investors. Along with our review letter, we included a partnership income check. Nothing much changed from quarter to quarter, so it was difficult to find new information to impart each time. My boss was fairly creative, but after some time even he got stymied. We finally bet each other that if we sent the same letter again and again, nobody would even notice. After four quarters, there were no comments from our investors. In the fifth quarter, we had to change the letter because we were also sending a K-1 along with it. Still no comments. Finally, we withheld a check because we were having some problems with our new computer system. We still sent the letter. Boy, did we get calls. The moral of the story? If you're sending money, nobody cares what you have to say.

Let's talk about communication. In my opinion, our relationships with clients are *all* about communication. From the first moment we sit down with them, we interview, talk, cajole, frame, empathize, badger, provoke, and even entertain them. I think it's important to know the various types of communication and why and how we can use them to our best advantage.

Our communication efforts begin with our prospects, long before they step foot in our office. In fact, I like employing pre–client loyalty techniques during the prospect courtship phase.

I was speaking with a planner friend the other day. He told me that at the end of each meeting with a happy client, he always says, "And do you know any other good people who would benefit from my helping them?" The problem is, with the market so volatile and consumer confidence so low, he hasn't felt that he has had a truly happy person in his office for months, maybe years. Obviously, getting client referrals is an important aspect of anyone's practice. Done appropriately, the prospect is presold because he has a friend who recommends you highly. But just asking for a referral doesn't mean you will get who you want, when you want.

One of the basic tenets of target marketing is to constantly be in a situation where your target market can talk about you. It can be a business situation, like belonging to the Chamber of Commerce or Rotary Club, or perhaps in a social setting, like a membership in the local golf club. Either way, prospects get to know you and get to know what you do. Unfortunately, every marketer knows this route, and often the time to acquire a new client through this route can equal the gestation period of an elephant.

The key to good referrals is going beyond conventional marketing techniques and creating preloyalty. Let's take a look at how that works. The lease on my husband's BMW Z3 was expiring. He hadn't found a new car that excited him, so he went back to the BMW dealership one afternoon, fully intending to lease a new one, same type, same color. The parking lot was full, so, eyeing a lot across the street, he pulled in there. While walking to the office, he passed a row of the oddest-looking cars he'd ever seen—small, rounded, retro looking—the new Mini Cooper. He fell in love, but unlike with the other auto experiences he'd had, this car needed to be ordered. Still, it was such a neat looking car, he decided to wait the eight to ten weeks and ordered one on the spot.

After he'd signed the paperwork, the saleswoman handed him a website address and a unique number to use. "This is the number of your car," she said. "Just type it in on the site, and it will allow you to follow the progress of your new little Mini." Of course, he went right home, got onto the site, but nothing was listed. He looked down at the paper—"please wait forty-eight hours." Two days later and perhaps to the minute he'd purchased the car, he was on the site, plugging in the number. Sure enough, his car was listed with a note beside the entry, "I am at the factory in England now, just being built to your specifications. This will take a while, but you can check up on my progress at any time."

Halfway through the waiting process, Mini Cooper sent my husband a travel mug with a funky looking bottom that will only fit in a Mini Cooper cup holder. This heightened the experience as he walked around his office day after day, carrying his cup and dreaming of the day he could use it.

The ten weeks flew by as my husband visited the site, nearly every week, to see the progress. One day the note informed him, "I'm on the ship now, heading to the U.S. so that I can be there on time for you." He was so excited, I swear, you'd think he was giving birth. When the car arrived at the dealership, my husband knew and called the saleswoman to see when he could pick up the little guy. He was already attached to the car, because he already "knew" it from birth.

Mini Cooper is creating customer loyalty *before* the car even reaches the owner's hands. And this little routine makes the waiting go much faster. For planners, client loyalty, which translates into client retention, has to be built over time. Or does it?

Let's examine this Mini Cooper experience and apply it to your advisory practice. First, BMW has a product that is unique and different. None of their other cars resemble this one. They keep some of them in the same lot as the others so that you simply can't miss them. They are eye-catching.

Now, look at your current offerings to clients. Are you providing the same products as everyone else? If so, how can you position them with other products and services so that your offering is unique? What do you do that would make someone choose you and your services above all others?

Second, the BMW people do not make the Mini Cooper available immediately. You have to order one. But, because you order one, you can choose the colors, trendy racing stripes, and other appealing additions in just the way you want them. As an adviser, you can mass-customize the choices your client can make about the kind of reports he wants from you, how those reports are presented, or perhaps how he receives his information from you—snail mail, e-mail, or faxing.

Third, because BMW makes you wait eight to ten weeks for your car, you get the idea that it is an exclusive car. You won't see them all over town because they are, in fact, making them to order. As an adviser, you can make it clear that you can't or won't work with everyone—that only people who meet your criteria can really benefit from working with you. And, you have a waiting list. You will need to set up an appointment weeks in advance. (Keep reading, and don't hold your breath. This *does* work.) The selection of the appointment time is important for two reasons: One, you want them to know that you are in demand, and two, you want to have time to "presell" them.

You should be prescreening your prospects so that you know whom you are targeting and whether they are a good fit for your practice. You can devise a prequalification form that asks a few pointed questions to determine if your prospects are viable prospects. For those who aren't appropriate, be sure to have names of other advisers you can refer them to. If you are getting referrals from current clients, be certain that they understand how you work and what the costs are, so that they are not referring inappropriate prospects. About once a year, we send our current clients a letter, telling them that we are well poised for growth, and stating how we currently work with clients and how we charge.

Notice, when BMW is making you wait the ten weeks for your car, they are continually giving you updates and giving you opportunities to get more information if you want it. You have your own unique number to get onto the Internet to see where your car is now. As an adviser, this is how you can make the most of your website, by having sections with information that is only available for clients. You can give your prospect a password to the exclusive part of the site, which will give him useful information and material available only to those who are exclusive to your practice.

Next, once a quarter, sponsor a lunch or dinner for some of your best clients, inviting a few prospects as well. You may even ask your clients to bring a few friends to these social occasions. Yes, I said "social occasions." You will make no presentations, just have a nice meal and give your best clients the opportunity to talk about you with some of their friends and your newfound prospects. You'd be surprised how many people will want to know how they can become part of this elite club.

Finally, look at the actual delivery of the Mini Cooper. You know, because of the information on the Internet, when your car will be at the dealer's. Your anticipation is high, because you have waited all these weeks to get it—and BMW has continually prepared you for this important event. You have been told just what will happen when you go to get the car. You go, and everything they said would happen does.

Mini is creating your expectations, meeting them, and managing them. Similarly, your prospects should know what happens at the first meeting, the second meeting, and subsequent meetings. Prior to their first meeting with us, we send a letter telling clients what to bring with them for the meeting. In fact, we usually have them fill out a short-form questionnaire so that we can be better prepared for the first meeting. At the first meeting, we give them a list of what happens at each subsequent meeting and what issues will be addressed. We have a flow chart that we provide, showing what generally happens in each meeting. Naturally, things change as we begin the engagement with the clients, but at least they have an inkling of what to expect as the relationship progresses.

Then Qualify 'Em and Interview 'Em

There's an old story about a man who picks up the phone at work one day.

"Son," says the voice on the other end, "I haven't been feeling too well."

"I'm sorry to hear that, Mom," he says. "What's the matter?"

"Well," she begins, "my leg hurts when I walk. The doctor says it's arthritis, and I'm just going to be in pain all the time."

"I'm sorry to hear that, Mom," says the man again.

"When are you coming to see me?" she asks.

"Gee, Mom," he replies, "I am awful busy with work. I've got some new contracts, and they really need some attention."

"But, son," she says, "you haven't been here in so long, and I really would like to see you."

"I know, Mom," he says, "But the kids play soccer on the weekends, and then there are the dance lessons, the skating lessons, the music lessons—you know."

"I understand," she says, "But I really miss you. And when you visit you really brighten my otherwise lonely day."

"Okay, Mom," he acquiesces, "I'll be there Saturday. I'll bring those cinnamon rolls you always love, and Jill will bake a chicken for you."

"Jill? Who's Jill?" asks the old woman.

"Why, Jill is my wife, Mom, you know that," says the man.

"No, your wife is Carole Sue," counters the old lady. "Isn't this Buddy?"

"Buddy?" says the man. "No, this is David. David Rhinehart." There is absolute stillness at the other end of the line.

"Oh," exclaims the old lady, "I must have the wrong number."

"That's okay," assures the man, preparing to hang up.

"But," she continues, "does this mean you aren't coming Saturday?"

We try to screen our prospects as much as possible before they waltz in the door. We have used a qualification questionnaire for years, one that we fondly call "the pink sheet" because it is printed on pink paper (see **Figure 12.1**). Pink was chosen in deference to my partner, Harold, because it's easily identifiable on a messy desk.

The form is two-sided. One side is used to record the identity of the caller and to record the disposition of the call. We use this side as an input form for our client relationship management (CRM) database. Here we note whether we will be sending a "puff package" and a preliminary data guide (**Figure 12.2**—see p. vi). We can also customize this data guide if we don't want to include all the pages. The pink sheet also documents whether we will be putting the prospect's name on our newsletter mailing list or referring him or her to someone else. If we make an appointment, we note with whom, the date, and the time. That information is then entered into our corporate calendar and the calendar of each responsible party. The flip side of this form gives us plenty of room to record details about our conversation with the prospect.

For me, there are a few essential questions to ask a prospect:

- How did you hear about us? This is obviously an important question if you're to track the success of your marketing efforts. If you have no marketing plan, you'd better get one (see Chapter 3). Our days of getting clients for free are about over. If you have a marketing plan and aren't tracking it, start now.

FIGURE 12.1 Evensky & Katz Prospect Form (The Pink Sheet)

EVENSKY & KATZ PROSPECT FORM

Person taking call:	Date:
Partner assigned:	Adviser assigned:
Name of caller:	

Address:	Telephone home:
	Telephone work:
	Fax #:
	E-mail address:

Communication preference: ___ regular mail ___ telephone ___ e-mail ___ fax

Result of First Communication:

a. Send puff package and data-gathering guide—CIRCLE PAGES TO INCLUDE

    #1. Client Info Sheet

    #2. Qualitative Survey

    #3. Assets

    #4. Cash Flow

    #5. Professional Advisers

    #6. Client Documents

b. Who are we referring* this prospect to: _____

c. Follow-up phone call. When:_____ Who: _____

d. Not compatible/do not need to send information.

Receipt of Data-Gathering Questionnaire

Date received in office: _____

Does it meet our requirements: Yes _____ No _____

Date prospect called: _____ By Whom: _____

    a. Set an appt. with:___ HRE ___ DBK ___ LJ Time: _____ Date: _____

    b. Other: _____

_____

Action:	Initials and date of person taking action:	
a. Puff sent (including data-gathering guide and return envelope)	_____	_____
b. Added to BAM (including DGQ reference in notes section)	_____	_____
c. Marked as prospect and In$ites	_____	_____
d. Thank-you card sent to referral for sending prospect	_____	_____
e. Letter/e-mail sent to referral informing them of our referring a prospect	_____	_____
f. Take off of prospect and/or In$ites list	_____	_____
g. Is any pertinent prospect information in the notes section of BAM?	_____	_____

ARE ALL THE BASES COVERED?

(continued)

■ | **FIGURE 12.1** Evensky & Katz Prospect Form (The Pink Sheet) (*Continued*)

How did you hear about us?

What kind of issues made you call us?

What prompted you to make this call?

What kinds of issues do you have?

Are you managing your own portfolio or is someone assisting you?

What are you hoping we can do for you?

- What prompted you to make this call? It's important to identify the caller's professed as well as hidden agendas. One day I got a call from a doctor who wanted an appointment with me. When I asked this question, he said, "My wife keeps hounding me to have a professional look at our portfolio." "How do you think you are doing?" I asked. "I think we're fine, but my wife is unhappy," he replied. "Do you think sitting down with a professional will make her more comfortable?" I asked. "I have no idea, but I'm sure my life will be more comfortable. She'll stop hounding me to see a professional," he said.

- Have you worked with a professional financial adviser before or are you now working with one? The last thing I want is someone else's problem. Originally, we did not ask this question. Then, one day we took on a new client. He seemed pleasant, and our first meeting was a pleasure. Early in the second meeting he asked me to recommend a securities attorney because he was planning to sue his last financial planner. I asked about the problem. He told me that the planner put him into some bad investments, and he wanted to be made whole. I asked how much he'd lost, and he said, nothing. His complaint was that the investments recommended by the adviser were too conservative and he didn't make the money that he thought he was going to make. The investments? A 50 percent allocation to large-cap core, 25 percent to small-cap core, and 25 percent to core international. "Everybody else is making a fortune, and my portfolio just sat there." This was during 1998 when Nasdaq left everything sitting in the dust. I decided that we didn't need a client with this kind of twenty-twenty hindsight. Another warning: Be sure you know your own motivation for selecting a client, and don't delude yourself. I once took a client from one of the big, high-profile brokers in town, simply because the client said he was unhappy, and I thought that I could do a better job than the broker. Okay, it was an ego thing. Well, that client turned out to be a big pain. Six months into the relationship he was complaining and fussing, saying all the things to me that he had said about the broker.

- If you are no longer working with a professional, what led to the change? Often people who have worked with an adviser before have a much better idea of how the engagement will go and what they can expect from it. Some of my best clients are physicians who have had poor experiences with a "hot shot" who pandered to their ego, not their long-term financial well-being.

- What do you think we can do for you? Better to know in advance if the client expects a 35 percent return and wants you to walk his dog, too.

Pre-Data Gathering

There are a few clever "pre-data-gathering" ideas that I thought I'd introduce here. Lou Stanasolovich of Legend Financial Advisors in Pittsburgh, Pennsylvania, tells me that he uses a rather detailed data-gathering form on the phone with prospects before he schedules the first meeting. He wants to sit in front of only serious prospects. Their willingness to complete the form before they have their first meeting demonstrates their intentions to follow through. David Bugen of RegentAtlantic Capital agrees. "It's like visiting a new physician," he maintains. "We want to make the best use of our time together, and we can only do that by having some advance information." David's firm uses a short data guide that they send out with the puff package.

On the other hand, I have a close personal friend who believes that a prospect's phone call should be rewarded with an appointment. She firmly believes that asking too many questions in advance of a first meeting discourages people who need help but who are uncomfortable with the process. She charges a nominal fee for the first visit, and if she's not going to work with prospects, she gives them a personal referral to a planner who can meet their needs. She also maintains that neither she nor the prospects think they are wasting their time if they are not a good fit.

Still, most advisers agree that the more you prescreen, the better the first appointment goes. It's much easier to help the client zero in on his issues once you have some background.

 ## The Client Fit Ratio System

Chris Dardaman of Brightworth Private Wealth Counsel (formerly Polstra & Dardaman) has devised a Client Fit Ratio[1] system to help the firm qualify clients (see **Figure 12.3**). You might consider using their process to develop your own client fitness test.

Chris has defined what he believes to be the attributes of his ideal client. He expresses these attributes in terms of four criteria:

- Available investment resources
- Desire and ability to delegate
- Reasonable expectations
- Personality/chemistry

Chris explains the genesis of his company's system: "Last year, a large Atlanta-based corporation we have worked with for ten years offered an early retirement package to hundreds of people. We knew it would be impossible for us to take all of the people who might call and were forced to be extremely focused as to whom we could accept as new clients. Even after referring out over 50 percent of the inquiries, we still ended up with a six-month waiting list to complete financial plans for new clients. The Client Fit Ratio system is a simple tool, designed to focus on what makes a good client-adviser relationship. Our firm has three partners. Having determined that each partner only wants to have about fifty to sixty clients, the Client Fit Ratio system forces us to look at each new prospect more closely."

Chris asserts that the "expectation gap," that is, the difference between what the client expects and what you provide, is narrowed considerably using this method. "The wider the gap, the more tension and friction in a relationship." Not only is everyone happier working with clients they like, but the company is more profitable because the principals are not spending valuable time with troublesome people.

Chris maintains that following this process is really the key to better client relationships, as you are consciously evaluating prospects and making concrete decisions about the fit. I have included a couple of Chris's examples so you can get an idea of how this process works.

In the following example, Chris determines that these potential clients will have investable assets available within a short period of time, do not have a strong relationship with anyone else, and have reasonable expectations of Chris and his

FIGURE 12.3 Client Fit Ratio

POLSTRA & DARDAMAN, LLC
Client Fit Ratio℠ **for** _____
As of _____

	Potential Score	Total Score
1. Available Investment Resources > $2 million	20	_____
Within 6 months 20		
Within 6–12 months 12		
Over 12 months 8		
2. Desire and Ability to Delegate		
Do they desire to outsource their personal finances?	10	_____
Are they busy with other things?	10	_____
Are we the sole trusted adviser?	10	_____
Are they comfortable paying for advice?	10	_____
3. Reasonable Expectations		
Of us and our services	10	_____
Of investment markets' ability to meet their cash		
flow needs	10	_____
4. Personality/Chemistry		
At peace with themselves and their life?	10	_____
Responsible and responsive to us?	10	_____
TOTAL SCORE	100	_____

Total Score	Client Fit
93–100	Excellent
85–92	Good
77–84	Average
70–77	Below Average
Below 70	Unacceptable

PDLLC Partner_____

_____ Accept

_____ Reject

_____ Refer to_____

Client Fit Ratio™ is a Trademark of Polstra & Dardaman, LLC

Source: Brightworth Private Wealth Counsel

firm. Additionally, other clients know these prospects, giving Chris a stronger reason to accept them as clients. They are accepted.

Client Fit Ratio: Accept	Potential Score	Total Score
1. Available Investment Resources > $2 million	20	20
Within 6 months	20	
Within 6–12 months	12	
Over 12 months	8	

He is retiring in 3 months and will have $3 million to roll over.

2. Desire and Ability to Delegate		
Do they desire to outsource their personal finances?	10	10
Are they busy with other things?	10	9
Are we the sole trusted adviser?	10	7
Are they comfortable paying for advice?	10	8

He does not want to spend time on finances in retirement. He has a stockbroker but not a strong relationship.

3. Reasonable Expectations		
Of us and our services	10	9
Of investment markets' ability to meet their cash flow needs	10	10

He is an experienced investor and has plenty of cash flow.

4. Personality/Chemistry		
At peace with themselves and their life?	10	10
Responsible and responsive to us?	10	9

The prospect and his wife seem happy, organized, etc., and have close family ties with children. They are longtime friend of our good clients, Sally and John Smith, who think they will be easy to work with.

TOTAL SCORE	100	92

Total Score	Client Fit
93–100	Excellent
85–92	Good
77–84	Average
70–77	Below Average
Below 70	Unacceptable

In this next example, Chris decides he has a closet "do-it-yourselfer" who does not have a good relationship with his spouse. In fact, they are talking of divorce, and she explains he abuses drugs. The husband has unrealistic expectations about returns, and Chris feels uncomfortable with them. They are rejected.

From our experience, if you do not have a formal way to evaluate prospects, you will inevitably wind up with some clients who are inappropriate. This is not profitable, but more important, not fun.

Client Fit Ratio: Reject	Potential Score	Total Score
1. Available Investment Resources > $2 million	20	5
Within 6 months	20	
Within 6–12 months	12	
Over 12 months	8	

They will have $900,000 in the next 12–24 months if he retires then.

2. Desire and Ability to Delegate		
Do they desire to outsource their personal finances?	10	2
Are they busy with other things?	10	3
Are we the sole trusted adviser?	10	1
Are they comfortable paying for advice?	10	4

He is an engineer, changes his own oil, and does his own tax return. He did their will from a $25 software package. His favorite show is CNBC *Squawk Box*. He reads numerous financial magazines and has accounts at five brokerage firms and eight different mutual fund families.

3. Reasonable Expectations		
Of us and our services	10	1
Of investment markets ability to meet their cash flow needs	10	3

He is looking for a one-time analysis of his stock options, etc., not an ongoing relationship. He said he expects a 20 percent return with little downside risk, and wants to take 10 percent withdrawals from his account each year.

4. Personality/Chemistry		
At peace with themselves and their life?	10	1
Responsible and responsive to us?	10	2

They yelled at each other in our meeting and are planning to get divorced. He complained about every other adviser they have ever had, and sued them for negligence. She said he has a problem with drugs.

TOTAL SCORE		100	22
Total Score	Client Fit		
93–100	Excellent		
85–92	Good		
77–84	Average		
70–77	Below Average		
Below 70	Unacceptable		

 ## The First Interview

In the early days of our profession, the first appointment was sales oriented. We would ask about their financial needs then tell the clients what we could do for them. Today, advisers have a more professional approach. The first meeting is now generally what I call the "tape recording session": You ask about them, and they ask about you, all for playback later. I spend more time listening to what the prospect says (or sometimes doesn't say) than anything else.

Preparation

As I noted earlier, David Bugen sent out a preliminary data questionnaire, requesting the client bring it with her or mail it in advance of the first appointment. Many advisers have found this to be a good way to avoid "tire kickers."

Lou Stanasolovich has a very good confirmation letter that is sent to prospects after the first appointment is scheduled. Lou also uses this opportunity to ask for documents for the first meeting by including a page with a financial document list. This lets the prospect know that this meeting is more than a "getting to know you" session. The following are the confirmation letter and the financial document list:

Cover Letter

Dear PROSPECT:

Thank you for inquiring about our services. As you requested, I am enclosing some background information on myself and my firm.

You may find of interest the enclosed article reprinted from *Barron's* entitled "Planning Your Financial Future: Meet The Alpha Group, The Nation's Most Powerful Financial Planners." As you will read in the article, I am one of the founding members of the Alpha Group. I have also enclosed my personal biography. You might also wish to know that I was selected by *Worth* magazine as one of the "Best Financial Advisers in America" in their October 1996, October 1997, September 1998, and September 1999 issues. I have also been chosen by *Medical Economics* magazine as one of "The Best Financial Advisers for Doctors in America" in their July 27, 1998, and November 8, 1999, issues. Furthermore, our investment process has been profiled in *Business Week, Morningstar Investor, USA Today,* and on the Internet on TheStreet.com.

It should be noted that Legend Financial Advisors is a fee-only, Securities and Exchange Commission–registered investment advisory firm. We provide two primary services:

1. Asset management services by which we assist you in creating an investment portfolio designed to help you achieve your financial goals. We then manage your investable monies on an ongoing basis and provide regular periodic performance reporting on the portfolio's performance, and

2. Development of a customized financial plan that will address all major areas of your finances.

We charge fees for both services so that we will provide you with unbiased advice.

As we discussed, I am enclosing directions to our offices as well as a list of documents for you to bring to our first meeting on _____ at a.m./p.m.

Please call me if you have any questions. I look forward to meeting you.

Cordially,

Financial Planner

Financial Document List

—Your most recent income tax return

—One month's worth of pay stubs

—A listing of all assets and liabilities

—The amount of money you will save and invest within retirement plans this year

—The amount of money you will save and invest outside of retirement plans this year

—Copies of the latest confirmation and/or monthly statements of any investments you own

—Insurance policies: life, disability, medical, long-term care, homeowners, auto, umbrella liability

—Wills, trusts, Powers of Attorney, if any

—Employee benefits information

—Your latest retirement plan statements, if applicable

—A listing of all family members, ages, official names, nicknames, grade in school, and health problems, if any

—Be prepared to talk about any obligations you might have with regard to other family members, such as parents or grandparents, now and in the future.

—Include a list of any expected cash windfalls such as inheritances, gifts, business successes, and invention or publishing royalties, etc., if any.

—A prioritized list of all financial goals: short-term (next twelve months), intermediate (twelve months to five years), and long-term (example: retirement, college funding, debt reduction, new home or second home purchase, etc.)

Many advisers I know confirm the first appointment via telephone a day or two before the meeting. This personal contact lets the prospect know that you expect him, respect his time, and respect your time, too. Some contact manager software such as ACT! or Outlook will allow you to e-mail your clients reminders of upcoming meetings and appointments.

What Brings You Here?

My partner Harold has a very sophisticated opening: "What brings you here?" This open-ended question is great for getting dialogue going. Ron Tamayo says of their first meetings, "We strongly encourage both spouses to attend. At the beginning of the meeting, we ask them if they have any specific questions they would like to ask us right away. We listen a lot and try to find out what their goals are or what motivated them to come see us. We also show them a sample client binder that contains a financial plan, investment policy statement, newsletter, and quarterly report."

Many advisers I know have a sample binder to show the prospects. It gives people a sense of what's to come. In our office we have a selection of various types of reports in the binder so that when the prospect becomes a client, he can select from among the various formats to customize his own reviews.

Data Gathering

Data gathering is one of the more critical aspects of planning. You get it wrong and all your work from then on is worthless. I'm beginning to see a resurgence of comprehensive planning software use among senior planners. I think this is because many planners, looking to add value in their relationship with their clients, feel a more formalized approach will enhance the experience. Second, and perhaps more important, there's much better stuff out there than there used to be. Consider NaviPlan, www.naviplan.com, developed by Emerging Information Systems Inc. (EISI), a Canadian company that has built a comprehensive, cash flow–based program that has attractive reports and good analytics. A fringe benefit of good software is that it provides a printable, comprehensive data-gathering guide that reduces the chance of missing important information.

More and more companies are producing Web-based comprehensive planning software. PIE Technologies (www.pietech.com), for example, has built a completely interactive planning system that allows you and your client to view the plan simultaneously over the Internet. It also allows the client to create and change scenarios on his own, so that he can discuss them with you later. Earlier I spoke about our client's need to have some control over his financial life—the CEO model, if you will. Some people will turn to planners to create the plan, but they'd like to have the control of creating and tweaking their own scenarios. An interactive system fits this need.

Getting the Data

How you collect your data is a question of style. Do you sit down with the clients and gather the data, or do you give the form to them to complete and bring in to you? When I started out in practice, particularly since I was working with little old ladies, I went to their homes, fished around in their cabinets and drawers to find source material, and completed the data gathering on my own. These days, I have neither the time nor the inclination to help clients sort through shoeboxes of statements and receipts. I'm now a firm believer in sweat equity. I mentioned earlier that we send an abbreviated data guide (Figure 12.2) at the initial contact. When the client sets the appointment, we ensure that we have the completed data form at least one week before the meeting. At our first "in person" meeting, we fill in the blanks, double-check the data, and determine what additional information we may need. As I've said, Lou Stanasolovich often sends his full-length questionnaire, along with a list of documents for the clients to bring to the meeting. Lou's cover letter lets them know exactly what will be happening at the meeting and manages their expectations:

> Dear CLIENT:
>
> We are looking forward to seeing you on _____ at ___:___ a.m./p.m. in our office to start the information-gathering process. To obtain a complete financial picture, we will ask many questions which may seem inappropriate at first. The purpose is to ascertain whether each type of asset or liability does or does not exist. Many questions seek a response regarding your goals and your attitudes toward various aspects of personal finance:
>
> - Savings philosophy and investment risk tolerances
> - Career, lifestyle, hobby, and retirement goals
>
> No one has all this information readily at hand, nor has everyone even considered many of the factors. Please do the best you can with the information form and the gathering of the appropriate documents. Do not worry about any omissions.
> Whenever you are not certain an item applies to you, simply place a large question mark in the margin. It will be covered in the meeting. Items which we discuss will all be covered in the written interview notes which you will receive subsequently.
> Cordially,
>
> Financial Planner

Data-Gathering Guides and Worksheets

- **Plain-vanilla data guide.** Moisand Fitzgerald Tamayo has a comprehensive data guide that I like because it is so complete (**Figure 12.4**—see p. vi). For example, it asks for information regarding insurance for long-term care, major medical expenses, and property-casualty, as well as asking for all the usual information about assets and income. A unique and particularly useful part is the "Planner Use Only." This four-page section of the worksheet allows the planner to make notes about specific tax treatments, such as holding periods for capital gains and marginal tax rates. I like the idea of a guide that clients complete with an additional section for the planner to make notes and observations, including unique assumptions such as returns or inflation factors.

- **Data gathering using a tax return.** My friend, Ben Tobias of Tobias Financial Advisors in Plantation, Florida, feels that he can accomplish all the data gathering he needs simply by analyzing the client's individual tax return. He believes that this is an excellent way to gather additional information or just to recheck the data the client provided in other forms. He also reports that he frequently finds errors in the returns that can benefit the client. Here's Ben's description of how it works:

I find that the 1040 form is a very useful tool for not only uncovering clients' assets and income sources, but also to use as a checklist to determine clients' risk-tolerance levels as well as attitudes toward investing.

The 1040 is used in my office as the primary data-gathering document, especially during a prospect meeting. It, of course, is supplemented with a checklist and various other forms, especially the ever-versatile lined yellow pad, but the individual income tax return becomes the focus of the data-gathering component of the financial planning process. It is virtually useless without the taxpayer present. More questions arise when reviewing a return than can be answered by the return itself.

The form. Starting off with prospects or clients, you're given the name, address, and Social Security number of the taxpayers. I will add, next to the Social Security numbers, the birth dates.

Filing status and exemptions. This area lets us know the family unit, whether or not there are minor children. If there are children, we ask their birth dates, where they are in school, what plans they have for college, public or private, etc. It is important at this point to ask whether there are any other dependents that are not indicated on the return. This may be an elderly parent or a sibling whose situation requires financial outlays.

Depending on the age of the client, we'll ask if there is a chance of increasing family size. We will also ask if there are any children from other marriages. This accomplishes two things. One, we immediately find out if there have been other marriages, which will start a whole new slew of questions, and two, we will be able to determine a client's attitude towards extended family members and his or her feelings of responsibility.

Line 7: wages. This tells us how much taxable income someone earns from a job. However, that's all it tells us. We would ask for a W-2 form to find out if there are tax-deferred plans, such as 401(k)s, reducing the income. I also use this time as an opportunity to discuss a person's job. This may also be done while going over a Schedule C.

It is important to note that the order of questions will vary from interview to interview. A lot of what we do here is intentionally redundant, and questions are asked in numerous ways at different times of the process. I warn clients to expect redundant questions. Frequently we find that a client remembers additional information as we are going along.

We try to find out about a person's occupation at this point—whether or not it looks as if the person will be staying in his position, whether he will be retiring soon, what his goals or desires are along those lines.

Line 8: interest. This tells us if a client has taxable interest. We then are able to estimate the size of a bank or bond portfolio and confirm those estimations right there and then with the client. Also, with a quick glance at Schedule B, we are able to see where the client invests, in what companies the client invests, or which brokerage firm the client uses.

Line 9: dividends. This tells us essentially the same as the interest number, but it brings up clients' attitudes. We have the opportunity to discuss the difference between stock and bonds, and guaranteed investments versus variable investments. Discussion at this time goes a long way to determine a client's risk tolerance. When we look at Schedule B and we see, for example, a line item that may say the name of a brokerage firm, I will ask for a copy of the client's brokerage statement to see the individual types of securities that are contained therein.

Line 11: alimony received. If we have not discussed previous marriages, at this point, we do.

Line 12: business income. Here we again discuss a person's work. At this point, seeing whether income is shown on a Schedule C or on a W-2 is not the real interest of the financial planners. We are simply gathering data to find out income sources as well as the individual's thoughts about his or her current position.

Line 13: capital gains. Here we will take a look at Schedule D. If there is a lot of trading on Schedule D, we will ask questions and try to tie that in with information we already found out about the client's portfolio and its size. If we see pages and pages of transactions from E*Trade Financial or something along those lines and we're dealing with a day trader, we know it's best to walk away very politely from the engagement. Also, for future tax planning purposes it is very important to peruse Schedule D to determine if there are any short-term or long-term capital loss carry-overs.

Lines 15 and 16: IRA, pension, and annuities. As we know, much of many individuals' worth is not reflected in a current income tax return. Amounts of IRAs, annuities, or pensions that they may be receiving at some time in the future do not appear anywhere on the original tax return. It is very important to remember this, and at this point, as well as at other points during the process, it is a good idea to ask these questions: Do you have an IRA? If so, where is it and what is its value? Do you have annuities? Do you have any type of pension at your place of employment or previous places of employment that may be coming to you?

Line 17: Schedule E. If anything was written in on line 17 relating to gains or losses, we immediately must go to Schedule E to see the origination. At this point, we ask the clients what types of other investments they may have made over the years or trusts that they are a part of. It is important to know which type of trust they are a part of, for example, and whether or not they are the beneficiary on an estate that has yet to distribute dollar one.

Line 18: farm income. I use this as another opportunity to talk about real estate in addition to primary residence. I bring up the question of vacant land and what its current value is.

Line 20: Social Security benefits. I try to get an idea of what the benefits will be if they have not yet been paid out, but I also will ask about, more important than the Social Security benefits, disability and income protection for those clients who are still working.

Lines 23–31: adjustments for adjusted gross income. I see what a person's IRA situation is. Again, this is redundant in terms of earlier questions, but it is surprising how many times new IRAs will pop up. I also will ask if they've ever paid penalties on early withdrawals of CDs. Almost everybody has, but they seem to forget about it. I think this is a good way to point out that CDs should not be considered liquid investments.

Page 2 of the tax return serves as a review, as a checklist for other items, and as confirmation of what we have already learned.

I will go over Schedule A in detail and ask questions. For example, in looking at the mortgage interest question, I will ask at that point about homeowner's and automobile and personal liability insurance. I will ask if there are other debts that are not recorded. For example, credit cards debts are not recorded on a Schedule A.

We will review the tax preparation fees and see if the clients feel that they are getting their money's worth. When I reviewed Al Gore's return, I found that he was paying $4,400 for a return that probably was worth $700 to $900. Pointing out these inflated fees is becoming more important since CPAs are no longer just a referral source but now represent competition. We will also find out about a client's charitable intent, whether through the use of cash, securities, or donated property. I will always have a discussion at this time about charities, to find out if it would be pertinent to bring up philanthropy conversations later concerning estate planning.

I find that about 20 percent of the returns contain errors in presentation or treatment. About half of these errors benefit the client.

We have been using Ben's method in our office to double-check against our own gathered data. It has been a great supplement to the data-gathering process.

Data Guide for Business Owners

Lou Stanasolovich told me that he hasn't found any planning software that effectively handles closely held small-business data. That's why he created his own small-business-data guide. I like it because it asks questions that often take us many months of dialogue just to get to (**Figure 12.5**—see p. vi).

Cash Flow Worksheet

Often clients have no idea of their own spending habits. Many advisers I know provide their clients with Quicken or Microsoft Money. We have also. But, for those clients who are unwilling to do the in-depth preparation, we devised a one-page worksheet to help them determine their cash flow needs and to remind them of where they are spending their money (see **Figure 12.6**).

Life Insurance Design Questionnaire

Larry Rybka of ValMark Securities has a nifty questionnaire for walking your clients through a life insurance analysis and matching them with a generic insurance solution (**Figure 12.7**—see p. vi). This isn't a capital needs analysis; it's a tool to assist your having meaningful discussions with your client about his insurance requirements. It also helps facilitate discussions about the types of insurance available that fit his needs. Larry provides this assessment tool to all his firm's representatives, but he has graciously agreed to let me include it in this book. Here's how it works.

The first page is an easy-to-understand chart, describing the various types of life insurance products. This helps you acquaint the client with the different products available; included is a table that compares the price of products based on age.

The twelve questions presented on pages 2 through 4 are designed to help you get a clear picture of the client's needs and preferences. For example, on page 2 you ask the client how long he wishes to pay premiums and what type of rating he would like the insurance company to have. Page 4 is focused on asset allocation, inflation, and cash value issues. Question 12 on page 4 helps the client prioritize and rank those issues that are most important to him when selecting insurance.

When you total the score for all your client's responses, the questionnaire helps you determine what types of insurance would be most appropriate to use. The questionnaire also provides a ranking for the client's answers to determine whether a variable life product is appropriate. If a variable product is used, the information helps determine what asset allocation within the product is most suitable.

As I noted earlier, the best aspect of this questionnaire is that it provides a good framework for having insurance discussions with your client. My friend Ben Baldwin, planner and insurance expert, maintains that all insurance is term; the rest is just packaging. Larry's Life Insurance Design Questionnaire reinforces that idea.

Vary Your Approach

Good data gathering is the essence of a good plan. Sometimes you need to vary the way you ask the questions to get the best answers. We usually have two advisers in the initial data-gathering meeting. We each hear something different, and we each have a different perspective about what we heard. We each write up our notes, then compare them before we actually begin the analysis. Try it yourself.

■ **FIGURE 12.6** Cash Flow Worksheet

CASH FLOW WORK SHEET

Monthly Income	Current	Retirement
Wages, salary, tips		
Cash dividends		
Interest received		
Social Security income		
Pension income		
Rents, royalties		
Other income		
Total Monthly Income	**$0.00**	**$0.00**

Fixed Monthly Expenses	Current	Retirement
Mortgage payment or rent		
2nd home mortgage		
Automobile note		
Personal loans		
Credit cards		
Life insurance		
Disability insurance		
Medical insurance		
Long-term care insurance		
Homeowner's insurance		
Automobile insurance		
Umbrella liability insurance		
Federal income taxes		
State income taxes		
FICA		
Real estate taxes		
Other taxes		
Savings (regularly)		
Investments (regularly)		
Retirement plan contributions		
Total Fixed Expenses	**$0 00**	**$0 00**

Variable Monthly Expenses	Current	Retirement
Electricity		
Gas		
Telephone		
Water		
Cable TV		
Home repairs and maintenance		
Home improvements		
Food		
Clothing		
Laundry		
Child care		
Personal care		
Automobile gas and oil		
Automobile repairs, etc.		
Other transportation		
Education expenses		
Entertainment/dining		
Recreation/travel		
Club/association dues		
Hobbies		
Gifts / Donations		
Unreimbursed medical and dental expenses		
Miscellaneous		
Total Variable Expenses	**$0 00**	**$0 00**

Net Cash Flow	Current	Retirement
Total monthly income	$0 00	$0 00
Total fixed expenses	$0 00	$0 00
Total variable expenses	$0 00	$0 00
Discretionary Income (Income - Expenses)	**$0 00**	**$0 00**

Few things are harder to put up with than the annoyance of a good example.

—Mark Twain, American humorist, writer, and lecturer

Educating your client from the first day he walks in your office ensures a better relationship and helps manage his expectations. A 1999 Gallup poll[1] showed that investors expected a more than 20 percent return each year for the next ten years. Right, we can do that.

To compound the problem, today your client can perform extensive investment research on the Net. Without your guidance, this abundance of information will only create more confusion for your client and higher expectations for your performance. As I've said, information is not knowledge, judgment, or empathy. If you are to have a successful long-term relationship, good client education is the key. The client who trusts you and with whom you have a good relationship will rely on you to provide the knowledge, judgment, and empathy.

 ## Risk-Coaching Questionnaire

I believe that the most important client education experience in our office is our risk-coaching process, built around our risk questionnaire. This process helps both us and the clients determine the more elusive of the two critical factors necessary to design an investment policy: their ability to withstand the reality of market volatility. (The other factor is the required return, and for this we use a traditional capital needs analysis.) After completing the capital needs analysis and the risk-tolerance questionnaire and comparing the results, if we're lucky, the conclusion is that our client can achieve his goals without taking a risk in excess of his comfort level. Unfortunately, it doesn't always work out that well. We've all had the experience of having to counsel clients who need to either reduce their expectations or accept more risk than they might like. By using our process, we help our clients understand these issues so they can decide whether they can live with the increased risk or must modify their goals. My partner Harold distills this to a simple question: "Do you want to sleep less well or eat less well?"

We have elected to use a formalized risk questionnaire to ensure that we cover all the aspects of risk that we think are important. For that reason, we call this document our Risk-Coaching Questionnaire (**Figure 13.1**—see p. vi). We also use it to help quantify the risk decisions and allow the client to participate in this critical element of the asset allocation design.

The questionnaire consists of twenty-two questions. It is designed to facilitate dialogue between the adviser and the client. Therefore, it is necessary for them to complete it together. Because this is such important stuff, I'll take some time and explain in detail our standard dialogue, what we expect to learn, and what we expect our client to learn from the exercise. This questionnaire is completed during the second or third meeting we have with the client.

• **Question 1.** Because it's critical that both you and the client have the same "investments" in mind as you go through the questionnaire, the first question begins the process by asking for a dollar amount of the investment portfolio. We explain that this is the total value of the assets for which we will be developing an investment policy. Because we're financial planners, we also must understand how the investment portfolio fits within the framework of the total investment universe, hence the second part of Question 1. If the answer is significantly less than 100 percent, we tell our client that although we may not be handling all his assets, it is necessary for us to know where everything is and how these assets work together for his objectives, so we'll need to get additional details on his other investments.

• **Question 2.** Many people don't realize how capricious their past investing has been. By asking clients to think back over past investing history, we frequently help them realize that they have made changes in their portfolios far more frequently than they realized.

• **Question 3.** This next question is an extension of the last one and gets to the heart of your client's investment rationale. By offering your client a number of choices to explain portfolio allocation changes, you can uncover important elements of his investment philosophy and history. The responses also provide additional opportunities for discussion:

I have learned more about investments. It is our experience that many novice investors begin slowly and then work up to greater equity positions. This is a good opportunity to delve into how much they do know.

I had a lifestyle change or I met a major financial goal (for example, paying for a wedding). It is appropriate to revisit allocations at major milestones and discuss the changes and the thinking behind the changes.

I was attempting to achieve superior returns through market timing. Make 'em face it. This is a good time to ask how it went. Most timers do not have a grasp of the costs of trading or the impact of timing on their returns. Many have not tracked returns.

I did not have enough funds to invest in certain asset classes. This is where we discuss the strategy of using index funds. We talk about different asset classes and how they affect volatility and return.

I did not pursue an asset allocation policy. Everyone has an allocation, whether it is designed analytically or just by whim. If you have not read Roger Gibson's books[2] on asset allocation, I strongly urge you to. His latest book, *Asset Allocation*, has an exercise that demonstrates the power of diversification. It is an effective tool that we often use with our clients.

Other. (I have never actually had anyone check this box until recently.) One of my newest clients checked "other" and then wrote beside it, "Fear." We had a good discussion about achieving an allocation that will allow her to sleep at night.

- **Question 4.** With this question, we get an opportunity to discuss the fallacy of the income portfolio. We don't believe in designing portfolios to spin off income. A popular but flawed strategy for retirees is to place assets in higher-yielding stocks, such as utilities and/or in bonds (often municipal bonds). The need to build the portfolio around these assets limits the growth potential of the portfolio. We discuss with our clients the concept of total return and explain that we will design their investment portfolio for total (tax-efficient) return. We then explain that we'll handle their cash flow needs by carving out of the investment funds up to twenty-four months of their cash flow requirements and placing that amount in a "reserve" cash account. I then go back and adjust the amount entered in Question 1 to reflect this carve-out. The balance of the portfolio is invested according to the asset allocation needed to maintain their long-term lifestyle. As we rebalance the portfolio, we replenish the reserve account as necessary.

- **Question 5.** I believe that an investment portfolio should have at least a five-year horizon. Therefore, it's important to know the client's lump sum needs in the near term. For example, if the client intends to withdraw $25,000 in two years for his daughter's wedding, it would be inappropriate to invest this sum in long-term investments. I would tell my client, "Let's carve out the $25,000 and decide how to invest it later. I want you to be comfortable that you're not likely to need any of the funds from your investment portfolio for at least the next five years." I would then go back and again adjust the amount entered in Question 1.

Admittedly there's nothing magic about five years. As with this entire questionnaire, it's simply a suggestion based on our experience. Customize it to your taste. For example, if you like three years better, simply adjust the questionnaire to meet your criteria.

- **Question 6.** If this seems to be asking the same thing as Question 5, you're right. In this case, redundancy is good. It's important to reinforce the time horizon of the investment portfolio, so we ask the same question in a little different way. It also helps our client realize that in reality the investment horizon is *really* long. Here's how we use it:

Suppose my client says, "Three years." My response is "Oh goodness, I'm sorry, I must have missed something earlier when we chatted about Question 5. I thought we'd pulled out of the portfolio everything you needed in the next five years." Usually the client admits that she really doesn't need anything in three years; she's just not used to acknowledging that fact.

If the client says, "Five years," I ask, "What happens then?" Typically the answer is "I don't know, it just seemed like a long time." Our goal is to emphasize that in most cases the portfolio better last for the balance of the client's life, or he'll get pretty hungry near the end.

- **Question 7.** My partner Harold tells of the time that he designed an investment plan for a new client. He carefully asked questions about risk, completed a capital needs analysis, and after many days of hard work handed the client a beautifully prepared (colored charts—the works) asset allocation recommendation.

The client looked at the long-term return expectations, jumped up from the table, slammed the plan on the desk and hollered, "Ten percent! My barber can do better than that!" From then on, we've always asked in advance if the client has something in mind regarding return expectations. We also use this question as an opportunity to explain the impact of inflation on investments over time and discuss the concept of real rate of return versus nominal rate. Note that this is an optional question. By that, we mean we don't want to force the client into providing an answer unless he really has an opinion.

• **Question 8.** This question requires some explanation, so I will run through it as though I am speaking with a client.

This table has a list of six phrases, each describing a common investment attribute. If the attribute or goal is extremely important to you, circle the number 6 next to it. If it is not important at all, circle 1. Circle any of the numbers in between to describe its level of importance to you. It's not necessary to prioritize these attributes. In fact, you may use any number in as many of the six categories as you wish, as long as it reflects how important or unimportant it is to you.

—*Capital Preservation.* Suppose you have $100,000 to invest today. How important is it to you that five years from now your investment will be worth at least $100,000? If your response is "extremely important," circle 6. Or would you think, "I don't care. After all, I'm investing with a twenty-year time horizon. As long as it's worth a lot more in twenty years, I don't care what it will be worth five years from now." In that case, circle a lower number.

—*Growth.* How important is it to you that five years from now your investment has some "growth?" If your response is, "That's extremely important. After all, that's why I am investing," circle 6. If instead you think, "I don't much care about growth. I just want to be sure that my original principal is preserved," circle 1. If you think that some growth would be desirable, circle 3, 4, or 5.

—*Low Volatility.* Volatility describes the reality that investment values may change daily, even from minute to minute. Ask, "Would you lose sleep if your portfolio declined in value from week to week, even if the portfolio later recovered from those short-term losses?" If the answer is yes, circle 6. If you know you would not pay attention to your portfolio in the short term, but would have confidence it would recover over time, circle 1. If you are like most investors and think you don't much like volatility, but are prepared to live with some in order to get better returns, circle a number in between.

—*Inflation Protection.* Again, suppose you have $100,000 to invest. How would you feel if, five years later, your investment had grown in value but, because of high inflation, your money now bought less than five years earlier? Choose 6 if you believe it is vitally important to avoid this, a lower number if inflation protection is less important.

—*Current Cash Flow.* Some people, particularly retired people, must take money from their investment portfolios in order to supplement their Social Security, pension and other noninvestment income. Most working investors have enough income from sources such as wages to allow all their investment returns to be reinvested in the portfolio for greater long-term growth. How about you? What percentage of your investment portfolio must you withdraw every year in order to maintain your current lifestyle? Divide that number by two. Use the answer to determine which number, 1 to 6, to select. For example, if you need 12 percent of the portfolio's value per year, circle 6. If you need only 2 percent less per year, circle 1.

—*Aggressive Growth.* I'm not talking about high growth, but rather aggressive strategies, such as options, short sales, and margin. Are you completely comfortable with such strategies? If so, circle 6. If the very idea makes you break into a cold sweat, circle 1.

It's important to discuss each answer with the client. For example, in our experience we've seen clients often answer 6 to both capital preservation and growth. We never lose the opportunity to point out that although they have strong concerns about each of these, it is impossible to achieve both equally in a single portfolio.

We always ask married couples to answer separately because, according to our experience, they seldom have the same risk tolerance. This makes for a useful discussion when they disagree significantly. It is also important that by the time we finish we have either reached some consensus or we have elected to design the portfolio initially around the individual with the lower risk tolerance.

Once the questionnaire has been completed, you can put the answers in the Excel risk algorithm (see **Figure 13.2**). It's based on our experience with

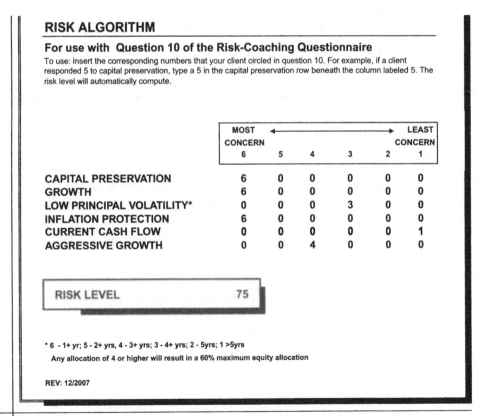

RISK ALGORITHM

For use with Question 10 of the Risk-Coaching Questionnaire

To use: Insert the corresponding numbers that your client circled in question 10. For example, if a client responded 5 to capital preservation, type a 5 in the capital preservation row beneath the column labeled 5. The risk level will automatically compute.

	MOST CONCERN					LEAST CONCERN
	6	5	4	3	2	1
CAPITAL PRESERVATION	6	0	0	0	0	0
GROWTH	6	0	0	0	0	0
LOW PRINCIPAL VOLATILITY*	0	0	0	3	0	0
INFLATION PROTECTION	6	0	0	0	0	0
CURRENT CASH FLOW	0	0	0	0	0	1
AGGRESSIVE GROWTH	0	0	4	0	0	0

RISK LEVEL	75

* 6 - 1+ yr; 5 - 2+ yrs, 4 - 3+ yrs; 3 - 4+ yrs; 2 - 5yrs; 1 >5yrs

   Any allocation of 4 or higher will result in a 60% maximum equity allocation

REV: 12/2007

■ | **FIGURE 13.2** Risk Algorithm

hundreds of clients and is designed to weight the combination of answers in such a way as to ultimately reach a single number from zero to one hundred. For each phrase or goal, insert the number that your client circled in Question 8. For example, if a client circled 3 for capital preservation, type a 3 in the capital preservation row beneath the 3 column. The score, or risk level, will compute automatically.

A score of zero would suggest 100 percent allocation to bonds, and a score of one hundred suggests 100 percent to equities. Normally, scores range from fifty to eighty, suggesting portfolios of 50 percent to 80 percent equities. This is not the final allocation; it is simply a guide. We compare this number to the other answers we receive to be sure that our findings are consistent.

- **Question 9.** This is another optional question. If the client has no strong feelings, we leave it blank. However, this question does provide us an opportunity to discuss different asset classes and whether or not the client has preconceived notions about them. It also allows us to "negotiate" with the client. For example, often clients will express concerns about small company and foreign stocks. It's often possible to get our client to agree to the inclusion of these investments if we agree to place constraints on the size of the allocation to these asset classes. Most important, even if our client suggests no constraints, we can be assured that our client understands these investments and how they operate within a portfolio.

- **Questions 10 and 11.** Yep, you're right again. These are redundant, too. We just want to reinforce the importance of a time horizon when designing a portfolio. We expect the answer to Question 10 to be 0 percent and to Question 11 to be 100 percent. If we get anything else, it's time for more discussion and education.

- **Question 12.** This has four scenarios. They must be ranked according to our client's level of concern. I usually ask our client to read through them first, and then select the one that worries him the most. Since we have had the first eleven questions to make our point, the answer we look for is "I would be very concerned with long-term volatility. . . ." If this isn't the answer, we talk further. Although it's possible that someone might be more concerned with a real return or even their targeted return, our experience is that, after discussing the issues, every client has ultimately acknowledged that long-term volatility is their number one worry. We then ask the client to choose the statement that worries them the least. We expect them to answer, "I would be very concerned with short-term volatility. . . ." If we get any other response, we again go into discussion mode. Even an all-bond portfolio has a reasonable probability of short-term volatility, and unless a client is willing to accept this fact, we can't be of much help.

- **Question 13.** Admittedly this one is a bit complicated. Sometimes it requires reading more than once. The goal of this question is to frame our client's response by providing him with historical market reality. As you can see from the boxed response at the bottom of the question, we're pretty obvious about what answers we don't expect. As with Question 12, we're looking to make clear that markets are volatile—all markets. And, unless our client is prepared to "sleep less well," they may have to "eat less well."

- **Question 14.** This one is almost a tongue twister. It may also require a few readings. We expect our clients to pick the second alternative. Everyone wants to pick choice number three (not included): "I want to be in the market when it goes up and out of the market when it goes down." By not including a third choice, this question makes clear to our clients that we do not believe in market timing. If you do, you may want to delete Question 14.

- **Question 15.** This question helps us understand a client's implicit time horizon and gives us an opportunity for further discussion and education. For example, if the client indicates that he looks at his portfolio more frequently than quarterly, we would want to know why.

- **Question 16.** Here we address volatility and time horizon. We discuss how the client would react to a 25 percent portfolio value drop over a one-year period. Although I maintain that most people cannot really anticipate how they will react to such an event, an answer that mentions getting upset and selling shares reflects a need for further discussion and education.

- **Question 17.** This question is similar to Question 8 in that it results in a quantifiable response. I explain to my clients that many people think of their risk tolerance in terms such as "low" or "moderate." The first column, "Overall Risk Level," lists our interpretation of those descriptions in terms of differing portfolios. The first adjective refers to their tolerance over a relatively short period (that is, a few years); the second, over a longer time frame. The second column, "Expected Compounded Return," is our estimate of the compounded total annual return of each portfolio over the next three to five years, assuming inflation is 3 percent. Since returns don't come nice and even, the next column provides an estimate of the range of returns our client might expect most of the time (our euphemism for one standard deviation). Finally, the last column is an indication of how bad it might be if we have a really rotten year. We use quotes around the descriptor *worst case* (our user-friendly term for two standard deviations) because it only reflects ninety-five out of a hundred years. There's a slim chance that it could be even bloodier.

As an example, I'll tell clients that if they're really, really conservative, I think we can design a portfolio that will give them a 6 percent return, and most of the time the worst I'd expect their portfolio to do is break even. In a really rotten environment, I'd expect it to be down only about 4 percent. If that seems too puny a reward, I think a return of 8.5 percent is reasonable if they can live with an occasional annual loss of 6 percent and a "worst case" loss of 20 percent. I'm always careful to remind them that this is a one-year estimated loss, not the loss the day after a crash. That short-term loss could look a lot uglier.

After all of this explanation, I hand my client the pen and ask him to pick one or two of the portfolios that best reflect his balance between risk and return. In most cases the response is consistent with the results of Question 8 and his other answers. If not, it's an opportunity to delve deeper and resolve the differences.

- **Question 18.** For a long time, we equated risk with downside market volatility and portfolio loss. As a result, all our coaching was focused on that interpretation of risk. At the end of the last century, we began to realize that our process was missing a significant risk; I guess you'd call it "tracking error risk." This is the risk that you're doing the smart thing (namely, diversifying), but the stupid market is rewarding the dumb thing (not diversifying). "Stupid" investors were making out like bandits while our clients' "smart" portfolios had performance numbers that would look abysmal when compared to "the market." As a consequence, we added a number of questions to anticipate the possibility of this form of market divergence in the future. Question 18 is the first of these new questions. It is a simple graphic that allows our client to choose between a series of risk/reward portfolios.

- **Question 19.** This builds on the response to Question 18 and addresses the problem of "performance envy." If a client answers that he would switch, we know that we need to discuss a potential tracking error risk with the client.

- **Question 20.** This question helps reframe the prior response by reminding the client that the go-go portfolio A might well have taken a significant tumble instead of a rocket rise.

- **Question 21.** This is my favorite; here's how it works. I explain to a client that I'm going to give him a two-part quiz. I then show him Number 1 (covering Number 2) and ask that he choose (a) or (b). Next I cover Number 1 and ask him to pick an answer for Number 2.

Almost all of my clients pick (a) for Number 1 and (b) for Number 2. I point out that, on the surface, this response seems contradictory, because the probability is the same in both cases. I then compliment them on passing the test. (If they "fail," I compliment them on being unique and proceed with my story.)

I explain that these responses confirm our experience that most investors are not "risk averse"; they're "loss averse." Selecting Number 1(a) in effect says, "I don't want to take a risk to make more money." Selecting Number 2(b) says, "I will take a risk in order to not lose money." Translating this conclusion to terms relating to our services, I point out that if a conservative investor were to walk into a brokerage office with $100,000 from a maturing CD, the adviser's recommendation is likely to be, "Whoa! You've been too conservative, let's put half of your investments in stock so we can make you some money." The conservative investor is likely to respond, "No thanks, I don't like taking risks!" If that same investor were to show up on our doorstep and our planning indicated that he needed to invest half of his funds in stock in order to maintain his standard of living, we'd make exactly the same recommendation, but for a totally different reason! We're not telling him to invest half the portfolio in stock to make him rich; we're trying to make sure he doesn't lose his lifestyle.

This is a powerful educational tool. After taking the test in Question 21, we've had many very conservative investors respond, "I get it now! I may be uncomfortable investing in stock, but I'm likely to be a lot more uncomfortable eating cat food. Let's go ahead with your recommendations."

Post Questionnaire

At the completion of this coaching exercise, we begin to see how compatible a client will be with our recommendations and how our investment plan will take form.

We have two questions that help to quantify the client's risk: Questions 8 and 17. Look over the answers the client gave you. Do these seem to be consistent? Now look at the answers to the other questions you've discussed. If these answers are not consistent with the quantifiable ones, you may need to revisit some of these concepts with the client. The idea is to get him on the same page with you regarding his risk parameters so that your investment policy will be useful to him.

Card Tricks

It is not easy to explain many of the investment concepts so important to the well-being of our clients in a way that's meaningful. While we can explain the issues, and our clients may intellectually understand concepts such as market volatility and real cash flow, getting the idea across at an emotional level is really tough. Over the years I've learned that as much as we would like a client to know how he will react in volatile times, he does not know. No matter how you pose the question, he is only guessing at how he will feel when his investment drops.

Our friends from PIE Technologies (www.pietech.com) worked with us to write the Monte Carlo Card Game, available on the MoneyGuidePro website at www.moneyguidepro.com. (Simply sign up for the free trial, and the card game will be made available to you.) The game is a program to demonstrate returns, risk, and volatility in a manner that allows our clients to experience how these attributes might feel in the future. The Monte Carlo Card Game comes closer than anything I have seen to giving the client a sense of virtual volatility. This program has proven to be a powerful educational experience for our clients. I'm going to run through it with you the way I would with a client.

The Monte Carlo Card Game

Welcome to Monte Carlo! Step right up and pick a table. Like a real casino, this tool offers your clients a wide range of games based on their taste for risk. In effect, each table represents the return profile for portfolios ranging from 100 percent bonds (Table 0%) to 100 percent equity allocation (Table 100%). The higher the number, the higher the risk. Prior to beginning play, we discuss with our clients the different risk and return expectations for each table. We then invite them to play a series of games, occasionally changing tables (that is, changing their risk and return expectations) so that they get a different set of possible returns. The games are such fun, you're likely to find your clients asking you to move over, leave them alone, and let them play by themselves.

We've used these games with many different clients, but they're particularly powerful when clients need visual impressions that they can own. For this book, I have created a number of scenarios to illustrate how you might use the game as a teaching tool with your clients. But first, let me take a minute to describe the mechanics of the Monte Carlo Card Game and the elements of the basic screen.

You'll see that there are numerous descriptive lines in the left-hand column in **Figure 13.3**. Each underlined item is a hyperlink to a new activity. Sandwiched between the "Introduction" (this is where you entered the program) and "Now

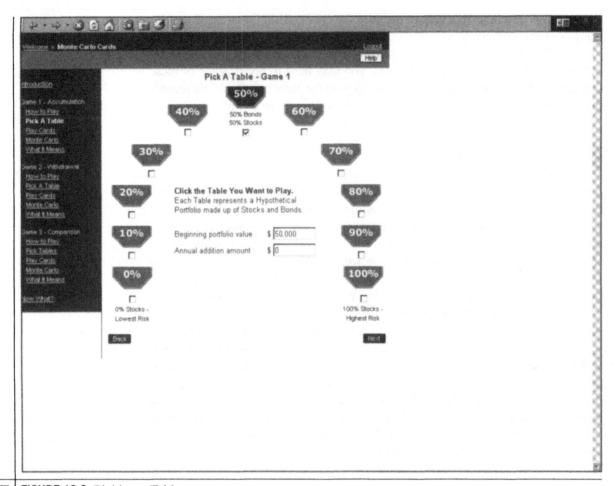

■ | **FIGURE 13.3** Picking a Table *Source: PIE Technologies*

What?" (a wrap-up commentary) are options for three different games. There are a number of games you can play—accumulation, withdrawal, or comparison. The format for each game is the same. For this discussion, select "Pick A Table" under "Game 1" in the menu.

Now, you'll have to decide what table you're going to play at (see Figure 13.3). Remember, the higher the number, the higher the risk. If you decide to change tables (that is, allocation) later on, it's easy to do from anywhere within the program by simply clicking "Pick a Table" on the left side of the screen. You can also change the value of the beginning portfolio. I'll use a beginning portfolio value of $100,000 and the Table 50% as an example.

At the beginning of a game, face down on the table, are thirty cards (see **Figure 13.4**). Each card has a number that represents the actual annual return for one year during the past thirty years for a portfolio allocated between bonds and stock in the percentage you selected. Taken together, the cards have numbers representing all of the annual returns for the past thirty years. The idea of the game is to allow clients to experience market volatility the way it might actually happen, and by using actual returns for the past thirty years the client can accept that the numbers are credible. By shuffling these real numbers, we allow our clients to invent and experience a hypothetical but credible future.

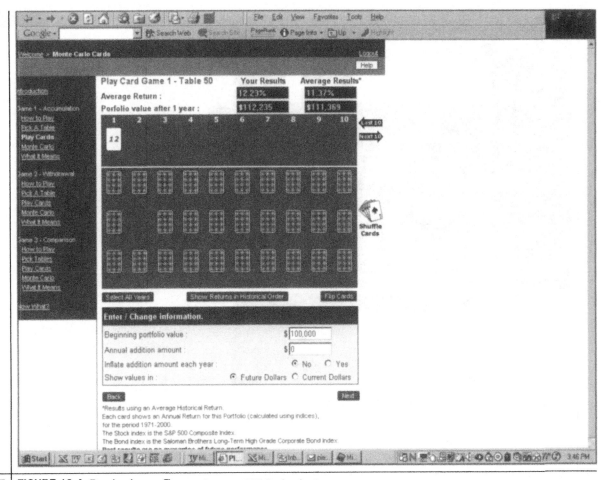

FIGURE 13.4 Beginning a Game *Source: PIE Technologies*

You play the game by clicking on a card (any card). Your selection will tell you your portfolio's return for the next year. Each subsequent click adds a new year's return. Unlike our real world, if you don't like your return (or would like to see what a different future might look like) once a card has been displayed, you can put it back in the deck by simply reclicking on it. Although not shown on the cards, included in the program is data reflecting the inflation rate for each year for the past thirty years. This data, linked to the return data, is the basis for calculating inflation-adjusted values.

On the main part of this screen (**Figure 13.5**) you'll also see the following items, approximately in the order discussed:

- Play Card Game 1–Table 50%. This lets you know what game and subsequent table is active.

- Average Return. This displays the annualized returns for the number of years the game's been played.

- Your Results. This first return is the annualized return based on the random sequence of cards you've selected. This will change constantly with each game and each card selected.

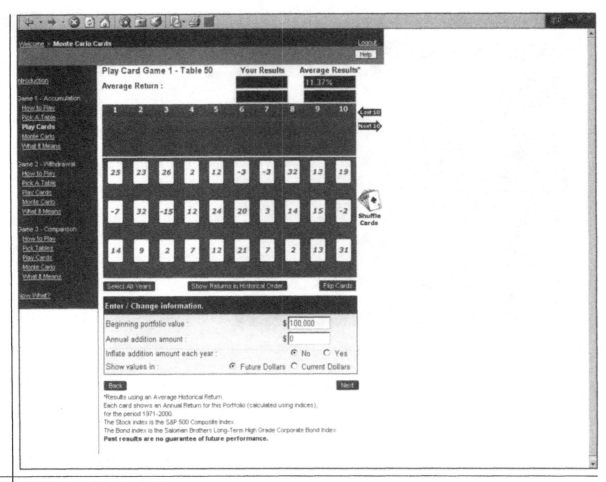

FIGURE 13.5 Flip Cards Figure *Source: PIE Technologies*

- Average Results. This second return is the historical annualized return for the past thirty years of a portfolio allocated between bonds and stock in the percentage noted in the left panel. You'll notice that as you play the average results do not change.

- Portfolio Value after X year(s). This appears once you begin selecting cards and displays the portfolio values for your hypothetical portfolio (based on the cards you've selected) and for a portfolio achieving average historical returns.

- Last 10/Next 10. These arrows let you toggle between the first, second, and third ten-year segments of a thirty-year series.

- Shuffle Cards. This icon lets you create a new future by reshuffling the deck and redisplaying the cards (that is, future returns) in a new random order.

- Select All Years. This handy button simply saves you the time of picking cards at random and automatically selects them all in the sequence they're displayed. When the cards are shuffled, they are in random order so the result is a random thirty-year sequence. By alternately shuffling and selecting all years, you can generate a continuing series of random futures.

- Show Returns in Historical Order. This is very cool. It turns over all of the cards, labels them by year, and displays them in actual historical sequence. In other words, it allows the player to play a what-if-I-had-invested-like-this-thirty-years-ago scenario.

- Flip Cards. This allows you to toggle between hiding and displaying the cards on the table. If you were to click on this button the result would look something like the illustration above.

- Enter/Change information. This section lets you change a number of input assumptions on the fly.

- Beginning portfolio value. How much money are you starting with? We generally change the investment amount to reflect the approximate value of the client's actual investment portfolio. We find this customization enhances the reality of the game for our clients.

- Annual addition amount. The amount of any regular additions. This is very useful for simulating dollar-cost averaging.

- Inflate addition amount each year. This allows you to simulate fixed real dollar savings.

- Show values in. This allows you to toggle the portfolio value between "Current Dollars" and "Future Dollars."

- Monte Carlo. Each game has a Monte Carlo option located in the left side of the screen. Although it's interesting and educational to play one game at a time, the results only reflect one possible reality out of an almost infinite number of possibilities. Clicking this button instructs the program to reshuffle the deck and run the game not once, but a thousand times. It then provides some very interesting results as well as a graph displaying the one thousand possible outcomes for each of the next thirty years. These graphs are powerful visual reminders that although on average one might reasonably expect a certain outcome, we don't live in average times. Everyone lives in a very unique time and the range of possible outcomes can be quite large. More on this when we look at Games 2 and 3.

Okay, that's the mechanics, let's play some games.

Game One

Scenario One: Let's Look Into The Future

"Mr. Client, all the planning we're doing is for the future, and it's a pretty murky future. In order to get an idea of what it might look and feel like, I've got a card game for you to play. Here's how it works at Monte Carlo Casino.

"As you see, you have a choice of eleven tables. As the numbers get bigger, the potential winnings get bigger. Of course, this is a casino so the risk gets bigger,

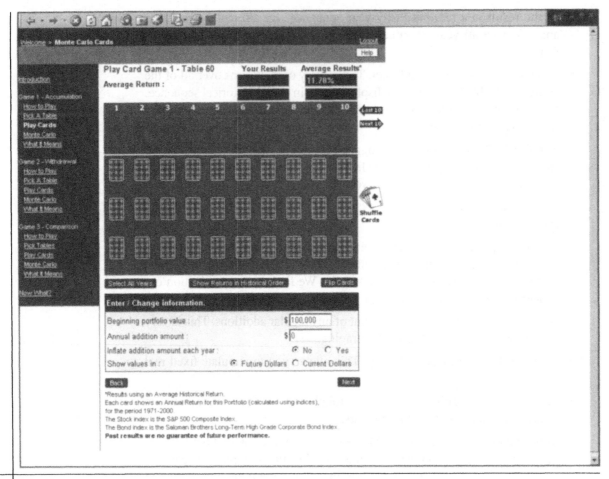

■ **FIGURE 13.6** Table 60% *Source: PIE Technologies*

too. For example, Table 0% is an all-bond table. You wouldn't expect much risk, but don't expect much return either. If you're looking for action, Table 100% is all stock. Table 60% represents a 40 percent bond, 60 percent stock portfolio. Okay, pick a table.

"Ah, you picked Table 60%, a portfolio with 40 percent in bonds and 60 percent in stock.

"You'll see there are thirty cards (see **Figure 13.6**). As this is Table 60%, the cards have numbers representing the actual market returns for a 40 percent bond/60 percent stock portfolio, for each year over the past thirty years. We chose thirty as a representative period of time in retirement. Take a look at the number in the top right-hand corner. The number 11.78 percent represents the historical annualized return over the past thirty years for a portfolio invested 40 percent in bonds and 60 percent in stock.

"I'm going to give you a stake of $100,000. Let's see how you do in the next thirty years at Table 60%. I want you to pick ten cards at random. Each card's return will tell you how you're doing each year of your hypothetical future."

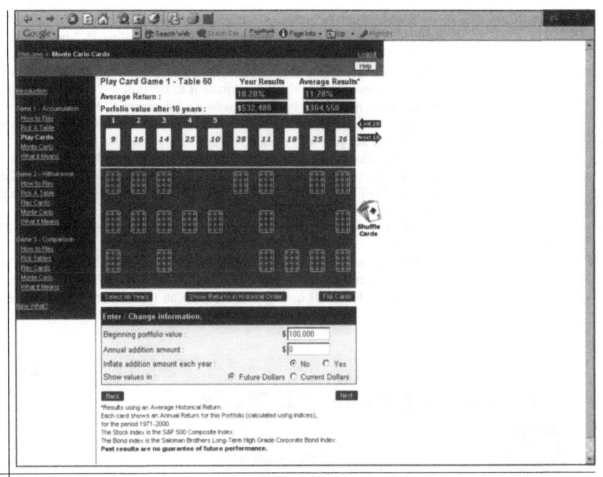

FIGURE 13.7 Ten Years of Positive Returns *Source: PIE Technologies*

In this example (see **Figure 13.7**), the client picks ten straight years of positive returns. As each card is selected, the conversation might go something like this:

Year One	Not bad, but you'd best hunker down and start doing better or you'll never get that 11.8 percent.
Year Two	Much better!
Year Three	You're doing fine.
Year Four	Great! We ought to hire you!
Year Five	Uh-oh, not negative but still well under the historical 11.8 percent. But don't worry, you have a good cushion.
Year Six	Well done!
Year Seven	It's okay, cushion's still there.
Year Eight	Very good.
Year Nine	You're back on the payroll!
Year Ten	Fantastic! You're going to head the investment committee!

In the example in Figure 13.7, the client's really happy. He has just picked all positive returns, and his total return is a benchmark-beating 18.2 percent for the ten-year period, giving him a total portfolio value of $532,480. I point out that if he'd actually realized this sequence of returns (a statistical possibility) in his personal investments, he'd likely attribute it to his skill and would be bragging to his friends how astute he was at investing. I then remind him that there could have been many other outcomes. In order to demonstrate an alternative outcome, I replace the last year with a negative return. You can do this by clicking on "Flip Cards" in order to find a losing year, and then clicking on the year you want to replace, followed by clicking on the card with the return you wish to use. "Let's just see," I tell him. "What happens if after nine years of a brilliant run you had a modest loss of 4 percent in the tenth year?"

"That one change dropped your overall return by over 3 percent!" (See **Figure 13.8.**)

Once we have played with the first ten years, we generally let our client play on for the next twenty years. Just click the arrow to get to each subsequent ten years. Your client will quickly discover that an extraordinary decade of great returns is likely to be followed by a decade of poor returns, and a decade of poor

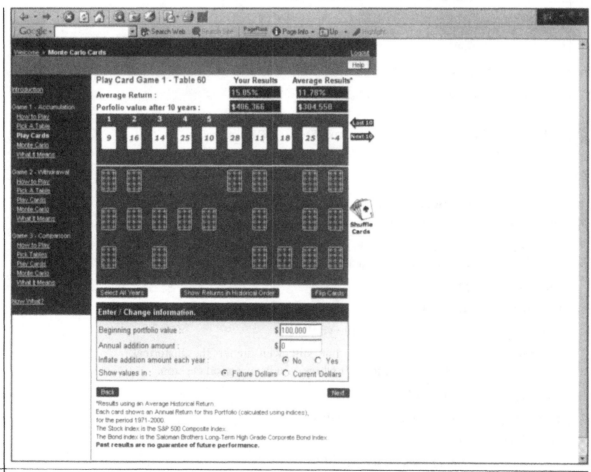

FIGURE 13.8 Modest Loss in Tenth Year *Source: PIE Technologies*

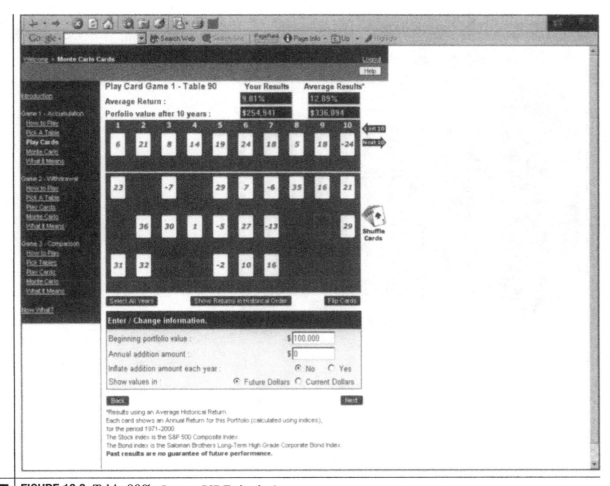

■ | **FIGURE 13.9** Table 90% *Source: PIE Technologies*

returns is likely to be followed by a decade of great returns, bringing the portfolio's long-term returns back into line with long-term expectations.

Scenario Two: I Want a Twenty-Year 25 Percent Annualized Return— A Get Real Exercise

"Ms. Client, so does everyone. The question is, is that realistic? To achieve such a high return you'll need a high equity exposure, so select Table 90% (**Figure 13.9**). Keep in mind that the return for a similar portfolio during the past thirty years was 12.9 percent.

"Now, let's see how close you'll come to meeting your goal. We'll start by having you turn over ten cards to see how you'll fare for the next ten years.

"In the future you've just created, you have nine positive-return years and one year with a huge loss (see Figure 13.9). Your annualized return is 9.8 percent. Let's suppose you weren't so unlucky and the last year you broke even with a return of 1 percent. Your portfolio return is now 13 percent. Suppose you really aced the last year with 36 percent (the highest probability for this portfolio). The return is 16.4 percent, still far short of your desired 25 percent. (**Figure 13.10** and **Figure 13.10a** show the returns remaining.) Do you really think that a 25 percent annualized return for twenty years is attainable?"

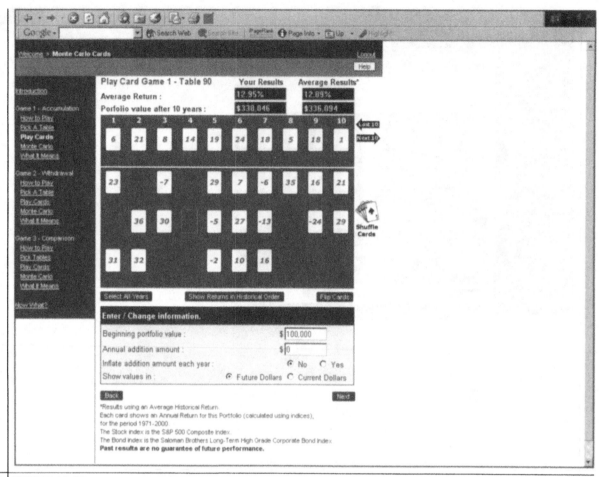

■ **FIGURE 13.10** Returns Remaining *Source: PIE Technologies*

By playing with the cards, you can demonstrate that based on the historically high returns of the past thirty years, her chances of seeing a 25 percent annualized return are almost zero. Even if she were to pick every best year for the past thirty, she'd drop below her target return in sixteen years, regressing to the target of 12.9 percent. Often percentages don't have the same impact as dollar amounts, which is why the program reports both the return and the cumulative portfolio value.

As I noted earlier, a powerful additional feature is the Monte Carlo simulation. By rerunning the card game one thousand times using random selections for future returns, your client can see a visual image of the probability of achieving a specific dollar amount at any given point in time (see **Figure 13.11**).

Scenario Three: What Happened to My 12 Percent Return? All I've Done Is Lose Money!

Welcome to the real world of market volatility. "Mr. Client, I know how frustrating, even scary, it is to have to live through the sort of volatility we've seen recently, especially since you started investing just as everything tanked. However, as you remember, we've often discussed the fact that volatility is inherent in long-term investing. What you have to keep your eye on is the long-term game plan.

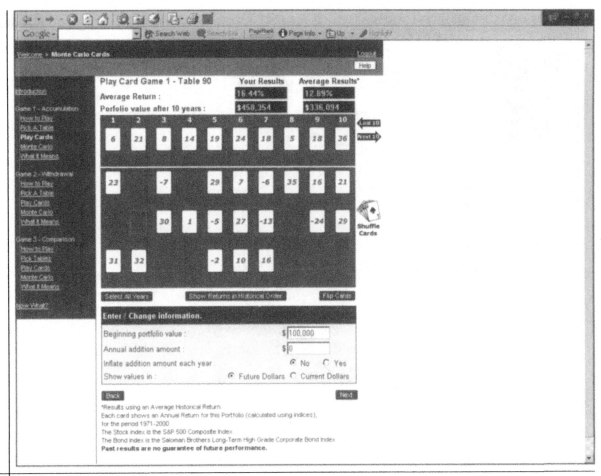

FIGURE 13.10a Returns Remaining *Source: PIE Technologies*

Let's look at a portfolio that resembles your allocation and rejiggle the returns of the past thirty years to see what the first few years might have looked like if you'd had some of the worst returns early on.

"Not too good: a three-year compounded loss of 8.3 percent (see **Figure 13.12**). Now suppose the markets begin to turn around. Let's see what kind of returns it would take to catch you up to the 11.8 percent of the past thirty years."

Obviously, this is not an unreasonable expectation (see **Figure 13.13**). The point is that markets fluctuate. No one can predict the future, but there is reason to believe that over time your portfolio returns will regress toward reasonable expectations.

Game Two

When our clients tell us they need a certain income in retirement, they usually think in terms of a steady stream of fixed dollars. For example, suppose we suggest that it's realistic during their retirement to plan on a long-term return of 10 percent. Further, they have a nest egg of $100,000 and need $10,000 per year to

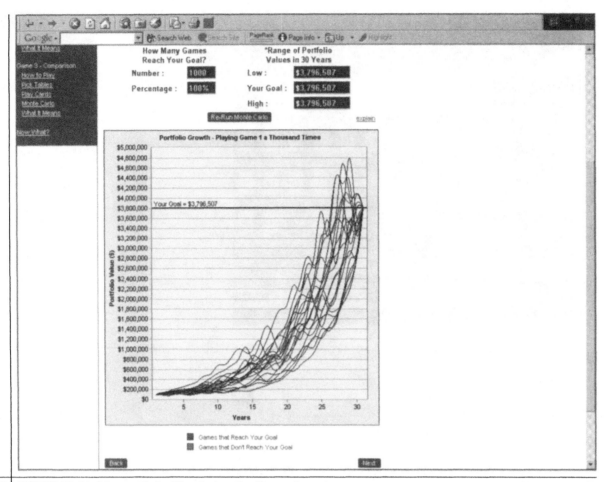

■ | **FIGURE 13.11** Monte Carlo Simulation for Game One *Source: PIE Technologies*

supplement their pension and Social Security. It's likely that the clients will conclude, happily, that they can invest, receive the necessary $10,000 like clockwork, and still pass on the main body to their heirs. Unfortunately they're obviously missing two critical realities—investment returns don't occur like clockwork, and they need a real return, not merely a fixed cash flow.

When planning for retirement withdrawals, timing is an important factor. Although we tend to think in terms of long-term averages, our clients don't live during average years; they live during real years. If they're so unfortunate as to begin their withdrawal during a black hole[3] (for example, a serious bear market), they may dip so heavily into their nest egg that there's too little capital remaining to grow during the ensuing bull market. Ask your client if any of their bills (utilities, food) ever go up as the years go by. Naturally they do, and obviously our clients want their retirement planning to take this into account.

Game 2 helps your clients see how these realities may affect their future well-being. The program utilizes the same thirty years of historical returns and incorporates historical inflation. It also allows the client to enter either a fixed or a real dollar withdrawal.

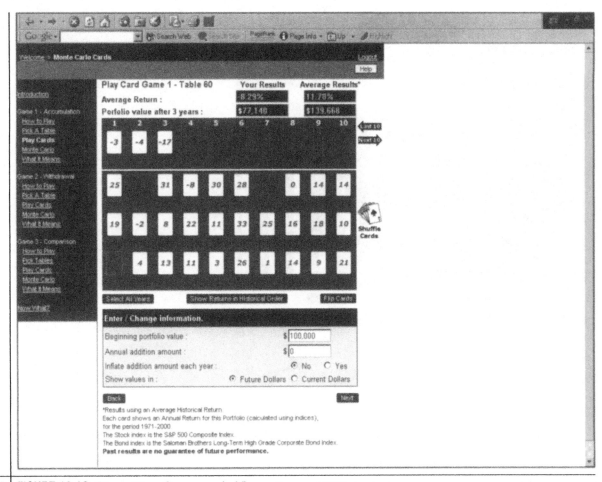

■ | **FIGURE 13.12** Three-Year Compounded Loss *Source: PIE Technologies*

Scenario Four: Black Holes

To play Game 2, select a table that reflects the allocation most representative of the one likely to be implemented by your client. For this example, I've assumed that the client is likely to utilize a 40 percent bond/60 percent stock allocation. First, determine what annual withdrawal rate your client is likely to find reasonable. As I indicated before, an effective default is a 10 percent fixed withdrawal, or in this case $10,000 per year. In the "Annual withdrawal amount" box enter the $10,000 and click next.

Now you're ready to set up the balance of the scenario. Toggle the "Inflate withdrawals each year" to "Yes." This will run the game based on withdrawals in real dollars (the kinds of dollars our clients really need). Click "Next 10" to display the values of all of the cards and allow you to finish your scenario creation. For this example (see **Figure 13.14**), I've selected a series of annual returns that results in an annualized return well in excess of the historical (15.1 percent versus 11.8 percent). If you ask your client about his comfort level if this were his portfolio, he's likely to be pretty pleased. After all, it's very much as he expects, and he has a nice cushion to boot (although, unfortunately, that cushion is in future dollars).

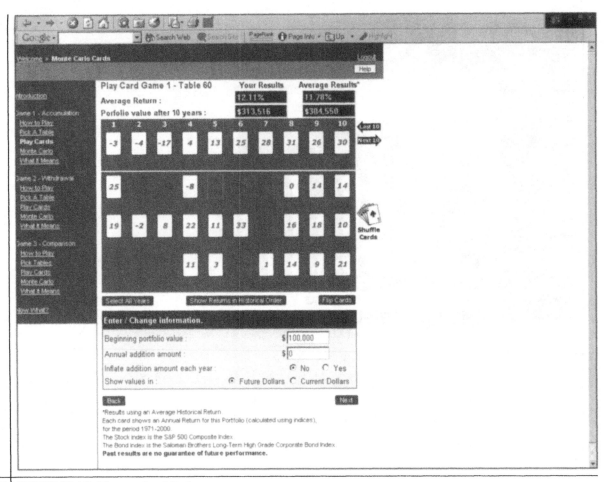

FIGURE 13.13 Fluctuating Market *Source: PIE Technologies*

Now let's show our client what might happen if she picked the wrong time to live and midway through the first ten years, the market entered a mild bear period.

In this scenario, even subsequent superior returns may not help (see **Figure 13.15**). This demonstrates that if you live at the wrong time, long-term averages won't make a diddly-squat's worth of difference.

Scenario Five: Fixed Returns Versus Real Returns

Although previous scenarios are affected by the differences between fixed and real returns, sometimes it's useful to focus on the issue. In order to set up this game, we need to determine what average fixed withdrawal rate a portfolio could have sustained over the past thirty years. That's easily determined using the game. Simply pick the appropriate table (I'll use a 40/60 portfolio) and in the "Change Information" section it will be calculated in the box labeled "The maximum withdrawal amount that will last 30 years when using a Fixed Average Return." In my example, the value is $12,213 (see **Figure 13.16**).

Now, in order to run a scenario using real dollars, we need to convert our $12,213 to real dollars. Do this by clicking on the "Yes" button next to "Inflate withdrawals each year."

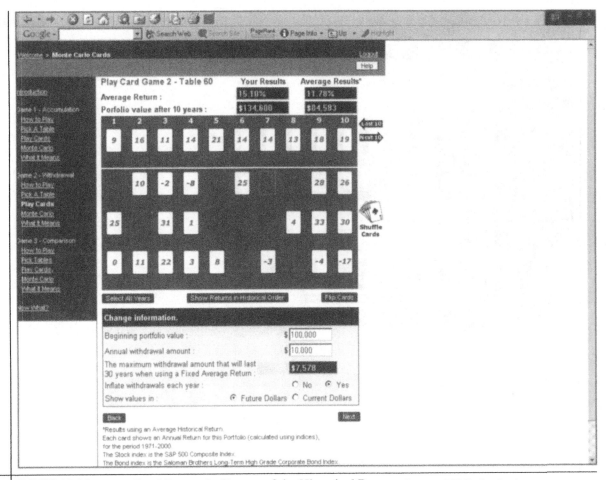

■ **FIGURE 13.14** Annualized Return in Excess of the Historical Return *Source: PIE Technologies*

At this stage, you could select a new series of cards (returns) either at random, or, by showing the cards, you could select a specific series of returns. Alternatively you can use an additional feature of the game, the "Show Returns in Historical Order" button. This will automatically select cards that reflect the actual series of returns over the past thirty years. For this scenario, the results are dramatic (see **Figure 13.17**).

Figure 13.17 demonstrates that an investor so unfortunate as to begin his investment and withdrawals in 1971 would have exhausted the entire portfolio in only seven years! If that doesn't impress your client, using the Monte Carlo simulation will. With it you can demonstrate that the probability of maintaining a real dollar withdrawal equal to the historical fixed average is effectively zero percent! (See **Figure 13.18**.)

Scenario Six: The Final Scenario—and the Pièce de Résistance
Once you've developed a familiarity with the card games, you'll most likely find yourself concluding your client education program with Game 3. This very powerful choice allows you to compare two alternatives. For example, many clients believe that the solution to unrealistic expectations is to simply increase their equity exposure. Rerunning the Monte Carlo simulation for scenario five in Game 3

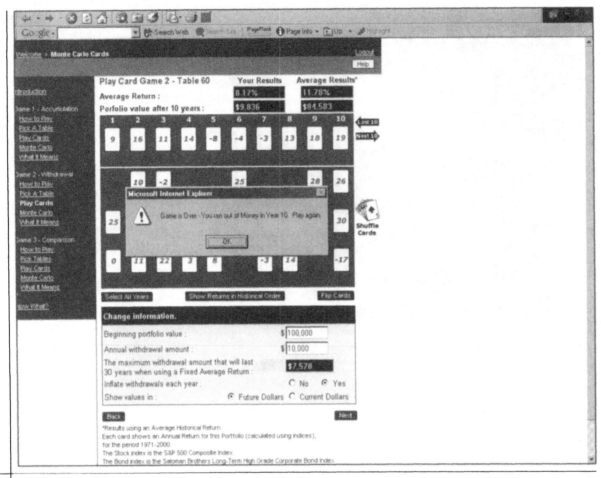

■ FIGURE 13.15 Mild Bear Market *Source: PIE Technologies*

and selecting an all-equity portfolio as a second choice may disabuse them of this notion (see **Figure 13.19**).

Even an all-equity portfolio results in a more than 90 percent failure rate![4] We've used these games to demonstrate many concepts, including:

- No portfolio attains an average return every year.
- Returns can vary widely from year to year.
- Great returns may reflect luck, not brains.
- Over time, returns tend to regress to the mean.
- The sequence of returns does not matter during the accumulation stage.
- The timing of returns is critical during the withdrawal stage.
- The use of Monte Carlo simulations can give you a better picture of the likelihood of achieving your goal than a point estimate can.

However, the possible uses are unlimited. The best part is that the games are, in default mode, completely random so that each time your client plays, a different scenario affords him another opportunity to experience the volatility of real world

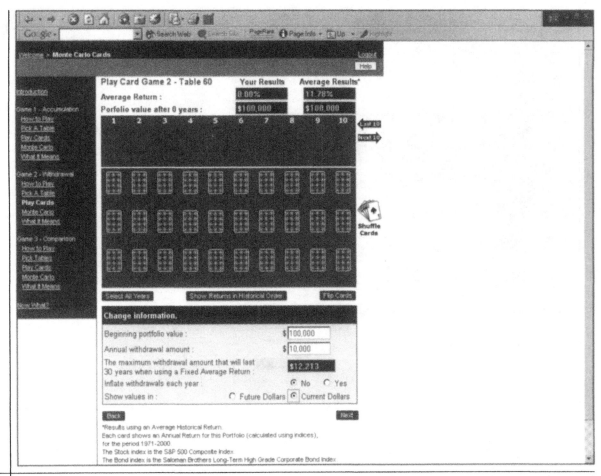

FIGURE 13.16 Maximum Withdrawal Amount *Source: PIE Technologies*

investing. The program is also flexible, so that you can force situations that will illustrate what you want.

We have literally played with this program for hours, figuring out what experiences we'd like the client to have so that when a scenario presents itself, we can change it around simply to make our point. Try it; you'll like it.

Investment Policies and Financial Plans

As I've said before, I think the way planners deliver planning to our clients has changed markedly over time. Planning is a process, not a product, so many advisers are beginning to believe that a formal comprehensive document is unnecessary and provides only a written investment policy. Other planning recommendations are delivered orally, using a white board or computer projector. A few advisers are beginning to use scenario software and interact with their clients via the Net.

This section focuses on form over substance. It will provide you with ideas you might incorporate into your investment policy and financial plan delivery. I

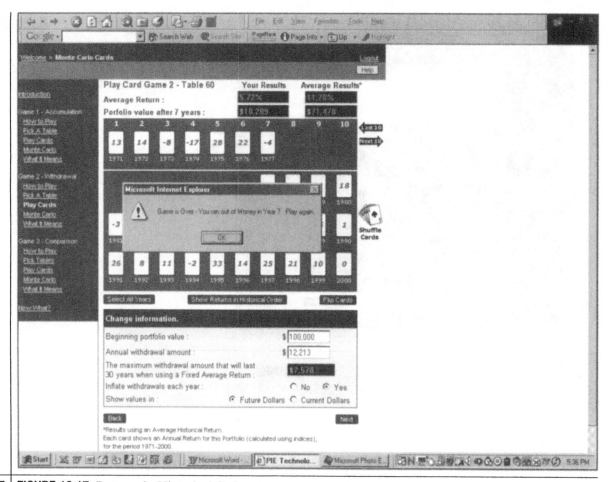

FIGURE 13.17 Returns in Historical Order *Source: PIE Technologies*

am not going into detail about the content of the components because that has been well covered by others.[5]

Paper Plan Delivery

Using a template to prepare the investment policy makes it so much easier than trying to reinvent the policy with each new client. However, it's important not to use too much boilerplate. There is a fine line between standardization and useless verbiage. Ron Tamayo of Moisand Fitzgerald Tamayo, reports that their clients believe their policy is well constructed and easy to follow. Their document begins with a description of the Investment Policy Statement (IPS), why individuals need a written policy, and what factors were taken into consideration to develop the policy. Their IPS discusses what asset classes will be used, what the asset allocation should be, and how the monitoring and rebalancing will be accomplished. At the end of the document, they list the duties of the adviser and the investor and require signatures from both.

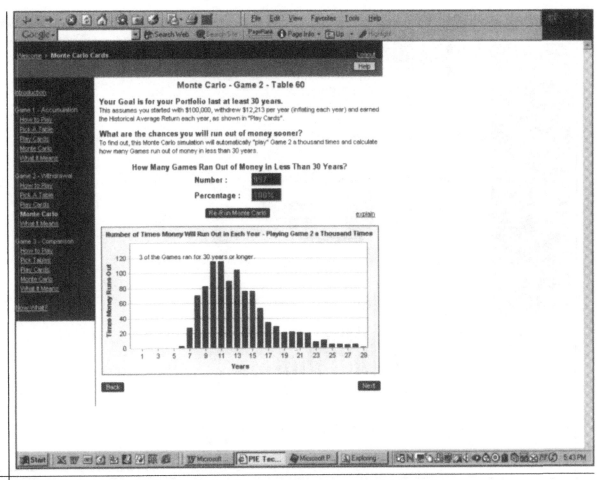

FIGURE 13.18 Monte Carlo Simulation for Game Two *Source: PIE Technologies*

Our investment policy contains both Word and Excel documents. The Word file (**Figure 13.20**) has text that we can customize for our current client circumstances, but has enough structure so that we are sure we don't miss something. The Excel forms include the strategy analysis page (**Figure 13.21,** explained below, and see p. vi) as well as charts with financial and retirement assumptions (**Figure 13.22**, **Figure 13.23**, and **Figure 13.24**) so we can share our analytical assumptions with the client in an understandable way.

The policy form also has a one-page summary sheet that requires the client's signature. We think having the client's signature is essential for managing expectations. As soon as the market takes a dip, your brand-new client will be beating a path to your office, convinced that a dip like this shouldn't be happening and that the world is coming to an end. You know your client's definition of a major correction? When stocks decline for a day. A bear market is when stocks decline for a week. The more you can do to disabuse him of that thinking, the better your relationship will be. We haul out his IPS, remind him that we discussed volatility (as his signature confirms), and walk through the thinking process to assure him that the world is not coming to an end. Our experience is that when our clients are reminded that their investment plan has anticipated these dips, they feel much better.

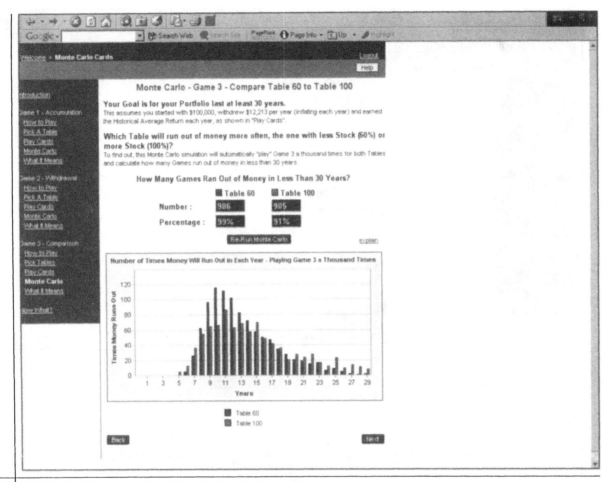

FIGURE 13.19 Monte Carlo Simulation for Game Three *Source: PIE Technologies*

As part of our IPS, we include a strategy analysis page (Figure 13.21) that lists the client's assets, the ownership, the amount, the asset class, and asset percentage of the total portfolio. This document is written in Excel. There are hidden columns in the document that allow you to put in the Committee on Uniform Security Identification Procedures (CUSIP) number of the asset so that you can use this document for trading as well. Since it breaks down the assets by ownership, it is a very useful tool for aggregating several portfolios. Because we also use the document for rebalancing, I have elected to further discuss its uses in the rebalancing section of Chapter 14.

The strategy spreadsheet allows you to enter your asset allocation by percentage of asset class or subasset class. When you put a dollar amount in the money market column, it automatically distributes that amount according to the policy. (Note that in Figure 13.21 I used $1,000,000 as an example.) Additionally, if you are reporting on a portfolio that contains more than one account (for example, an IRA and a joint account), you can note the ownership in the "Owner" column, and hidden columns (you can open on the right of the form) will keep track of how much is owned by whom. This is also a nifty form to use for rebalancing, because it will let you balance the portfolio as a whole without overallocating or underallocating dollars by account.

■ FIGURE 13.20 Evensky & Katz Investment Policy Summary

INVESTMENT POLICY SUMMARY

JANUARY 2008

Investor	**A. Sample Client**
Type of Assets	Trust, IRA
Current Assets	Approximately $2,000,000
Investment Time Horizon	Greater than ten years
Return Objective	4.8% over CPI

Risk Tolerance Intermediate Term: Moderate; Long Term: Moderate
Losses not to exceed 13%/year (90% Confidence Level)

Asset Allocation

Cash Equivalents	2%
Fixed Income	37%
CORE	
U.S. Broad Market	24%
U.S. Broad Value	4%
U.S. Small Value	8%
International Developed	13%
SATELLITE	12%

Allocation Variance	**Style**	**Subclass**	**Major Class**
CORE			**70%–90%**
Fixed Income			± 6%
Equity			± 6%
U.S. Broad Market		± 7%	
U.S. Broad Value	± 3%		
U.S. Small Value	± 4%		
International Developed		± 5%	
SATELLITE			**10%–30%**

I have reviewed my investment policy and understand the risk and return parameters of the proposed investment strategy. I also recognize that this policy assumes at least a five-year investment horizon. I will notify Evensky & Katz if my circumstances change. Investment policy is based on taxable returns.

Accepted_____   Date_____

FIGURE 13.21 Strategy Analysis

STRATEGY ANALYSIS — 39% Fixed — 1/30/2008

POLICY	OWNER	STYLE	TOTAL	DESCRIPTION	SYMBOL	CURRENT $	CURRENT %	POLICY $	POLICY %	PROPOSED $	PROPOSED %	TOTAL	SAMPLE Taxable ($980,000)
CASH/MMKT	#N/A	MMA	100.0%	SCHWAB MONEY MKT	SWMXX	$1,000,000	100.0%	$20,000	2.0%	$20,000	2.0%	2.0%	$20,000
FIXED	SAMPLE	SHT	0.0%	SCHRODER SHORT MUNI BOND	STMIX			$70,000	7.0%	$70,000	7.0%	7.0%	$70,000
	SAMPLE	INTER	0.0%	THORNBURG LTD TERM MUNI-INSTL	LTMIX			$90,000	9.0%	$90,000	9.0%	9.0%	$90,000
	SAMPLE		0.0%	SCHRODER INT MUNI BOND	SMBIX			$170,000	17.0%	$170,000	17.0%	17.0%	$170,000
	SAMPLE	GBL	0.0%	JULIUS BAER TR BOND-INSTL	JBGIX			$40,000	4.0%	$40,000	4.0%	4.0%	$40,000
FIXED INCOME			100.0%			$1,000,000	100.0%	$390,000	39.0%	$390,000	39.0%	39.0%	
CORE	SAMPLE	CORE-U.S.	0.0%	RUSSELL 3000 ISHARES	IWV			$220,000	22.0%	$220,000	22.0%	22.0%	$220,000
	SAMPLE	LG-MID VAL	0.0%	ISHARES S&P MID VALUE	IJJ			$40,000	4.0%	$40,000	4.0%	4.0%	$40,000
	SAMPLE	SM VAL	0.0%	DFA US SMALL XM VALUE	DFFVX			$60,000	6.0%	$60,000	6.0%	6.0%	$60,000
	SAMPLE	INTL DEV	0.0%	JULIUS BAER INTL II -INSTL	JETIX			$130,000	13.0%	$130,000	13.0%	13.0%	$130,000
	SAMPLE		0.0%	DFA INTL CORE EQ	DFIEX			$40,000	4.0%	$40,000	4.0%	4.0%	$40,000
SATELLITE	SAMPLE	LG GWTH	0.0%	RUSSELL 1000 GROWTH ISHARES	IWF			$20,000	2.0%	$20,000	2.0%	2.0%	$20,000
	SAMPLE	L/S-DEF	0.0%	OM ANALYTIC DEFENSIVE EQ - INS	ANIEX			$20,000	2.0%	$20,000	2.0%	2.0%	$20,000
	SAMPLE	EM CURR	0.0%	PIMCO DEV LOCAL MKTS -INSTL	PLMIX			$20,000	2.0%	$20,000	2.0%	2.0%	$20,000
	SAMPLE	TACT	0.0%	GOLDMAN SACHS SATELLITE	GXSIX			$20,000	2.0%	$20,000	2.0%	2.0%	$20,000
	SAMPLE	L/S-INTL	0.0%	GOLDMAN SACHS INTL EQ FLEX	GIFLX			$20,000	2.0%	$20,000	2.0%	2.0%	$20,000
	SAMPLE	FUND IDX	0.0%	PIMCO FUNDAMENTAL INDEX PLUS	PFPIX			$20,000	2.0%	$20,000	2.0%	2.0%	$20,000
EQUITY			0.0%			$0	0.0%	$610,000	61.0%	$610,000	61.0%	61.0%	
TOTAL			100.0%			$1,000,000	100.0%	$1,000,000	100.0%	$1,000,000	100.0%	100.0%	$0

<1>
1

FINANCIAL MARKET PROJECTIONS

FIXED INCOME INVESTMENTS	ROR	STD DEV
MONEY MARKET	5.0%	3.4%
GOVT SHORT	4.3%	6.3%
CORP SHORT	4.6%	7.0%
MUNICIPAL SHORT*	5.0%	6.6%
GOVT SHORT/ INTERMEDIATE	5.7%	9.0%
CORP SHORT/INTERMEDIATE	5.8%	9.2%
MUNICIPAL SHORT/INTERMEDIATE*	6.2%	9.4%
GOVT INTERMEDIATE	6.4%	12.6%
CORP INTERMEDIATE	6.8%	13.5%
MUNICIPAL INTERMEDIATE*	7.2%	13.5%
GROWTH INVESTMENTS		
INDEX	9.8%	19.6%
VALUE	10.2%	16.0%
GROWTH	11.4%	21.3%
SMALL CAP - VALUE	11.5%	23.0%
SMALL CAP - GROWTH	12.2%	26.0%
INTERNATIONAL- DEVELOPED	11.4%	20.3%
INTERNATIONAL - EMERGING	12.5%	43.0%
COMMODITIES	9.8%	36.5%

PERSONAL INFLATION	2.5%
EDUCATION INFLATION	5.5%

*Taxable Equivalent   Month 20xx

FIGURE 13.22 Financial Market Projections

Electronic Plan Delivery

We recently experimented with our investment policy by transferring it to Power-Point slides so we can make verbal presentations to clients without the necessity of the full written plan. I have included our PowerPoint slides so that you can see what is important to include on the slides (**Figure 13.25**—see p. vi). So far, it seems to be a successful experiment. Clients like the interaction of this type of plan delivery, and, frankly, I've had my fill of reading the plan upside down while explaining it to the client.

There are many more adviser tools offered on the Web these days. I predict that in the near future you won't have any software resident on your

RETIREMENT PLANNING PROJECTIONS

	BEFORE TAX RETURN	AFTER TAX RETURN
FIXED INCOME		
SHORT TERM	4.6%	3.4%
SHORT/INTER	5.6%	4.2%
INTERMEDIATE TERM	6.2%	4.7%
LONG TERM	6.0%	4.5%
GROWTH INVESTMENTS		
EQUITIES	10.6%	8.1%

INFLATION	**2.7%**

Month 20xx

FIGURE 13.23 Retirement Planning Projections

system—you will just pull up your Web tools on demand. And, because of the Web format, these tools will allow you to interact with your client when and how you want.

One of the interactive Web-based financial plans I've worked with recently, a goal planner, allows the client to create scenarios based on the personal data we've entered. Written by our friends at MoneyGuidePro (www.moneyguidepro .com), these what-ifs let our client change assumptions and financial data to get a better feel for his options, without disturbing the integrity of our original input. We either provide our clients a copy of the software with their personal data or give them access via the Web. If you subscribe to MoneyGuidePro's program,

FIGURE 13.24 Asset History

ASSET CLASS	1926–2007		1998–2007	
	ROR	REAL ROR	ROR	REAL ROR
US T BILLS	3.7	0.7	3.5	0.8
INTERMEDIATE GOVT BONDS	5.3	2.3	6.0	3.3
LONG-TERM GOVT BONDS	5.5	2.5	7.3	4.6
LONG-TERM CORP BONDS	5.9	2.9	6.7	4.0
COMMON STOCK	10.4	7.4	5.9	2.8
SMALL-COMPANY STOCK	12.5	9.5	10.6	7.9
INFLATION	3.0		2.7	

ASSET CLASS	ROLLING PERIOD 5-YR RETURNS		ROLLING PERIOD 10-YR RETURNS	
	MAX	MIN	MAX	MIN
US T BILLS	11.1%	0.1%	9.2%	0.2%
INTER GOVT BONDS	17.0%	1.0%	13.1%	1.3%
LONG GOVT BONDS	21.6%	−2.1%	15.6%	−0.1%
LONG CORP BONDS	22.5%	−2.2%	16.3%	1.0%
COMMON STOCK	28.5%	−12.5%	20.1%	−0.9%
SMALL COMPANY	45.9%	−27.5%	30.4%	−5.7%
INFLATION	10.1%	−5.4%	8.7%	−2.6%

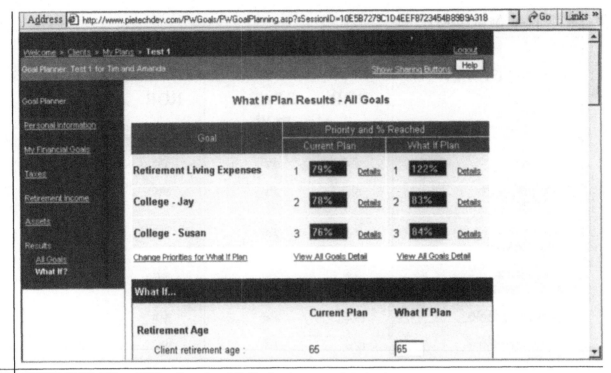

you and your client can go through the website and view the data simultaneously. **Figure 13.26** and **Figure 13.27** are screenshots showing how this works.

Figure 13.26 is a copy of the user-friendly screen that allows the client to play with changes. Assets can be assigned to goals, which can be prioritized. The client assigns the priority. Running the program shows the client how much of his goals he can accomplish under the present scenario (see Figure 13.27).

To tweak the plan, the client may change nearly every variable. For example, if he wishes to extend his retirement age, he simply makes the change on the screen. If he wishes to make increases to his projected retirement plan contributions, he can do that. He can even change the return assumptions. He can also elect to increase savings at various times or increase spending on specific goals (**Figure 13.28**).

Finally, when the variable has been addressed, the new calculations provide the plan results in the form of an easily understandable graph. The client can view the impact of all changes, or just one at a time. This graph is a powerful visual (see **Figure 13.29**).

And, for those engineer clients, there is a table of returns (see **Figure 13.30**).

The best part is that your client can play alone and go over it with you at a later time. Or, he can meet you on the Web and you can change the scenarios together, because it allows both of you to view and change them at once. You create a duplicate copy of the file so the client won't disturb the original input on the PIE website.

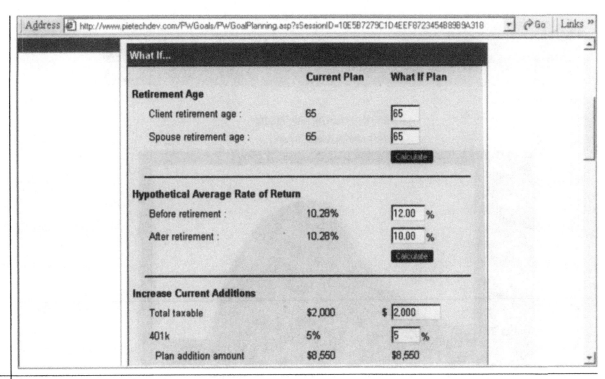

FIGURE 13.27 Assigning Assets *Source: PIE Technologies*

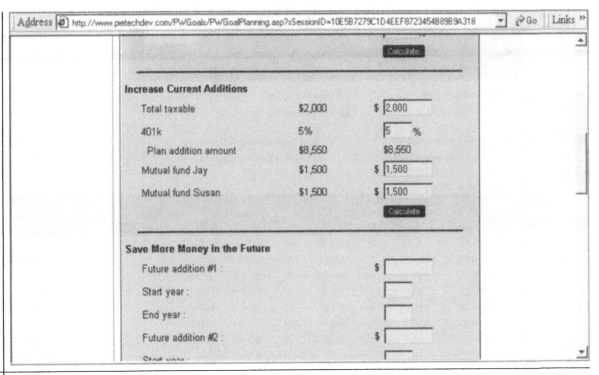

FIGURE 13.28 Change in Variables *Source: PIE Technologies*

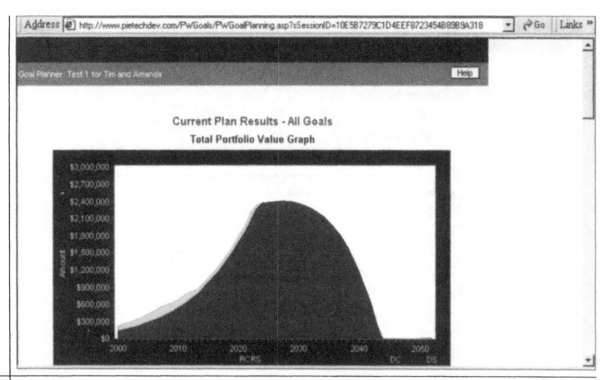

FIGURE 13.29 Graph of Plan Results *Source: PIE Technologies*

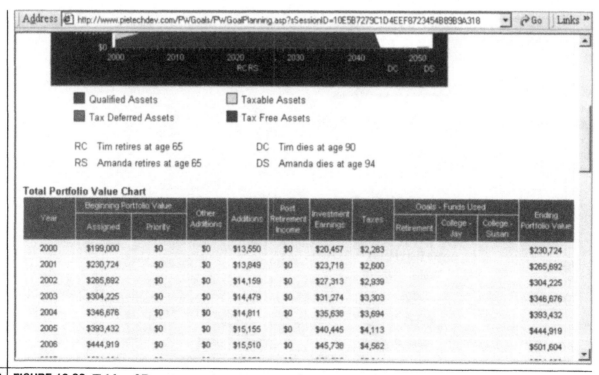

FIGURE 13.30 Table of Returns *Source: PIE Technologies*

Not every client will want to play with these scenarios. But for those who do, you can be certain that this input, unlike other calculators on the Web, is solid and you can participate in the action along with your client.

Deliver the Goods

It doesn't matter how you deliver the plan to your client. Your style should dictate which method to use. Regardless, I think it is essential to focus on the process of the plan, not the plan itself.

Yada, yada, yada.
—Jerry Seinfeld, comedian

Ongoing Client Communication

The late David Norton of Norton Partners in Clevedon, England, devised a short questionnaire that he completed with the client during the first meeting (see **Figure 14.1**). He felt this helped him to narrow the client's focus since often the individual did not clearly define his objectives prior to their meeting. It definitely helped David get a better picture of the client.

We like to follow up our first appointment with a confirmation letter that recaps what we've discussed and outlines the work that we will do. We refer to the issues that the client has raised and how we will address those issues. I have included a sample letter here.

Dear Prospect:

As a follow-up to our meeting on _____, this letter will outline the services Evensky & Katz (E&K) would provide to you. We would be honored to be chosen as your investment adviser and look forward to what is, hopefully, the first step in a long relationship together.

As we discussed, we propose to provide certain services and information pertaining to your investment portfolio. We will recommend that your assets be segregated into two pools. The first is those assets that are restricted or to which we will not act as fiduciary. This includes your _____ 401(k) and _____ 403(b) portfolio. We are not making a judgment regarding these investments; however, we understand you do not wish to liquidate these assets. We will consult with you on these securities if requested but will not take fiduciary responsibility. The second pool would be the remaining assets of approximately $_____ and shall be referred to as the "managed assets." We would recommend that institutional accounts be established in your name with Fidelity Investments. Our services are independent of Fidelity. We do not receive any commissions or other compensation from any vendor, including Fidelity. Based on our discussion, for the managed assets, we will provide the following services to you:

1. Analyze the current position: The investment management process begins with a thorough understanding of your current situation and future needs. The typical examination will include discussions with you, risk and return statistics for the managed assets, and a discussion of capital market history. We will discuss the requirements of the Uniform Code of Fiduciary Conduct.

2. Design the portfolio: It is generally agreed by theoreticians and practitioners alike that the asset allocation decision is by far the most

---

CLIENT OBJECTIVES

A key to successful financial planning is to identify your personal objectives, so that you are better placed to achieve them. Norton Partners have found that clients wish to set many of the following objectives. Which apply in your own case?

INCREASE my net spendable income

IMPROVE my quality of life

SAVE tax (including income tax, capital gains tax and inheritance tax)

INCREASE the return on my investments

SAVE money by using it effectively

INCREASE my expected income in retirement

GAIN peace of mind by feeling financially comfortable

REDUCE paperwork

IMPROVE my insight into present and future values of my pension schemes

INCREASE my financial security

REDUCE time spent worrying about my financial affairs

ACHIEVE financial independence

IMPROVE my business performance

SAFEGUARD my family and dependants

IMPROVE the organisation of my financial affairs

INCREASE my financial awareness

REDUCE personal, business and investment risks

INCREASE the net amounts I give to charity

Source: Norton Partners

important decision made by the investor. Based on the information gathered above, E&K will prepare the portfolio's asset allocation. The allocation is very dependent on four factors: risk tolerance, asset class preferences, time horizons of major disbursements, and the expected returns.

3. Develop an Investment Policy Statement (IPS): The most important duty of the fiduciary or trustee is the development and ongoing maintenance of this policy. The IPS provides a paper trail of policies, practices, and procedures for investment decisions. The document can be critical evidence used in the defense against litigation or accusations of imprudence. It serves as an excellent example of compliance for auditors. The IPS negates second-guessing or "Monday morning quarterbacking," and ensures continuity of the investment strategy. The IPS reassures corporate and public contributors as well as individual donors affected by the investment performance of investment stewardship. The IPS provides a baseline from which to monitor investment performance of the overall portfolio, as well as the performance of individual money managers. E&K will prepare the IPS in consultation with your other professional advisers, continue to monitor the IPS, and maintain documentation as to investment decisions.

4. Implement manager search and selection: Investment returns and risks are largely determined by asset allocation decisions. These will include decisions regarding active versus passive investment strategies, due diligence, and portfolio structure. E&K will search for, select, and upon approval by the Trustees, hire and monitor investment managers. E&K has access to most investment managers; however, due to the size of the portfolio and minimum requirements of world-class portfolio managers, we would recommend the universe of no-load and institutional mutual funds.

5. Monitor the portfolio: Once the portfolio has been designed and the investment policy statement prepared and implemented, the final critical step is the ongoing monitoring and supervision of the investment process. We will continue to update you regarding fiduciary requirements, maintain performance attribution, recommend terminating managers when appropriate, measure money manager performance, update the asset allocation, rebalance the portfolio, compute performance calculation, prepare for meetings with you on a quarterly basis, and create performance measurement reports.

The fee for providing these items and conducting quarterly meetings with you shall be based on the total of the managed assets. Our fee shall be _____percent (basis points) of the total billable assets (approximately $_____) payable quarterly in advance and subject to a minimum of $_____ quarterly.

For disclosure purposes, we are, with this letter, providing you with a copy of Part II of our Form ADV that has been filed with the Securities and Exchange Commission. Also attached is a selection of actions required of a fiduciary, drawn from Harold Evensky's book, *Wealth Management*.

Thank you for the opportunity to submit our proposal to you for investment management services.

Cordially,

Financial Planner

Remain in Control

However you qualify clients and whatever you cover in the first appointment, you'll want to remain in control of the relationship. We've found the dialogue goes better when we direct the questioning with open-ended questions and let the conversation flow. There's an old Sir Arthur Conan Doyle story about Sherlock Holmes who solves the mystery because something expected did not happen: the dog didn't bark. Listen to what your prospects aren't saying, too. That may be telling you a great deal about them. If you manage the relationship from the first "touch," you will have more rewarding experiences and so, I believe, will your clients.

I used to give talks on the merits and use of long-term care insurance. One of my recommendations was for advisers to determine how insurers treat existing policyholders. For example, when a new product is introduced, do they allow old policyholders to upgrade? This can give you a better idea of how the relationship with their insurers will be handled. Once while I was giving this talk, an adviser asked me, "What determines the difference between an old policyholder and a new insurance policyholder?" Without a thought, I replied, "the signature at the bottom of the contract, of course." As soon as your client signs the contract, he's an "old" policyholder, and he's usually treated very differently. Sometimes, this is what happens to our prospects once they become clients.

 ## In the Beginning

Once a client has agreed to engage you as an adviser, you'll want to prepare a contract with him outlining the obligations you each have to the relationship. Greenbaum and Orecchio has provided a contract format that is not laden with legalese (**Figure 14.2**—see p. vi). The "Fiduciary Oath" section outlines a very specific relationship with the client, with a pledge of full disclosure. We have also elected to include a fiduciary oath as part of our contracts. I have included our two contracts: one for financial planning services (see **Figure 14.3**) and one for investment management services only (see **Figure 14.4**).

Okay, here comes the sermon: I believe that it is important for advisers to recognize their fiduciary role with clients and, more important, to make sure that the client is made aware of this position as well. It's fairly clear now that if you hold yourself out as someone giving financial advice, you accept the role of fiduciary. It's a good idea to have that statement in your materials.

> Fiduciary Oath:
> Evensky & Katz will exercise its best efforts to act in good faith and in the best interests of our clients.
> We will provide written disclosure to our clients prior to our engagement, and thereafter throughout the term of the engagement, of any conflicts of interest that may compromise our impartiality or independence.
> We do not receive any compensation or other remuneration that is contingent on any of our client's purchase or sale of a financial product.
> We do not receive a referral fee or other compensation from another party based on the referral of our client or our client's business.

■ | **FIGURE 14.3** Investment Policy Agreement

EVENSKY & KATZ
INVESTMENT POLICY AGREEMENT

1.   Nature of Agreement

This agreement is for the development of an investment policy and is entered into between the undersigned and Evensky & Katz.

Evensky & Katz is a registered investment advisor under the Investment Advisors Act of 1940, and provides the investment planning services provided in this agreement.

This agreement is intended to outline the responsibilities of the respective parties with regard to the investment planning services to be provided to you by Evensky & Katz.

2.   Purpose

You are desirous of having an investment policy prepared to assist you in attaining your financial goals, and hereby retain Evensky & Katz to assist in the preparation of such a policy. We agree to prepare a professional policy statement which will reflect your specific goals, risk tolerance and investment constraints.

3.   Confidentiality

We agree to keep confidential all information received from you and your advisors pertaining to your financial affairs except as otherwise required by law. The firm, as part of its services, may consult with attorneys or other professionals regarding the client's financial affairs. You agree to the disclosure of any information which Evensky & Katz deems appropriate for carrying out the objectives of the advisory agreement.

4.   What Evensky & Katz Will Do

Based upon the data supplied by you, we will review and evaluate your stated investment situation. We will prepare a written investment policy which both summarizes our findings and presents recommendations which we believe will assist you in attaining your stated goals.

Based upon stated goals and objectives provided to us by you and upon our analysis of the information supplied, we will make specific recommendations concerning generic products, services, and/or strategies which we believe will best assist you in attaining your goals and objectives.

(*continued*)

5.   What You Agree To Do

You agree to cooperate in the preparation of your plan by completing an INVESTOR QUESTIONNAIRE (provided by Evensky & Katz) and by providing all other relevant documentation which may be required by us, and you hereby authorize us, in appropriate circumstances, to contact your other advisors. You acknowledge that the accuracy and usefulness of your analysis is dependent upon the information which you provide us.

6.   Your Responsibilities and Choices

Throughout the planning process, you are entirely at liberty either to follow or disregard, wholly or in part, the information, recommendations and advice given by us. Additionally, you, in your sole discretion, shall make and be responsible for all decisions relating to the advice given. Please note that the recommendations made by us may be interrelated; therefore, if only part of the policy recommendations are carried out, your objectives may not be fulfilled or could have unintended disadvantaged results. In this regard, you are encouraged to consult with your other advisors in their respective areas of expertise. If you decide to undertake any or all of our recommendations you are free to do so through any brokerage, insurance or other financial services institution.

If you decide to implement any of our recommendations we will charge investment management fees which will be agreed to in advance of the implementation. A discussion of our management fee structure is detailed in our brochure previously provided to you.

7.   Time Necessary to Prepare Your Investment Policy

We agree to prepare your written investment policy and to have it available for you within a time period that will not normally exceed sixty days after we receive from you all necessary documents and other information which we stated to be required. It is understood that under certain circumstances a longer period of time may be necessary to complete our work. In instances where a longer preparation period is required, you will be so informed at least ten days prior to the end of the sixty day period, and our time for performance will be extended for up to thirty days. If we do not complete your policy within the time outlined, your agreement fee will be returned.

8.   Professional Fees

As a compensation for preparation of your investment policy, you agree to pay us the sum of $_____ one half due upon your signing of this agreement, and the balance due upon delivery of the completed policy.

■ **FIGURE 14.3** Investment Policy Agreement (*Continued*)

9. Cancellation

You have the unconditional right to cancel this agreement within five business days after you sign it, and to receive a complete refund of any fee actually paid. Thereafter, you will have the right to cancel this agreement at any time prior to the policy presentation. If such notice of cancellation is given after five business days, fees are refundable for any portion of advanced fees attributable to services not performed prior to termination of the agreement.

We will have the right to cancel this agreement if we do not receive the documents or other required information you have agreed to supply within thirty days of our written request for such information. In such cases, we may retain a portion of the policy fee previously paid to compensate the firm for administrative and managerial services performed.

10. Limitation of Liability

Since the services rendered under this agreement are judgmental in nature, you expressly agree that Evensky & Katz will not be held liable in any way relating to the performance of the services hereunder, as long as those services are rendered by it in good faith, and provided that Evensky & Katz is in no way in violation of applicable laws. You agree that your personal attorney/accountant will be solely responsible for the rendering and/or preparation of all the following:

Legal Advice	Legal Opinions and Documents
Accounting Advice	Accounting Opinions and Documents

You understand that neither Evensky & Katz nor its associates are practicing attorneys. Likewise, you should rely on a competent tax professional for all tax advice and tax preparation.

11. Assignability

This agreement is not assignable by either party without the written consent of the other party.

12. Governing Law and Construction of Agreement

This agreement shall be governed by and constructed and enforced in accordance with the laws of the State of Florida. This agreement contains all the understandings of the parties as to this engagement.

(*continued*)

13.   Arbitration

Any controversy arising out of the execution of Agreement or relating to this Agreement or breach thereof shall be submitted to and settled by arbitration pursuant to the rules, then in effect, of the National Association of Securities Dealers, Inc., or the Board of the Governors of the New York Stock Exchange, Inc., or the American Arbitration Association as you may elect. If you do not make such an election by registered mail addressed to us at our main office at 2333 Ponce de Leon Boulevard, Penthouse Suite 1100, Coral Gables, Florida 33134, within five days after we demand that you make such election, then we may make such election. The parties thereto, and all who claim under them, shall be conclusively bound by such arbitration. Judgement upon any award rendered by the arbitrators may be entered in any court having jurisdiction thereof. This clause is not intended to take away any rights under Federal Securities Laws.

14.   Acceptance of Agreement

By signing this agreement you acknowledge that you have received Part II of Evensky & Katz Form ADV Registration Application as an Investment Advisor under the Investment Advisors Act of 1940, or its equivalent.

Date: _____

Client: _____   Client: _____

Print: _____   Print: _____

Accepted: Evensky & Katz

Date: _____

Advisor: _____

Print: _____

■ **FIGURE 14.4** Investment Advisory Agreement

EVENSKY & KATZ
INVESTMENT ADVISORY AGREEMENT

THIS INVESTMENT ADVISORY AGREEMENT is between **EVENSKY & KATZ (we or us)** and   **(you) and is dated as of the date executed by Evensky & Katz.** Evensky & Katz is registered with the Securities and Exchange Commission under the Investment Advisors Act of 1940 and you wish to retain us to act as your investment advisor for various accounts in accordance with the terms and conditions of this Agreement.

This Agreement sets forth responsibilities of the parties with regard to the investment management services to be provided by Evensky & Katz.

(1) We will give you the benefit of our continuing study of economic conditions, security markets, and other investment issues. On the basis of these studies, we shall provide advice from time to time regarding the allocation and investments of your assets including money market accounts, CDs, municipal and government securities, unit investment trusts, REITs, mutual funds, annuities, limited partnerships, insurance investments and other investments introduced in the future. Generally, advice on specific stocks will not be given.

(2) We will, after consulting with you, recommend that you maintain and/or establish, in your name, accounts into which you shall deposit funds and/or securities, which shall be referred to as "managed assets."

(3) You may at any time increase or decrease your managed assets. Your managed assets will, at all times, be held solely in your name and will require your authorization for withdrawal.

(4) We will periodically provide you with a statement setting forth the funds and securities, which constitute your managed assets at the end of each period. You shall in addition receive directly from all corresponding brokers, banks, mutual funds, partnership sponsors and/or insurance companies which hold your investments, a statement reflecting your investment(s) in their custody.

(5) In accordance with the documents executed at Charles Schwab & Co., you will grant to us the limited discretionary power, authority to make exchanges and transfers of your managed assets, and authority to bill our fee to your account.

(6) You shall pay Evensky & Katz for its services a quarterly fee based upon the market value of your managed assets, in accordance with Evensky, Brown & Katz current fee schedule (attached). Fees are due in advance, and billing will commence with the beginning of the quarter of the contract date. Fees may be subject to a minimum in accordance with the schedule. You may arrange to have the fees deducted from an appropriate account.

(continued)

(7) You understand that the past performance of investments recommended by Evensky & Katz should not be construed as an indication of future results, which may prove to be better or worse than the past. We make no promises, representations or warranties that any of our services will result in a profit to you.

(8) We may rely on information furnished to us which is reasonably believed to be accurate and reliable, and we shall only be held liable for losses suffered by you caused by our negligence, misconduct or unlawful acts. You agree to indemnify and hold us harmless from any loss or liability, including attorneys' fees and other expenses, arising from compliance with the terms of this Agreement or compliance with instructions given to us unless caused by our negligence or misconduct. This clause is not intended to take away any rights from you as promulgated under Federal Securities Laws.

(9) Any controversy arising out of the execution of Agreement or breach thereof shall be submitted to and settled by arbitration pursuant to the rules, then in effect, of the American Arbitration Association or the National Association of Securities Dealers, Inc. The choice of Associations will be yours. If you do not elect to submit to arbitration within five days after we request that you make such election, then we may make such election. All parties shall be conclusively bound by such arbitration. This clause is not intended to take away any rights from you as promulgated under Federal Security Laws.

(10) This agreement may be modified upon such terms as may be mutually agreed upon in writing. This Agreement may be terminated without penalty upon written notice by either party. If termination occurs prior to the end of a quarter, fees will be prorated in an amount equal to the portion of the fee attributable to the unprovided services. This agreement will not be assigned by either party without the written consent of the other party.

(11) If this Agreement is established by the undersigned in a fiduciary capacity, you hereby certify that (i) all beneficial interests in the estate, trust, or other account for which you are acting as such fiduciary are owned by the individuals or by non-profit organizations, and (ii) the undersigned is legally empowered to enter into or perform this Agreement in such capacity. If this Agreement is established by a corporation, the undersigned certifies that the Agreement has been duly authorized, executed and delivered on behalf of such corporation and that attached to this Agreement is a validly certified copy of a resolution of the Board of Directors of the corporation to that effect and authorizing the appropriate officers of the corporation to act on its behalf in connection with this Agreement.

(12) This Agreement shall be governed by the laws of Florida. This Agreement contains all the understanding of the parties as to this engagement.

(13) You certify that the Social Security Number (Tax Identification Number) set forth below is correct and that you are not subject to "backup withholding" under section 340(a)(1)(C) of the Internal Revenue Code or any successor provision. You are a citizen of the United States.

■ | FIGURE 14.4 Investment Advisory Agreement (*Continued*)

Social Security # : _____

Social Security # : _____

Your legal residence is: _____

_____

By signing this agreement you acknowledge that you have received Part II of Evensky & Katz Form ADV Registration Application as an Investment Advisor under the Investment Advisors Act of 1940, or its equivalent.

By signing this agreement we acknowledge our fiduciary responsibility as outlined by our Fiduciary Oath.

Fiduciary Oath

Evensky & Katz shall exercise its best efforts to act in good faith and in the best interests of the client. The advisor shall provide written disclosure to the client prior to the engagement of the advisor, and thereafter throughout the term of the engagement, of any conflicts of interest which will or reasonably may compromise the impartiality or independence of the advisor.

Evensky & Katz, or any party in which E&K has a financial interest, does not receive compensation or other remuneration that is contingent on any client's purchase or sale of a financial product. The firm does not receive a fee or other compensation from another party based on the referral of a client or the client's business.

Client: _____   *Date:* _____

Client: _____   *Date:* _____

Evensky & Katz

By: _____   *Date:* _____

Approximate Initial Assets Under Management: $ _____

Introduction to the Firm

When a new client joins us, we immediately send a welcome letter. This letter reminds the client of our services and introduces him to the people in the firm. We list all staff members, their backgrounds, and what job responsibilities they have within the organization. Finally, we include e-mail addresses so that clients can reach them easily by electronic mail. One of the reasons we do this is to reinforce our team concept. We are politely inviting our clients to call others in our firm for services that they need, instead of constantly calling an adviser who will just have to involve others anyway.

Welcome Letter

Dear CLIENT:

I'd like to take this opportunity, on behalf of everyone at Evensky & Katz, to express how much we are looking forward to working with you. We believe it's important for you to know what to look forward to in being our client.

We all work on a team basis here. You will be supported by Lane Jones, Taylor Gang, associate adviser Brett Horowitz, and a client service adviser, Veronica Vilchez. Our support staff performs multiple, interactive tasks to ensure all client database information—from birthdays to IRA beneficiaries—is correct and complete. Our team approach strives to leave no stone unturned, and no questions unanswered.

Attached is a list describing our staff's diverse responsibilities. You may never have a reason to work with them directly; however, you may be greeted by one or more of them when calling or visiting our main Coral Gables office. And the entire staff of Evensky & Katz is always available to assist you with any questions, comments, or concerns you may have.

Communication means everything to us. Aside from phone calls, we often mail interesting media pieces, and use the Internet to send informational "flash" reports to keep you up-to-date with relevant current events. If you have an e-mail address, please let us know.

In addition, you will receive our quarterly *Insites* newsletter, which features articles on a variety of topics—from taxes and estate planning to insurance and retirement issues. Many of the featured articles are written by the partners and advisers of E&K, and we occasionally ask other professionals at the top of their fields to share their thoughts and ideas as well. If you would like to see a specific subject discussed, feel free to let us know—your opinions and feedback are appreciated.

We want to be there for you. If at any time we fall short, please call me personally.

Cordially yours,

Financial Planner

Another Client Letter

I have also included a welcome letter used by Legacy Wealth Management in Memphis to give you an idea of how you might spruce up your welcome letter.

Dear CLIENT,

Legacy Wealth Management welcomes you to our family. We appreciate your retaining us and look forward to working together with you. I will be your primary contact at Legacy Wealth and my assistant is Deborah Wilson. Deborah is fully capable of answering operations questions and can fulfill requests for information. Since I am often in client meetings, I encourage you to call Deborah with questions or requests. Please find her business card enclosed.

As our new client, please allow us to build a firm foundation with you by sharing some background information about Legacy Wealth Management.

WHY THE NAME *LEGACY WEALTH MANAGEMENT?*

Our name represents exactly what we do, which is provide counsel for the overall financial well-being of our clients and their heirs. The wealth management process begins with a thorough exploration of a client's goals and dreams, progressing through the identification of a client's risk tolerance and desired return, and culminating with an extensive review of his or her resources. A comprehensive list of topics can be addressed that includes education of children or grandchildren, adequacy of retirement assets, risk management, cash flow planning, estate planning, transfer of assets, and investment management.

OUR LOGO:

It's an egg. Yet so much more. It's how we view what our clients have entrusted with us. A child's future. A secure retirement. An international adventure. A backyard paradise. A wish for one more scholarship. A prayer for one less incurable disease. It's hopes and dreams. We'll provide the care and nurturing to reach these goals.

MORE ON CONFIDENTIALITY:

We view the confidentiality of our clients' financial affairs to be of paramount importance. Client documents are shredded at the client's request. Also, from time to time, clients have requested us to fax personal financial documents to their offices. To ensure your privacy, we will be happy to call you before sending such information.

SMART PROCEDURES:

As you know, we do not take custody of client monies or securities. If you are depositing securities or checks into your account, we ask you to send them directly to Charles Schwab:

Charles Schwab & Co., Inc.
Institutional Service Group, Team 5
P.O. Box 628290
Orlando, FL 32862-9905

Also, we want to remind clients never to sign the back of stock or bond certificates. Once this is done, the certificate becomes a cash equivalent. We have stock and bond powers you can sign instead. You can then mail the certificate and the stock or bond power separately to Schwab where they can match them. These procedures serve the same purpose as signing the back of the certificate, but are significantly safer. Please write your account number on all items mailed to Schwab.

Another procedure we recommend, to make everyone's life easier, is to hold all securities at Schwab in a brokerage account. We do not charge clients for this service because we are not currently charged. Dividends will then be paid into a money market account automatically so you will not have to cash numerous individual dividend checks. The value of your accounts is at our fingertips if you or we need that information quickly. Lastly, each client account at Schwab is insured up to $100,000,000.

FRIDAY DRESS:

If you should drop into our offices on a Friday, you may notice that we are dressed in more casual clothes. As they are for many other businesses, Fridays are casual days for both our advisers and staff.

WE HAVE VOICE MAIL AND E-MAIL:

During regular business hours, a receptionist will answer the telephone and will direct your calls. Additionally, we have voice mail and e-mail systems in our office to enhance communication. We ask that you provide as much information as possible on voice mail or e-mail so we can respond promptly and efficiently.

ADVISERS AND STAFF:

For your convenience, we have enclosed a Staff Reference List as a supplement to this letter. This listing provides background information as well as each individual's function within the organization.

ADV PART II FORMS AVAILABLE FOR CLIENTS:

Our ADV Form Part II is available. This is our official disclosure document and is updated at least annually. To request one, please call our office.

We hope you find this information helpful. If at any time you have a question, please call us. We are here to serve you. Thank you once again for choosing Legacy Wealth Management.

Sincerely,

Financial Planner

 During the Relationship

Action Plans

I think the action plan is the most critical paper you produce. It certainly lets the client in on the game plan, but it is so much more. Particularly now, when many advisers are scrambling to figure out their added value in the adviser-client relationship, having an action plan that spans a year or two helps the client understand the process of planning. Many consumers are still under the impression that a financial plan is a product; we only reinforce that thinking when we provide a big book with all their issues addressed. It seems to me that the use of action plans makes a better statement.

It is vitally important to document ongoing activities with clients. We tend to outline our recommended actions in a letter to the client as opposed to having a formal document for this. The following is an example of an action letter that we sent to a client:

Dear CLIENT:

Harold and I enjoyed meeting with you yesterday and are pleased to welcome you as a client. As we discussed in our meeting, you are particularly concerned with decisions regarding your estate planning, in light of your new windfall. We have prioritized your concerns and agreed on the following course of action:

1) We will have both the Net Income with Makeup Charitable Remainder Unitrust (NIMCRUT) and the Irrevocable Life Insurance Trust (ILIT) reviewed by our consultants at KPMG. Any changes to the NIMCRUT should be addressed prior to its funding with the shares of XX stock.

2) Additionally, as Harold mentioned, we will review the strategy of utilizing an Irrevocable Life Insurance Trust.

3) We recommend that you immediately review your property and casualty liability coverage with your agent and consider, at a minimum, raising your umbrella liability limits to $5 million of coverage from the $1 million of current protection.

4) We recommend that you speak with Joe Lawyer about the preparation of a living trust. We do not recommend consideration of the trust as a probate avoidance tool or for privacy reasons but rather to facilitate management of your assets in the event of your incapacitation. In addition, we recommend that at a minimum you have prepared and execute a Durable Power of Attorney, living wills, and health-care powers for both of you. Once the trust is created, you will need to retitle your non-tax-sheltered assets into the name of the trust. This will not prevent you from funding the NIMCRUT once our analysis is complete and will not create an additional tax liability. Ultimately, the trust will hold title to those assets not transferred to the NIMCRUT. We'll be pleased to assist in this matter.

5) I have also enclosed a number of forms for your execution along with a return envelope. These include:

• Limited Power of Attorney forms granting us specific authorizations over XX existing Fidelity accounts.

• A Fidelity account application for the NIMCRUT. Once the charitable trust has been funded and the initial sale of the XX shares is completed, we will provide you with wiring instructions in order to fund this new account.

• A Fidelity account application for your IRA and a transfer form for bringing over your current balance from the Vanguard Group funds.

• A Fidelity account application to open a personal account in the name of XX. This account will hold the assets not transferred into the NIMCRUT and will be retitled in the name of your living trust upon its completion.

• Two copies of our basic advisory agreement. One is for your records, and the other is to be returned to us.

• A client information sheet required by the SEC to be filled out in its entirety.

• A copy of our ADV Part II.

We'll be in touch with you soon to follow up on our review of the NIMCRUT and the ILIT. Please call should you have any questions in the interim.

Cordially yours,

Financial Planner

Action Plan and Agenda

Ross Levin of Accredited Investors in Edina, Minnesota, has developed action plan formats from his Access program so that each issue that requires action will continue to be listed on the client's internal review document until it is marked "complete." The actions are assigned to Ross, staff members, or the client at the time they are created and are tied to an annual goal that Ross and the client have forged together at the beginning of the year. Ross covers how this works in his book *The Wealth Management Index.*[1]

Ross sends an agenda to each client before his review meeting. The action tasks that have not been completed are listed on this letter, so the client knows what topics will be discussed. He finds that this method helps to manage the client's expectations and demonstrates the value of their periodic meetings together.

Client Diaries

If you are not keeping copious notes on your interactions with clients, I believe you should rethink your procedures. Obviously keeping good records is a prudent move for liability reasons, but we have found over the years that the more we chronicle interactions with our clients, the better we can control the relationship with them. For example, we list family members, important dates, travel experiences, and other nonfinancial information so that we can make our contact with the client more personal. We also have used our client diaries to spot trends in client behavior that we need to address. If a client is constantly going over the same ground, we know that we have been unsuccessful in communicating with him. If a client continually expresses fear about the markets, the economy, or his portfolio, we set up a special risk coaching appointment because this behavior may be an indication that we need to reinforce some old concepts.

Client Letters on Tough Subjects

The good people at what was formerly Kochis Fitz/Quintile write some of the best client letters I have ever read and on some of the toughest topics. This retainer letter that Tim Kochis shared with us is an effort to explain and justify a change in fees. The letter is well prepared, reflects much thought and care, and includes a list of new services they offer (see **Figure 14.5**). It might prove helpful to you in your practice.

Retainer Letter

Dear CLIENT,

Over the years, our business has grown substantially . . . in terms of the number of clients we serve, the volume and intensity of services we offer, and in the size of our staff. We are making every attempt to ensure that, as we grow, we continue to provide all of our clients with the quality of service they have a right to expect.

Today, all of our new clients engage us to provide both initial and ongoing comprehensive personal financial planning services and discretionary management of their investment portfolios. The planning services are paid for by fees calculated by the hour of professional service, and the portfolio management services are compensated by a small annual percentage of the assets under management. Ongoing updating and refinement of the nonportfolio aspects of the client's financial plan are now usually paid for by an annual "retainer," billed at the start of the year.

This overall formulation has evolved for our clients because it provides many substantial benefits for them:

• The overall plan is regularly reviewed and updated because a very key component—the investment portfolio—gets regular and intense attention.

• The investment plan—usually the centerpiece and engine of the overall financial plan—is implemented, monitored, and refined as appropriate in a timely, cost-efficient, and dispassionate fashion.

• As the discretionary manager of the portfolio, we are able to access "institutional" mutual funds that, in several cases, are less costly and/or better performers than those available for us to merely recommend to non–discretionary management clients.

• The annual updating retainer both provides for our continuous attention to the client's overall planning situation and removes any fee sensitivity to the client's calling us whenever questions arise or a new planning issue requires attention. We are "on call"; the fee for the year has already been paid.

Because this has worked so well for other clients, we urge you to adopt this program as well. In recognition of our existing relationship, we are prepared to offer a substantial discount from the normal "minimums" that would apply to new clients. While we will want to discuss the specifics of your ongoing planning needs to arrive at a firm number for your circumstances, we may be able to settle on an annual retainer as low as $1,500. Similarly, where we now normally require at least a $____ million investment portfolio for new clients, we will be happy, in your case, to accept discretionary management responsibility for a portfolio at a $____ threshold. Our fees would be _____ percent per year for the first $1 million, and then _____percent per year for amounts above that level.

We realize that even these discounted terms may amount to your incurring costs greater than you have in the past. We believe, strongly, that the much-enhanced package of services will be well worth the greater expense.

In summary, we are convinced that these new arrangements will better meet your ongoing needs and will keep your financial plan and its most important implementation up-to-date.

FIGURE 14.5 Comprehensive "New" Service Program

Feature	Comprehensive "New" Service Program	Current Program (To be discontinued no later than 12/31/XXXX)
Investment Services	Discretionary management by Kochis Fitz	Kochis Fitz recommends portfolio construction
	Best available, institutional quality mutual funds, at institutional pricing	Best available retail funds
	Ongoing portfolio monitoring and adjustment, initiated by Kochis Fitz (includes capture of available tax losses and timing of capital gains)	N/A
	Periodic performance monitoring against relevant benchmarks, using industry standards for performance calculations	N/A
Comprehensive Personal Financial Planning Services	Pre-paid, "on call" status for all personal financial issues	N/A
	Quarterly letters commenting on your portfolio's investment performance and prompting a meeting to review your overall financial plan	N/A
	At least one pre-paid face-to-face meeting per year to thoroughly review all relevant financial issues, initiated by Kochis Fitz	Meetings *when* and *if* you call; at incremental fee cost
	Annual summary of all major financial decisions and status report of all pending issues	N/A
Background, Reference, Educational Materials	Updated editions of *Concepts* and Periodic tax planning "Alerts" *Investment Commentary* ... quarterly	Same Same Year-end issue only

Source: Kochis Fitz

We understand that you may have a number of questions about this new program and that it may require some time for you to decide to go forward on these terms. Consequently, we've postponed the deadline for these new arrangements until January 1 of next year. In the meantime, if you would like us to do work for you under existing arrangements, we are very happy to do so. If you ultimately decide not to adopt the new program, we will, with regret, provide you with a list of alternative planners whom we believe are in a good position to help you.

Please call with any questions. We're eager to get you underway in this new service program as soon as you're ready.

Sincerely,

Financial Planner

Tim graciously shared another letter on a topic other advisers have had some trouble addressing, the issue of raising minimums. This letter carefully outlines the need to change the minimums, and then uses the opportunity to explain the concept of a "team" approach to client relationships. It ends by mentioning the fact that they have expanded their professional staff, and introduces the new members on a second page. Tim told me that this letter was sent to their referral sources as well as to existing clients to be certain that everyone who might refer a client will know to send someone to Tim who meets the firm's new criteria.

Raising of Minimums Letter

Dear Clients and Friends:

We're writing to inform you of our decision to raise the minimum financial advisory fees and the minimum investment management portfolio size for new clients of the firm. In order to ensure that all of our clients receive the quality of attention they have a right to expect of us, effective July 1, _____, we can no longer accept new client engagements for which the initial financial consulting fees would be less than $_____ or the size of the portfolio to be managed would be less than $____ million.

In order to ensure that we're appropriately allocating our key resources, we can only offer the direct involvement of one of our principals, as the primary client contact, in cases where the engagement includes the management of investment portfolios of at least $2.5 million, in the case of Linda and Tom, and $4 million in the case of Tim.

These new thresholds do not apply in the case of corporate-sponsored financial planning engagements. There we have no specific expectation of managing a client's investment portfolio, and economies of scale and of delivery method permit considerable customization in pricing.

Further, these new portfolio size thresholds for Linda, Tom, and Tim do not change our vitally important rule that all clients "belong" to the firm as a whole. In all cases, all of our clients—current and new—have the benefit of the insight and experience of our entire team.

While each of you has probably come to regard some one person in our firm as your primary contact and we have come to view that same person as the one primarily responsible for responding to your needs, each of you has a claim on the entire reservoir of our combined professional talents and, at all times, the work that we do for you is the result of the collaborative effort of at least two of our people. All investment management decisions, for example, are the result of collegial input and seasoned judgment from the entire professional staff. We're convinced that this whole is much better than any one of its parts. Nevertheless, the principals exercise, again in all cases, final authority to execute those decisions.

As you know from earlier communications, we have substantially expanded our professional staff within the past several months. The enclosed summary displays the credentials of this enhanced team. That expansion and this increase in our new client thresholds are two parts of a deliberate effort to make sure that the quality and timely responsiveness of our services to all clients do not suffer. As business people, we are of course interested in new clients, but not at the expense of continuing to provide highest quality service to the clients who have already given us their loyalty and support. Our first responsibility is to you.

Thank you,

Financial Planner

A Big Change is Coming Letter

Over the years I think we all have discovered that some clients can get very disturbed over change. I was speaking with an adviser not long ago about staff changes. "We take a picture of our staff every year for our holiday card. I've looked over them for the past several years," he said. "The same old partners are in the front, and the sea of faces changes constantly in the back." I know that when we have had staff changes, clients have been practically disoriented. But, what if you change your business structure? What if you change partners? David Drucker and Mary Malgoire amicably separated their practices a few years ago. David decided to move his practice to Albuquerque, New Mexico, so he needed to tell his clients about the split and the move. I liked David's letter and thought you might find it useful one day.

Dear CLIENT:

As we've discussed recently in person and by mail, Malgoire Drucker Inc. has "subdivided" into two new firms—The Family Firm, Inc., which will represent all of Mary Malgoire's clients, and Sunset Financial Management, Inc. ("Sunset"), which will represent all of my clients. The purpose of this letter is to forward to you the first of two sets of forms that need to be signed to make this change, and to tell you a little about Sunset.

The enclosed forms are a new Letter of Understanding and a letter of termination to Malgoire Drucker Inc. The signing of these documents is merely a formality—there are no substantive differences between the enclosed Letter of Understanding and your existing Letter of Understanding other than a name change and, in some cases, an increased level of service (with no fee increase) designed to create greater uniformity among all of my client contracts. If you see any changes that concern you, please call me to discuss them.

The termination letter simply fulfills your duty under your existing Letter of Understanding to give notice of your desire to terminate that contractual arrangement. It also signifies your understanding of the "dual management" that will exist in the future. This refers to the arrangement

Sunset will have with Charles Schwab whereby the MDI staff, who have served you in the past by providing investment support services to me, can continue to do so. To make this possible, both Sunset and The Family Firm will have a Limited Power of Attorney (called "dual management") under a joint master account with Schwab.

The second set of forms you will receive in a week or two will be primarily related to your accounts at Charles Schwab and moving them to the new Sunset master account mentioned above.

As you can imagine, this restructuring is a complicated matter, since we need to coordinate a number of regulatory and investment account changes. It will be very helpful if you will return these forms in the envelope provided as soon as possible. Mary and I appreciate your prompt attention to this.

As you know, I will be working in my customary locations until my family and I occupy our Albuquerque, New Mexico, home in July of 1998. The staff you've come to know at Malgoire Drucker Inc—Lisa St. Claire, Lexy Burke, Steve Thalheimer, Doris Lerman, and our new office manager, Wanda Mumford—will all join me in continuing to serve you both before and after my move.

Our Mission Statement

You may or may not recall MDI's mission statement that has been posted in our reception area for many years, and which we include in the letters we write to you each year when we tell you what's new with our firm and its services. That mission statement is . . .

"Providing individuals and families with a trusted and enduring advisory relationship so that they may not only achieve long-term financial well-being but also realize personal aspirations."

Note that this mission statement is not just about money. We might have said, "Our mission is to maximize your wealth," but we all know that that is not enough. We must be able to use our money to make our dreams come true. If we don't figure out a way to make the two come together, then increasing our financial wealth—by itself—is an empty achievement.

As a wise person once said, "When we lie dying one day, will we wish that we'd spent more hours at our jobs?" To the contrary, our regrets will probably be about wanting more connectedness with our loved ones and friends, and having a greater quality of life together. For my wife and me, this move to the Southwest is a small step in the direction of making this mission statement real for us. It is going from a familiar and "safe" place that has simply become too fast-paced for us, to a more relaxed place of many unknowns but great promise—a place we believe will be ideal for raising our daughter. (And don't worry, "more relaxed" doesn't mean inattentive to your needs!)

In any job like mine, where teaching and guidance are involved, it is important to practice what one preaches. I've always done that with my personal investing. I use the exact same models, research, procedures, and investment vehicles in my personal investment program that I recommend for each of my clients. But, with this move, I would like to think I am modeling much more than reasoned investing habits—I'm hopefully modeling the mission statement that Mary and I have professed for many years. I believe we must all strive to make financial security a foundation for a more meaningful life.

Accessibility

The most important service you receive from me is my advice to you. Of course, to advise you, I must be accessible to you. It has always been my goal to make it easy for you to reach me (one phone number that finds me wherever I am) and to reply promptly. This must never change because it is essential to our relationship. In that regard, beginning next July, I will have an "800" number at which you will find me always.

Services

You may wonder how my move is going to affect you, in spite of assurances I've given you in the past that my service to you will be unchanged. The services you receive will not be unchanged but, rather, improved.

As effective as Mary's and my partnership has been over the years, and as highly as we have regarded each other to this day, it is a partnership, and you must expect a slower pace to needed change and innovation than in a firm with one "CEO" acting on his or her vision, alone, as to how things should work. Thus, my corporate changes will benefit you as I move forward, just as I think Mary's clients will benefit from the same freedom of innovation that she will enjoy, e.g., without the need for my constant "okay."

My first new service, of which most clients are already aware, is my site on the World Wide Web. This will not benefit all of my clients because not all use computers or "surf" the Internet but, for those who do, they will get the same information I will provide to everyone—just a little bit faster.

My most beneficial service to you will always be to help you make important decisions and thereby free you up to use your time more productively or in a more satisfying way. Almost everything of value to us in our fast-paced existence meets one of these objectives. To this end, I am continuing to make contacts in a variety of other personal service businesses that can benefit you in ways described above. I will make available to you referrals to these persons or business, as those relationships solidify, in areas such as

- bill-paying services
- personal computer setup and consultation
- eldercare social workers and related services
- medical claims processing
- and a growing list of other personal service providers

If this reminds you of any services you have been seeking that are not on this list, please let me know so that I can add them and help you find the expertise you need.

More frequent contact is on my list of operational items on which to expand. In surveys I have conducted with all of my clients over the last several years, the one need that arises most often is more frequent contact. It will be a primary goal to achieve this, using a variety of mechanisms, including direct contact by phone and meetings (when in town each quarter), more mailings, more e-mail bulletins to those clients using e-mail (in addition to my Web page), more mailings of articles of interest to you, and other means of contact.

As always, feel free to tell me what you want my service to be for you, and what you value the most. I welcome such feedback at all times.

And before I conclude this letter, I want to thank you again for your patronage and support, and for giving me the opportunity to serve you.

Sincerely,

Financial Planner

Termination Letter

Dear Financial Planner:

I have been advised that Malgoire Drucker Inc. has "subdivided" into two new firms—The Family Firm, Inc., which will represent all of Mary Malgoire's clients, and Sunset Financial Management, Inc., which will represent all of David Drucker's clients. I further understand that Ms. Malgoire and Mr. Drucker have amicably and, by design, effected this subdivision and that each desires that his or her clients affiliate themselves with their respective firms.

Accordingly, in order to continue my relationship with David J. Drucker as a client of Sunset Financial Management, Inc., I hereby give notice to Malgoire Drucker Inc. (now The Family Firm, Inc.) that I am terminating my relationship as a client of that firm. Also, I understand that my investments at Charles Schwab & Co. will be dually managed, with Sunset Financial Management, Inc. being primary, and The Family Firm, Inc. being secondary, solely for the purpose of enabling the staff of Malgoire Drucker Inc. (now the staff of The Family Firm, Inc.) to continue to provide the same investment support services to Sunset that I enjoyed prior to the subdivision of the two firms.

Sincerely,

{Client Name}

Nervous Nellie Letters

Occasionally events happen in the world that directly affect our clients' lives. We feel it is especially important to respond to these as quickly as possible. If we believe the event will disturb clients, we immediately write a letter, then send it by snail mail, flash fax, or e-mail—however the client prefers to get his information. We figure that our clients will be getting many opinions about the event and want to be seen as proactive. We want to let them know we're aware of current events and are actively considering how these events might affect their lives. We also want to help them formulate their own opinions. Here are a couple of letters that my partner Harold created in response to specific events.

Dear CLIENT:

It would be hard not to be concerned about the impact on the markets of our government's machinations over its debt management. We thought you would like to know our thoughts.

- This isn't a first. A similar crisis occurred twice during the Reagan administration and once under Bush.

- The probability of an actual default on capital market obligations is very slim. There are numerous sources of emergency reserves that would allow the government to limp along for a while.
- The potential upside is that this posturing will lead to a meaningful deficit reduction package, one that balances the budget by 2002. If so, that will be good news for both the bond and stock markets.

There are a few possible downside scenarios:

- Even without an actual default, the current crisis will result in the markets demanding a risk premium on government paper, thus driving up Treasury rates. As U.S. government bonds tend to set the base for all bonds, it would result in a general increase for all bonds and ultimately a push upwards for inflation.
- There is no significant budget reduction. That would result in a negative for the bond and stock markets.
- There is a real default. The consequences of this scenario are unknown, but the market disruptions could be significant.

We have spoken to most of our managers and, across the board, they agree with us that no significant action is appropriate at this time. The markets in general, obviously, agree based on their actions for the last few days.

Most important, keep in mind the E&K mantra—FIVE YEARS, FIVE YEARS, FIVE YEARS—and rest assured, we'll continue to monitor the markets, our managers, and your portfolios.

Please give us a call if you have any questions or concerns or would just like to chat.

Cordially yours,

Financial Planner

Dear CLIENT:

The recent market volatility is certainly not a secret. Unfortunately it's such a "good story" that the media, as expected, seem to be doing everything in their power to panic the world. While we could be on the verge of a bear market, we want to assure you that you're well positioned as a long-term investor with a diversified portfolio, invested in hundreds of high investment grade bonds and thousands of good companies throughout the world. Your portfolio is prepared to weather any storm or to take advantage of any sudden surge to the upside.

Still, we recognize that everyone prefers markets that trend steadily upwards. Although we may not be able to do anything about the market direction (at least in the short term), we want you to know that, as always, we are carefully monitoring all of your investments closely. In addition, during periods of particularly volatile markets such as the last week, we initiate a special program of increased performance monitoring and benchmarking of our managers and attribution analysis of our clients' portfolios.

Most important, we wanted to remind you what we've told you all. "We don't make our clients rich, but we don't make them poor. We help them sleep well at night and go about enjoying their life without worrying about their investments." We consider it our primary responsibility to help you "sleep well" during poor markets. Towards that end, please call us to chat or stop in if the recent or future market volatility causes you any concern. In fact, call to say hi or stop in even if it doesn't.

Cordially yours,

Financial Planner

My partner and I were away from the office when the Dow Jones Industrial Average fell over 400 points in 2007. Funny, we also were both away from the office when it fell 500 points in 1987. If we were into drawing big conclusions from small case data, we could say for certain we caused it by being away, but we know we didn't. Our newest client did. And we know that because he told us the day before that the market would go down as soon as we invested his funds in it.

My partner, Harold, has been warning clients that this would happen for twenty years, "I know what you're thinking, 'as soon as we invest your money, the market will collapse,' and you're right! As soon as we invest your money, the market will go down 20 percent, and it will be your fault. Not only that, we will send letters to all of our other clients telling them that it's your fault . . ." It is amazing how much impact that line has always had. Intellectually framing the absurdity in these thoughts really does work to ease a client's mind about it. Except last week Harold wasn't there to say it. And no one else in our firm said it either.

The day after the 400-point drop, our advisers were on the phone once again assuring everyone that Microsoft is still in business; the phone's still working, yada, yada. Our clients are used to this dialogue, too. "No, I'm not worried; I know I have enough cash in reserve for about two years of my income needs. I have to go now; I am taking my grandchildren to lunch." These were the easy calls.

For a few clients we prepared some on-the-spot stress-testing sensitivity analysis to see just how far down it could go before they headed for the windows. We use the sensitivity analysis feature in MoneyGuidePro, continually adjusting the expected returns downward until the client blanches. We remind our clients that the funds they have in the domestic stock market are the funds they will need in the distant future. "In order to get market returns, you have to be *in* the market."

Framing the event is essential. "This is only one of the markets you are in. Here's what's happening with the others." This gives us an entrée to discuss asset allocation, diversification, and other theories the clients won't remember. They will remember that we called to talk, and that's the important part of the process.

It's so easy to avoid the "bad news" calls. I've known plenty of advisers who rationalize that contacting clients the day following an event like this is overreacting. They prefer to "wait it out" to see what happens next. If there are more than a few days of negative territory, they will consider an e-mail or a letter. If the market plunges further, they'll finally make a call. Personally, I believe that when there is an elephant in the living room, praying that it will go away before you have to introduce it to somebody is probably Webster's definition of *denial*. You control client behavior *with* your call, not without it.

By midmorning, it was clear that our most important call of the day would be to our newest client who had just dumped a million dollars into a market that dropped a little over 3 percent the following day. I'd love to tell you that this was the first call we made, but it wasn't. We weren't avoiding it either; we just needed to plan it carefully to make the best impact. We purposely waited until midday so that we didn't convey a feeling of panic. We're not insensitive to pain; however, it is important to think through how you manage stressful events because this is where you set the tone for the continued relationship. If you overreact or panic, your clients will too.

I listened as Harold and our key advisers strategized the call. We always start with the positive perspective. "Well, he should be pleased," said Lane, our COO. "It wasn't 20 percent." "Of course if we had actually said 'possible 20 percent drop,' it would have been better," countered another adviser. We once again used our sensitivity analysis to determine the impact on the portfolio. Our client was not taking money from his investments (his IRA account) and would not until his required minimum distribution (RMD) in about twenty years. Our expected real rate of return (ROR) for his portfolio was 4.8 percent. If the market were to turn much uglier for the balance of the year and actually tank by 20 percent, followed by a second year with a 10 percent loss, as shown in **Figure 14.6**, we estimated that he would still just about be on target. That's assuming we made no interim adjustments to his plan, which of course we would.

As only 60 percent of his portfolio was in equities, we also pointed out how unrealistic such a loss scenario would be.

We also felt that it was important for us to use this event to demonstrate how volatile markets can be over the smallest event. The media quickly announced that the drop was precipitated by the announcement that China was going to take measures to cool down its economy. The market reacted by wild selling. I always try to explain these events in ways I think my client will respond to. So my explanation of the drop last week was something like this: As a kid my sister was a smart, adorable little devil who constantly got into trouble and blamed every bad thing on her two-year-old brother. "Bobby did it," she would say, looking straight into my father's face with eyes that said, "How could you even consider me as the culprit?" Once my sister climbed up onto the kitchen counter, grabbed a handful of freshly frosted cake and jammed it into her mouth. To ensure his guilt and her innocence, she wiped her hands on Bobby's face, leaving streaks of frosting everywhere. "Bobby did it," she carefully explained, paying no attention to the trail of cake on her dress. I think many investors felt that the market was overvalued; many wanted to take some profits, others were simply looking for an excuse to reduce their equity exposure. Since huge market movements are seldom at the hand of individual investors, I suspect the money managers also needed a good excuse so they blamed it on China. Whatever it was, you should now know how serendipitous the market can really be. Nobody saw this coming.

By the end of our adviser discussion, we had set our course, our tone, and our attitude and were ready to talk to the client. Lane made the call since he was senior adviser in the relationship. "Mr. Fleming," be began, "I am sure you noticed the hiccup in the Dow Jones yesterday and that's why I am calling. . . . "

You Won't Take My Advice?

Lou Stanasolovich has a solution for people who do not want to follow his advice. He sends them a "no-action" letter. I tend to think more along the lines of my good friend Lynn Hopewell who usually told someone who refused to take his advice: "You don't need me. It's obvious you know more than I do." Personally, I don't think I'd keep someone as a client who hired me for my advice and then refused to take it, but I think Lou's letter is a good one. I just hope I never have to use it.

■ | **FIGURE 14.6** Sensitivity Analysis

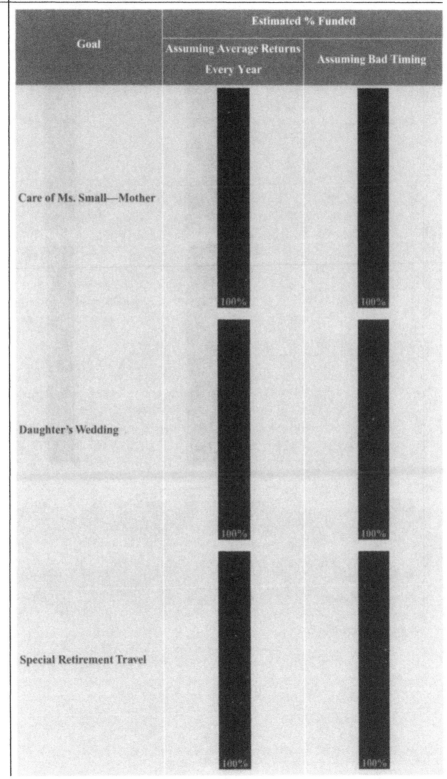

(*continued*)

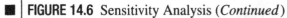

FIGURE 14.6 Sensitivity Analysis (*Continued*)

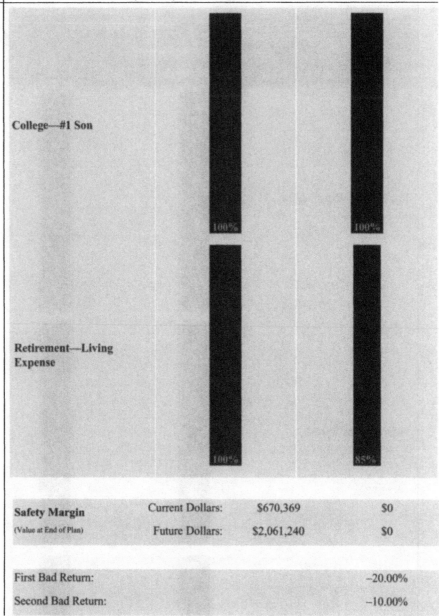

Source: MoneyGuidePro

No-Action Letter

Dear CLIENT:

Everyone's financial circumstances involve a balance between risk and reward, opportunity and protection.

You have two items to be protected: the present assets you have acquired and the future income you will receive. Opportunities which are lost may not come again, or if they do, the remaining time for growth has been foreshortened.

The job of a financial planner is to measure these risks and communicate them effectively to you. We try to help you form a balance between the risk exposure and the expense of insurance or the inconvenience of risk avoidance.

You have indicated your desire not to take action at this time on a recommendation we consider critical to your future. Naturally, this is your prerogative. Please give this matter further thought, and if you continue to feel the same way, please contact me.

Cordially,

Financial Planner

Client Reviews

I firmly believe that if you focus on portfolio performance in your reviews, your clients will also focus on them. That's why our quarterly reviews include a plethora of information unrelated to market performance. Further, we believe that the reviews we provide should reflect the client's choice of information. We have standard forms, but the client is also offered the opportunity to pick and choose what will appear in his review package from these forms.

It's the Doctor, Not the System: The Importance of Client Reviews

One of my clients is a physician. At one of our quarterly meetings, he confided to me that he was finding it harder and harder to be an effective doctor. "The health-care system in the United States is falling apart," he told me. "Health insurance is ridiculously expensive and is covering less and less. To make things worse, there is no patient loyalty anymore. If a patient changes insurance carriers and I am not a listed provider, they simply ask me for a referral to someone else. They never ask me if I can get on their new list. They never ask if they can make other arrangements. I can be their doctor for years, and then poof . . . they're gone. Am I that interchangeable?"

I thought about my own experiences with my personal physician. She doesn't honor any insurance. If I go to see her I have to file my own insurance claims, and I have to pay more. I still go. In fact, I wouldn't want to go anywhere else. I thought about why I have such fierce loyalty. It could be because when I am sick, I get to talk with her on the phone and not three receptionists and a nurse-practitioner. It could be that before my scheduled visit, she has me take all my lab tests, so she can make the visit more meaningful. It could be that she gives me all the time I need when I am in her office and has her assistant call if she is running too late. It could be that when I call her office to set appointments, I hear a nice, friendly voice who knows who I am and handles my requests cordially and efficiently. It could be that she makes follow-up calls to see that I have taken the tests I need or gotten the medicine she ordered. She arranges appointments for me to see specialists when I need them. I have her beeper number, her cell number, her back-office number, and her e-mail address. I never abuse the privilege of having them, but I do use them when I have an emergency.

Then, as I often do, I thought about my practice and wondered if some of the clients who left me thought I was interchangeable, too. Something makes your clients stay with you year after year. The key is not to just know what it is, but to be sure that you continue to give it to them, and continually exceed their expectations.

Just as you might go for a periodic medical checkup, a periodic review is a perfect opportunity to develop an ongoing relationship with your clients and to gain their continued trust. It is not the time to stun them with overwhelming data and information, or numerous pages of benchmarks and dialogue that they won't be able to decipher without a course in modern portfolio theory. It is important, though, to provide a meaningful formal report that will make it easy for your clients to gauge their progress.

Most of our formal report reviews are prepared on a quarterly basis. During the first year of working with clients, we request personal meetings, to ensure that we are meeting their expectations and that no important issues are being ignored. After that, although we encourage quarterly visits, we are also flexible in offering phone appointments or occasionally postponing a face-to-face meeting. In any case, we make sure that clients know we are available at any time for a review meeting, even if it's not our regular "checkup."

For clients who we believe will spend too much time viewing their positions and worrying about month-to-month volatility, we purposely create their review quarter so that it is not on the calendar quarter. That way, it is not easy for them to compare calendar quarter returns to their current report, which may end February 28, for example. This is one of our techniques to educate clients about the dangers of focusing too closely on short-term returns.

If you are holding yourself out as a portfolio manager, then performance is of major importance in your reviews. However, as a planner, I tell my clients that while performance is important, it is only important in the context of meeting their goals and objectives. We don't need to maximize returns; we just need to get them where they want to go. Consequently, our performance page is the last page in the formal review. Additionally, because we do not want clients to think about short-term volatility, we do not provide year-to-date returns, only one year and longer.

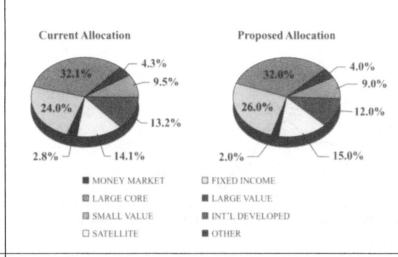

FIGURE 14.7 Current and Proposed Allocations

Our first page of the review sets the stage for the other pages to follow. It is a narrative, written by one of our advisers, that highlights the economy and the markets over the past quarter. This report discusses broad asset classes, global economic trends, and events that may have had a positive or negative effect on markets in the past quarter. Our macro look at the economy helps put the client's returns (when we finally report them) in context.

During the initial work with our clients, we develop an investment policy for them. We believe that the discipline of adhering to the policy may mean success or failure in reaching their goals, so the second page of the review reflects the current-policy allocation compared to the target allocation. We do this by showing two pie charts (**Figure 14.7**). From these pie charts, we can demonstrate that it may be time to rebalance the portfolio.

By designing the review to emphasize the allocation and rebalancing issue, we are also demonstrating that the performance is of lesser importance in the short term.

The next page of the review, again in our order of prioritized importance, is a chart that shows the client's return against the consumer price index (CPI), our measure of inflation (**Figure 14.8**). This demonstrates how well the portfolio is protecting his or her purchasing power, since our concern about the effects of inflation far outweighs our other portfolio concerns.

The fourth page is our list of assets by asset class and by percentage of that class within the portfolio. We also list the benchmark for each asset class. With this page we are encouraging the client to look at the portfolio as a sum of its allocated parts, rather than to look at each individual asset. Clients learn to understand that although, individually, assets may be negatively or positively correlated, they do work together to make a more stable portfolio.

Our final page is the annual performance for the portfolio. As stated earlier, we do not provide year-to-date or any short-term returns.

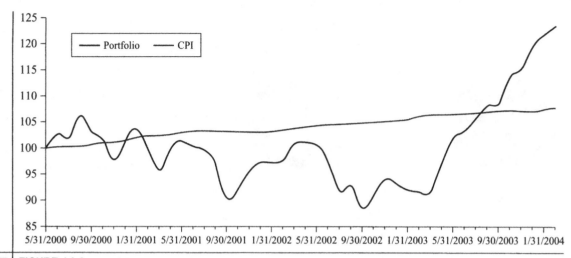

FIGURE 14.8 Portfolio Versus Inflation

During the review meeting, we also discuss our Action List. The Action List is developed at the beginning of the engagement with the client and is reviewed and redesigned each year, according to the client's needs and circumstances. For example, an Action List may indicate that the client needs to purchase insurance, revisit cash flow, or have a will prepared. If these items involve other specialists like attorneys or accountants, we may arrange for these meetings at the same time as our review meeting. Action items remain on the list until completion. In that way, the client is periodically reminded and the task isn't overlooked.

We also use the review meeting to ask about family members, travels, hobbies, and other items of interest. Often clients bring new pictures of their grandchildren or latest trips so that we can enjoy their experiences with them. We find that the more we talk about the personal aspects of our clients' lives, the richer and fuller our relationship with them becomes.

Finally, we always leave time in the meeting for the clients to bring up any current needs or concerns. Many times they will share family problems or other personal circumstances. Since our clients know that confidentiality is of utmost concern to us, they feel comfortable using us a sounding board or even a resource to address some of their most personal issues.

I've thought about my doctor-client relationship many times recently, comparing his experience as a physician to mine as a financial planner. Just like a physician, we often tend to our clients' needs on an on-demand basis; they have a critical issue or situation that needs attention immediately. Those situations are not likely to form lasting bonds with them, however. It's the ongoing "checkups," the consistent availability and investment of time in the relationship through our periodic reviews that ultimately build the trust and loyalty that makes clients stay with us, through good times and bad. Something makes your clients stay with you year-after-year. Good client reviews can ensure it.

Review Notification

Many advisers simply send out their reviews when they are completed. Many insist that the client come in for a review meeting to discuss the material. We've done both. Now

> Dear: _____ Date: _____
>
> We are preparing your current review.
>
> If you would like to visit our office and have us review it with you or if you would like to schedule a phone review, please call us at (305) 448-8882.
>
> Should you prefer to see the review and call with any questions you might have, we will mail the review on its completion.
>
> ## EVENSKY & KATZ

■ **FIGURE 14.9** Review Notification Card

we ask the client if she wants to meet. By sending a card about two weeks in advance of the completion of the reviews, the client can decide if she wants to call a meeting. Of course, we don't use these if we want to call a meeting (see **Figure 14.9**).

The Review Cover Letter—Setting the Stage

Our review letter functions as a cover letter for the review package we provide clients. Our partner, Lane Jones, usually writes whatever is on his mind each month when reviews are being prepared. As a result, this review letter often seems like an informal conversation with a sage investor who has experience and perspective. Many times it is a comment on markets, like the highlights letter below. Sometimes it is a talk about financial planning issues or world events.

Highlights Letter

Dear CLIENT:

Years ago Cisco Systems, a technology firm founded at Stanford University in 1984, went public. In March, for a brief period, the company passed Microsoft (another relative newcomer) for the title of the world's most valuable enterprise in terms of stock market value. While this accomplishment is laudable, what really impresses is the contribution Cisco and similar companies have made to the quality of our lives. Cellular phones and the Internet are just two innovations that have radically altered our lifestyles and will continue to improve the way we do business and communicate. Biotech companies are cataloging information about our genetic code, which should ultimately lead to the discovery of cures for diseases that today are considered untreatable.

The potential of these technological advances has not been lost on the investing public during the last few years.

Lately, however, we have been witnessing some wild gyrations in the market prices of these technology stocks. At some point the true value of these high fliers should become evident. Companies that have something meaningful to offer us will become the General Electrics of tomorrow, and those that don't probably won't survive. Benjamin Graham, the father of fundamental investment analysis, summed it up best when he stated that "in the short run the stock market is a voting machine and in the long run, a weighing machine." This is a major reason we believe that a thoughtfully constructed, diversified portfolio will provide returns that should enable you to achieve your long-term goals.

Cordially,

Financial Planner

Our reviews also include a one-page epistle from Lane, who puts the economy in perspective. We call it "Highlights of the Economy and the Markets." We find this to be a helpful commentary, particularly when clients are trying to "measure" their portfolios against what's happening in the rest of the economy. If their portfolio is off, it helps them to understand what sectors of the economy contributed to the decline. I've reproduced a sample for you below.

Highlights of the Economy and the Markets

We must admit that the first five months of the year 2000 were a bit more interesting than your average period of late. The U.S. economy continued to power ahead, generating substantial growth in output, income, and employment. Meanwhile, the financial markets went through some wild gyrations—some good, some bad. There was even a hint in the air that the long-dormant value style of investing might be supplanting growth as the wave of the future. Surely, this was just another one of those recurring dreams that turn out not to be true when morning arrives.

Those hot technology stocks began the year just as they finished the last; roaring ahead like the party would never end. For this group the term "price-to-earnings ratio" disappeared from the lexicon and was replaced by "price-to-sales ratio." After a while, even this measure of a company's worth started to appear a bit scary. Then as the first quarter wound down, some air pockets developed and a number of the highest flying Internet and biotech stocks started plunging—the losses in many cases approaching 70 percent from peak values. For the first five months of the year virtually every major domestic index was down. More specifically, the S&P 500 lost 2.8 percent, the small-cap Russell 2000 Index, 5.2 percent, and the Nasdaq, 16.4 percent.

World markets didn't fare much better than those in the United States. The Morgan Stanley Capital International (MSCI) indexes of developed markets and emerging markets fell 7.7 percent and 11.1 percent, respectively, in the first five months of 2000. Rather than focusing on particular countries, global investors seemed to pay more attention to specific industry segments. As in the United States, the most popular sectors were technology, telecommunications, and media, both on the upside and the downside.

The major driving force behind the early year's domestic bond market performance was the Treasury's repurchase of some longer maturity issues. For the first time in many years the government found itself with more money than it knew what to do with—thus the buy-back program. The result of this initiative was an inverted yield curve, with the 10-year Treasury yielding 6.28 percent, and the 30-year, 6.01 percent at the end of May.

Once again, with a few cracks starting to show in the domestic markets, are we approaching a "dip-buying" environment or beginning the long-expected correction? At this juncture, it doesn't seem like much assistance will come from the Fed, which after raising the discount rate 50 basis points in May is threatening to boost interest rates once again this summer. If those rates get much higher, some of those investor dollars may exit stocks and find their way into the bond market.

Moisand Fitzgerald Tamayo put their quarterly review commentary in the form of a newsletter. Ron Tamayo tells me they include a market report and an economic report, along with an editorial corner and company news. This gives their clients more material to read about than just portfolio performance. See **Figure 14.10**.

Policy Review

Most portfolio management software programs have a report that will provide an asset allocation pie chart as part of the review to show the client where his portfolio is currently against his target portfolio allocation. This helps you focus the client on allocation rather than performance. If you don't have such a report, we've included **Figure 14.11**, a sample of a policy analysis report that you could easily create in Excel. This report includes two pie charts, one for the target (policy) allocation, and one that is the current position, based upon the numbers you input.

Manager Reviews

We also include manager review pages as part of our review documents (**Figure 14.12**—see p. vi). We prepare a one-page document for each manager and include a narrative that discusses, among other things, the manager's style and buy-and-sell discipline. The page also includes a sector breakdown in a colorful pie chart and a list of the top ten holdings within the portfolio. We have found this very useful, particularly when a client wants to buy a hot stock. We can show that individual that he probably owns it already within a professionally managed portfolio.

Occasionally, one of our advisers prepares a "Manager Spotlight," a more in-depth view of one of our approved managers (see **Figure 14.13**). Again, including material on the managers and their styles helps take the focus off a client's portfolio performance.

FIGURE 14.10 Quarterly Newsletter

Moisand Fitzgerald Tamayo – First Quarter 2000 Newsletter
Page 1

INTRODUCTION

Nature can be a powerful and strangely efficient force. Forest fires provide a perfect example. Despite the most advanced technologies, techniques and strategies humans can offer, given the wrong conditions forest fires can rage uncontrolled for days or weeks. But, eventually, the forces of nature inevitably shift and the fire runs its course. The effects can be double edged. While acres may be damaged, the positive underlying effect is that it clears the way for new growth that over time can be a source of renewal and opportunity.

The same is true for the stock market. We've had a forest fire this year. While stock prices and portfolio values were damaged, it created an opportunity to buy good quality companies and benefit from new growth. We believe the current market correction will enable a clearer distinction between market leaders and laggards and may have broken the back of reckless speculation.

MARKET REPORT

What caused the latest correction? We believe there was no single event or news that triggered the sell-off. Instead, it was the culmination of several destabilizing factors ending with the March Consumer Price Index (CPI) report. With the core CPI rate rising 0.4 percent, the largest gain in more than five years, visions of a more aggressive Fed flooded the press. This touched off a wave of selling, which was greatly exaggerated by margin calls, as individual investors and day-traders panicked. It was exacerbated by investor liquidations to pay taxes on tremendous capital gains from 1999.

The following are some highlights and comments about the market this year and what to expect for the remainder.

▲ The NASDAQ closed at a record high 5048 on March 10; Dow Jones Industrial Average closed at a record high 11722 on January 14.
▲ The Standard & Poor's 500 index closed at a record high of 1527 on March 23.
▲ The NASDAQ, DJIA and S&P 500 suffered market corrections of 37 percent, 16 percent and 12 percent, respectively, in the first quarter.
▲ We continue to believe the NASDAQ will again lead the DJIA and the S&P 500 indices this year.
▲ We also believe the Federal Reserve is likely to raise rates again in May. However, we see inflation concerns moderating in the second half of this year.
▲ We continue to remain very optimistic about long-term market prospects. The economic backdrop remains very favorable for the bull market to continue.

ASSET CLASS RETURNS PERIOD ENDED 03/31/00					
Asset Class	**Index**	**1Q00 (%)**	**1 Year (%)**	**3 Year (%)**	**5 Year (%)**
Large Company Stocks	Dow Jones Industrial Average	–5.0	11.6	18.4	21.3
	S&P 500 Index	2.0	16.5	25.6	24.5
	NASDAQ Composite	12.4	85.7	55.8	41.7
Small Company Stocks	Russell 2000 Index	7.1	37.3	17.8	17.2
Foreign Stocks	Morgan Stanley EAFE Equity	–0.1	25.4	16.6	12.7
Domestic Bonds	Lehman Govt/Corp Bond Index	2.7	1.7	6.8	7.1
	INFLATION (CPI)	1.1	3.1	2.1	2.4

Source: Weisenberger

FIGURE 14.10 Quarterly Newsletter (*Continued*)

Moisand Fitzgerald Tamayo—First Quarter 2000 Newsletter
Page 2

ECONOMIC REPORT

The following is a summary of economic data for first quarter 2000 and some perspective on investing this year.

▲ On a seasonally adjusted basis, the Consumer Price Index rose 0.7 percent in March, following an increase of 0.5 percent in February.
▲ Rising energy costs—up 4.9 percent in March—accounted for more than half of the monthly change in the overall CPI for the second consecutive month.
▲ The index for petroleum-based energy increased 9.1 percent, and the index for energy services rose 0.5 percent.
▲ Excluding food and energy, the CPI rose 0.4 percent in March.
▲ We believe rising oil prices are filtering into other consumer prices, but anticipate a moderation of this effect in the second half of this year.
▲ The current economic environment of strong growth with low inflation remains very positive for stocks.

FINANCIAL PLANNING CORNER

An area of planning which has increased in popularity over the past few years is the family limited partnership (FLP). A partnership is generally defined as persons working together for a common economic benefit. A partnership agreement sets out the rights and powers of the general and limited partners. The general partnership interest usually retains all of the management rights of the partnership. Unlike a corporation, a partnership is not an independently taxable entity and the income taxes flow through to the individual partners.

Following are some of the goals that may be accomplished through the use of a family limited partnership:

▲ **Reduction of estate taxes**—The transfer of an interest in a partnership takes partnership assets out of the gross estate of the donor.
▲ **Reduction of gift taxes**—The donor can gift to donees every year, thus reducing the donor's estate by the use of the annual exclusion.
▲ **Maintenance of control**—The donor can remain the general partner, with all management rights over the assets.
▲ **Asset protection**—Limited partners of an FLP have limited liability. General partners' liability can be limited through a corporation as the general partner.
▲ **Creditor protection**—Creditors of a partner cannot force liquidation of the partnership. They can only attach partnership income.
▲ **Family retention of assets**—Stock transfer restrictions and buy-sell agreements can be used to prevent involuntary transfers.
▲ **Flexibility**—The donor can retain control by being a general partner; can change the form of the entity at any time; can choose when to make gifts to the partnership; and can always modify the plan accordingly.
▲ **Probate avoidance**—Assets that are owned by an FLP are not probated.
▲ **Valuation discounts**—Tax discounts may be available to both the retained and transferred interests.

In order to establish an FLP, the following documentation is needed: (1) a partnership agreement; (2) a deed of gift or assignment evidencing the transfer of the assets into the partnership; and (3) a partnership certificate. These issues, as well as issues relating to the tax reduction and asset protection effectiveness of FLPs, are very complex and should only be planned and drafted by qualified professionals. Our firm works with several attorneys who are board certified in estate planning and qualified to prepare such complicated legal documents.

(*continued*)

FIGURE 14.10 Quarterly Newsletter (*Continued*)

Moisand Fitzgerald Tamayo – First Quarter 2000 Newsletter
Page 3

INVESTMENT SPOTLIGHT

Many of you have asked us about JDS Uniphase, a company we have added to some of your portfolios, so we take this opportunity to spotlight the company. JDS Uniphase is the world's leading provider of optical components and modules, supplying the basic building blocks for fiber optic networks. Probably the best way to describe what they do is to use the analogy of highway traffic. If you think of the Internet as a highway (i.e., information highway), you know that as Internet traffic grows, data will move slower unless you expand the number of lanes over which traffic moves. Building completely new traffic lanes (laying new fiber optic cable) is an expensive proposition. JDS Uniphase components expand the number of traffic lanes without building new ones. Telecommunications service providers are transitioning their networks from electrical to optical technologies in an attempt to meet soaring bandwidth requirements. This is prompting robust demand for optical components. In our view, JDS Uniphase is exceptionally well positioned in a fast growing market with formidable barriers to entry. We expect revenue and earnings growth of over 100 percent this year. The company is only constrained by its ability to increase manufacturing capacity fast enough to meet demands. This is a good problem, which we believe their strong management team can solve.

EDITORIAL CORNER *BY RON TAMAYO*

In our last newsletter, Susan Spraker explained the vast difference between a *Growth* stock and a "*Fashionable*" stock. I thought an update was timely given the recent market correction. As a refresher, Susan wrote, "a fashionable stock frequently becomes disconnected from its basic business value." This is very evident of a company she wrote about, Red Hat Software. At its 52-week high, Red Hat Software had a market capitalization of almost $20 billion with annual revenues of less than $43 million. In other words, the stock price disconnected from its basic value. Today the company has a market capitalization of about $4 billion or a decline of over 78 percent this year alone! This sort of reckless speculation and excess is what needed to be wrung out of the market recently. We believe this is very healthy for the market in the long term. In the meantime, we sit tight and hold on to solid companies with strong fundamentals and real earnings.

COMPANY NEWS

We are very pleased to introduce our new team member, Mabel Rasmussen, who joined us April 6, as Client Services Associate. She replaces Linda Harter, who joined her daughter in a new business venture. We wish Linda well. She helped us form our new company and now moves on to help her daughter do the same. Mabel is from Michigan but has been a Floridian since 1979. She is an R.N., and for 14 years was everything from Public Health Nurse on the back streets of Chicago to Nursing Director for both Indian River Memorial Hospital in Vero Beach, and South Seminole Community Hospital in Longwood. Needless to say, Mabel loves to help people, is highly organized, detail oriented, and thrives in positions with lots going on. She certainly found the right place, and we sure feel like we found the right person. Mabel will be calling to introduce herself, but if you have a spare moment and feel inclined, call to say hello. We promise she won't ask any medical questions!

Source: Moisand Fitzgerald Tamayo

Schwab Account Access – Just a reminder you can access essential information about your portfolio on the web at www.schwaballiance.com. If you have any questions about the SchwabAlliance website or if you want to establish online access for your account(s), please call 1-800-515-2157.

CLIENT NAME
POLICY ANALYSIS
DATE

	DESCRIPTION	POLICY ALLOCATION	CURRENT $	CURRENT ALLOCATION
FIXED	MONEY MARKET	3%	$21,782	3%
	U.S. FIXED INCOME	31%	$189,721	26%
	INTERNATIONAL	5%	$37,791	5%
	TOTAL FIXED	**39%**		**34%**
EQUITY	US LARGE CAP	26%	$244,965	33%
	US SMALL CAP	9%	$96,854	13%
	INTERNATIONAL	19%	$107,788	15%
	REAL ESTATE	7%	$40,166	5%
	TOTAL EQUITY	**61%**		**66%**
	TOTAL PORTFOLIO	**100%**	**$739,067**	**100%**

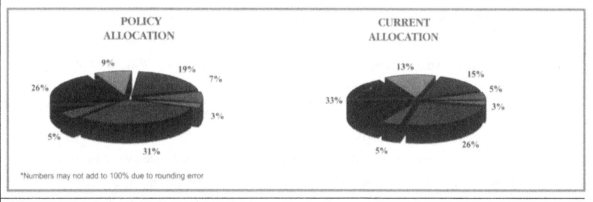

POLICY ALLOCATION: 9%, 19%, 7%, 26%, 3%, 5%, 31%

CURRENT ALLOCATION: 13%, 15%, 5%, 33%, 3%, 5%, 26%

*Numbers may not add to 100% due to rounding error

 FIGURE 14.11 Client Policy Analysis

Rebalancing

We don't believe in micromanaging investments, which is why we are slow to make changes within a portfolio. We do set rebalancing parameters when we create an investment policy, and our clients' portfolios are reviewed on a quarterly cycle. It's during this review that we determine if the portfolio allocation has exceeded its rebalancing parameters. We divide the asset classes into major classes and subclasses, so we are not making minute changes too frequently. **Figure 14.14** is an example of an allocation variance taken from an investment policy statement.

You will note that the portfolio must be overweighted or underweighted by 7 percent in debt to equity and/or by 2 percent, 3 percent, or 5 percent in subclasses

■ | FIGURE 14.13 Manager Spotlight

Manager Spotlight

Accessor Small–Mid Cap Fund   October 2000

Management:	Symphony Asset Management
	San Fransisco, CA
	Praveen Gottipalli, Dir. Of Investments
	David Wang, Portfolio Manager
Asset Class:	Small-Cap Core
Benchmark:	Wilshire 4500
Total Assets:	$375M

Evensky & Katz hired Symphony Asset Management in February 1999 to actively manage a core small cap strategy. This strategy was intended to provide our clients with an exposure to the universe of domestic stocks characterized by the Wilshire 4500 index. This universe is considered the total U.S. investable market minus the S&P 500 Index (Wilshire 5000 – S&P 500 = Wilshire 4500). Previously, all U.S. small company exposure in our clients' portfolios was provided via style specific management, either a growth style or a value style. As markets swing between favored styles, we at E&K felt it important to add a core small-cap component to steady the performance deviations in your portfolio. Symphony's portfolio seeks to add value above the index, but maintains strict alignment with the index's sector and sub-sector weightings to control the portfolio's risk parameters. This is an element monitored closely by E&K and the fund's management company, Seattle-based Accessor Capital.

Accessor Capital also tracks the portfolio's performance relative to the benchmark to determine Symphony's management fee. Symphony is compensated on a performance-fee basis, earning the maximum fee only when exceeding the benchmark (W4500) by 9% over a three-year period. This is a strong incentive for Symphony's management to stay consistent with their philosophy and not engage in speculative

■ | **FIGURE 14.13** Manager Spotlight (*Continued*)

positions that might result in increased risk and/or style drift. As of August 31, 2000 the fund's performance ranks 28 out of 702 peer funds for the trailing sixty months. It is this long-term track record of solid performance, consistent management, and risk controls that led to the fund's approval by the E&K Investment Committee.

Investment Strategy

As explained every quarter in the manager summaries contained in your review, Symphony uses a multifaceted process in developing this segment of your portfolio. Management focuses on superior stock selection to add return rather than making industry or sector bets.

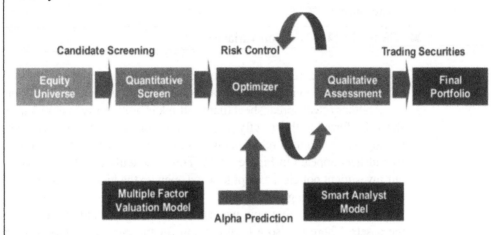

In the fourth quarter of 1999, the portfolio's performance began to deviate from the Wilshire 4500 due to the increasing exposure of the index to IPOs and new issues. The model Symphony employed traditionally screened out these stocks because of their lack of earnings and extraordinary valuations immediately following public offering. Accessor and Symphony began to integrate a second model used specifically to value emerging industries and younger companies that has since brought the portfolio in line with the index.

As we proceed through what will undoubtedly be a turbulent period in the domestic equity markets, we are convinced that your portfolio will benefit from a solid core holding providing a diversified exposure to all industries across the small domestic company market.

Lane M. Jones, CFP

Asset Class	Style	Subclass	Major Class
Fixed Income			+ 7%
Equity			+ 7
U.S Large Cap		+ 5%	
U.S. Large Cap Growth	+ 3%		
U.S. Large Cap Value	+ 3		
U.S. Small Cap		+ 5	
U.S. Small Cap Growth	+ 3		
U.S. Small Cap Value	+ 3		
International		+ 5	
Emerging Market		+ 3	
Real Estate	+ 2		
Alternative	+ 2		

■ | **FIGURE 14.14** Allocation Variance

for us to consider rebalancing. We then factor in the impact of trading costs, including transaction fees, spreads, and taxes, before we initiate any trades.

Another Excel spreadsheet that we think is pretty nifty is our strategy analysis sheet. I referred to this briefly in Chapter 13, but since we also use this form as a trading ticket and as a rebalancing tool, I thought I would mention it again. The spreadsheet appears in Figure 13.21. This is actually the strategy page we put in our investment policies, except now we open up the hidden columns to allow us to use it for rebalancing and trading.

You will notice that now we can view the owners and the ticker symbols for the assets. There is also a total column for the current dollars, and one for the proposed allocation. Off to the right are columns that allow you to break out the assets by ownership. Our current portfolio software is linked to this Excel sheet so that our client's holdings are dropped into the template. Then, we can use this page as a rebalancing page.

Unfortunately, it's all too easy to accidentally rebalance multiple accounts by using the funds in an IRA to fill the need in a personal account. To avoid this error, each account is totaled at the bottom of the page to ensure that you have not mixed dollars from accounts with different ownership. Once we are happy with the results, we simply turn it over to our trading department, which closes up some of the columns and uses it as a trading document.

Recently, we adopted an amazing product called, iRebal (www.irebal.com). It makes the process much easier by automating the intelligence behind the rebalancing procedures. It's pricy, but still worth the dollars if you have a substantial firm.

Transfer and Termination

It's never easy to lose a client. It's not even easy if you are the one who is terminating the relationship. I have found, though, that if you are honest and straightforward, you have no regrets later. I have included some sample termination letters in this chapter that I thought might be useful to you at some point in your career.

Termination Letter

Whenever a client has terminated us, we immediately send a letter to the custodian of his account resigning our discretionary authority over the account. At the same time, we also offer to help facilitate our client's move to a new firm and/or his new adviser to ensure that the transfer runs as smoothly as possible. We are in a small community, and we do not want to leave any relationship on a sour note. I will say that once in a while it's hard to hide the excitement and celebration dance we do when losing a client relationship that we have not enjoyed. This hasn't happened to us very often, but when it does, writing that termination letter is cathartic. Here is an example of a letter we write when the client calls us or, if by chance, the custodian informs us that the client has requested that our name be removed from the account as adviser.

> Dear CLIENT,
>
> It is my understanding that you have terminated your relationship with Evensky & Katz, effective DATE.
> In order to facilitate the preparation of your future income tax returns, I am enclosing realized gain and loss reports for the current year. In addition, I am including unrealized gain and loss reports, which provide the cost basis for your current holdings.
> Please acknowledge your receipt of this letter by signing below and returning it in the enclosed envelope. Upon receiving your signed letter, any prepaid fees, as of the termination date stated above, will be returned.
> In the meantime, if there is anything further we can do to ease your transition, please feel free to contact us. PARTNER, ADVISER, and our staff at Evensky & Katz were pleased to serve as your financial advisers and wish you the best in your future endeavors.
> Cordially,
>
> Financial Planner

Letter Releasing Account to Client

Lou Stanasolovich has a specific letter for a terminating client who does not communicate directly with his adviser, but instead just asks that the account be released to the client exclusively. I have always felt uncomfortable on the rare occasions on which someone has done this. It just affirms that we did not have good communication from the beginning.

> Dear CLIENT:
>
> Custodian informed me that you were transferring your accounts from Custodian, which means you are terminating your contract with Legend. Therefore, I am enclosing an invoice for the unpaid portion of your asset management fee (the fee calculation is enclosed). The fee will be billed from your Custodian Institutional Services account as it has been in the past.
> For your convenience, we have included all cost basis information that originated from your managed accounts.

We would also like to remind you that we will no longer be responsible for providing distributions from your Custodian Institutional Services accounts. You will have to initiate those yourself.

For your convenience, we will keep all your accounts as adviser accounts until (Month Day, Year). They will then be switched over to retail accounts (trading fees are more expensive and we will not receive copies of statements).

We at Legend wish you nothing but the best of luck. Please let us know if there is anything we can do for you in the future.

Cordially,

Financial Planner

Fee Refunds

When a client terminates, there is generally a question of whether rebated fees are due to him. We bill ahead, so this is usually the case, as in this letter that Lou Stanasolovich provides:

Dear CLIENT:

(As you requested), I am enclosing a check for the unearned portion of your asset management fee (the fee calculation is enclosed). (We did not charge you any financial planning fees; therefore, there is not a refund for this service.) (Also enclosed is a check for the unearned portion of your financial planning fee. The fee calculation is enclosed.)

For your convenience, we have included all cost basis information that originated from your managed accounts. We have also enclosed cost basis information as best we have it for those securities which you had purchased outside of Legend.

(We would also like to remind you that we will no longer be responsible for providing distributions from your Custodian Institutional Services accounts. You will have to initiate those yourself. Nor will we be responsible for calculating or initiating IRA distributions from your IRA accounts.) You will also need to contact Vanguard yourselves when you require anything other than the normal check-writing privileges or to make deposits.

For your convenience, we will keep all your accounts as adviser accounts until _____. They will then be switched over to retail accounts (trading fees are more expensive and we will not receive copies of statements).

We at Legend wish you nothing but the best of luck. Please let us know if there is anything we can do for you in the future.

Cordially,

Financial Planner

Unpaid Fees

If you bill in arrears, often when a client terminates, fees will be due to you. Lou prefers to handle this by asking the client for a check, rather than by making a final billing to the account. Here is a sample of how he handles that.

Dear CLIENT:

(As you requested), I am enclosing an invoice for the unpaid portion of your asset management fee (the fee calculation is enclosed). The fee will be billed from your Custodian Institutional Services account as it has been n the past. (Please send us a check for the amount due in the enclosed postage-paid return envelope. We will not bill this amount from your account.)

For your convenience, we have included all cost basis information that originated from your managed accounts. We have also enclosed cost basis information as best we have it for those securities which you had purchased outside of Legend.

(We would also like to remind you that we will no longer be responsible for providing distributions from your Custodian Institutional Services accounts. You will have to initiate those yourself. Nor will we be responsible for calculating or initiating IRA distributions from your IRA accounts.) You will also need to contact Vanguard yourselves when you require anything other than the normal check-writing privileges or to make deposits.

For your convenience, we will keep all your accounts as adviser accounts until _____. They will then be switched over to retail accounts (trading fees are more expensive and we will not receive copies of statements).

We at Legend wish you nothing but the best of luck. Please let us know if there is anything we can do for you in the future.

Cordially,

Financial Planner

One Letter You'd Like to Write

I have been talking about how gracious you should be when a client is terminating. One year, for venting purposes only, I wrote the following letter to a departing client. Of course we never sent it, but it sure made me feel good.

Dear CLIENT:

I was ecstatic to hear that you removed our name as adviser from your account. Since we have been working together, I have been frustrated and grumpy, and have put on ten pounds. In reviewing our client diary, I note that you called twelve times, challenging our use of value funds. Finally, you called Schwab and traded these funds yourself, buying your own stock picks. I was happy to hear that you bought Home Depot at its all-time high. I figure you've lost about $320,000 by now.

Just for the record, I did not enjoy helping your daughter, a selfish, spoiled, and thoroughly unpleasant teenager, invest her bat mitzvah money in your cousin's new Internet IPO. I got a little tired of explaining to her why the price went way, way, down after the initial offering.

As for working with your anal-retentive wife, I can only blame myself for continuing to accept her calls after she wanted us to find the $1.22 error in her money market account, calling us inaccurate and unprofessional. I resisted the temptation to point out that she has overdrawn this same money market account five times in the past year.

My staff and I wish you the success in the market that you so richly deserve.

With great relief,

Financial Planner

Remember, this was strictly a venting letter. I did not send it, and the client never saw it. Sometimes, you just gotta get it out! I think I've gotten better at managing the relationships and client expectations through reviews and other periodic communications with clients. I also think that over the years I have gotten better at recognizing the signals of relationships that aren't going to work.

 ## Managing the Relationship

In years past, many advisers put great emphasis on the almighty review process. I think today we feel that periodic reviews are essential for managing the client's expectations, but they do not have to focus heavily on performance. They're much better used to educate and reinforce other aspects of your relationship with the client.

Finally, I know I've learned an important lesson over the years about relationships with clients. If it isn't working, gracefully let it go, move on, and try not to take it too personally.

*Do less than customers expect and service is seen as bad.
Do exactly what customers expect and service is seen as
good. But do more than customers anticipate and service
is seen to be superior.*
—Paul Dorrian, *Intensive Customer Care*[1]

I wanted to devote an entire chapter to client retention. It is easy to lose sight of its importance while your business is experiencing extraordinary growth. Research suggests that it's five times more expensive to acquire a new customer than to keep an existing client.[2] Corporate America has recognized this and made a buzzword of CRM, or customer relationship management. As John Bermudez, senior director of product strategy at Oracle Corporation, recently noted, "Stronger customer loyalty, increased competitive edge, improved profitability . . . these are the dividends of customer relationship management. The secret, according to *Fortune* magazine, is that we need to touch customers the way they want to be touched."

For our firm, the core of client retention is communication and management of client expectations. The comedian Danny Thomas told a wonderful story about expectations. A guy is driving down an old country road at midnight when his car breaks down. He discovers that his tire has blown out and he reaches in the trunk for a jack so that he can change it. While he's opening the trunk, a hard rain begins. He then discovers there is no jack in the trunk. Standing in the muddy road, drenched and forlorn, he spots a light in a farmhouse in the distance and heads toward it. While walking, he speculates about his encounter with the farmer. "Well, it's pretty late," he mutters. "The farmer will have been asleep. Yet farmers are nice fellows as a general rule, so if I give him five bucks, he probably won't mind loaning me a jack." He walks on, still talking with himself. "Of course, farmers probably go to bed very early; even so, he's had a few hours of sleep anyway, but he probably will be aggravated that I woke him up at midnight. So, what could he want, twenty, thirty bucks?" As he knocks at the door, he realizes it's raining harder and getting colder. "That farmer will probably be very angry. He's got to get up at 3:00 a.m. to milk the cows. It's rainy and cold. He'll probably want a hundred bucks for that jack! A hundred bucks! That's highway robbery!" Just then, the farmer raises a second story window and calls out, "Yeah? What do you want?" The man looks up at the farmer and yells, "Keep your damn jack!"

It is human nature to build a "jack story" when no one is available to put things in proper perspective. Our job as advisers is to help our clients keep their perspective, and in essence, to manage their expectations. We don't want the client to have to come to us when the markets are volatile or down. We contact them first, and we tell them how to assess what's happening.

 ## Behavioral Finance

It's difficult to talk about managing client expectations without discussing behavioral finance. It's important to understand and to apply psychological as well as economic principles to improve financial decision making. Most of us learned in economics classes that humans are rational investors. We developed investing strategies based on classical influences until the mid-1980s, when Amos Tversky and Daniel Kahneman identified behavioral finance principles, which included the heuristics, or mental shortcuts, that investors use to process information. Tversky and Kahneman demonstrated that although investors are not rational, they are predictable. They maintained that the more we understand how investors process information, the better they can make decisions. With this knowledge, we can be more effective advisers.

One of the best-known Tversky and Kahneman studies demonstrates that the average investor is loss averse, not risk averse. A study group was offered two choices, both with the same expected value. The difference was in how the question was framed. Participants were asked to choose A or B in a two-part question as follows:

Part One

A. You win $800.

B. You have an 80 percent chance of winning $1,000.

Part Two

A. You lose $800.

B. You have an 80 percent chance of losing $1,000.

Ninety-five percent of the participants choose A in part one and B in part two. Tversky and Kahneman concluded that people would not take a chance to win more, but were willing to take a chance not to lose. In other words, investors are loss averse, not risk averse. We use a modified version of this question as part of our risk coaching questionnaire (Figure 13.1) to help our clients understand the importance of investing some funds in what they perceive as risky investments so they will not lose their standard of living during retirement.

Although I believe the principles of behavioral finance should be the foundation for managing client expectations, a detailed discussion is clearly outside the scope of this book. However, here are a few features of typical investors that you may want to investigate further:

- Information availability. Making decisions based on recent information rather than taking the time to research and analyze

- Anchoring. "Anchoring" decisions to the last guesstimate, rather than evaluating them independently

- Confirmation bias. Crediting information that confirms the original judgment and ignoring or discounting that which does not

- Contagious enthusiasm. Following the crowd. Buying when an investment story is "hot"

- Mental accounting (adding and subtracting). Placing a higher psychological value on losses than on gains, which results in the reluctance to cut losses

- Mental accounting (multiple accounts). Mentally creating multiple accounts based on the nature of the account, such as IRA and personal, or on how the funds were received, such as through salary or bonus

- Overconfidence. Tendency to believe that one can consistently produce superior returns or hire somebody to produce such returns

- Regret, pride, and shame. Assigning personal characteristics or social commentary to investments. "I won't buy that stock; it's a dog."

- Representativeness. Predicting the future from the past. A stock will be up tomorrow because it was up yesterday.

The Importance of Client Retention

Most advisers get their prospects from client referrals or spheres of influence (accountants, attorneys, or others who advise potential clients). A study by Rydex AdvisorBenchmarking (www.advisorbenchmarking.com) found that 78 percent of new adviser business comes from referrals (see **Figure 15.1**).

This means that we must be doing a very good job of taking care of our current clients, and we need to continue to do so because we rely on referral sources so heavily. I call using your current clients "hothouse" marketing. It's a good method, but generally cannot be your only marketing source. Marketing to referral sources gives you access to much more opportunity. Try putting together a newsletter for professionals, giving them information that will make them look pretty smart to their clients. You will catch their attention. My partner Harold has started a monthly newsletter, written in letter form. Each month he grabs bits and pieces of things he's read that he believes people will find of interest. For example, last month, mixed in with the market views and woes, he added information on where to find a website jam-packed with all those travel-sized articles you can't live without. Another time, he reported that some federal wiretaps were shut down by the phone company for nonpayment. He followed that with a report that the

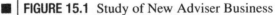
FIGURE 15.1 Study of New Adviser Business

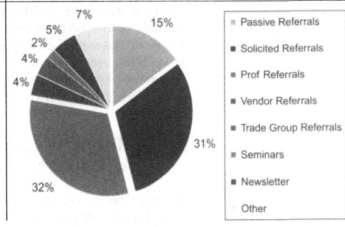

Source: Rydex AdvisorBenchmarking

American Dialect Society voted *subprime* as the word of the year and that the most creative word was *Googlegänger*—that's a person with your name who shows up when you Google yourself. (And who hasn't done that?)

Harold sends his newsletters to influencers—professionals who work with folks who might be our potential clients. He has received tons of responses to his musings, but one classic from an attorney who somehow ended up with one. "Mr. Evensky: I know for a certainty that I have *never* thanked anyone for sending me an unsolicited newsletter, but here goes. . . . Thanks for including me on the list to receive a very interesting, thought provoking, and eclectic publication. I look forward to the opportunity of meeting you and thanking you in person." This guy, Harold tells me, has not only become a client, he has become a great source of referrals as well.

Nurturing

Our concept of client service originated with my observation of my mother's actions in my childhood home in Michigan. The concept grew as I observed occasions of unique service over the years, and coalesced when I visited a top hotel in New York about five years ago.

When I was nine years old, my family had the luxury of a guest bedroom. One evening, my mother announced that she was going to spend the night in that room. We all thought she was a little nuts. The next morning Mom rearranged the furniture, added an extra washcloth in the bathtub area, and brought in a lamp for the bedside table. "Deena," she said, "you can never tell how your guests feel until you spend a night in your own guest room."

Taking Mom's advice, we put a critical eye to our practice from the client's perspective and began to develop a new approach to client service and support. While working on this process, my husband and I spent a weekend in a New York hotel renowned for its fine service. During our stay, I was waiting in the lobby one morning when a woman approached the concierge desk, railing about various things wrong in her room. She continued venting her frustration, yelling about a charge to her account that she didn't think should be there. Before she was finished, she had rattled off half a dozen problems she demanded be rectified immediately. The concierge, rather than referring her to the housekeeper, cashier, and assistant manager, picked up his pen, made notes, and then assured her he would call her by three o'clock in the afternoon to report how things had been handled to her satisfaction. Not once did he indicate these problems were someone else's responsibility. He simply told her he would take care of them and report back to her at a specific time. What emerged from my mother's guestroom idea, coupled with my observations in New York, was our concierge service, and a complete shift in client support.

Taking Responsibility—The Elements of Concierge Service

Our first tenet is "You pick up the phone, you own the problem." That doesn't mean that the staff person is solely responsible for resolving the problem. He is expected to solicit help. It simply means that the client sees seamless service. Our policy is that the original person to take the call will report back to the client. I am sure the woman at the New York hotel did not care which employees made things right for her, just that everything was made right, period. One of the conclusions we reached from "spending the night in our guest room" was the realization that a receptionist without authority or responsibility is merely a barrier to our clients. A traditional receptionist, by the very nature of her job, can *only* pass the client on to someone else. We no longer have a "warm body" receptionist. The person greeting our clients and prospects when they call or enter the office is a full-fledged member of our concierge team. Depending upon the nature of the call and the request from the client, she either handles it herself or finds the person who can.

Phone Etiquette

Our concierge philosophy strengthens the loyalty of both our clients and our employees. We know that people want to be treated in a special way. Our concierge service is a tangible demonstration that we appreciate and want to keep our most valuable asset—our clients. Our special attention starts with phone calls. Think about how important that first phone call is. It sets the tone for your entire office.

One evening I arrived home to find that our television cable service was out. I called the cable service number. A recorded voice told me to press number one if I have no picture, press number two if the picture is distorted, press number three if there is no picture but audio, and so on. I pressed number one. A recorded voice told me to press number one if only one television was out, or number two if all of the televisions were out. I pressed two. Then a recorded voice informed me that no problems with the service had been reported in our neighborhood and to hold for the next available service representative. I'm not sure which was more irritating after that—the elevator music or the intermittent commercial extolling the praises of the cable company. After twenty minutes, no human voice picked up the line. After thirty minutes, I felt like a fool and hung up. These barriers can just give the wrong impression to our clients. We have neither a traditional receptionist, nor an automated answering machine.

Anyone answering the phone in our office will be familiar with all our clients and with the basics of the client's personal circumstances (e.g., spouse's name, recent trips, new grandchildren) or will be able to quickly access this information. Consequently, the person can answer in a less formal and more personal way. As a fail-safe backup, we have voice mail, but only if the caller asks to leave someone a voice mail message.

Uncommon Courtesy

This is going to sound simple, but did you ever notice that some people can smile right through a phone? You can hear instantly that they are in a good mood and are happy to talk with you. I love that, because even if I am having a bad day, it's pretty hard not to respond positively to someone who has been trained to smile through the phone.

A friendly smile does not mean a casual or inappropriately familiar attitude. I am constantly amazed at the number of companies whose receptionists, whom I've never met nor am ever likely to, address me casually as "Deena." It is a rule in our office that no one, especially clients, is called by his first name unless he has invited us to do so. A flip side to this is that our staff always give their full names when asked. There is nothing more unprofessional than telling the caller who asks for a staff member's name, "I'm Candy."

Tell Them How You Feel

Being too formal in our relationships with others can be a barrier, too. When I moved from Chicago to Miami, I needed to find a new doctor. Using recommendations from clients and friends, I visited several doctors' offices. Most of the visits were the same. The offices were attractive, the staff competent, and the doctors professional. The visit with the last doctor proved to be the best, and the one that gave me an insight that I incorporated into the way I run my practice.

Prior to the physical exam, I sat in the doctor's office while he took an extensive health history. After the exam, I sat again with him while he went over his findings. Then he said something very unusual. "I would like to be your doctor. I would value you as a patient, and I believe that together we can keep you healthy." I almost fell out of my chair. No doctor has ever expressed his willingness, let alone eagerness, to have me as a patient. It's a simple thing, but since then, we always tell our prospective clients that we want to be their adviser and that we will value them as clients. They like to hear this, and potential barriers melt right away.

Greetings

When available, our concierge director personally greets prospective clients and introduces them to the assigned adviser. Together, the clients and the adviser meet the partner for the initial interview. We try to have the prospects meet as many of our partners and staff as possible on the first visit. We want to demonstrate our depth of knowledge and expertise, as well as encourage the clients to embrace the team approach.

This seems like good sense to me, but how many times have you sat in some waiting room while people scurried around, not acknowledging your presence? Let's face it, how many people do we have descending on us at one time? Our practices are not based on walk-in traffic. We pretty much know who's supposed to show up and when. It doesn't take much effort for a staff member to greet our visitors, welcome them by name, and make them feel wanted. Our database keeps a list of their beverage preferences, so we can offer them what they like when they visit. Once the initial greeting has taken place, one of the staff sits with them, engaging them in conversation until their meeting begins. Rarely do we leave clients or prospects sitting in the waiting area by themselves.

Be Indispensable

Roy Diliberto of RTD Financial Advisors says the key to retention is becoming indispensable to his clients. Roy maintains that the stronger the relationship, the more clients tend to rely on you for everything. "One of my clients died last year. Of course, I went to the funeral. It was amazing. I had never met my client's kids, but every one of them knew me by name. Obviously, I had been an important part of his life."

Roy tells another story of a client who inherited a huge sum of money. The client decided that, for diversification, he would invest some of it with Sanford Bernstein and the rest with Roy's firm. He called to tell Roy of his decision and to make an appointment to bring in the Bernstein application so Roy could help him complete it.

Cater to Their Egos

Many years ago, I visited Stan Corey of Great Falls Financial Services. Stan's practice at the time was composed of many physician clients. While we were talking, his receptionist interrupted with a call from "Dr. Holloway, an Eagle client." When he got off the phone, I asked Stan what an Eagle client was. "Oh, that," he said. "Doctor's egos arrive three weeks before they do. So I've devised a little program to make them feel special. It's called 'Eagle clients.' I tell them when we start working together that they will be Eagle clients. That means when they call, if I am not on the phone, I will take their call immediately. If I am on the phone, their call will be the next one I return. I tell them that they will receive special treatment, but they must identify themselves as an Eagle client when they call."

"The truth is," he added, "I treat all my clients special. I take their calls right away or I call them back as soon as I am free. It works, though. These doctors all identify themselves as Eagle clients." Stan has redefined his Eagle clients in recent years, based on revenue to the firm. Clients are not informed that they are Eagle clients until they become one. The premise hasn't changed, however. Stan explains, "It is more of a mental benefit for the clients, but it's tangible. They appreciate knowing that you recognize their importance to the business."

Are You Providing a Hotel or a Bed?

One of the major reasons for our company's thrust toward superior, intensive client care is our philosophy regarding portfolio performance. We tell our clients from day one: we don't provide performance; we report it. We do not maximize return; we don't have to, and neither do they. Our clients need portfolio performance sufficient to achieve their objectives. We don't believe in market timing either; our clients are fully invested in the market, good times and bad.

The clients' expectation that you can consistently provide superior performance for them is attributed to the heuristic "overconfidence." In order to challenge this behavioral characteristic, we must emphasize something other than performance. For us, that has been continual support and extraordinary service.

One of my clients is a nationally known consultant to the hospitality industry. He has written textbooks used at the Cornell University Center for Hospitality Research, one of the finest in the world. When I described our concierge idea as a philosophy and a commitment, he immediately fell in love with it and agreed that it was an appropriate model for our profession. When I related my experience with the concierge in New York, he told me that the Ritz-Carlton hotel chain far exceeds what I had witnessed. Not only the concierge is charged with completely seamless service; it is required of every staff member. If, for example, I ask a maid where to find a certain room, she is instructed to stop what she is doing and walk me to the place I'd requested.

My client went on to tell me of an incident at the Hyatt Hotel in Coral Gables, Florida. The Hyatt is a posh hotel, with a beautiful marble and brass lobby. One evening at 10:00 p.m. a man appeared at the check-in desk in his pajamas. He was irate. It seemed he'd just returned from dinner to get ready for bed and found that his bed had not been turned down. "For 290 bucks a night," he argued, "I deserve a turndown." The hotel manager told my client, the consultant, that she has thought about this incident quite often since then. "People walk into this lovely hotel, see this beautiful lobby, and immediately have certain expectations. What we must to do," she added, "is to make reality exceed their expectations." She recognized that the Hyatt is not just in the business of providing a room and a bed; they are providing a *hotel*. This is the essence of our concierge service. In the financial advisory business, providing asset management is merely providing the bed. To be successful, we have to provide far more. Our "hotel" is the planning and peace of mind we provide our clients, through good markets and bad.

Lifestyle Consultant

Paul Brady, in Australia, calls himself a lifestyle consultant. Paul told me there are three pictures on his office wall. One is a map of the world, and two are pictures of Portofino, Italy, his favorite place. On the opposite wall are masks he's collected. "I am in the business of helping people dial up their lifestyle." He always talks with his clients in terms of an annual travel budget for arriving at their financial destination. If they tell him they need a $40,000 income at retirement, he says, "Let's see, that's about a $5,000 travel budget. Is that enough?" All his important discussions revolve around clients' travels. He points to the wall, telling his clients, "I practice what I preach. I love to travel. I've collected my masks from all over the world. When we work together, we'll help you reach your goals. You tell me one of those goals is having the money and flexibility to travel, so when you're out and about, I hope you will keep me in mind when you see an interesting mask." Try to find a metaphor that replaces a client's preconceptions with something useful, illuminating, and distinctly yours.

In our office, we have a lifestyle collage. This is a compilation of pictures of our clients doing the activities they like best. Some are playing golf; some are gardening, carving wooden pens, or horseback riding. If anyone asks to see our "track record," we point to the collage. The collage is an elegant testimony to the fact that our clients accomplish their goals.

Judgmental Overlay

The primary responsibility of our director of concierge services is to heighten the client sensitivity to our practice. She provides the "judgmental overlay" to our other activities. For example, if we are preparing letters, newsletters, or any other communications for our clients, her job is to look at them from the clients' viewpoint. In addition, she has her own small advisory group composed of a number of our long-term clients. The participants, all thoughtful and perceptive, are carefully selected to ensure that they vary in age, status (self-employed, retired, married, or widowed), and interests. We explain to them that we are asking for their honest feedback. Our single goal is to continuously improve our service. We look to this advisory group to help us exceed expectations. They quite often beta test changes in our forms or documents. They offer substantive input, and we listen. This is critical, as our concierge service is a major element of our client retention strategy.

Levels of Client Service

In nice American Hotels, if you pay for a concierge-level room, you receive a key that will take you to a special floor. Extra amenities such as thick terry cloth robes and French milled soaps are placed in your room. A hospitality suite is open for continental breakfasts and afternoon cocktail hours. If you don't pay for the concierge level, you still have a very nice room and basic services. Although we provide all our clients with a basic level of concierge service, not all our clients provide the same revenue to the firm. Therefore, in 1990, when we decided to analyze the demographics of our clients, we devised a system of levels of client service, based upon revenues.

Analyzing the Client Base

It became clear after reviewing our client list that we'd grown like Topsy, with no rhyme or reason. We had, more or less, a microcosm of society, and we were delivering services developed more out of client request than our own philosophy and capabilities. To analyze our client base, I divided the clients into ages, assets under management, needs of services, and types (e.g., widows, divorced, couples). I discovered that most of our clients were over age fifty and came to us in preparation for retirement. A significant portion had sold a business, retired with a substantial pension, inherited, or in some other way experienced a windfall that they felt was too overwhelming to manage. I then looked at the quality of our relationships with every client. Some were entirely rewarding. I looked forward to talking with Mrs. Nathan. I found Mr. Zachery's questions challenging. I noted how often staff came in to my office to vent about how rude Mrs. Logan was. I tracked my own behavior as well. Why did I feel like ducking calls when any of the Tylers called? Eleanor Blayney said she went through much the same activity. When she discovered that she picked up her phone calls and voice mails from a particular client with dread, she recognized that it was time to reevaluate the relationship.

The next thing I realized was that as we had increased our minimums over the years, our newer clients had less and less in common with our early clients. The newer ones were more concerned with estate preservation and multigenerational issues than with strategies to make their money last a lifetime. My partner Harold commented that these newer clients could reach their goals by stuffing cash in a mattress, or for diversification, three mattresses. We needed to make a decision about how we wanted to be serving our clients' needs into the future, and then envision what types of clients they would be. We also needed to know what types of relationships were profitable, rewarding, or both.

Judy Shine caters to mostly small business owners and corporate executives as clients. "One day I recognized a common personality trait in these clients. They were highly intelligent, used to being in control, and wanted to be involved but did not want to manage their investments. I began to see myself as a facilitator. They would come to me with some ideas, ask me to research them, and give them my professional opinion on them." Judy has developed a way to keep these control people interested and involved in their portfolios by buying some individual lots of blue chip stock for them. "These are corporate people, they hear things, they get information, and they love to talk about stocks." Judy's philosophy is, "I always want to control the part of the portfolio that interests my clients. If stock excites them, I don't want them to take that excitement to a broker."

One of the best exercises you can do is to segment your client base. Nearly every adviser I talk with tells me he has segmented his client base—A, B, and C clients, usually. Most admit, however, that outside of identifying the segments, they have done little to prioritize the service around the client mix. One of the biggest obstacles to this strategy is that all clients are used to getting all services; that's pretty hard to change. On the other hand, carefully crafted, you can bring new clients into the mix with your new strategy, and slowly tease the rest away from the usual service mix.

In the early years when we were charging solely on assets under management, it made some sense to segment our clients by their assets. Prior to changing our segmenting from assets to income to the firm, our scale looked like this:

Diamond	$15,000,000 and above
Platinum	$10,000,000–$25,000,000
Gold	$1,000,000–$10,000,000
Silver	$750,000–$1,000,000
Copper	Under $750,000

Now, the problem with this method is that although you have information about how big your client's assets are, you have no information about how much money that client is worth to you in income. This method was wonderful for helping to determine how to reward or provide extra service, but it didn't give you much information about the revenue to the firm or the value of the client on a purely monetary basis.

We then devised our new segmentation focusing on the revenue:

Sovereign	Greater than $25,000 annual revenue
Imperial	$15,000–$25,000
Monarch	$10,000–$15,000
Regal	$4,000–$10,000
Charter	Under $4,000

Now, let's assume that you have $300 million under management and two hundred clients. Your annual minimum fee is $10,000. (If you are charging an asset fee, this is 1 percent of a $1 million dollar client.) The breakdown by segment of these clients is as follows:

		Rev %	
Sovereign	9	4.5%	
Imperial	38	19%	
Monarch	24	12%	
			35.5%
Regal	81	40.5%	
Charter	48	24%	
			64.5%
	200	100%	100%

You're probably familiar with the well-known concept of the Pareto principle. This concept was adopted from an observation in Venice in 1906 that only about 20 percent of the residents of Venice owned 80 percent of the wealth. The principle was named for the Italian economist Vilfredo Pareto who made the observation but adapted by management thinker Joseph M. Juran.

If you ascribe to the Pareto rule, you are admitting that you are willing to accept that 80 percent of your client base will not fall into your sweet spot, or to put it another way, 80 percent are people you would not accept as clients today. Seems self-defeating to growth strategies, doesn't it?

If your minimum annual fee is $10,000, almost 65 percent of your revenue comes from clients who do not currently meet your minimum. Many may be clients you have had for a long time, and you are reluctant to make any changes in your relationships with them. You might consider some cost-saving changes such as assigning a junior adviser as their primary adviser, or adjusting the services they receive, such as meeting only twice a year or receiving reports less frequently. Or, you might consider raising their fees. Whatever you decide, you will need to be prepared for those clients to decline your changes and look elsewhere for assistance.

We have been using this simple "Pareto report" for years (see **Figure 15.2**). Let's see what happens to our client mix over the following three years as we focus on our target market.

■ | FIGURE 15.2 Pareto Report

Year 2: Client Mix

		Rev %	
Sovereign	**15%**		
Imperial	**18%**		
Monarch	**23%**	*83.0%*	**117 Clients**
Regal	**30%**		
Charter	**14%**	*17.0%*	**92 Clients**
	100%	**100.0%**	

Sovereign is > $25,000 fees

Imperial is $15,000 to 25,000

Monarch is $10,000 to 15,000

Regal is $4,000 to $10,000

Charter is under $4,000

AFTER 3 Years: Client Mix

		Rev %	
Sovereign	**17%**		
Imperial	**17%**		
Monarch	**25%**	*85.5%*	**133 Clients**
Regal	**27%**		
Charter	**13%**	*14.5%*	**91 Clients**
	100%	**100.0%**	

Sovereign is > $25,000 fees

Imperial is $15,000 to 25,000

Monarch is $10,000 to 15,000

Regal is $4,000 to $10,000

Charter is under $4,000

Now let's look further at the information you should gather about your client bases. Mark Tibergien, formerly of Moss Adams, recommends that you look at your clients as a ratio in terms of staff productivity and client productivity. Since Moss Adams prepared the study for 2002, and we assume it will continue to provide this information as long as it is useful, you will be able to benchmark your practice against other best practices.

Still using the same scenario, $300 million under management, two hundred clients, and $2 million in revenue, we now add the number of staff we have to service those clients. Let's assume you have ten staff members. Four are professional; the rest are administrative or operational. Then the ratio analysis looks like this:

RATIO ANALYSIS:

	December	2002
Month:		
Year:	2003	FPA Study
Staff Productivity		
# of Clients per Staff	20	35
# of Clients per Professional Staff	50	53
AUM per Staff	$30,000,000	$29,230,113
AUM per Professional Staff	$75,000,000	$47,223,818
Revenue per Staff	$200,000	$224,718
Revenue per Professional Staff	$500,000	$344,820
Operating Profit per Staff	0	0
Operating Profit per Professional Staff	0	0
Client Productivity		
AUM per Client	$2,000,000	$909,262
Revenue per Client	$10,000	$6,060
Operating Profit per Client	0	0
Operating Profit per Active Client	0	0

 Retention Budget

Just as for any other initiative you have in your business, there are costs involved. For retention, it's expressed in time and dollars. The dollars are the easy part. In Chapter 12, we discussed what it costs to bring on new clients and to service them on an annual basis. The hard part is determining where you will spend time on retaining your relationships. To determine how you will budget your retention activities, divide them into four parts:

1. Ear time: phone
2. Eye time: newsletter, letters, flash reports, reviews

3. Face time: reviews, updates, special events

4. Screen time: website visits

Now decide how you will spend your retention budget in keeping your clients happy, comfortable, and loyal. You may want to devise a task sequence for each of your clients that determines how much of your time and staff time you will allocate.

Remember, a retention-focused practice has a different emphasis than an acquisition-focused one. In acquisition, the goal is to gather quality prospects and convert them into clients. In retention, the goal is to keep the client base constantly aware of the adviser's value and additional service and/or product offerings.

In 1995, I recognized that our practice was growing at an even faster pace than it had in the prior five years. We were hiring more staff, working harder, and making less. I felt we needed direction if we were ever to be profitable. I decided it was time to reanalyze our client base. First, I determined the reasonable number of clients that each of the three partners could handle with existing staff and facilities. At the time, we averaged forty clients each, or a total of 120. Our average client size was approximately $300,000. That was also our minimum account at the time. I estimated that we could comfortably add another twenty clients per partner without adding staff or facilities. If I added sixty clients at our minimum size, each would generate $3,000 in new fees. Our additional income would be $180,000.

I thought about this and realized that if we left our minimums at $300,000, at the rate we were acquiring new clients, we would very soon reach capacity. I recognized that the only commodity we have that cannot expand is our time, so if we wished to grow, we needed clients with more assets. I also recognized that if we raised our minimum to $500,000, it might take a little longer to reach capacity but the profit would be larger because we would have significantly greater revenues without having to add new staff. So I raised the minimums to $500,000. As I mentioned before, this was not a slam-dunk choice. Our voices cracked the first few times we turned away $300,000 clients. We had continually to remind ourselves that at the higher minimum we could be increasing our annual revenue stream by an additional $300,000, not $180,000. Once we increased the minimums, an amazing thing happened. The pace of new clients increased! It seemed that the higher the minimum, the more professional we looked to prospects. Subsequently we've revisited and modified our minimums many times. Our current minimum is $2 million. Of course, we have clients in all ranges, which we regularly review in terms of the cost in partner time. Our challenge is how to deliver the extraordinary service our new larger clients expect, while continuing to work with smaller clients who have helped us grow.

Eileen Sharkey, of Sharkey, Howes & Javer, points out the dilemma presented by a desire to adequately serve small clients while maintaining, as she does, that nearly every client relationship should be profitable. "If not all your clients are profitable, let's just call it therapy and forget it." She also echoes the results of the Bain study[3] and notes that it costs more to develop a new client relationship than it does to maintain an old one. Our commitment was to provide good basic services to all clients. However, we admitted that all clients did not necessarily want to receive the same services. As with our other efforts at triage, we determined appropriate levels of service by categorizing our client base by fees to the firm, as we discussed above.

We then elaborated the types of service that would be provided for each category. Through the years, we have refined that list and the services many times, and we understand it to be a starting point, not a straitjacket. The types of service and the way we deliver that service are unique to each client. One of our platinum clients told me that she thought it was odd that we sent her a birthday card. "Birthday cards to me are very personal. Only my closest friends and family send them." Our concierge told me that we will stop sending cards until she considers us close friends.

 ## Add Services Sparingly

Before you initiate a new service—any new service, including adding new reports and reviews—determine whether you will be able to sustain this activity. You might consider the following questions:

- How complicated is it to deliver?
- Is it best delivered by outsourcing?
- Do you have the capacity to handle this activity?
- Is it expensive to produce or deliver?
- Will there eventually be some economies of scale?
- Will it add value to your relationships?

 ## Customized Gifts

Clients of ours who are Monarch Level and above receive customized birthday cards, holiday cards, gifts, and an anniversary card commemorating their years with us. In the past we have sent gifts for special events, such as the birth of a grandchild, as well as specialty items at holidays. All our cards are created with our Hallmark Card Studio software or American Greetings CreateaCard software and printed on our color printers. That way, we can customize them with names and events and even pictures. If we need to be a bit more formal, the cards are handwritten on our company card stock.

Many of our clients were becoming grandparents. To acknowledge this event, we did the obvious. We did the obvious very well. We'd send a lovely silver rattle to the new grandchild. One day our client service adviser challenged this tradition. "What message are we giving our client by sending a gift to the grandchild? Many times we don't even know the child's parents. Alternatively, if we sent a grandparent's package with a picture frame and a journal for our client to chronicle his or her life for the family, we are sharing the event with our client. And the gift is for him or her, to share with the newcomer." This one idea has brought us wonderful responses from our clients. One grandmother client told me, "This birth brings us mixed feelings. Our daughter now has a daughter.

So it was so nice to get little gifts just for us to share with our grandchild. It makes us feel special, too."

When we take an extended trip, we take some address labels for all the gold, platinum, and diamond clients. It usually takes us two or three days to personally hand write a short note to everyone, affix a stamp, and mail them back home, but the clients love them. They also love that we thought of them while we were on the road.

It's important to note that although the quantity of our services may vary by account size, the quality of our financial planning and investment advice is consistent and uniform throughout. All clients are invited to contact us with questions or issues, and we are prepared to provide any additional planning or counsel as part of their retainer fee. Our staff provides *concierge level* service and are prepared to do what it takes to satisfy the client, regardless of asset size. If at any time, we think a client is abusing our time, we talk with them about it. Rarely do we find it necessary to charge additional fees to reflect the extra time we are spending.

Each year my partners and I, along with our advisory staff, write down a description of our "perfect client" in personality, temperament, net worth, and complexity of issues. We then compare our client base to our descriptions and attempt to weed-out those relationships that are personally and emotionally unrewarding. (See Chapter 12 for more on this.)

 ## Peppering the Client

Overlaying our basic concierge services we also add a bit of extra spice. We use every opportunity to "pepper" clients with articles, notes, or other items of interest. Using our Internet resources, we have many articles on hand to pique their interests. Because we have some high-profile clients, our concierge scans the papers daily, looking for articles with client names in them. She sends these along with little notes of congratulations.

 ## Managing Client Expectations with Communications

Communications are essential to maintaining the best relationship with our clients. We use them to reinforce our philosophy and manage our clients' expectations. Our communications strategy has changed drastically over the years. What's interesting is that while originally our communications appeared highly structured to clients, now they are highly structured for us, but appear to be more fluid, comfortable, and natural for our clients.

"Crisis" Conversations

Richard Busillo of RTD Financial Advisors in Philadelphia maintains that it is vitally important to control your clients' expectations from the beginning of the relationship, and especially when people panic during market volatility. "One of my clients is a high-powered attorney, used to getting his own way." After significant planning, Rich determined that the client had a long-term time horizon. The investment policy called for the client to invest $700,000 in the domestic market in February 1994. In March, the portfolio was down more than 10 percent, and the client called. Coincidentally, Philadelphia was having a major winter storm, with a foot of snow on the ground and more coming. The client, clearly agitated, yelled, "I just got my statement. Just what are you advising your clients, considering what's going on out there?" "Well," said Rich, "I'm telling them, when you shovel, just make sure you use your legs and not your back." The client laughed, and Rich notes that this client has not been overwrought about short-term volatility since.

Right after the 500-point drop on October 19, 1987, my partner Harold called all his clients. "It's not the end of the world," he explained. "AT&T must still be in business because we're on the phone. People are still taking pictures at Disney World, so Disney and Kodak are still around. That's what you own: AT&T, Disney, Kodak."

"Five years," he told them. "Remember, you have at least a five-year time horizon."

Reviews to Manage Client Expectations

Almost everyone in our industry prepares quarterly performance reviews. In the past few years, we have all struggled with what information to include in these reviews. Many advisers I interviewed expressed concern about finding the right balance between customization and standardization. I briefly discussed our reports and standardized review appointments in Chapter 14. Be sure that your reviews are organized in a way to de-emphasize short-term performance and focus more on long-term success.

Flash Reports

At the beginning of our relationship with clients, we ask how they would like to receive intermittent information from us. We offer them e-mail, fax, and snail mail. Periodically, when we want to explain the economic climate, transmit interesting material from a portfolio manager, or just stay in touch, we issue a "Flash Report." If we have information that we think will need some discussion, we always supplement the flash with a phone call. We have a special form for this communication so the client will know that it is something important enough to read. We only send these a few times a year.

Newsletters

Norm Boone of Mosaic Financial Partners spends significant time designing and writing his own newsletter. Most of the advisers I know write their own. "My newsletter is a reflection of me, my company, and our philosophy. It is our opportunity to show our personality and reinforce ideas," said Norm. "I have a section in each newsletter that talks about my family. I get more reaction to that than nearly anything else."

You can create and reinforce your image through your newsletter. Powers & Phillips, a law firm specializing in securities law, consists of three partners: a husband and wife team and one other woman partner. They position themselves as "two bitches from hell and a short fat guy." Their newsletter, *The Bitches from Hell Reporter*, has a unique format, with columns like "Dear Flabby," advice for men working with professional women; and "The Dragon Lady Speaks," stories about the firm's clients. They believe that lawyers are viewed as stuffy and intimidating, so they've elected to use their newsletter to inject humor and single themselves out in a professional world where everyone seems the same. They report that this has not tarnished their image, but it does attract a great deal of attention. They now send over four thousand copies of their newsletter to people all over the country.

To add interest and depth, we have asked some of our clients to contribute articles for our newsletter. They enjoy it. In fact, our clients have written some of our best newsletters. Retired clients have useful perspectives to share with others contemplating retirement. Our clients have written articles on Elderhostel, local adult education programs, the value of personal medical checkups, and the emotional aspects of retiring. No one can tell it better than someone with experience. Our clients tell us they love writing for us and reading first-hand accounts.

If you don't feel comfortable writing your own newsletter, contact a local college or university and outsource it to a student. You don't have to produce newsletters monthly, or even regularly. Our first newsletter included the words "Published Intermittently" in the masthead. In any case, most advisers believe it is better to have no newsletter than use a service where you just slap your name and/or picture on the top.

Client Advisory Boards

Roy Diliberto developed his client advisory board a few years ago. His board is very structured, with clients serving three-year staggered terms. Roy says the development of the board was a practical decision. He and his partners would argue about what services and reports to provide to the clients. Now, "we just ask them what they want." The board has vetted every report, correcting grammar and making it user-friendly.

One year Roy asked his board, "Why did you hire us?" He continued, "We had the most revealing responses. 'Trust, integrity, clarity, understanding, continuity, and reasonable rates of return.' Notice, they didn't say, performance, performance, or performance." Roy admits his board is handpicked, but he says he and his partners try to choose an adequate mix by age, sex, and asset size. "Advisory boards are wonderful," Roy adds. "Clients buy the dream; now they can claim ownership of it, too." Karen Spero had an advisory board for years. She recommended treating the board professionally and compensating them for their participation.

Client Surveys

A few years ago we developed a survey and sent it to clients. We received two criticisms. One client remarked that he did not like the Schwab statements, and he gets too much paper when we trade. That was it. Everyone else thought we were wonderful and did everything to perfection. I learned a valuable lesson. Our own surveys are much less useful because clients who have issues will not usually want to tell you directly what their problem is. However, we did learn a few things in our subsequent surveys that were quite useful. We asked questions about value and what it means to our clients individually. Some of our answers, although surprising, did help us understand our "value gap" in service. When we asked, "What would you tell a prospect about our experience together?" we heard:

- Genius investment guru
- Helped me retire to Maine
- Don't have to look for a parking place when visiting you
- I sleep well at night
- My wife stopped nagging me about my bad investment choices
- Would not recommend: you might get too big and not have any time for me.

Of all the answers, the most perplexing was the "valet parking." When we asked ourselves what we believe clients value in our relationship together, I guarantee, "valet parking" never occurred to us. The most interesting response was from the client who was worried that we would outgrow him. We are very careful now to periodically tell our clients that we intend to grow at an intentional, reasonable pace.

Now, as a matter of course, we periodically survey our clients to see where we can improve, but we always use a third party. I believe that client surveys are essential in the growth plans for your practice. Today we use a third-party provider to accomplish that. I highly recommend, Advisor Impact, a New York company owned by Julie Littlechild (www.advisorimpact.com). Advisor Impact helps you design your unique survey to get the best responses. They administer the survey and compile the data, but, most important, they interpret the data, telling you ways that you can improve relationships and servicing to manage client expectations and improve your bottom line.

 ## Just *What* Are You Saying?

A few years ago, the Hershey Company had a great ad, titled, "Change is Bad," picturing a paper coffee cup with the following notice printed on its side:

Warning. Please take notice that by accepting the hot beverage in this container, the recipient of the aforementioned beverage agrees to waive any liability that might arise, including, but not limited to, any burning, scalding, marring or any other physical and/or mental damage to the aforementioned recipient. Enjoy.

I agree with Hershey's. Whom are these container people kidding? It's a good lesson for us. I know that the financial advisory business is highly regulated. I know that we must have certain documents in place to protect our clients and ourselves. But, I don't believe that these documents need to be mired down in legalese. They must be straightforward and easy to understand. Any document that creates a barrier between our clients and us or that can serve as the basis for misunderstanding is detrimental to our relationship with them. Take a good long look at your engagement letters, contracts, and initial communication with your clients. Spend the night in your guest room. Just what message are you communicating to them? I wouldn't even attempt to suggest how you should have your legal documents written. However, I firmly believe that you can ensure that your contracts protect you without being formal and unfriendly.

Train Your Clients: Don't Let Them Train You

The concierge at the Beverly Wilshire in the movie *Pretty Woman* does everything from arranging for a young prostitute to buy a dress, to teaching her which utensils to use for dinner. Although we do not have a formal concierge, our planner advisers are the resident problem solvers. They generally hear from the client first and are obligated to see the issue through until it is resolved. They function as part of a well-oiled team, so they know where to go to get solutions.

Despite this high level of service and interaction, we never confuse providing exceptional service with agreeing to provide some information or design reports that we don't believe are appropriate or in the client's best interest. We've been asked, for example, to include numerous benchmarks on our performance reports. We will not. We have been asked to calculate estimated tax payments, complete real estate appraisals, and hire maids. We do not have expertise in those areas, and we won't do it. We will help clients find the appropriate person, however.

A few months ago I hired a new landscaper. While we were looking around the property, I pointed out that the sprinkler system wasn't working very well and the lights around the plants needed replacing. I asked him if he did that. He replied, "Ma'am, I want this job. If that's what it requires to get it, I'll do it." I then asked him if he knew any good outdoor lighting and sprinkler people. He quickly rattled off a few names of people he'd worked with before. "If you don't normally provide this service and you know good people who do it, why did you offer to do it anyway?" I asked. "Some people like one-stop shopping. I try to be accommodating because I want the work," he replied. "It usually doesn't work though," he went on. "I'm a great landscaper but only fair at sprinklers and lights." I hired him. The lawn looks great, and whenever there is a problem with lights or sprinklers, I pay him to find the right people to fix them.

Our Biggest Challenge

You'll think it's odd, but the biggest impediment to growth is not lack of new clients, it's poor client retention. It is immeasurably more time consuming and costly to find the next client than it is to take good care of the current ones. Increased competition and volatile markets can only be managed with proactive, consistent initiatives.

If you give a mouse a cookie, he's going to ask for a glass of milk.

—Laura Joffe Numeroff, children's book author

Sometimes we either don't see or don't want to see the obvious, that our client base includes inappropriate clients. This failure may drag down a practice's ability to grow. It is wise to evaluate your client base on four things:

1. Profitability
2. Relationship
3. Both
4. Neither

If you have profitable clients, that's great. If they happen to be people that you really like working with, that's fantastic! On the other hand, if you have a corral filled with clients, reevaluate them on the basis of relationship. We all have clients we love and adore, who bring us a great deal of personal satisfaction, even though they are not the most profitable ones. But, if you have relationships with people who are neither profitable, nor personally satisfying, think about "freeing up their future." This chapter is all about how to do it.

One day David Bugen, of RegentAtlantic Capital in Chatham, New Jersey, was having a particularly rough day. His most difficult client arrived unannounced to bark about recent market performance. David had always been patient with the guy, who seemed to go ballistic without warning and rarely for any good reason. At the start of their relationship he threw a fit because a transfer of funds was delayed by the sending institution. He'd miss appointments, but show up days later expecting to be seen. At the end of this altercation, David wandered into his partner's office, visibly shaken. "Just what am I going to do with this guy?" His partner said, "David, you train people by your behavior. You have trained this guy to treat you miserably. Treating him like a child will elicit childlike behavior. He just had another tantrum."

A friend once told me that a wise investor repurchases his portfolio every day. The same could be said for your client base. Why would you want to throw time, resources, and money at a relationship that clearly is not working? At some point in our professional lives, we find it necessary to fire a client. From talking with others in practice, it's safe for me to say that most of us put up with a great deal more than we should before hollering "uncle." We usually have had enough long before we actually find the words and recognize the moment to end it.

I asked thirty top advisers what, in their minds, would necessitate firing a client. Every adviser told me they would instantly sever a relationship with someone who was disrespectful to staff. That's an easy one. We all agreed that we have taken clients over the years that we absolutely shouldn't have. Jerry Neill, a planner in Kansas City, suggests that he would consider firing a client "if I can't educate him, I find I don't like working with him, or he's a lawsuit waiting to happen. Many times you don't see this going into the relationship, but as time goes by, you need to do something about it." Of course, most of us would not have had the courage to do this early in our practices. As Paul Brady from Sydney, Australia says, "The ability to fire a client is one of the benefits of a mature business."

The ability to fire does allow you great freedom. You know that you can terminate a relationship if it's not working, or you can attempt to salvage it. Sometimes it's hard to tell which path you should be taking. Here are some early warning signs for troubled relationships:

- You get a sinking feeling each time that client calls.

- Each time he is up for review, you hope he won't want an appointment.

- There is an increase in the frequency of the times your staff appears in your office to tell you about yet another unpleasant call with Mr. Client.

- Each time you meet with him you find yourself going over the same issues.

- After a meeting with him, you'd like to put your hand or his head through a wall.

Eleanor Blayney explains that she and her partners assign a "hassle factor" to their clients. How difficult or unpleasant is this person? How many times does the client call with the same questions? The higher the factor, the more likely the fees for additional services are charged, or the client is released. Eleanor explains that she does not want to work with any client who seems to be using money in a destructive, greedy, or fraudulent way. She feels that she and her clients must share the same basic values in order for the work to be productive.

There are several issues to consider before you actually decide to release a client:

- Do you really want to work with the person? Eleanor says her gut "is never wrong." If she is not feeling good about this relationship, it has to go.

- Does your client have unrealistic expectations that can be handled over time, but over the long haul will consume more effort than they repay?

- Does having this relationship prevent you from spending more time with other clients? "There's only so much time," says Paul Brady. "I can spend it trying to make this one guy comfortable, or I can spend it providing ongoing services to several clients who are already comfortable."

- Can you or do you want to diffuse this situation with humor? In 1997 Richard Busillo of RTD Financial Advisors received a call from a client unhappy with his mediocre returns from a well-diversified portfolio at a time when the domestic stock market was reaching new highs. "I could've put my money in a shoebox and done better," he barked at Rich. That afternoon, Rich visited the client's office, shoebox under his arm. "What'll it be?" he asked his client. The client broke into a hearty laugh, and Rich talked with him about his short-term time horizon.

- Has the relationship broken down? Sometimes relationships that appear to be good at the beginning deteriorate. Ross Levin considers severing the relationship if the client is not forthcoming about information or if there is a "value disconnect," when Ross and the client do not continue to share the same priorities and outlook.

- If communication has broken down, is this a control issue or an economic one? Dave Diesslin maintains that conflicts with clients generally stem from one or the other. It's helpful for you to be clear in your mind on how and why the relationship is broken. Mark Ralphs explains that he will never quibble over a fee. If his price tag becomes an issue, he gives the fee back to the client and refuses the engagement.

Ross Levin mentioned that not long ago, he and his partner decided to end a relationship with two of their biggest and most difficult clients. "Anticipating the break was terrible, but it's very liberating once you've done it. The hard part is convincing yourself that you will be able to replace those clients with other, more rewarding relationships." Ross did, we did, and you can too.

But, What Do You Say?

Let's assume that you've gone through the checklists and determined that you need to release a client. What do you say? The late David Norton of Norton Partners, in Clevedon, Great Britain, said he took his cue from the health care industry. When a family member was too much of a problem to keep in the long-term care facility, the administrator called in the family and told them, "We simply cannot meet Mr. Baker's needs any longer." That's just what David said to clients who couldn't seem to get comfortable with the relationship.

In our office, we keep copious notes on all conversations with clients. When a relationship has broken down, we can usually tell by the number of times we've referred to the notes. Once a year we review those notes with staff and decide which client we are going to set free. Staff is very much a part of this decision because they are usually the ones who have been abused more than the partners.

We are honest and straightforward. We just tell them that the relationship is not working and we don't think we can help any longer. We usually follow that statement with some examples from our notes. As much as possible, we prefer to do this in person, rather than on the phone. We then recommend that the client seek advice elsewhere and offer a list of advisers who may be more suitable.

For clients who just can't seem to get comfortable taking any advice, we review these situations and point out that it is unnecessary for them to be paying for advice when they only want to follow their own. To them, we suggest they seek a discount brokerage arrangement.

David Diesslin looks at all his client relationships once a year in terms of the economics and pleasure, rating each aspect positively or negatively. If both are negative, David "graduates" them. "The key is to make them feel good about graduating, not upset about being fired." David feels that most advisers stay with their relationships longer than they should. "It's like a bad marriage; we're more afraid of the unknown, so we do nothing until it gets so bad that we can't ignore it any longer." Dave maintains that two percent of the client base is responsible for 98 percent of the headaches.

Here are some good suggestions from experienced practitioners for severing that two percent:

- Mark Ralphs, Financial Planning Corporation, in the United Kingdom, also graduates his clients. "You don't really need me anymore; you can handle this yourself." Be firm, though—sometimes they need a little push from the nest.

- Ron Tamayo, Moisand Fitzgerald Tamayo, LLC in Maitland, Florida, has used "There is just not a chemistry for this relationship to work."

- Roy Diliberto describes the communication that is failing between himself and the client. He then explains, "I really don't think I can provide value for the fees you are paying."

- Eleanor Blayney says she prefers to position it in such a way that it appears the client is releasing her firm. "We are unable to do what you want," she says.

- In some cases, Jerry Neill explains that he is "slowing down," looking toward semi-retirement, and offers to let them work with another person in the firm or move on.

- David Norton suggested you "engineer it so they will fire you. That way, you can at least try to keep good relationships, even if you are not working together any longer. I certainly don't refer them to anyone else, particularly if they are a problem. Who wants to wish that on anybody?"

 ## What If They Fire You?

So far this chapter has dealt with your decision to part with a client. What if they want to dump you? A couple of years ago, Ross Levin of Accredited Investors in Minneapolis called to talk. "I just lost a client and I feel terrible about it. I looked back over the three years this guy has been a client. I feel I did everything right. When he left, he told me he wanted to do it himself, but I keep thinking, 'What did I do wrong?'" We all lose clients, and it is not unusual to look to yourself when a relationship is broken. It's helpful to take Dave Diesslin's suggestion and ask yourself, "Is it economic, or is it control?"

Ross has spent some time trying to think this though. When you lose a client you want to keep, there are two alternatives, in hindsight: you either had control over the relationship, or you didn't. "The one you agonize about is the one you had control over, but just blew it." Ross admits that systematizing your practice can help you keep clients. He also points out that no matter how hard you try, there will once in a while be that "black cloud" client. "Every mistake possible happens with that guy. There's just not much you can do about it."

"Losing a client may be evidence that you are doing a good job with your business," offers Eleanor Blayney. It means that you have defined your business well and some people just won't fit. If you don't lose a client, you lose yourself." Eleanor also suggests that for some clients there may be a point at which you have done everything you can do for them. An ongoing relationship is just not practical for either of you. Often times, we just don't want to admit it.

Harry Beckwith, in his remarkable little book *Selling the Invisible*,[1] says that when service fails, everyone takes it personally. "So rarely we take product failures personally. The services we use, by contrast, usually are provided by people we have met or at least spoken with. When that person fails to do what she promised, we often take it personally. We ask, 'How could she do this to me?'"

As I've spoken to many senior advisers that I admire around the country, it was very comforting to hear them admit to losing clients that they really wanted to keep. How enlightening! Even the best advisers can lose clients! Because this business is highly personal, it is very difficult to ignore the hurt when a client with whom you have enjoyed a good relationship summarily dismisses you. I used to try to talk clients out of this decision. In fact, I vividly remember speaking with the daughter of one of my clients who had called to tell me that her mother was moving her account to another firm in town. I expressed my concern that her mother needed a great deal of handholding and attention that she may not get with a different firm. I discussed our personal relationship that spanned several years, including the tumultuous period after the death of her husband. "Look," said the daughter, "I've got a guy who can get Mom a 15 percent return with low risk. Can you do that?" I confessed I couldn't, nor did I have any confidence that any one else could either. That conversation taught me that it is not necessarily my personal failure that encourages a client to change advisers. I also learned that occasionally people outgrow you. Although the client needed my attention and mothering during her personally challenging times, she was now declaring her independence.

If a client wishes to release us today, I no longer use rhetoric to convince them to stay. I recognize how hard it must be for them to say this to me, so I make it easy. I express my regret that we could not meet their needs and I tell them we will always be available should they wish to reconsider. We follow it up with a nice cordial letter, reconfirming that we are releasing their account. We also offer to assist with the transition to a new adviser.

Refusing a Client

It is better to refuse an inappropriate relationship at the outset than to try to figure out creative ways to sever it when it's not working. When a prospect's profile is not appropriate for us, we apologize for being too narrowly specialized to give him or her the best service. We say that we're sorry we are so focused that we can't accommodate them, rather than indicating they don't have enough money or in some way are lacking. It's bad for business to make people feel embarrassed or uncomfortable about their money, or lack of it.

We make it clear to a prospect that even though we are unable to help, our commitment is to find them a more appropriate adviser relationship. We keep a list of people we know and trust and share it with them, adding that if the recommendations don't work out, they may check back and we will be happy to suggest others. It's our commitment to them for their confidence in calling us initially. Most of the time, people take us up on it. It is, nevertheless, a challenge to refuse a relationship, especially when the prospect somehow made it through your screening process and is sitting across from you. Eleanor admits she uses her "gut" much more than she used to. "I have my own comfort level. When that's disturbed, I try to find a pleasant way to say no. I might say, 'I don't think we can help you' or 'clearly, this isn't a good fit.'"

David Norton confided that he frequently refused relationships based on his estimation of the situation as he talked with prospects. David would refuse a relationship if he didn't like or trust someone, or if the prospect appeared to be a "messer" (someone who couldn't make decisions). He would also refuse if he perceived that his services were not a good value for the client.

Paul Brady tends to be more blunt. He recommends being honest and frank about it. "I simply tell them this is not a good match." Jerry Neill prefers a less direct approach. "I usually price my service out of the market or explain we can't take on that project now, but perhaps in a few months. . . ." Jerry also points out that if you have bundled services, you can use that as an excuse as well. A client who only wants you to manage money will probably not want to do a comprehensive plan with you. Roy Diliberto will simply not take a new client unless they agree to a comprehensive plan.

David Bugen looks for compatibility. "If a prospect's expectations do not mesh with ours, we say, no, sorry. Sure, we love to take new clients, but we don't want today's solution to be tomorrow's problem."

Many advisers screen heavily prior to the first meeting. David Bugen sends out a questionnaire for the prospect to complete prior to that session. We do, too. If someone balks at this, we explain that "when you visit a new doctor, he needs information to make an assessment of your medical situation. This information will help us determine if we can help you. We don't want to waste your time or ours. We believe that if you are not prepared to commit your time to providing the information we consider critical, we are not likely to be the right firm for your needs." This really discourages "tire kickers."

It's Not What You Say . . .

Be very careful in what you say to prospects because it may just backfire on you. A few years ago I needed to have a colonoscopy. I had never met the doctor before, but I undressed and put on one of those gowns that won't cover a gnat's behind. The doctor walked in, took one look at me and said, "I know you. I came to see you a couple years ago, but you said I didn't have enough money to work with you."

I hope you are picturing this, because you can easily see the look on my face, contemplating whether I should continue with this procedure or just run. I know that this is a statement that I would *never* have made. But, this event was a huge "Ah-Ha" for me: it's not what you say, it's what they hear. Be mindful of how you construct your refusal, but also realize, they may hear something completely different in what you have to say. (Yes, I did have the procedure and he did eventually become a client.)

Just Say No

As hard as it might be to fire clients or refuse new relationships, it is necessary for developing your practice. Remember, part of Pareto's law states that roughly 20 percent of your income in ten years will come from your current client base. You'll want to weed out, then concentrate on retention. Managing your client base effectively will make your business more efficient, and better yet, more fun.

THE PROCESS

The secret to a successful and profitable practice lies in the processes that you adopt. Don't be fooled into thinking that technology alone can do this for you. Technology is a tool, not a solution. Design your work flow around the tools you have available. The following chapters offer some ideas to incorporate into your operations that just may make a difference in your profitability, quality output, and, ultimately, client satisfaction and loyalty.

When it comes to personal computers, there have been many killer apps, starting with the spreadsheet, but there haven't been any new ones in a long time, which is a problem.

—Robert X. Cringely, technology journalist

I have been in this business since 1979. In the early days of practice, everything we did was by hand. Month by month. By the time we got our information documented, organized, and typed, we were ready to start another month. After several grueling years, we "bit the bullet" and bought our own computer system.

Our first computer was a Digital Equipment Corp. PDP8-I, consisting of a monster mainframe the size of a small Toyota, with a paper tape backup and an IBM printer, equally monstrous, that produced "garbage-truck pickup" sounds as it printed reports. We quickly outgrew that model and embraced a new DEC computer with 256K storage! (That's so small that today it hardly warrants a jump drive!)

As soon as software companies began to write software we could use in our industry, we have all been looking for "The Killer Software," the fully integrated program that would solve all our back-office problems and take out the garbage, too. A few years ago, Moss Adams completed an operational study of the industry for Pershing, called "Mission Possible" (you can get this from a Pershing representative: start with www.pershing.com), which discussed adviser operational issues, including software needs. Pershing discovered that most advisers don't use much of the capability of any of their software programs. Most learn enough to get the job done and that's it. The learning curve for most software programs is high, and advisers just don't allocate enough time to get the most out of each one. Pershing's conclusions? What advisers need is "The Killer Process."

Before I talk about processes, I want to talk about the types of software I think every good practice should have to operate efficiently. I won't make specific suggestions because new software is made available all the time, but I will give you a contact to stay current with the best and brightest: www.virtualofficenews.com. It's the brainchild of David Drucker and Joel Bruckenstein, who track new software, test it, and then report whether you should give it a spin.

There are three types of software I believe are essential to every planning practice:

1. Customer relationship management (CRM) software with the capability to track and store information about your client, handle client systems and processes, and handle interoffice and external communications.

2. Financial planning software with the ability to assist you in making planning recommendations for clients, including retirement calculations, life insurance needs, college funding, and tax and estate planning strategies.

3. Portfolio management software specifically designed to download client positions and pricing and generate reports with time-weighted and dollar-weighted performance data at intervals you set.

There are a few software packages that combine the three above, but so far I have not been impressed. Custodians and broker-dealers have their own software to facilitate trading and interface with your portfolio management software. Some may have proprietary planning or CRM software or give you access to various kinds at a discounted rate. While there are other resource software programs that you will find useful, these few are essential to your smooth operations.

You will need some programs to help you in research, but you can go crazy trying to select the kinds of software you could use for research in the preparation of your portfolios. I recommend that if you are primarily working with mutual funds (or even if you're not, because your potential clients will have them) buy Morningstar (www.morningstar.com). They offer many different types of software packages, including Advisor Workstation and Principia, so check with the good people at Morningstar, who can help you choose what's best for you and your practice.

If you are bogged down with performance reporting, consider iRebal, the Rolls-Royce of rebalancing software. iRebal uploads from all custodians, creates a trail of executed transactions, and rebalances according to the parameters that you build into the system. It's costly, but if you have in excess of $300 million under management, you will want to investigate it. TD Ameritrade owns the program but makes it available to all.

Beginning the Process

Once you have your software in place, focus on your processes. An easy way to begin is to build a flow chart of the major activities you have in your practice. We start with our review process because it is lengthy and cumbersome to manage. The idea is to track how each job is handled and who handles it so you can assess where you might make improvements to reduce time and energy.

If you have never tracked your processes, or if you are starting from scratch, try creating an information flow chart. You can flow chart any function. For example, take a look at my personal wake-up process in **Figure 17.1**.

You may want to start with the simplest process, acquiring a new client. **Figure 17.2** is ours.

The point here is that in order for you to see how information flows, you are going to have to document it. Once this is done, review it with your staff to see how you can manipulate the flow to become more efficient. Try to automate as much as possible. Ask these questions:

1. What functions must I perform?

2. What functions can someone with lesser skills do?

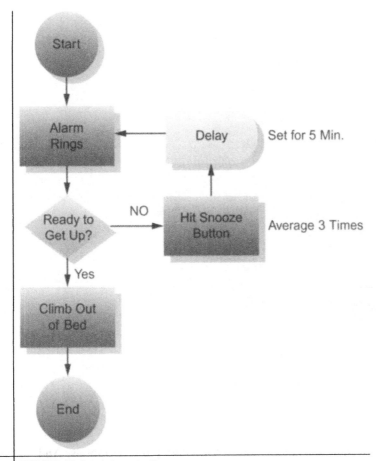

■ **FIGURE 17.1** Wake-Up Process

3. What functions can a machine accomplish?

4. What functions are redundant?

5. Are there any systems of checks and balances we need to incorporate?

6. Does the information flow logically and efficiently?

7. Can or should any of these functions be outsourced?

Once you have visually reviewed your systems, you can begin to document how each function is accomplished. Look at the chart in Figure 17.2. The first shape indicates that someone is entering the client into the customer relationship management software and coding the entry for a newsletter. If we were to break this job down, we would document how to start the software, how to enter the new client, and how to code the client as a prospect. We would indicate that she is to receive a number of mailings from us, including our newsletter, and enter a decision date by which time she will be required to actively ask for a continuation of the mailings.

Each job that must be accomplished within your process should be documented. It sounds daunting, I know, but think of how much easier it will be to train new people when you have training manuals ready to assist. The summary

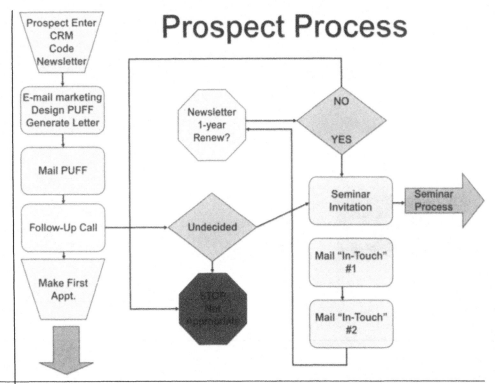

■ | **FIGURE 17.2** Prospect Process

of each of these functions helps you to formulate job descriptions. And, having well-constructed job descriptions will assist you in hiring the best people for the positions you need to fill.

Outsourcing

Years ago most advisers were absolutely opposed to outsourcing, particularly any-thing that involved client information. The fact is, many third-party vendors have a much better chance at protecting your data than you do. It's very costly to put technol-ogy and firewalls in place to protect data, and let's face it, if Bank of America couldn't protect theirs, a few years ago, what makes you think you can do any better?

So one of the questions to ask while reviewing your processes is whether any of the functions should be outsourced. Outsourcing can help you focus on core competencies, become more profitable, and streamline your processes. Look at each of the processes you've developed and consider them in terms of outsourc-ing. Use the guide in **Figure 17.3** to help you.

Almost anything can be outsourced and many advisers have found areas where outsourcing improves profits, and oftentimes morale. Here is a list of things you might consider:

- Data management
- Portfolio management

Outsourcing Guide

- Is this a core competency? **YES** → **KEEP IT**

- Can it be done more cheaply externally? **YES** → **OUTSOURCE IT**

- Does it waste time and money? **YES** → **OUTSOURCE IT**

- Does it take a more highly skilled person than you have in-house to do it? **YES** → **OUTSOURCE IT**

- Is it a temporary need? **YES** → **OUTSOURCE IT**

- Is this something that no one wants to do? **YES** → **OUTSOURCE IT**

FIGURE 17.3 Outsourcing Guide

- Accounting, payable and receivable
- Payroll and benefits
- Human resources
- Training
- Compliance

Of all these items, compliance is the one area in which you can outsource the activities, but you can never outsource the responsibility. I will talk about compliance later.

 ## Sequencing

Devising sequencing steps to track workflow was one process that helped us immensely and allowed us to build a sequence profile in our CRM software to alert us to jobs that needed to be done. Let me tell you how this works.

Whether you do a job once a week or once a year, it is efficient to document the steps needed to perform that task from beginning to end. Once that is complete, you are assured you will never forget a step, nor do you have to rethink each time the task occurs. If you do the task infrequently, a sequencing document is a real time-saver. And, if more than one person works on the task, it's essential. I am a private pilot. Each time I step into the cockpit, I pull out my checklist that is permanently affixed to the visor. Even though I have many hours in the air, I always refer to my checklist for take-off procedures. Just one time, relying on memory alone could mean disaster for me. I'm not sure you would crash if you forgot a step in preparation for your reviews or a client meeting, but you get the idea.

Our sequences are then loaded into Junxure (our CRM of choice). Then, when it's time to perform a task, Junxure sends out e-mails to all people involved. Each e-mail sets a time frame in which the work needs to be done. The e-mail keeps popping up until the task is completed. (That can be very irritating if you are behind, but it works just the same.)

Here's an example of our sequence for operations tasks.

Operations—Position Independent

- Retrieve index and manager reports information
- Check pricing of annuities and other irregular account information
- Run intervals (three months)
- Check the value of "all managed accounts," entering values of $0.00 securities or calling to find out if a security has been deemed "worthless"
- Create the EK monthly review spreadsheet
- Review recommendations

Operations—Position Dependent

Director of Operations

- Run reconciliation reports
- Review any extraordinary account changes
- Check added/decreased cash
- Review accounts that have changed management

Assistant Director of Operations

- Rerun intervals of any affected account from price changes in parametric/all
- Change the price of one "separately managed account" for any client in the all-user defined category whose value has changed
- Check portfolios and accounts in review
- Check if there is a position that is less than $0.50
- Revise or edit an account

Special Projects Manager

- Update Principia, Excel index-related accounts, and securities in rebalancing form
- Create special account files (sovereign, imperial, monarch)
- Evaluate reports and security classifications, and advise operations on the review process

- Perform client-support administrative tasks
- Prepare reviews for the appropriate adviser

Adviser

- Evaluate the review
- Notify operations of any account changes, unusual numbers, or additions and deletions not previously listed

Operations Data Guide

I've included an operations data guide to help you determine what operational items you are missing and which ones may require some attention. Use this to help formulate your back-office needs and make processing easier. (See **Figure 17.4**.)

Back-Office Models

As you think about operations, it is wise to review your current structure. Moss Adams has identified three basic back-office models:

1. Adviser-centric—Designed for one adviser. If there are more advisers, each process is replicated with each adviser.

2. Client-centric—Clients direct activities, either choosing from a service or options menu or asking for "one-offs," and advisers and staff accommodate.

3. Process-centric—Standardized process with few or no exceptions.

Moss Adams discovered in its survey of advisers that the most efficient and most profitable arrangement is process-centric, allowing for the most standardization and for less duplication of efforts. Process-centric offices are centralized with support areas servicing many advisers (**Figure 17.5**).

Naturally if you are a sole practitioner, you will need to use your back-office resources differently. But you will want to be as highly processed as possible. Whatever the size, highly processed firms are more profitable.

 Process and Communication

There is no question that e-mail has improved intraoffice communication drastically. Yet as valuable as we find e-mail to be, it was necessary for us to learn to use it properly. It is never a replacement for face-to-face communication. When we first got our e-mail system running, I would leave long directives to my new secretary each evening. She would answer these directives each morning. I would answer, and then she would ask for clarification. This went on for three days until I realized I hadn't seen her during that time. I walked into her office and remarked

FIGURE 17.4 Operations Data Guide

Operations Data Guide

Entity Name: _____

❑ RIA   ❑ Corporate   ❑ Individual

Licensed in the following states: _____

_____

Software

General ledger: _____

Payroll: _____

CRM database: _____

Financial planning: _____

Portfolio management: _____

Billing management: _____

Contract management: _____

Custodial/broker-dealer relationships: _____

Data download: ❑ In-house   ❑ Outsourced

Systems

Network: _____

Number of users: _____

IT specialist: ❑ In-house   ❑ Outsourced

Hardware

Desktop units: _____

Servers: _____

Backup system: _____

Printers: _____

Scanners: _____

Shredders: _____

Copiers: ❑ Server   ❑ Stand-alone

Faxes: ❑ Fax   ❑ From desktop

Compliance

Compliance officer: _____

Compliance manual: _____

■ | **FIGURE 17.4** Operations Data Guide (*Continued*)

Disaster policy: _____

Mandated policies (manual): _____

Privacy policy: _____

Proxy policies: _____

E-mail documentation policy: _____

Website

Website designer: _____

Internet provider: _____

Operational Systems

Trading policies: _____

Electronic trading: _____

Systems Procedures:

What are your investment criteria? _____

_____

Investment Policy

What investment software do you
use? _____

_____

Asset Allocation Strategies

Investment philosophy for:　❑ Risk　　❑ Return

What is your recommendation
process? _____

_____

Tax Status and Implementation

Process Behind the Philosophy

How are trades executed? _____

_____

Asset Allocation

　Bond allocation to taxables: _____

　When is the account
　rebalanced? _____

_____

　Equity to fixed income: _____

(continued)

FIGURE 17.4 Operations Data Guide (*Continued*)

Investment strategy: _____

What is your client data
gathering process? _____

_____

Allocation of company size: _____

Allocation of style: _____

_____

_____

Allocation of U.S. to foreign: _____

Allocation of alternatives: _____

What is your analysis
process? _____

Accounting rebalancing: _____

Fund/stock retention policy: _____

What is your estate
planning process? _____

_____

Selection based on risk: _____

Selection based on returns: _____

Will services vary by AUM,
client fees, or account type? _____

_____

Taxable account: _____

Nontaxable account: _____

Reporting period: _____

If yes, do you have a
process for diversification? _____

_____

FIGURE 17.4 Operations Data Guide (*Continued*)

Benchmarks: _____

Frequency of reports: _____

Taxes: _____

Outsourced services:
- ❑ Comprehensive planning
- ❑ Data maintenance
- ❑ Marketing
- ❑ Payroll
- ❑ Preparation
- ❑ Legal services
- ❑ Human resources
- ❑ Insurance

Graphs and client reports: _____

Trades based on taxes: _____

Monitoring process: _____

Policy revisions procedure: _____

Investment committee: _____

Application issues: _____

Account minimum: _____

Account maximum: _____

Fund/stock research: _____

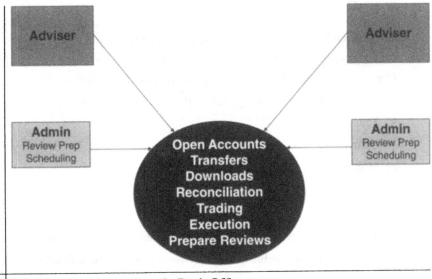

FIGURE 17.5 Process-Centric Back Office

that she hadn't been in to see me all week. "Oh," she replied, "I thought you felt more comfortable communicating from a distance, you know, the *Wizard of Oz* management style."

Even Bill Gates, at his Microsoft CEO Summit in Seattle in 1998, has acknowledged a problem with the emphasis we often place on e-mail today. "Sometimes people must meet face-to-face. If they are going back and forth more than three or four times on e-mail and are disagreeing, the wise thing is to get together and discuss the matter, because it's very hard to come to an agreement in an electronic mail exchange."

Clarity begins at home, inside the office, by promoting face-to-face conversation among staff. All our office systems are based on checks, balances, and cross-training. No one person is totally responsible for the completion of any single project. For small companies or work groups, this is important. If someone is absent, the work can still be completed.

Time Management and Processes

Julie Littlechild of Advisor Impact produced a time management report in 2007[1] based upon the surveys done with U.S. advisers. In the summary findings, advisers concluded that many time management problems would be solved through better systems and processes.

As part of the report, Advisor Impact provided a self-assessment in time management to help advisers understand where they can make improvements. The thirty questions in the report are reprinted here with permission for your use.

1. I have clearly established goals for my own retirement.

2. I have clearly established goals for my business, which link directly to my personal retirement goals.

3. I have a clear definition of my ideal client and this links to my client selection criteria.

4. My clients are segmented based on the value they bring to the business, and service levels are clearly defined for each segment.

5. I have clearly defined processes within my business for routine activities (e.g., welcoming a new client or updating a financial plan).

6. I set specific time aside in my schedule to plan the upcoming:

    a. Year?

    b. Quarter?

    c. Month?

    d. Week?

    e. Day?

7. I spend at least thirty minutes in "planning activities" each week.

8. The roles and responsibilities on my team are clearly defined and documented.

9. I delegate all or most activities that I am not uniquely qualified to do.

10. The majority of my time is invested in activities that I believe will actively support my business management and growth goals.

11. My clients are educated as to how we work together as a team to manage the relationship.

12. I hold regular meetings with my team to review priorities for the week or day.

13. My team members all have sufficient training to do their jobs very well.

14. If a client calls and asks me to do something that is not part of my role description, I pass him or her over to the appropriate team member.

15. I have invested time in tracking how I spend my time now in order to identify inefficiencies.

16. I have a set schedule of meetings and tasks for each workday.

17. I only deviate from my schedule if there is an urgent situation involving an important client.

18. I have a manageable number of to-do items on my list each day and can reasonably expect to complete all items on that list.

19. The tasks on my to-do list are clearly prioritized.

20. I have defined and measurable goals for the number of client and prospect meetings I will hold each week.

21. I schedule all or most of my activities, including personal activities, so that I know what needs to be accomplished each day.

22. I schedule my meetings back-to-back or with a defined amount of time between each meeting.

23. I schedule all or most of my activities using an electronic calendar.

24. We "preschedule" client meetings well in advance so that nothing falls through the cracks with our clients.

25. I set specific time aside to respond to phone calls and e-mails, rather than dealing with them as they come in.

26. I have defined "time blocks" for core activities, such as meetings, business planning, or research.

27. I hold my client meetings at defined times each week (either on specific days of the week or in defined time blocks throughout the week).

28. My office and desk are clean and organized.

29. I do not need to work on evenings and weekends just to keep up with my workload.

30. I schedule enough time to "recharge my batteries" and be with my family.

From your answers, you can pretty much assess where you could use improvement.

Systems Make the Difference

Systematizing your practice is essential for client retention, for saving money, for efficiency, for consistency, and ultimately, for transfer or sale. I've given you some ideas about systematizing your own practice. As you review what you're doing now, keep the following hints in mind:

- Any activity that has multiple steps should have a checklist so that no steps are forgotten.

- To the extent possible, important tasks should employ a system of checks and balances, necessitating more than one pair of eyes to review.

- For critical tasks, have a designated backup person and complete documentation.

- Consider outsourcing activities that are time-consuming and unproductive. In the long run, buying these services may save you money.

*Ideas are a dime a dozen. People who put them
into action are priceless.*
—Unknown

When I was a kid, we always had roast beef on Sundays. Every Sunday. I think it was because my folks were ministers and my mom could prepare it, shove it in the oven, and have it ready by the time we got home from church. One year, when my sister was about ten, she asked our mom to teach her to cook the roast. Mom set all the ingredients on the kitchen counter. She trimmed the roast, seasoned it, and at the very end of the process, cut both ends off. "Why do you cut off the ends?" asked my sister, Sharon. "My mom always does it that way," Mom replied. Unsatisfied with the answer, my sister called Grandma for an explanation. "My mom always does it that way," answered Grandma. By then my sister, frustrated, called Great Grandma. "Why do you cut the ends of the roast?" Sharon asked. "Why," explained Great Grandma, "my pan was too small."

We're fortunate to be in a profession in which practitioners share so openly with each other. I've certainly been lucky in my professional life to have so many advisers share their creative projects with me.

I am certain it has given me an advantage with my staff and with my clients. That's why I'm particularly pleased to be able to pass some of the things I learned along to you. No question, it's much more efficient to "honestly steal" good ideas than to try to invent all these things yourself. More important, you can adapt ideas and concepts that others have taken time, effort, and considerable thought to develop. You don't have to cut off the ends of the roast without an explanation of why.

One good thing about writing a book is that you get to include materials in it that you appreciate. If you've chosen well, others will find them useful, too. They might even enjoy them. In the previous chapters, I grouped together numerous ideas under themes. Not surprisingly, many of the most interesting ideas don't fit so neatly into specific categories. In this last chapter, I want to share some of the more eclectic thoughts, insights, and reflections that I have collected over the years, in listening to speakers, reading articles, and networking with friends. In New Orleans, they'd call this "lagniappe," just a little bit extra, the thirteenth doughnut in the baker's dozen. Maybe you'll find something in here that will speak volumes to you.

Concepts to Own

- Question basic assumptions.
- Question certainties.
- Become better informed with less certainty.
- Honor the beginner's mind.
- Ask me anything.
- Question anything.
- Allow mistakes.

 On Planning

Two gems from Mark Tibergien, now at Pershing in Jersey City, New Jersey: "Don't begin your planning when you're three cars behind the flowers," and "Life Cycle of a planning firm—Wonder, Blunder, Thunder, Plunder."

 On the Value of Advice on the Internet

"The irony of the information age is that it has given new respectability to uninformed opinion," said a veteran reporter John Lawton, sixty-eight, speaking to the American Association of Broadcast Journalists in 1995.

 How Long Will Your Money Last?

Admittedly the minipresentation in **Figure 18.1** is a little self-serving inasmuch as I'm stealing it from a book I did on retirement planning.[1] Still, I've found it to be very helpful in demonstrating to some clients the multiple impacts of inflation and the need for real cash flow.

The table in Figure 18.1 gives you a quick way to estimate how long your assets will last, depending upon what they are earning and how much you withdraw annually. You may have seen something like this in the past, but this one is different because it is indexed for an annual inflation rate of 3 percent. The column at the top lists rates of return from 1 percent to 12 percent. The rows on the left list withdrawal rates, from a high of 12 percent of principal a year at the top to a 1 percent of principal at the bottom.

 Opportunity Costs

My partner Harold wrote a small book for Y2K to help our clients deal with their concerns about the unknown impact it might have on the market. Although Y2K is long gone (and with not even a ripple), one of the tools he developed for the book has proved useful in helping some clients deal with their asset allocation

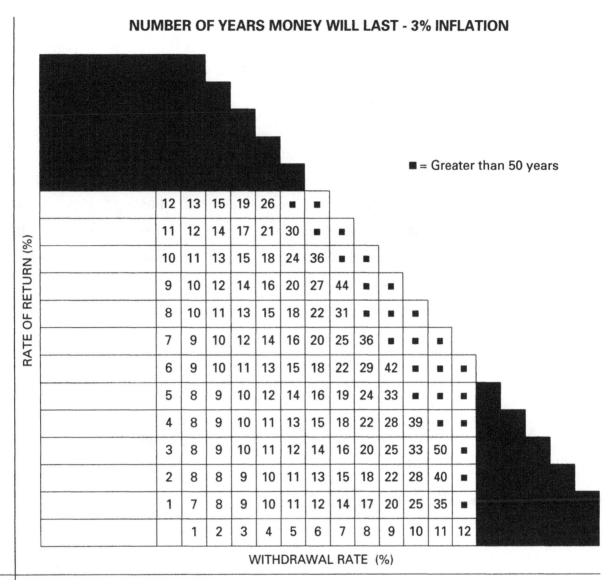

NUMBER OF YEARS MONEY WILL LAST - 3% INFLATION

■ = Greater than 50 years

FIGURE 18.1 Number of Years Money Will Last

decision (see **Figure 18.2**). The tool provides a simple calculation that gives the client an idea of how much potential return (opportunity cost) he will be giving up should he increase his allocation from stocks to bonds. Because the table in Harold's system is based on specific market expectations, I'm providing it to you as an idea, not a solution. If you find the idea useful, it will be easy to redesign the table to meet your market expectations.

To use this table, a client would determine the amount of his portfolio and his current allocation. For example, assume $100,000 is invested 40 percent in bonds and 60 percent in stocks. He would then determine how big a shift he was considering. For example, he might contemplate a shift from the 40/60 allocation to a 60/40 allocation. Using the factors in the table, he would then determine the projected guesstimate for the future value of each portfolio by multiplying the appropriate factor times the portfolio value (see **Figure 18.3**).

Market Expectations:

Asset Class	Average	Good
Bonds	5%	7%
Stock	11%	23%

Portfolio Allocation:

	Average Results	Good Results
All Bonds	1.05	1.07
90% Cash/10% Stocks	1.06	1.09
80% Cash/20% Stocks	1.06	1.10
70% Cash/30% Stocks	1.07	1.12
60% Cash/40% Stocks	1.07	1.13
50% Cash/50% Stocks	1.08	1.15
40% Cash/60% Stocks	1.09	1.17
30% Cash/70% Stocks	1.09	1.18
20% Cash/80% Stocks	1.10	1.20
10% Cash/90% Stocks	1.10	1.21
All Stock	1.11	1.23

■ **FIGURE 18.2** Opportunity Cost Factors

Current Portfolio Value = $100,000

40/60 Average Result Factor = 1.09   40/60 Good Result Factor = 1.17

60/40 Average Result Factor = 1.07   60/40 Good Result Factor = 1.13

	Current Portfolio	Proposed Portfolio	Opportunity Cost
Average Market Results	$109,000	$107,000	$2,000
Good Market Results	$117,000	$113,000	$4,000

■ **FIGURE 18.3** Opportunity Cost Calculation

Been There, Done That, Got the T-Shirt—A New Era

We have been talking about the "new era" for the past few years. I don't know, as you read this book, what phase of the new era you think we will be in, but I thought I would like to share a few observations on the subject that I've recently read:

From *How to Secure Continuous Profits in Modern Markets*, by John Durand:[2]

> . . . we live in a "new era," says Dr. Anderson, in which the laws of economics are suspended, in which all financial records are broken, and in which an indefinite continuance of the breaking of financial records may be confidently looked forward to and believed by a good many people.

From *Business Week:*

> For five years, at least, American business has been in the grip of an apocalyptic, holy-rolling exaltation over the unparalleled prosperity of the "new era," upon which we, or it, or somebody has entered. Discussions of economic conditions in the press, on the platform, and by public officials have carried us into a cloudland of fantasy where all appraisal of present and future accomplishment is suffused with the vague implication that a North American millennium is imminent. Clear, critical, realistic, and rational recognition of current problems and perplexities is rare.

It's sobering to reflect that both of these observations were published in September 1929.

Food for Thought

People who know me would believe it unlikely for me to write a book without some reference to food. You might think about this idea for clients, for staff, or even for your building manager. We keep a crystal dish of candy on our receptionist's desk. Daily, the building engineer visits to pick up his sugar fix. As a result, he always knows if a light is out or the sink is stopped up. Guess who gets great service? The FedEx, UPS, and mail carriers appreciate treats, too. They stop in, even if they don't have a package for us and don't mind taking something as an unscheduled pickup.

Cookie Man

Jerry Friday, former sales director for ACT Learning Centers in Duluth, Georgia, takes cookies with him to meet with prospective clients. It's been a great success and clients call him "the cookie man." Instead of asking prospective clients if they would like something ten minutes into the meeting (don't wait too long or it might break the meeting mood), our receptionist waltzes in with a tray of cookies or pastries. She then asks if anyone would like a drink to go with it. Call Mrs. Fields.

Moving Up the Food Chain

Lew Wallensky, a certified financial planner with Lewis Wallensky & Associates in Los Angeles, California, shared this idea with me. As I read it, I wondered, "Do they serve better food at the tables with people who've been around longer?" (Just kidding, Lew.)

> Two years ago, we had a thirtieth anniversary party for our clients. There were over 200 in attendance. This in itself is not unusual. Many planners have client appreciation nights. But what we have done is seat clients at tables according to how many years they have been clients. Over 75 percent of the people there were at tables of fifteen years or longer. We are proud of that record. Thus people sat at thirty-, twenty-five-, twenty-, fifteen-, ten-, or five-year tables. We had two full tables of clients who have been with us twenty-five to thirty years. We even had two tables where we sat three generations of the same family. Prior to the thirtieth anniversary, we had the twenty-fifth, twentieth, fifteenth. As each five years passed, clients wanted to move up to the next level. This has been a wonderful experience and tradition. This year we are planning to do the thirty-third (note it is not a multiple of five) which is of course a third of a century.

Coffee Anyone?

When anyone walks into our office, he is handed our beverage menu. If it's a client, our receptionist already knows what drinks he or she prefers (we keep that information in our database), but we always give guests a chance to change their minds. We find that when a client looks at the menu, he often makes a suggestion for additions. For example, because of an idea from a caffeine-free client, we now have several flavors of decaffeinated green tea for our health enthusiasts.

Lastly, on the subject of food, remember—never underestimate the value of edible perks.

Branding

Here's an overused but important word for your repertoire: *branding.* The more competition we have, the more important branding becomes. I read this great book on branding, *22 Immutable Laws of Branding: How to Build a Product or Service into a World-Class Brand,* by Al Ries and Laura Ries. They use an analogy to describe the concept: ". . . branding in the marketplace is very similar to branding on a ranch. A branding program should be designed to differentiate your cow from all the other cattle on the range. Even if all the cattle on the range look pretty much alike."[3] The idea is to get people to think of your "cow" when they think of a good planning firm. Some product companies have been very successful at this.

Xerox is so well known that the word has become a replacement for the generic term *photocopy*. Band-Aid should really be *adhesive bandages*. Wite-Out is any liquid stuff you can use to cover your paper errors. I wouldn't mind if the world described what we do as getting a "Katz-Plan." Spend some time thinking about how you can position yourself and your business to build your brand and grow your business.

Fidelity has a Brand Development Toolkit available as part of their Practice-Mark support for advisers who work with them. It has great templates for you to get your arms around developing your own brand. Visit www.fiws.fidelity.com.

Coaching

Years ago I attended a session with a professional certified coach, Will Mattox of Cheshire, Oregon (will@coachingservices.com). I liked Will immediately when he announced to the group, "I help people make change and move forward." "Hey," we all said, "that's what we do." "Ah, but," Will countered, "how many of you do it for yourselves?" He had us there. Will walked us through five basic coaching activities that we can use for ourselves and with our clients.

Immediately, we all found them useful in dealing with problems, but more importantly, in helping formulate effective solutions. I thought I'd share them with you.

Balance Wheel

This activity helps you to quantify the things that are distressing you or preventing you from moving forward. Draw a circle, and then divide it into eight parts. Fill each section with those things that are of concern to you. Here is the one I did (see **Figure 18.4**). Next you'll want to rank these items according to your level of concern and mark the segment on the pie accordingly (see **Figure 18.5**). The center represents zero (most concern). The outer edge represents a ten, or least concern.

Now you can address the items that you feel need work. On this chart, staff is about a four. Using the concern about staff as an example, let's break down these issues and prepare a "Staff Concern" wheel (see **Figure 18.6**).

Using this method, you can narrow the focus on issues in your practice that require some strategic thinking.

Create SMART Goals

We planners may not have invented the acronym, but creating goals is what we planners do every day. Goals should be:

- Specific
- Measurable
- Achievable

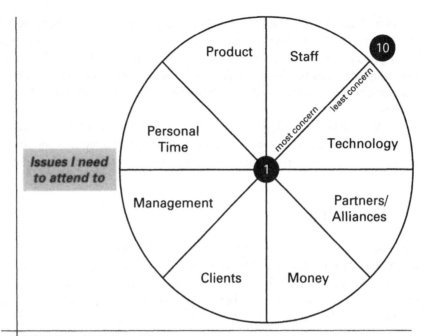

FIGURE 18.4 Balance Wheel

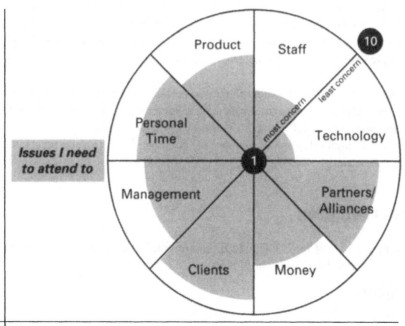

FIGURE 18.5 Balance Wheel Rankings

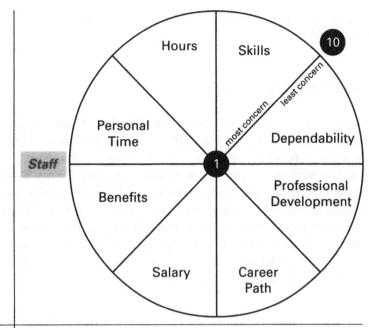

FIGURE 18.6 Balance Wheel Breakdown

- Realistic
- Timely

Will recommends that you create three-month, one-year, and five-year goals using this method.

Ask Powerful Questions

These are questions that begin with "What" or "How." Some of the more obvious ones are:

- What do you want?
- What are your first steps?
- What do you expect?
- How will you get there?

Break Down Your Tasks into Single Daily Actions (SDA)

For example, one adviser in our group said technology (or lack thereof) was plaguing him. He had settled on some new software, but he was waiting until he knew it was compatible with the software that he was currently using. He thought he was "on hold" until he realized that he could be performing SDAs to get him a bit further every day. After some thinking, he decided to read about his targeted portfolio software for fifteen minutes every morning.

Keep an Accountability Log

Will maintains that change comes from two sources. The first of these would be an event with strong emotional impact. For example, last year I was involved in an auto accident when some idiot plowed into me at an intersection. Now, each time I come to an intersection, not just the one where I was hit, I move slower and look longer than I did before the accident. Secondly, change happens through repetition. It's estimated that it takes about twenty-one days to break an old habit or to create a new, more productive habit in its place. If you are not accountable for taking the new actions, you will seldom acquire the new habit. By keeping an accountability log, you are consciously tracking the positive changes that will take you to the goal. The repetitive action ensures success.

 Shift Inventory

I attended the FPA Oregon Regional Retreat years ago and spoke with many advisers about their practices. Most expressed concern about managing changes within their organizations, and in particular, about how to delegate and become more efficient. Advisers in general often register the same concerns, so I called Dick Zalack, president of Focus Four, who is one of our profession's best-known practice management consultants. Based in Cleveland, Dick helps sole practitioners become better small-business owners and entrepreneurs. Check Dick out at www .dickzalack.com. I discussed our dilemma with Dick, who told me about "Shift Inventory." I then asked him if he would contribute his concept to this book. He agreed. **Figure 18.7** is a worksheet to help you with this concept.

The following is the excerpt from Dick's book:

One of Parkinson's Laws says, "Work tends to expand to fill the time available." Zalack's corollary says, "The harder you work at reducing the length of your to-do list, the longer it becomes." Or, "The more successful you are, the more work you generate." As the head of your own financial planning business, you are more than familiar with those facets of being in business for yourself.

The question is not, "How can I work harder and longer?" but "What can I do to get back to doing what I do best?"

When you started the business, you were able to spend almost all of your available working hours using your unique talents, whatever they were—creating great financial plans, finding highly profitable investments, signing up new clients, creating new leads. As you became more successful, you had to start doing more of the things at which you were merely excellent—sales, sales calls, sales training. Your further success then required you to spend more of your time on those things at which you were only competent—meetings, reports, etc. And finally, you discovered you needed to spend

■ | FIGURE 18.7 Shift Inventory: Results Plus

RESULTS PLUS

Shift Inventory

Task	Should we be doing it? Yes/No	If yes, why?	Should I? Yes/No	If yes, why?	If no, why?	When?

Source: Focus Four

your valuable time, energy, and creativity on those things at which you were incompetent!

For me, that included filling out forms, spelling, and anything that had to do with graphic design. The problem we have in this downward progression is that our unique skill gets lost in what I like to call administrivia—the details of running a business. And it was that unique skill that allowed us to start our business and be successful in the first place.

What needs to be done, then, is to get back to using our core skills and spend more time doing what makes us who we are. The goal of programs like Focus Four is to help the entrepreneur build a structure around himself which insulates him from the "stuff" of business and allows him as much time as possible to use his time, energy, and creativity (unique talents) to build the business. After all, the sole responsibility of the business owner is to ensure the future viability of the business. That is our ultimate job. No matter how successful we are at generating revenue, if we do not spend time, energy, and creativity in planning for the growth and future of the company, there will come a time when the business will stagnate and perhaps even cease to exist.

When you are insulated from administrivia and free to use your unique talents, you will be able to ensure your company's future success. And you do that with something I call the "Shift Inventory." The Shift Inventory allows you to look at all the myriad details of your everyday activities and shift as many as possible to someone else's to-do list.

Let's be honest here. All those details, the ones at which you are incompetent to excellent at, need to be addressed and then acted upon. They just don't need to be done by you! So the first thing you must do is discover what is included in the list of things you no longer need, should, or want to do.

The first step in the Shift Inventory is the inventory. Begin by reviewing your to-do lists for the last month. Look at everything you "had to" do. Write down each activity and then follow that with the answer to this question, "Should we (the company) be doing this?" If the answer is "No," stop doing it. If the answer is "Yes," write down why it needs to be done. Be brutally honest. Don't rationalize.

Then comes a harder set of questions and answers: "Should I be doing it?" If you think the answer is "yes," then write down why you should be the one to do it. If your answer is "no," then write down who should be doing it and "when." If you have the person in place, then shift the activity to him or her. If you don't have someone, then you need to get someone. You can either hire (look for someone with values and attitude that match yours and then train him or her to be competent in this area) or bring in experts.

In my case, I do both. I bring in advertising and public relations people to plan campaigns, graphic designers to create the material, writers to create the words, and marketing experts for our direct mail campaigns. I create a virtual company using outside experts to help me be successful in areas in which I am only excellent, competent, or incompetent.

The most important person I have, however, is someone I hired, my administrative assistant. This person helps me coordinate all my activities, keeps my calendar straight, sets up my paydays, focuses my foundation days, and performs the two most important functions someone can do for a business owner—keeping me free from administrivia and giving me as much free time as possible to use my unique talents. In addition, my administrative assistant holds me accountable for doing what I say I will do. I now have the time I need to do what only I can do—think strategically and create plans to achieve the goals of the company.

As your business progresses, you will see a major change occur. Most of us started our businesses because we were the chief gunslinger in producing revenue. We could generate income like no one else. We were the main producer. But as time goes on and the business grows, what becomes apparent is that we can hire people to produce revenue. Maybe not up to our individual gunslinging capacity, so we hire two or three producers, but what we discover is that what we can't do is hire anyone to create the vision for the company. From the very beginning, we were the only person who knew where the business was ultimately going. What we need to do now is spend more time in thinking about the future and creating plans to achieve our goals. We are the only ones who can do that. We just need more time in our schedule. That's the function of the Shift Inventory and the administrative assistant.

If it's been a while since you've thought about the future of your business, now would be a good time to be crystal clear about what kind of business you want to create and what the model will be. What volume of sales do you want? What size staff? What kind of market will you go after? What kind of products will you carry? What will be your image in the community? What kind of customer service will you have? What kind of staff training? And so on.

Once you have the model clearly identified and written down, you should invest your time, energy, and creativity in creating processes and systems that will help achieve your goals. The infrastructure you create to protect you and ensure the success of the business will have two goals of its own:

- To ensure a consistent and repeated stream of income-generating opportunities, and

- To retain those clients who came to you as a result of these systems and processes.

As you shift from primary producer to leader, you will need to invest more of your time, energy, and creativity in steering your business instead of rowing it. You will hire more producers and train them well. And you will spend more of your time coaching them and developing your staff. And you will discover that when your business is working the best, you are spending more of your time supporting your staff and helping them to work and less and less time doing the actual producing.

You can achieve success like this by using the Shift Inventory to eliminate those things from your daily schedule that can be done by others and to free up your time so that you can create the vision and develop the plan necessary to steer your business to your preferred future.

Business Analyses

My friend Mark Ralphs of Financial Planning Corporation in Southport, United Kingdom, has created an unusual way of managing the revenues from his client base. I thought it might stimulate you to a new and perhaps more profitable practice.

Yield Management in an Independent Financial Adviser (IFA) Practice

Have you ever wondered why when flying with some of the more successful airlines, few of the passengers have paid the same fare? Yet on some less successful airlines (often national and subsidized) most of the passengers are on a flat discount ticket. The answer is "yield management." Where capacity is restricted, it is good practice to manage the supply of your service to those customers who can and will pay premium prices for your service.

My business partner Moira O'Shaughnessy piloted such an exercise for our firm and although we intuitively knew that we always had to be rigorous in our dealings with clients, the results genuinely took us aback.

Often quoted is Pareto's Principle of the top 20 percent of your customers producing 80 percent of your income. Which is broadly correct. What it does not show is from where the top 20 percent of your profit comes. Here you need to differentiate between different classes of clients and apply a measure of ARGE—asset revenue generating efficiency.[4]

We have developed a weighted model for our own purposes, but in its simplest form consider the following information:

Whether you are fee based, commission based, or charge on the basis of assets managed, you should be able to have a standard measure of input. It may be the number of appointments or hours allotted to a client. **Figure 18.8** shows that the highest revenue earner was client Davies with $25,000, but he required more effort to service than some others, so he only averaged $625 per unit, putting him in eighth ranking for unit value.

Simply ranking revenue or unit value does not tell the whole story, and that is why Pareto alone is misleading. A simple ARGE can be calculated by adding together the ranking of revenue and the ranking of unit value, and then ranking the score in ascending order. This shows what you would expect: that Fawcett, Davies, and Jennings are all worthwhile clients. It has been said that what you do not know can hurt you the most. The clients like Brinson who have a high revenue figure can be expensive clients to have.

In our own investigations, we discovered what we would expect from the top two quartiles. Intuitively, we knew to spend more than 50 percent of our time with these clients, and the results of those efforts accounted for more than 85 percent of our revenues. What shocked us was the bottom quartile. It still consumed 18 percent of our effort, reflecting our subconscious belief that we should not spend too much time with these clients. However their contribution to revenue was only 2 percent.

REVENUE RANK	CLIENT	REVENUE	INPUT	AVERAGE	UNIT VALUE RANK	ARGE	ARGE RANK
5	Able	$12,000	8	$1,500	3	8	3
7	Brinson	$7,000	12	$583	9	16	–7
11	Crown	$4,250	10	$425	11	22	9
1	Davies	$25,000	40	$625	8	9	4
8	Erikson	$7,000	20	$350	12	20	8
3	Fawcett	$18,000	10	$1,800	2	5	–1
12	Garrett	$1,500	8	$188	13	25	11
13	Hughes	$1,200	9	$133	14	27	12
2	Ibbotson	$22,000	25	$880	5	7	2
4	Jennings	$17,500	5	$3,500	1	5	–1
6	Kray	$9,500	12	$792	6	12	5
9	Lewis	$6,000	9	$667	7	16	–7
10	MacKay	$4,500	4	$1,125	4	14	6
14	Nimmo	$1,000	2	$500	10	24	10

■ | **FIGURE 18.8** Yield Management Model *Source: Financial Planning Corporation*

Our response was to ignore the bottom quartile entirely. Unless they contacted us, we made no contact. The third quartile was evaluated, and if they had referred us to first- or second-quartile clients, they remained; otherwise they were introduced to a new pricing policy that ensured that they at least matched the unit values of the bottom members of the second quartile. If this goal was not met, they were tactfully "graduated."

We are now five years on from the initial program, and we still find the necessity to purge from time to time. This focuses our minds when recruiting new clients, to ensure that they are of "investment grade."

Mark offers another bit of perspective, this time on targeting business performance using moving averages (**Figure 18.9**).

Moving Averages

Not everyone has the luxury of a constant, predictable stream of income. Some may rely upon project-based fees or commissions. The traditional planning tools sold or distributed by the sales support industry usually have annual targets, and each week or month the calculation is made as to whether or not the individual being assessed is ahead or behind his or her target.

There are many problems with this method of measurement. If the individual is ahead of "target," she may become complacent. Likewise, if she is behind, it can become overwhelmingly difficult to meet what once seemed like reasonable annual targets.

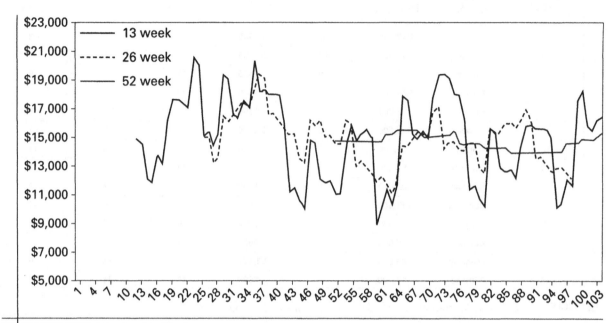

■ FIGURE 18.9 Monitoring Performance *Source: Financial Planning Corporation*

For many years we have done two specific things that allow us to move ahead. The first is to have quarterly targets. These are set each quarter, and if they are achieved, all is well and good. If they are not, we draw a line under the failure and move on to a nice fresh quarter. Ninety days is long enough to plan and execute and not so long that you can't just draw a veil over it if the success was not apparent.

The second key stage is our monitoring of performance (see Figure 18.9). For this we do not use cumulative or year-to-date figures but a series of moving averages. We measure all activity on a weekly basis and review the moving average over 13 weeks, 26 weeks, 52 weeks, and a trendline.

From this chart of moving averages we can deduce a number of things; there are a number of seasonal shifts in production, and by the second year (beyond week 53) we can see that both the 13-week and 26-week averages are well down. This means that production is low. However, by week 70 things have improved. We've found that if the 13- and 26-week lines are above the 52-week line, things are likely to improve over the longer term.

What Sorts of Things Can Alter the Charts?

The 13- or 26-week line can drop quite dramatically when a particularly high production week falls out of the frame. This is most apparent when the 13-week line is going up, yet the 26-week line takes a sudden drop.

By feeding in past sales data or banking data, it is possible to use a simple Excel program to draw these charts and even to do regression analysis.

If performance is not as good as you wish, it is an indication that analysis of marketing position and technical competence, or maybe an organizational rebalancing, is required, but it also serves to remind us that this is a marathon and not a sprint and we need to keep the bigger picture in view.

A word of caution. Whilst these charts are helpful in seeing the bigger picture, they are no replacement for the conventional cash flow analysis and profit and loss accounting. They just provide another dimension.

Compliance and Back-Office Forms

Because our industry is so highly regulated, there are certain completed forms that you must have in order to comply with SEC regulations (check out www.sec .gov/rules/extra/iarules.htm for more information). We've developed a few forms over time that may make it easier for you to develop your own compliance and procedure manual. Here are a few I like.

Insider Trading

This simple trade request form was designed in order to track employee trades according to the Securities Exchange Act of 1934 on insider trading (see **Figure 18.10**). Each time an employee makes a trade, a form must be completed and signed by a principal. We also require that all employees sign an acknowledgement of this policy (see **Figure 18.11**). We print the pertinent portion of the act and present it, along with a copy of our Insider Trading Policy, to every staff member.

Privacy Letter

Every financial advisory firm is required to send a privacy letter each year to inform clients how they are protecting information. This one is from MetLife. I like how easy it is to understand.

THIS NOTICE IS FOR YOUR INFORMATION. NO RESPONSE IS REQUIRED.

Privacy Notice to Our Customers   **MetLife and Affiliates**

Metropolitan Life Insurance Company ("MetLife") and each member of the MetLife family of companies (an "Affiliate") strongly believe in protecting the confidentiality and security of information we collect about you. This notice refers separately to MetLife and each of the Affiliates listed below by using the terms "us," "we," or "our." This notice describes our privacy policy and describes how we treat the information we receive ("Information") about you.

Why We Collect and How We Use Information: We collect and use Information for business purposes with respect to our insurance and other business relationships involving you. These business purposes

■ | FIGURE 18.10 Trade Request Form for Principals and Employees

EVENSKY & KATZ
Trade Request Form for Principals and Employees of E&K

Trade Date:_____
Account #: _____   **Name:**_____

	Quantity	*Description*	*Total Amount*
BUY	_____	_____	_____
BUY	_____	_____	_____
BUY	_____	_____	_____
BUY	_____	_____	_____
BUY	_____	_____	_____
BUY	_____	_____	_____
BUY	_____	_____	_____
BUY	_____	_____	_____
SELL	_____	_____	_____
SELL	_____	_____	_____
SELL	_____	_____	_____
SELL	_____	_____	_____
SELL	_____	_____	_____
SELL	_____	_____	_____
SELL	_____	_____	_____
SELL	_____	_____	_____

This form has to be approved by the president of E&K prior to placing an order in your account. Please use one form per account.

Approved by:_____   **Date:** _____

■ | **FIGURE 18.11** Insider Trading Policy

FEDERAL ACTS

SECURITIES ACT OF 1934

Trading on Non-Public Information

"127. If a person buys or sells a security, including an option contract, while in possession of material non-public information, the individual will be held liable to any buyer or seller of the security."

"131. If the SEC concludes that an individual has violated the 1934 Act by buying or selling securities while in possession of "material non-public information," or has communicated "material non-public information" to another individual, the SEC may bring an action in a federal court. Any penalty for insider trading (i.e., trading on material non-public information) will be determined by the court based on the facts and circumstances of the particular case. The penalty may be up to three times the profit gained or loss avoided in the illegal transaction. If an employee engages in insider trading, the employer or persons in authority to direct the employee's actions will also be subject to penalties as controlling persons. Civil penalties against controlling persons may be up to $1 million or three times the amount of profit gained (or loss avoided) on the transaction, whichever is larger. Controlling persons will be liable for these penalties only where they knowingly or recklessly failed to enforce procedures and policies to prevent insider trading."

Evensky & Katz
Insider Trading Policy

A. Insider trading is prohibited for all officers, shareholders, directors, associated persons, clerical personnel and customers.

B. All officers, shareholders, directors, associated persons and clerical personnel will be required to sign an attestation of knowledge and understanding of Federal and State law requirements regarding insider trading.

<u>ATTESTATION</u>

I hereby acknowledge that I am aware of Federal and State law requirements and Evensky & Katz policy and procedures relating to the use of material, non-public information in the trading of securities.

Therefore, I shall not engage either for a client or on my own behalf in a securities transaction that would be promulgated by having material, non-public information. I understand that if I have been discovered in such practice, I shall be subject to immediate dismissal and the relevant trading information shall be disclosed to the State of Florida and the SEC.

EMPLOYEE   DATE

include evaluating a request for our insurance or other products or services, evaluating benefit claims, administering our products or services, and processing transactions requested by you. We may also use Information to offer you other products or services we provide.

How We Collect Information: We get most Information directly from you. The Information that you give us when applying for our products or services generally provides the Information we need. If we need to verify Information or need additional Information, we may obtain Information from third parties such as adult family members, employers, other insurers, consumer reporting agencies, physicians, hospitals, and other medical personnel. Information collected may relate to your finances, employment, health, avocations, or other personal characteristics as well as transactions with us or with others, including our Affiliates.

How We Protect Information: We treat Information in a confidential manner. Our employees are required to protect the confidentiality of Information. Employees may access Information only when there is an appropriate reason to do so, such as to administer or offer our products or services. We also maintain physical, electronic, and procedural safeguards to protect Information; these safeguards comply with all applicable laws. Employees are required to comply with our established policies.

Information Disclosure: We may disclose any Information when we believe it necessary for the conduct of our business, or where disclosure is required by law. For example, Information may be disclosed to others to enable them to provide business services for us, such as helping us to evaluate requests for insurance or benefits, performing general administrative activities for us, and assisting us in processing a transaction requested by you. Information may also be disclosed for audit or research purposes; or to law enforcement and regulatory agencies— for example, to help us prevent fraud. Information may be disclosed to Affiliates as well as to others that are outside of the MetLife family of companies, such as companies that process data for us, companies that provide general administrative services for us, other insurers, and consumer reporting agencies. Our affiliates include financial services companies such as life and property and casualty insurers, securities firms, broker-dealers, and financial advisors and may also include companies that are not financial services companies. We may make other disclosures of Information as permitted by law.

Information may also be shared with our Affiliates so that they may offer you products or services from the MetLife family of companies. We may also provide Information: (i) to others outside of the MetLife family of companies, such as marketing companies, to assist us in offering our products and services to you, and (ii) to financial services companies outside of the MetLife family of companies with which we have a joint marketing agreement. For example, an agreement with another insurer to enable us to offer you certain of that insurer's products. We do not make any other disclosures of Information to other companies who may want to sell their products or services to you. For example, we will not sell your name to a catalog company. We may disclose any Information, other than a consumer report or health information, for the purposes described in this paragraph.

Access to and Correction of Information: Generally, upon your written request, we will make available Information for your review.

Information collected in connection with, or in anticipation of, any claim or legal proceeding will not be made available. If you notify us that the Information is incorrect, we will review it. If we agree, we will correct our records. If we do not agree, you may submit a short statement of dispute, which we will include in any future disclosure of Information.

Further Information: In addition to any other privacy notice we may provide, a recently enacted federal law established new privacy standards and requires us to provide this summary of our privacy policy once each year. You may have additional rights under other applicable laws.

For additional information regarding our privacy policy, please contact us at our website, www.metlife.com, or write to us at

MetLife, PO Box 318,
Warwick, R.I. 02887-9954.
Metropolitan Life Insurance Company, NY, NY
Metropolitan Insurance and Annuity Company, NY, NY
Metropolitan Tower Life Insurance Company, NY, NY

For contrast, here is the one we use:

Evensky & Katz

Privacy Notice

Evensky & Katz ("E&K") maintains physical, electronic, and procedural safeguards that comply with federal standards to protect its clients' nonpublic personal information ("information"). Through this policy and its underlying procedures, E&K attempts to secure the confidentiality of customer records and information and protect against anticipated threats or hazards to the security or integrity of customer records and information.

It is the policy of E&K to restrict access to all current and former clients' information (i.e., information and records pertaining to personal background, investment objectives, financial situation, tax information/returns, investment holdings, account numbers, account balances, etc.) to those employees and affiliated/nonaffiliated entities who need to know that information in order to provide products or services to the client. E&K may disclose the client's information if E&K is (1) previously authorized to disclose the information to individuals and/or entities not affiliated with E&K, including, but not limited to, the client's other professional advisors and/or service providers (i.e., attorney, accountant, insurance agent, broker-dealer, investment adviser, account custodian, etc.); (2) required to do so by judicial or regulatory process; or (3) otherwise permitted to do so in accordance with the parameters of applicable federal and/or state privacy regulations. The disclosure of information contained in any document completed by the client for processing and/or transmittal by E&K in order to facilitate the commencement/continuation/termination of a business relationship between the client and a nonaffiliated third party service provider (i.e., broker-dealer, investment adviser, account custodian, insurance company, etc.), including information contained in any document completed and/or executed by the client for E&K (i.e., advisory agreement, client information form, etc.), shall be deemed as having been automatically authorized by the client with respect to the corresponding nonaffiliated third party service provider.

E&K permits only authorized employees and affiliates who have signed a copy of E&K's Privacy Policy to have access to client information. Employees violating E&K's Privacy Policy will be subject to E&K's disciplinary process. Additionally, whenever E&K hires other organizations to provide services to E&K's clients, E&K will require them to sign confidentiality agreements and/or the Privacy Policy.

Should you have any questions regarding the above, please contact Lane M. Jones, CFA, CFP,
Chief Operating Officer of E&K, at 305-448-8882.

 ## A Stranger at the Door

Not long ago, I was sitting at my desk quietly attending to my daily work when our new receptionist ran excitedly into my office. "There's a guy here who says he's from the SEC. I don't know what that is, but he looks important and intimidating." The best preparation for a surprise SEC audit is to have your documentation in apple pie order. Our comptroller, Mena Bielow, suggests that you prepare a compliance book that has copies of the forms that an SEC auditor would want to see during a surprise audit. Mena, in fact, keeps a document checklist in the book, indicating what is needed when the auditor drops in the door, and where these files and information are kept. This book is so thorough that if she were on vacation, we would easily be able to locate everything and complete the audit without her. (Not that we'd want to.) Here is a copy of the table of contents of Mena's compliance book:

Evensky & Katz
Rule 206(4)-7 Policies and Procedures
Table of Contents

And, speaking of compliance, I have only two things to say here. Take this seriously and get help. The SEC is auditing more often and issuing penalties, rather than hand slaps. Get a securities attorney or use one of the compliance support groups like MarketCounsel (www.marketcounsel.com) to get your material in order. I am not kidding and neither is the SEC.

 ## Value Added

The late David Norton of Norton Partners, in Clevedon, United Kingdom, devised the Excel form in **Figure 18.12** to help clients understand the adviser's value. David tried to quantify the relationship. David would fill this out with the client after the first year of the engagement. He then added the tangible value (e.g., "tax savings") with the intangible ("having a trusted adviser") to direct the client's focus to the added value that his adviser provided. David put his fees on the line "Fixed Price Investment for the Year."

 ## More on Client Surveys

The best way to find out whether your clients are happy with your relationship and service is to ask them. I think surveys are the best way to do this, although I am not certain whether sending them yourself is the best strategy. When we did it, all our clients responded that we were wonderful. I believe they were too intimidated to respond honestly, knowing that the forms came back directly to us. We then sent a survey they could respond to anonymously through a service that tallied the results and summarized the responses. I think we got a much clearer picture of how our clients feel than when we did it ourselves.

Kirk Hulett, vice president of human resources and practice management at Securities America, believes that surveys are one of the best ways to get a large amount of data about your clients in a small amount of time. You can find out about the satisfaction with your services or whether you should be adding new ones. You can also ask about their buying or saving habits, educational background, or other personal information that you may not have already addressed with them. Most advisers use surveys to find out about client's perception of the firm's services and custodian services, and to determine new services to add, or services to discard. The following are a few useful examples: Kirk has provided us with sample surveys (**Figure 18.13**—see p. vi), letter templates (see **Figure 18.14**) you can use for this purpose, and a sample agenda (see **Figure 18.15**) for a client advisory group. Fidelity Investments Institutional

FIGURE 18.12 Value Pricing—Value-Added Services

Client Name		
Value Pricing - Value Added Services in year ended	**Date:** mm/dd/yy	
Value of portfolio (one year ago)	$1,000,000	

1. Financial Returns

		Value Added $
Investment return (note ** below)		0
Pension investment return (note ** below)		0
Tax efficient investment		0
Tax savings - income tax		0
Tax savings - capital gains tax		0
Tax savings - inheritance tax		0
Tax benefits of pension contributions		0
Reinvested commission savings		0
Discounts obtained		0
Charges saved		0
Commissions received and offset		0
Other financial returns (specify)		0
		0

** Note that short term investment returns are not within our control and so a long term view (five years cumulatively) needs to be taken of these areas.

2. Other Valued Benefits

Valued benefits of knowing that your tax affairs are being dealt with efficiently and effectively	0.0%	0
Valued benefits of not having to deal with the Inland Revenue	0.0%	0
Valued benefits of unlimited access to our time and expertise	0.0%	0
Valued benefits of having financial matters dealt with straightforwardly and without jargon	0.0%	0
Valued benefits of knowing that there are no unexpected fee charges from us	0.0%	0
Valued benefits of knowing you are on course to achieve your objectives	0.0%	0
Valued benefits of knowing how much income you will need in retirement	0.0%	0
Valued benefits of knowing whether or not you can afford a particular course of action	0.0%	0
Valued benefits of knowing that the market is researched thoroughly and well on your behalf	0.0%	0
Valued benefits of knowing whether you can afford to finance your desired lifestyle	0.0%	0
Valued benefits of knowing that you can relax and not have to read the weekend financial press	0.0%	0
Valued benefits of impartial, non-product driven advice	0.0%	0
Valued benefits of having a trusted adviser	0.0%	0
Valued benefits of our role as facilitator	0.0%	0
Valued benefits of time saving from outsourced chores compared with cost of own time	0.0%	0
Valued benefits of extra leisure time achieved	0.0%	0
Valued benefits of peace of mind	0.0%	0
Valued benefits of security from proper insurance cover	0.0%	0
Valued benefits to business owner (value of business, peace of mind, leisure)	0.0%	0
Valued benefits - other (describe)	0.0%	0

Total Value Added		$
Fixed Price Investment for the Year		
Net Value Added		$

Source: Norton Partners

■ FIGURE 18.14 Sample Letters

Sample Letters
Letters to accompany your survey and to remind clients to return your survey.
**These letters should be preapproved by a registered principal
before distribution to clients.**

[DATE]

Mrs. Any Client
1220 Any Street
Any Town, Any State

Dear Ms. Client:

I'm writing today to ask you a favor.

In approximately one week, you will be receiving a survey from me to find out how satisfied you are with my services. My number one priority is to serve the needs of my clients.

To help me do this, I am asking all of my clients to please fill out a survey about how I'm doing right now, and how I could serve you better. It should take about ten minutes to complete.

A stamped envelope is also enclosed. Please return the completed survey in this envelope.

Thank you in advance for your assistance with the survey. I will be circulating a summary of the results to you and to other clients later this year. Please call me if you have any questions.

Best regards,

Roberta Representative
Registered Principal

FIGURE 18.14 Sample Letters (*Continued*)

[DATE]

Dr. Andy Noon
1234 Main Street
Omaha, NE 68134

Dear Dr. Noon:

Within the next few days, you will receive a request to complete a brief survey. I am mailing it to you in an effort to learn the needs of my clients.

This survey is being conducted to better inform me of the type of services you need and want.

I would greatly appreciate your taking the few minutes necessary to complete and return the survey.

Thank you in advance for your help.

Best regards,

Ronald Representative
Account Executive

FIGURE 18.14 Sample Letters (*Continued*)

[DATE]

Mrs. Any Client
1220 Any Street
Any Town, Any State

Dear Ms. Client:

Approximately one week ago, I sent you a letter explaining that you would be receiving a client survey. I would like to ask you to take a few minutes to complete the attached survey to help me become a better representative.

My number one priority is to serve the needs of my clients. To help me do this, I am writing you to ask you to please take ten minutes to complete the enclosed survey of how I'm doing right now and how I could serve you better.

A stamped envelope accompanies the survey, for your convenience.

Thank you in advance for your assistance with this survey. I will be circulating a summary of the results to you and to other clients later this year. Please call me if you have any questions.

Best regards,

Regis Representative
Registered Principal

P. S.   As a small thank you for taking the time to respond to this survey, ten of the respondents will be randomly selected to receive gift certificates for dinner for two at their favorite restaurants. Thanks again for your assistance.

(*continued*)

[DATE]

Dr. Andy Noon
1234 Main Street
Suite 202
Omaha, NE 68134

Dear Dr. Noon:

Enclosed please find a survey that is being sent to all of my clients. It is an attempt to find out their needs. The answers to these questions will help me serve you and all my clients better. I would appreciate your assistance.

Thank you for your time,

Sincerely,

Rachel Representative
Registered Representative

SAMPLE POSTCARD

Dear Valued Client:

I would like to take this opportunity to remind you to please fill out the survey I sent you approximately two weeks ago.

This survey is very important to help ensure that I'm providing the highest possible level of service.

If you have already returned the survey, I greatly appreciate it. If you have not, please take a few moments to complete it.

In thanks and appreciation,
RR Representative

P.S. If you need a new survey please call me at 402-555-2222.

Source: Securities America

■ | **Figure 18.15** Sample Agenda

Sample Agenda for Client Advisory Group Meeting

MoneyPenny Retirement Planning
Client Advisory Group
September 8, 2001
Oak Hills Country Club

Purpose Statement*: The Client Advisory Board provides advice, opinions, and ideas to MoneyPenny Advisory Group on client service, marketing, and all aspects of the client-adviser relationship.*

Agenda

5:30   Cocktails and Appetizers

6:00   Welcome and Introductions

6:30   Dinner

7:30   Marketing
    ❖ Review Marketing Plan
    ❖ Review New Brochure

8:00 Client Service
    ❖ Describe positive and negative client service experiences
    ❖ Review format of quarterly performance reports

8:20 Open Discussion

8:30 Conclude

Source: Securities America

Brokerage Group provides a Client Satisfaction form as part of their Practice-Mark marketing site, which they have allowed me to reproduce for you (see **Figure 18.16**). Our client survey is provided as **Figure 18.17**. Both ask about relationship and services, although Fidelity's works great for 401(k) clients because it asks about plan administrators.

Advisor Impact (www.advisorimpact.com) is great at third-party surveys and will help you interpret the results as well.

 ## Doing Better Business

When I was a teacher just out of college, I found that the more time and thought I put into my lesson plans, the better the experience was for the kids, and for me. One year I had so many kids in my classroom that I went home exhausted every evening. Consequently, I didn't have time to plan, prepare, and reflect. It showed up in the interactions I had with my students, other teachers, and the administration. I learned that running to keep up isn't good for anyone. I hope some of these business- and client-related tips and tools will help you and your staff take a breather and figure out where you are going next. I expect the effort will result in a better experience for everyone, especially your clients.

 ## On the Future

More pearls from Mark Tibergien: "When you want to buy a red car, all you see are red cars. Are you going to recognize an opportunity when you see it?" Mark, commenting on the future of the small practitioner in this highly competitive marketplace: "Sole practitioners will always make a living; they just won't make an impact."

 ## A Final Word

I talked about the undiscovered managers' white papers earlier in this book. While I believe that Mark Hurley and the gang there have made some good observations about the future of this industry, there is one which I fervently hope they got absolutely wrong: the closing of our open environment of sharing advice, information, and expertise that we have enjoyed all these years. I would never have survived in this industry if it had not been for all the mentors who talked me through the good, the bad, and the bizarre of my practice; all the friends who've shared their failures so I could avoid their mistakes; and all the industry leaders whose vision extended far beyond my own.

Look at where you are today in your practice. If you're a silver-haired (or in my case, silver-haired masquerading as a redhead) planner, remember that someone was there years ago to help you get where you are. Return the favor. If you're just starting out, find a mentor and as you gain knowledge and expertise, continue to share what you know with others. You'll benefit and certainly the profession will benefit.

■ **Figure 18.16** Client Satisfaction Form

CLIENT SATISFACTION WORKSHEET

client satisfaction

PLEASE FILL IN (YOU CAN TYPE RIGHT ON THE LINE)

Your current clients are your most valuable assets. Have you checked with your clients lately to determine if their satisfaction level is where it should be? Use the following questions to help you understand where your clients' perspective is, and what you can do to make your relationship as strong as possible. This worksheet can be an effective tool to help you learn what attributes of your practice your best clients appreciate—which can provide you with a powerful sales message to target future prospects.

HOW WOULD YOU RATE YOUR RELATIONSHIP WITH US?

☐ Excellent   ☐ Very Good   ☐ Average   ☐ Below Average   ☐ Poor

Comments: _____

_____

_____

HOW SATISFIED ARE YOU WITH OUR CUSTOMER SERVICE?

☐ Very Satisfied   ☐ Somewhat Satisfied   ☐ Satisfied   ☐ Slightly Less than Satisfied   ☐ Unsatisfied

Comments: _____

_____

_____

HOW WOULD YOU RATE THE FOLLOWING STATEMENTS:

1=Strongly Disagree, 2=Somewhat Disagree, 3=Neither Disagree nor Agree, 4=Agree, 5=Somewhat Agree, 6=Strongly Agree

- I am satisfied with the level of client service my financial adviser provides.   _____
- I would like to hear from my financial adviser more often.   _____
- In the past six months, I have considered consolidating the management of my assets.   _____
- I am satisfied with the performance of my portfolio.   _____
- My financial adviser's personnel handle my affairs with professionalism and intelligence.   _____
- I would recommend associates or family members to my adviser.   _____
- My financial adviser is able to meet all my financial planning needs.   _____

Comments: _____

_____

_____

OVERALL, HOW WOULD YOU RATE US?

☐ Exceed expectations   ☐ Meet expectations   ☐ Do not meet expectations

Comments: _____

_____

_____

Source: Fidelity Investments Institutional Brokerage Group

Figure 18.17 Client Survey

Evensky & Katz Client Survey

PLEASE RATE YOUR TEAM'S PERFORMANCE IN THE FOLLOWING AREAS:

	VERY SATISFIED	SATISFIED	NEUTRAL	DISSATISFIED	VERY DISSATISFIED	NOT APPLICABLE
1. Overall staff rating	_____	_____	_____	_____	_____	_____

PERSONNEL

2. Courtesy of staff	_____	_____	_____	_____	_____	_____
3. Knowledge of staff members	_____	_____	_____	_____	_____	_____
4. Promptness answering phones	_____	_____	_____	_____	_____	_____
5. Timeliness of follow-up calls	_____	_____	_____	_____	_____	_____

TIMELINESS

6. Setting up new accounts	_____	_____	_____	_____	_____	_____
7. Follow-up on account transfers	_____	_____	_____	_____	_____	_____
8. Processing disbursements	_____	_____	_____	_____	_____	_____

ACCURACY

9. Setting up account transfers	_____	_____	_____	_____	_____	_____
10. Processing disbursements	_____	_____	_____	_____	_____	_____

Do you have any suggestions to improve our service to you?

_____

_____

_____

_____

What is your opinion of how Schwab is handling your account (e.g., statements, accuracy, and timeliness)?

_____

_____

_____

_____

 **NOTES**

CHAPTER 1

1. John Guy, *Thoughtful Wealth Planning & Management* 2 (October 1998).

2. Russ Alan Prince and Karen Maru File, *Cultivating the Affluent* (New York: Institutional Investor, Inc., 1995).

3. Russ Alan Prince and Lewis Schiff, *Middle-Class Millionaire: The Rise of the New Rich and How They Are Changing America* (New York: Doubleday Business, 2008).

4. Harold Evensky, *Wealth Management: The Financial Advisor's Guide to Investing and Managing Client Assets* (New York: McGraw-Hill, 1997).

CHAPTER 2

1. Steve Moeller, "When Clients Move Center Stage," *Dow Jones Investment Advisor* (April 1998).

CHAPTER 3

1. Mark Hurley, "The Future of the Financial Advisory Business and the Delivery of Advice to the Semi-Affluent Investor," white paper for Undiscovered Managers (1999).

CHAPTER 4

1. Don Peppers and Martha Rogers, *Enterprise One to One* (New York: Doubleday, 1997).

2. Larry Chambers, *The Guide to Financial Public Relations: How to Stand Out in the Midst of Competitive Clutter* (Boca Raton, FL: St. Lucie Press, 1999).

3. Lisbeth Chapman, *Get Media Smart!: Create News Coverage That Builds Business* (Wellfleet, MA: Ink & Air, 1997).

CHAPTER 6

1. Mark Tibergien and Rebecca Pomering, *Practice Made Perfect: The Discipline of Business Management for Financial Advisors* (New York: Bloomberg Press, 2005).

CHAPTER 7

1. Tibergien and Pomering, *Practice Made Perfect* (see chap. 6, n. 1).

2. Roger Gibson, *Asset Allocation: Balancing Financial Risk* (New York: McGraw-Hill, 2008).

3. Evensky, *Wealth Management* (see chap. 1, n. 4).

4. Charles Ellis, *Investment Policy: How to Win the Loser's Game* (New York: Dow Jones-Irwin, 1985).

5. Donald Trone, William Allbright, and Philip Taylor, *The Management of Investment Decisions* (Chicago: Irwin Professional Publishing, 1996).

CHAPTER 9

1. Meredith Belbin, *Management Teams: Why They Succeed or Fail* (Oxford; Boston: Butterworth-Heinemann, 2004).

CHAPTER 10

1. Michael Barrier, "Reviewing the Annual Review," *Nation's Business* (September 1998): 32–34.

CHAPTER 11

1. Harry Beckwith, *Selling the Invisible: A Field Guide to Modern Marketing* (New York: Warner Books, 1997).

CHAPTER 12

1. Client Fit Ratio^SM is a trademark of Brightworth Private Wealth Counsel. If you choose to adapt their form to create a fitness test for your firm, Brightworth Private Wealth Counsel requests that you credit them when sharing your system with others.

CHAPTER 13

1. Twentieth *Index of Investor Optimism*, 1999 Gallup Poll in cooperation with Paine Webber.

2. Gibson, *Asset Allocation* (see chap. 7, n. 2); *Simple Asset Allocation Strategies: Easy Steps for Winning Portfolios* (Columbia, MD: Marketplace Books/Traders Library, 2000).

3. A term used in William P. Bengen's excellent articles on this subject: "Determining Withdrawal Rates Using Historical Data," *Journal of Financial Planning* (October 1994); "Asset Allocation for a Lifetime," *Journal of Financial Planning* (August 1996); and "Conserving Client Portfolios During Retirement, Part III," *Journal of Financial Planning* (December 1997).

4. You'll note that the Monte Carlo failure rate result for the 40/60 portfolio in the illustration "Monte Carlo Simulation for Game Two," Figure 13.18, is slightly different from that in the illustration "Monte Carlo Simulation for Game Three," Figure 13.19 (100 percent versus 99 percent). This is a result of having run only one thousand games.

5. The following are a few books that discuss the Investment Policy Statement (IPS) in detail: Evensky, *Wealth Management* (see chap. 1, n. 4); Trone, Allbright, and Taylor, *The Management of Investment Decisions* (see chap. 7, n. 5); and Norman Boone and Linda Lubitz, *The Investment Policy Statement Guidebook* (available on www.amazon.com).

CHAPTER 14

1. Ross Levin, *The Wealth Management Index: The Financial Advisor's System for Assessing & Managing Your Client's Plans & Goals* (Chicago: Irwin Professional Publishing, 1997).

CHAPTER 15

1. Paul Dorrian, *Intensive Customer Care* (Cape Town, South Africa: Zebra Press 1996).

2. Deloitte and Touche, "Relationship Marketing Report," (1997).

3. Darrell K. Rigby, "What's Today's Special at the Consultants' Cafe?" *Fortune 138* (September 7, 1998): 162–63.

CHAPTER 16

1. Beckwith, *Selling the Invisible* (see chap. 11, n. 1), pp. xix–xx.

CHAPTER 17

1. Julie Littlechild, "Practice Update 2007: Time Management and Personal Productivity," www.advisorimpact.com.

CHAPTER 18

1. Deena Katz, *Taking Charge of Your Retirement* (New York: Lee Simmons Associates, 1997).

2. John Durand, *How to Secure Continuous Profits in Modern Markets* (Whitefish, MT: Kessinger Publishing, 2003). This is a reprint of the original, which was published in 1929.

3. Al Ries and Laura Ries, *22 Immutable Laws of Branding: How to Build a Product or Service into a World-Class Brand* (New York: HarperCollins, 1998), p. 7.

4. For a full explanation of ARGE, see C.H. Lovelock, *Managing Services: Marketing, Operations, and Human Resources* (New York: Prentice Hall, 1992).

Trademarks

Access is a trademark of, and Excel, Office Outlook, and PowerPoint are registered trademarks of Microsoft.

ACT! is a trademark of Sage Software.

AdviserView is a service mark of Jackson National Life Insurance Company.

Advisor Workstation is a service mark, and Principia is a registered trademark of Morningstar.

American Greetings and CreataCard are registered trademarks of Riverdeep Interactive Learning Limited.

BAND-AID is a registered trademark of Johnson & Johnson Consumer Companies.

BranchNet is a trademark of Linsco/Private Ledger.

CARE BEARS is a registered trademark of Those Characters from Cleveland.

CFP and Certified Financial Planner are registered trademarks of CERTIFIED FINANCIAL PLANNER BOARD OF STANDARDS, INC. The certification mark, to be used by authorized persons, certifies that the person displaying the mark has completed education course work requirements and work experience requirements of the certifier, has completed examinations administered by the certifier in satisfactory manner, has agreed to adhere to the certifier's standards for professional responsibility, continuing education and other post-certification requirements.

Client Fit Ratio is a service mark of Brightworth Private Wealth Counsel.

Domino's is a registered trademark of Domino's IP Holder.

FieldNet is a service mark of National Guardian Life Insurance Company.

GoldMine is a registered trademark of FrontRange Solutions USA.

Hallmark is a registered trademark of Creative Home.

INFINET21 is a registered trademark of Independent Financial Marketing Group.

IPS AdvisorPro is a trademark of BLIPS Partners.

iRebal is a trademark of TD AMERITRADE.

Junxure is a trademark of CRM SOFTWARE.

Just Do It is a trademark of NIKE.

Little Caesars is a registered trademark of Little Caesar Enterprises.

MasterTrak is a copyright of MRA Software.

MetLife is a registered trademark of Metropolitan Life Insurance Company.

Mini Cooper is a registered trademark of BMW.

MoneyGuidePro is a trademark of PIE Technologies.

Myers-Briggs Type Indicator (MBTI) is a registered trademark of Myers-Briggs Type Indicator Trust.

NaviPlan is a registered trademark of Emerging Information Systems.

Pizza Hut is a trademark of Pizza Hut.

PracticeMark is a service mark of Fidelity Institutional Wealth Services.

Quicken is a registered trademark of Intuit.

SunGard software is a copyright of SunGard Data Systems.

VISION2020 is a service mark of American International Group.

WebEx is a registered trademark of Cisco Systems.

Wite-Out is a registered trademark of BIC USA.

INDEX

ABOUT BLOOMBERG

Bloomberg L.P., founded in 1981, is a global information services, news, and media company. Headquartered in New York, the company has sales and news operations worldwide.

Serving customers on six continents, Bloomberg, through its wholly-owned subsidiary Bloomberg Finance L.P., holds a unique position within the financial services industry by providing an unparalleled range of features in a single package known as the Bloomberg Professional® service. By addressing the demand for investment performance and efficiency through an exceptional combination of information, analytic, electronic trading, and Straight Through Processing tools, Bloomberg has built a worldwide customer base of corporations, issuers, financial intermediaries, and institutional investors.

Bloomberg News®, founded in 1990, provides stories and columns on business, general news, politics, and sports to leading newspapers and magazines throughout the world. Bloomberg Television®, a 24-hour business and financial news network, is produced and distributed globally in seven languages. Bloomberg Radio℠ is an international radio network anchored by flagship station Bloomberg® 1130 (WBBR-AM) in New York.

In addition to the Bloomberg Press® line of books, Bloomberg publishes *Bloomberg Markets®* magazine. To learn more about Bloomberg, call a sales representative at:

London:	+44-20-7330-7500
New York:	+1-212-318-2000
Tokyo:	+81-3-3201-8900

ABOUT THE AUTHOR

Deena Katz, CFP, is an associate professor in the Division of Personal Financial Planning at Texas Tech University in Lubbock, Texas. She is also a partner of Evensky & Katz, a wealth-management firm in Coral Gables, Florida. She is an internationally recognized financial adviser and practice-management expert and the author of six books on financial planning and practice-management topics. Her book edited with Harold Evensky, *Retirement Income Redesigned: Master Plans for Distribution*, has just received an Axiom Business Book Award for 2008. Katz served as the editor in chief of the *Journal of Retirement Planning*, and has been a contributing writer for *Financial Advisor, Investment Advisor, Financial Planning* magazine, and *National Underwriter*. Currently, she is a columnist for *Financial Planning* magazine.

Working with Moss Adams, Katz has served as a consultant to many companies within the financial services industry, including institutional custodians and brokers, money managers, and insurance companies.

Katz was one of the advisers named as *Financial Planning* magazine's "Movers and Shakers" for 2001 and 2008, as well as one of *Accounting Today*'s "top ten names to know in financial planning," in 2001 and 2002. She has been on the *Investment Advisor*'s IA 25 list of "most influential people in the industry" for the past five out of six years, including the current one. She has been included on *Worth* magazine's list of top financial advisers numerous times. She is frequently quoted by major national news media, and has made various television appearances on local and national network programs for CBS, ABC, and PBS.

Katz is a nationally recognized speaker in the United States. She has also been called upon by global financial services organizations to speak at international financial forums held in various locations, including Australia, Canada, Japan, England, India, Ireland, Singapore, New Zealand, Malaysia, and South Africa.

She is on the national board of directors of the Financial Planning Association, is an immediate past member of the board of trustees for the Foundation for Financial Planning, and is past member of the Advisory Board for Fidelity Research. In 2007–2008, she served as an adviser to the comptroller of the state of Texas on the state's college funding plans.

Katz was the first female member of RotaryOne, Chicago, as well as the first woman to serve as a director of a United States Rotary Club. She received her bachelor's degree from Adrian College and was the 1993 recipient of the college's Young Alumni Achievement Award. Katz has been a trustee of Adrian College and received a doctorate of humane letters from the college in 2001.

Made in the USA
Monee, IL
17 May 2024

58558868R00203